A Roman villa and other Iron Age and Roman discoveries at Bredon's Norton, Fiddington and Pamington along the Gloucester Security of Supply pipeline

by Tim Allen, Kate Brady and Stuart Foreman

with contributions by
*Leigh Allen, Edward Biddulph, Sheila Boardman, Paul Booth,
Geraldine Crann, Mark Gibson, Kath Hunter, Cynthia Poole,
Rebecca Nicholson, Ian R Scott, Ruth Shaffrey and Lena Strid*

and illustrations by
*Julia Collins, Markus Dylewski, Hannah Kennedy
and Magdalena Wachnik*

Oxford Archaeology Monograph No. 25
2016

The publication of this volume was generously funded by Severn Trent Water.
Published by Oxford Archaeology as part of the Oxford Archaeology Monograph series.

Designed by Oxford Archaeology Graphics Office

Edited by Ruth Shaffrey

This book is part of a series of monographs about the Thames Valley Landscapes which can be bought
from all good bookshops and internet bookshops. For more information visit www.oxfordarch.co.uk

Front cover: Roman plunge bath with flagged floor and cistern at Bredon's Norton, Worcestershire
Back cover: Roman burial of a young adult at Bredon's Norton, Worcestershire

ISBN 978-0-904220-76-6
Typeset by Production Line, Oxford

Printed in Great Britain by Hobbs the Printers Ltd, Totton, Hampshire SO40 3WX. www.hobbs.uk.com

Contents

Chapter 1 Introduction and Background *by Paul Booth and Stuart Foreman*

Chapter 2 Archaeological description *by Kate Brady and Tim Allen*

Chapter 3 Finds reports

Chapter 4 Environmental reports

List of Figures

List of Plates

List of Tables

Summary

This report presents the results of a programme of archaeological mitigation along the line of the 17km long Gloucester Security of Supply Water Pipeline in the vicinity of Tewkesbury. The archaeological mitigation works were commissioned by Severn Trent Water (STW) in compliance with environmental screening proposals for the pipeline scheme. The largest part of the pipeline route and two of the three excavated sites (Fiddington and Pamington) lie within the county of Gloucestershire, whereas the most substantial archaeological remains were discovered at Bredon's Norton in Worcestershire.

The site at Pamington consisted of a pair of small ditched enclosures dating from the mid-late Iron Age, perhaps stock enclosures or seasonal settlements. The site at Fiddington comprised a complex of enclosures of varying dates from the 1st to the 4th century AD, and including a circular 4th century example. A single early Saxon pottery sherd was also recovered.

The Bredon's Norton site constituted a narrow transect through an extensive series of Iron Age and Romano-British settlement enclosures. Geophysical surveys of the surrounding area indicate the likely limits of the settlement to the north, south and west, and it appears to have extended under the modern village to the east. The minimum enclosed settlement area is c 2Ha, of which the excavation was only able to examine 15%.

The excavated Iron Age remains include a number of enclosure ditches, a middle Iron Age crouched burial, unusually accompanied by a saw, and another burial of probable late Iron Age date. Some of the late Iron age ditches continued into the early Roman period, and other features include an early Roman circular enclosure surrounding a central pit, possibly indicating a roundhouse, a scatter of ditches and a few crouched inhumation burials. In the middle Roman period there was a switch to larger enclosures, a cremation and more inhumation burials, including a group of seven neonatal burials at the corner of an enclosure.

Apart from a small corndryer found at the north-west edge of the site, later Roman activity is mainly focussed upon the remains of a substantial masonry building near the south-east end of the site. A sunken-floored room within the structure was probably the plunge pool of a bathhouse with a stone-flagged floor, drain and plastered and painted walls. This was later drained and had a small circular stone-lined cistern inserted into the middle.

South of the plunge pool the building has been heavily robbed, but a few surviving hypocaust pilae and stone blocks, together with box-flue tiles in the demolition debris, suggest a group of heated rooms, strengthening interpretation as a bathhouse. On stratigraphic grounds the building could have been constructed as early as the early 2nd century AD, although the dating is not clear. Most of the associated finds are of 4th century date, but derive from secondary use of the building and from demolition deposits.

In its latest phase the sunken room, or more likely the loft above it, appears to have been used as a grain store, the stored spelt crop being unusually well-preserved by the fire that destroyed the building. Radiocarbon dates suggest that this occurred at the very end of the Roman period.

Acknowledgements

Oxford Archaeology (OA) would like to thank Severn Trent Water for giving them the opportunity to carry out the archaeological work. Richard O'Neill of Wessex Archaeology acted as consultant to Severn Trent Water throughout the project, and his support is gratefully acknowledged.

Stuart Foreman managed the project in the field. He would like to thank Mike Glyde, Historic Environment Planning Officer for Worcestershire County Council, Charles Parry, Senior Archaeological Officer at Gloucestershire County Council and Tony Fleming, Inspector of Ancient Monuments for English Heritage, for their assistance and advice when monitoring the project.

Stuart would also like to thank Dan Sykes, who ran the project in the field on a day-to-day basis, Leo Heatley, who ran the survey, and all the members of the field team for their hard work/dedication. He is grateful to Paul Booth and Dan Sykes for preparing the post-excavation assessment report, from which Paul's Archaeological and Historical Background is reproduced in this report.

The original gradiometer survey of the pipeline easement was carried out by Phase Site Investigations, and the evaluation by Cotswold Archaeology. OA would also like to thank Stratascan, who carried out the resistance survey, and Richard Hart, who conducted the wider area gradiometer survey at Bredon's Norton.

Kate Brady wrote a draft of the archaeological description and organised the finds and environmental specialists. Tim Allen managed the project in the post-excavation analysis phase, edited, expanded and in some places rewrote the description, compiled the finds and environmental reports and the illustrations, and wrote the discussion. He would like to thank Gary Jones for his assistance with the site drawings made in GIS; other site drawings were created by Markus Dylewski and Julia Collins. Thanks are also due to Magdalena Wachnik, who drew the finds, and Hannah Kennedy, who photographed them. The authors would like to thank all of the specialists for their contributions to the report.

We would like to thank all those whose comments helped improve the report: Alex Smith (academic referee), Richard O'Neill, Charles Parry, Victoria Bryant of Worcestershire County Council and Lisa Moffett of Historic England. The opinions expressed in the report however remain those of the authors, who take full responsibility for any errors that may remain.

Chapter 1

Introduction and Background

by Paul Booth and Stuart Foreman

PROJECT BACKGROUND

The pipeline route forms an arc, *c* 17km long, which passes to the east of Tewkesbury, from the Strensham Water Treatment Works (Worcestershire) in the north (NGR SO 9175 3948) to Coombe Hill, Knightsbridge (Gloucestershire) in the south (Fig. 1.1, NGR SO 8917 2686). The route passes through predominantly rural areas comprising a mixture of pasture and arable land, crossing several roads and a railway. Several watercourses are crossed by the route, including the Carrant Brook, which forms the present county boundary between Worcestershire and Gloucestershire. The largest part of the pipeline route and two of the three excavated sites (Fidd-

ington and Pamington) lie within the county of Gloucestershire, whereas the most substantial archaeological remains were discovered at Bredon's Norton in Worcestershire (Plate 1.1). An archaeological watching brief was maintained along the remainder of the route (Fig.1.1), but did not reveal any other archaeological sites.

The archaeological mitigation works were commissioned by Severn Trent Water (STW) in compliance with environmental screening proposals for the pipeline scheme. A desk-based assessment (DBA), undertaken by ARCUS in 2008, considered three alternative route options. The DBA data was used, in conjunction with desk-based assessments

Plate 1.1 Bredon's Norton – low level aerial photograph of the site during excavation

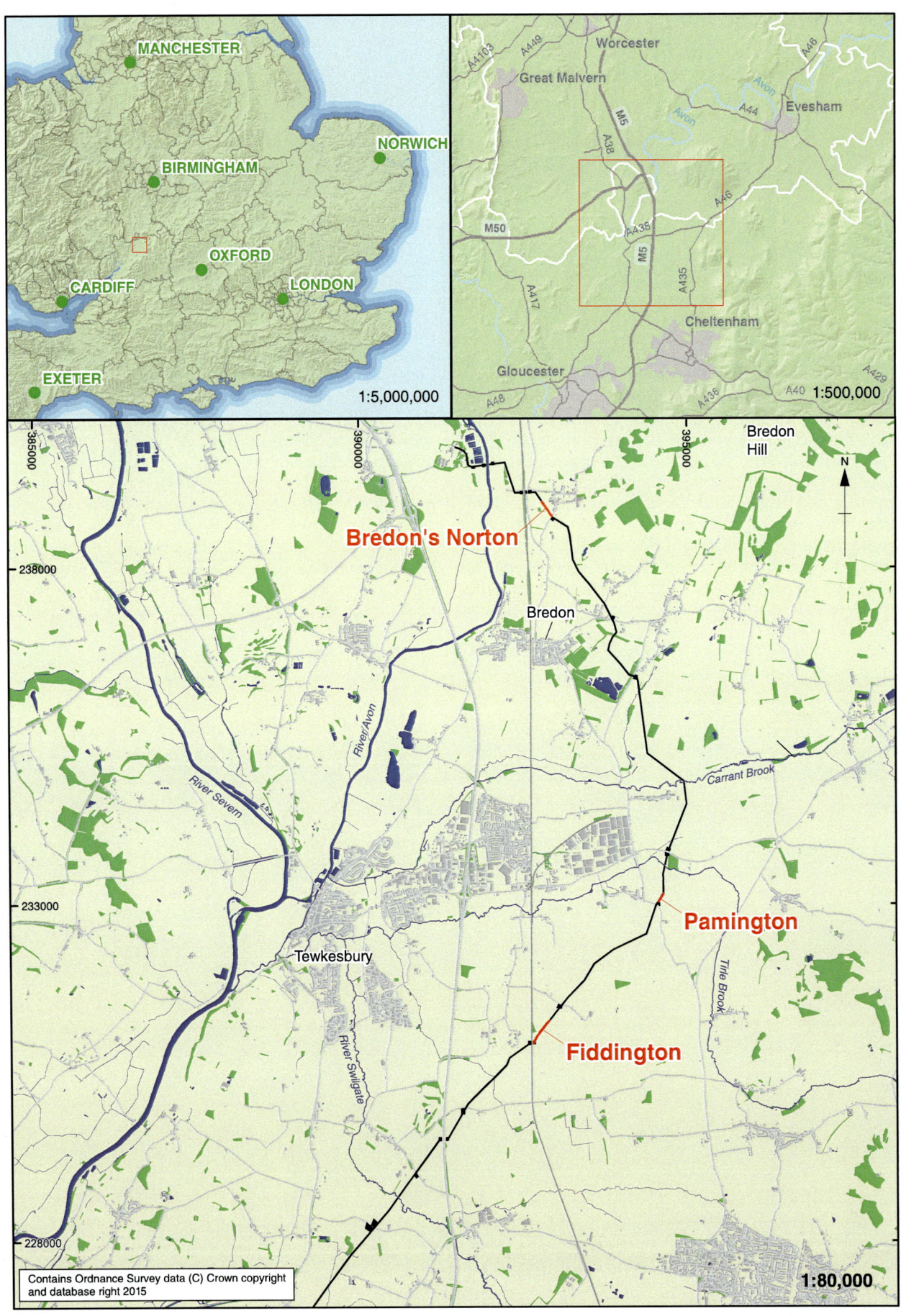

Contains Ordnance Survey data (C) Crown copyright
and database right 2015

of environmental and engineering constraints, to select the preferred route.

A staged programme of further investigation was undertaken in relation to the preferred route in 2008–9. This comprised geophysical survey (Phase Site Investigations 2009a; 2009b) followed by evaluation by trenching (Cotswold Archaeology 2009; see also below), which identified a series of archaeological sites (see below). On the basis of evidence presented in the evaluation reports, none of these was considered sufficiently important to justify re-routing the scheme.

Wessex Archaeology, acting as consultant to STW, then prepared a Written Scheme of Investigation (WSI; Wessex Archaeology 2010), the outline scope of which was agreed with the Senior Archaeological Officer for Gloucestershire County Council and the Historic Environment Planning Advisor for Worcestershire County Council.

The WSI (Wessex Archaeology 2010) outlined the requirements for archaeological mitigation, including the definition of three mitigation areas that would be subject to 'strip, map and sample' excavation.

AIMS

The stated aims of the work (*ibid.*, 6) were as follows:

- The aim of the programme is to offset the impact of the proposed pipeline by preserving *by record* three specified areas of archaeological significance that have been identified (strip, map and sample Mitigation Areas 1 [Fiddington], 2 [Pamington] and 3 [Bredon's Norton]). In addition the entire length of pipeline trench in Gloucestershire will be stripped to allow recording of archaeological remains.

- The investigations will further characterise archaeological remains identified during previous works in Fields 31 (centred NGR 39270 23098) – 33 (NGR 39286 23124) [ie at Fiddington], Field 45 (centred NGR 39456 23312) [at Pamington] and Fields 76 (centred NGR 39283 23876) – 77 (NGR 39286 23890) [south-west of Bredon's Norton].

- Each of the specified sites has distinct archaeological potential. It is the aim of the programme and subsequent post-excavation works to address that potential in relation to local, regional, and wider research objectives:

Mitigation area	Fields	Aim
1 – Fiddington	31-33	Targeted sample excavation of Middle to Late Iron Age settlement; Iron Age ditch; Romano-British enclosure ditches; and medieval fields.

Mitigation area	Fields	Aim
2 – Pamington	45	Targeted sample excavation of Middle to Late Iron Age settlement deposits; Romano–British sub-rectangular enclosures and linear ditches; and medieval fields.
3 – Bredon's	76-77	Targeted sample excavation of a Late Bronze Age to Early Iron Age Norton ditch; Middle–Late Iron Age settlement evidence; a potential high status Romano-British settlement; medieval fields; an undated burial; unexcavated ditches and pits.

- A report on the results of the programme of strip, map and sample (and other archaeological mitigation works) will be prepared, the aim of which will be to present and assess the results in the form of a Post-excavation Assessment Report to include, as appropriate, an Updated Project Design for further analysis and publication.

The width of the excavation areas was defined by the pipeline easement width, which was variable depending on site constraints, but typically *c* 15m.

In Worcestershire, designated lengths of the pipeline easement were selected for archaeological watching brief, as some parts had previously been subject to significant recent disturbance. The designated lengths are given in the WSI (Wessex Archaeology 2010, fig. 4).

The regional research objectives for the West Midlands were not published until 2011 (Watt (ed.) 2011), and those for the South West (Webster (ed.) 2007) are general, hence the lack of specific reference to these in the WSI or the PX assessment (Wessex 2010, Sykes *et al.* 2011). Due to the nature of the proposed excavation areas, which were laid out for the purpose of pipeline construction, and provided only a relatively narrow transect across the three sites selected for further mitigation, the opportunity to answer such questions was in any case limited, and dependent upon the particular types of remains uncovered.

Following the discovery of the masonry building at Bredon's Norton, additional work was requested by the Worcestershire Historic Environment Planning Advisor and the English Heritage Inspector of Ancient Monuments to facilitate a strategy for preserving the remains *in s itu*, and to inform management of the site in future. This work comprised the following tasks and aims:

Fig. 1.1 (opposite) Location of the scheme

- Excavate most of rubble in-fill, and basal organic layer, from the sunken-floored room, retaining a section through the in-fill deposits at the west end. Preserve excavated remains by record.

  Clarify date and primary function of cistern feature and sunken floor.

  Clarify relationship between masonry building, flagstone floor and underlying possible spring feature. If possible without dismantling the floor, monolith sample the underlying deposits.

  Clarify extent and significance of wall plaster – examine for designs that might shed light on the building's primary function.

  Recover further dating evidence and samples to characterise secondary use of the structure — organic deposit sealing flagstone floor suggest use as a grain store, and/or for crop processing

- South of the sunken room, remove shallow surface deposits to fully expose rubble base layer

  Clarify building plan, construction, and the extent of terracing.

- Remove rubble debris from room interior in Area C (sequence appears to deepen from E-W).

  Investigate possible masonry drain features to clarify building function, relationship to possible underlying spring, and/or water management.

- Remove rubble debris from vicinity of masonry 'door jamb'.

  Clarify building plan and extent of *pilae* (*hypocaust floor? base for wooden steps?*)

  Resistivity survey designed to look for further evidence of masonry structures on either side of the pipeline route (Smalley 2011).

  Establish ground plan and extent of masonry structures (function, extents).

To minimise disturbance to the identified structures, Severn Trent Water agreed to route the main pipe trench beyond the western limits of the building.

GEOLOGY AND TOPOGRAPHY

The solid geology along the route comprises clays of the Charmouth Mudstone Formation (formerly known as Lower Lias deposits) of the Jurassic period (British Geological Survey, Geology of Britain online viewer; Figs 1.2 and 1.3). This is typically a blueish-grey clay, but was commonly encountered in the pipeline route in weathered form as a surface deposit of orange-brown clay with no overlying superficial deposits. The route lies to the east of the River Avon and in places crosses a range of superficial geological deposits, including river alluvium in the floodplain of the Avon at the extreme northern end of the route, and Second Terrace river deposits (predominantly sands and gravels) in the southern section of the route, associated with the Avon itself, and tributaries including the Carrant Brook, the Tirle Brook and the River Swilgate, which join the Avon close to its confluence with the River Severn.

Bredon Hill forms the only substantial area of high ground in the vicinity, rising to 305m OD and dominating the landscape in the northern section of the pipeline route (Fig. 1.3). It is an outlying part of the Cotswold escarpment, the main mass of which is formed from clays and silts, overlain by sandy limestone (Marlstone Rock). The junction between the limestone and the underlying clay forms a natural spring-line around the southern flanks of the hill (Bishop 2009). A group of historic villages (including Bredon and Bredon's Norton) are located in a ring around the base of the hill and the associated parish boundaries divide the hill into a series of eight segments, which meet near the summit.

Bredon's Norton (Site 3) was located on a patch of Quaternary Head deposits (clay, silt, sand and gravel), on a south-west facing slope between Bredon Hill and the River Avon. The distribution of the archaeological features through which the pipeline passes correlates closely with the extent of the Head deposits in these fields. Overall, the extent of the Head deposits as mapped by BGS, is broadly co-terminous with the modern village of Bredon's Norton except on the south-east, where the Head deposits extend further. The Charmouth Mudstone was visible in hand-excavated sections as a blue-grey clay, where it was overlain by gravel. Elsewhere within the pipeline easement it was encountered as a weathered orange-brown clay, typical of most of the pipeline route.

Fiddington (Site 1) was located on weathered clay of the Charmouth Mudstone Formation overlain in places by shallow, patchy spreads of dark brown silty clay of uncertain origin (Fig. 1.2). The site is on flat, relatively low-lying ground so the superficial deposits are not likely to be colluvium. However, the site is not immediately adjacent to a watercourse either. The deposits could be alluvium associated with formerly boggy ground.

Pamington (Site 2) is also located on fairly low-lying level ground (Fig. 1.2). The archaeological features were cut into orange-brown weathered clay derived from the Charmouth Mudstone Formation, typical of much of the pipeline route.

The present landscape of field boundaries crossed by the pipeline route is largely a product of 19th century enclosure. Prior to establishment of this field pattern the lower-lying areas adjacent to

Fig. 1.2 (opposite) Geology and topography: Fiddington and Pamington

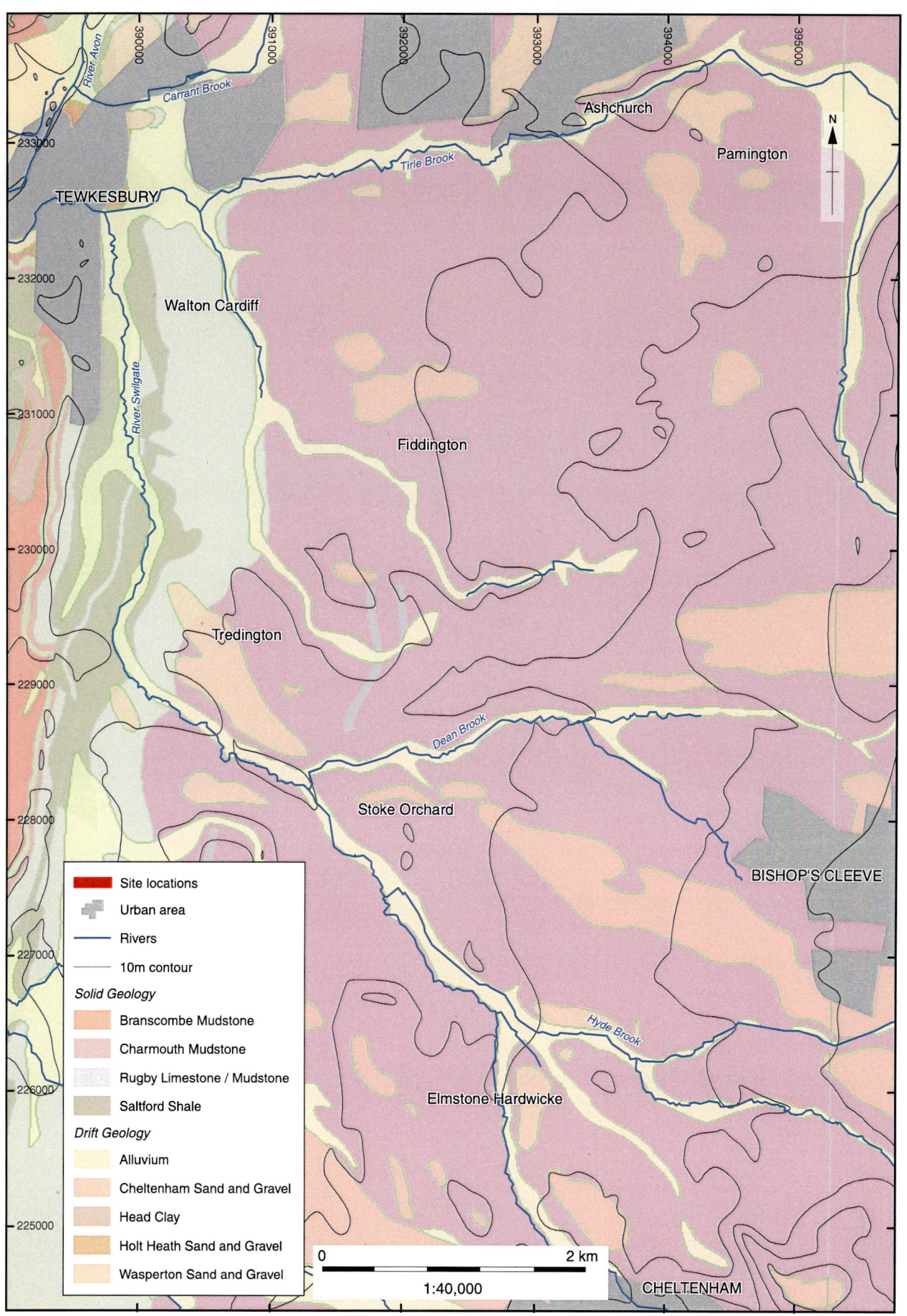

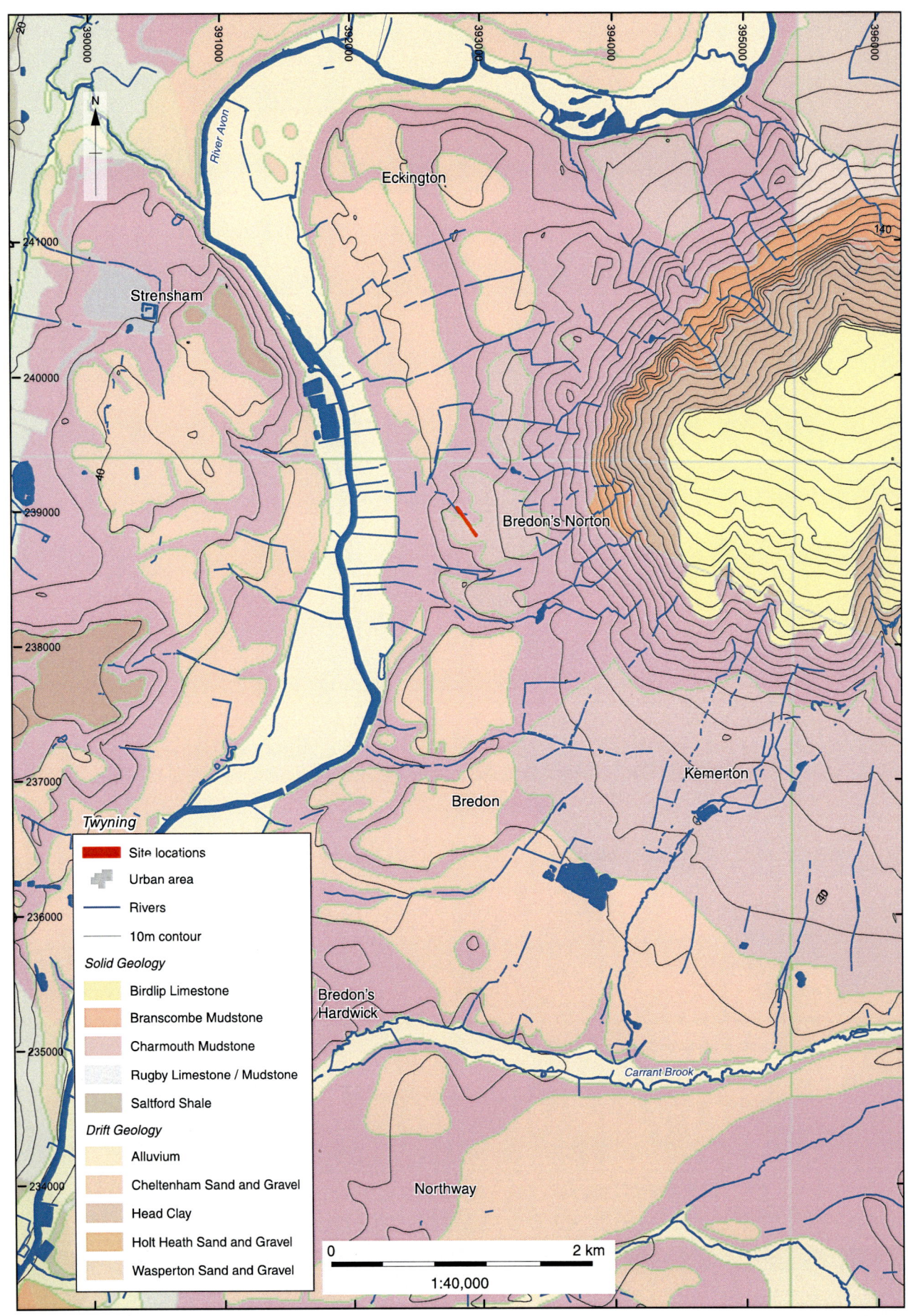

Site locations

Urban area

Rivers

10m contour

Solid Geology

Birdlip Limestone

Branscombe Mudstone

Charmouth Mudstone

Rugby Limestone / Mudstone

Saltford Shale

Drift Geology

Alluvium

Cheltenham Sand and Gravel

Head Clay

Holt Heath Sand and Gravel

Wasperton Sand and Gravel

0   2 km

1:40,000

the River Avon and Carrant Brook were open fields, while the higher ground around Bredon Hill was devoted to pasture (Phase Site Investigations 2009a and 2009b; Page 1913; Elrington 1968). Traces of ridge and furrow were found along most of the pipeline route during the evaluation and excavations. Although rarely surviving as recognisable earthworks, the ridges and furrows are particularly clear on the geophysical survey plots. Ploughing has clearly had a detrimental effect on the preservation of archaeological features at all three of the excavated sites.

ARCHAEOLOGICAL AND HISTORICAL BACKGROUND *by Paul Booth*

The Worcestershire section of the pipeline route includes the Bredon Hill/Carrant Brook area, which has seen considerable archaeological investigation, and is among the richest archaeological landscapes in the county. Trackways and enclosures identified from cropmarks have been recorded extensively in this area. Most are thought to be field systems and enclosures of later prehistoric and Roman date and are mostly concentrated in areas of River Terrace gravels, which are particularly conducive to the formation of cropmarks (Bishop 2009). Extensive archaeological excavations in this area have resulted predominantly from gravel quarrying and pipeline construction.

Palaeolithic/Mesolithic

Palaeolithic finds, including handaxes and other stone tools, have been found in Aston Mill Quarry and Beckford Quarry. Mesolithic flints have come from Aston Mill Quarry, Huntsman's Quarry in Kemerton and from Beckford Quarry, all located in the valley of the Carrant Brook (Worcestershire Historic Environment and Archaeology Service Historic Environment Record [hereafter WHEAS HER]; Dinn and Evans 1990).

Neolithic/Bronze Age

A small Neolithic henge or hengi-form monument was found in a quarry at Westmancote, and another has been found at Bredon (Bishop 2009). Traces of Late Neolithic barrows, surviving as plough-eroded ring-ditches, have been found at Aston Mill Quarry and Huntsman's Quarry, Kemerton. Beaker period burials have been found on Bredon Hill and at Huntsman's Quarry, and a possible early Neolithic flat grave was identified in the Wormington to Tirley Pipeline (Coleman *et al.* 2006).

Huntsman's Quarry also produced extensive evidence for late Bronze Age settlement, comprising fields, droveways, waterholes, roundhouses, structures and pits. Radiocarbon dating suggests that settlement activity started in the 12th century BC

and reached a peak in the 11th century BC, presumably declining or relocating thereafter. The settlement is interpreted as having a predominantly pastoral economy, and produced evidence for textile and bronze working. The artefact assemblage suggested contacts over a wide area (WHEAS, HER).

In the Gloucestershire section of the pipeline, the route mostly crosses heavy clay soils. The archaeological potential of the clays to the south-east of Tewkesbury was explored in 1996-7 by Cotswold Archaeology during excavations along the route of the Tewkesbury Eastern Relief Road, which lies *c* 4km west of the pipeline (Walker *et al.* 2004). A series of Bronze Age and Roman sites were located along a low clay ridge, surrounded on three sides by the flood-plains of the Tirle Brook and the River Swilgate (Walker *et al.* 2004). Within the four excavation areas three distinct locations produced earlier prehistoric pottery (late Neolithic/beaker/early Bronze Age), albeit in very small quantities, two of which which revealed features and artefacts of Bronze Age date, while a third site produced a few residual late Neolithic/Bronze Age artefacts but no features. The Bronze Age activity apparently intensified from the early 2nd millennium BC, and was represented in archaeological terms by ditches, pits, at least one small D-shaped enclosure, and a significant bronze-working site (Walker *et al.* 2004).

Iron Age

There are two certain and one possible Iron Age hillforts on Bredon Hill (Kemerton Camp, Conderton Camp and possibly Elmley Castle):

Conderton Camp, a small middle Iron Age hillfort which enclosed 1.9 hectares, was excavated in 1958-9 and provides a potential example of a 'central place' of the early-middle Iron Age (Thomas 2005). Roughly oval, and aligned along a spur, it was constructed between the late 6th and 4th century BC. It had simple entrances at each end and at least ten circular stone houses built within the ramparts, with over 140 rock-cut pits among them. A large pottery assemblage and objects of bone, iron, bronze and stone suggest a materially fairly rich, self-contained agricultural community. Finds from outside the immediate region were limited, but include a glass eye bead from Glastonbury (Somerset) and two sherds of briquetage containers for salt from Cheshire (Thomas 2005). Conderton Camp was abandoned before the late Iron Age and only occasional Roman finds and features were identified.

The largest of the hillforts on Bredon Hill is Kemerton Camp, near the summit and the closest to the pipeline route (3km east of Bredon's Norton), which was investigated in 1935-7 (Hencken 1938). According to the NMR record (based on Hencken's excavation report):

Fig. 1.3 (opposite) Geology and topography: Bredon's Norton

'The first camp at Bredon Hill [ie Kemerton Camp] was constructed *c* 100 BC and was a simple rectangular univallate promontory fort with overlapping entrance. The pottery and metal-work found is of 'South-West' type and there is evidence that these settlers came into an Iron Age 'A' area and absorbed the earlier inhabitants. The reconstructed fort (1st century AD), now about 22 acres and bivallate, yielded pottery which reverts to an older tradition and sheds its La Tene decoration. Similarly the rampart style of the second phase seems to be a reversion too, from earthen rampart to one with berm and drystone wall revetment in front. Mutilated remains of some 50 adults were found where they had fallen in its main entrance, evidence of inter-tribal fighting as no Roman remains were found' (NMR Record 118075).

The archive has recently been re-assessed by Hurst and Jackson who confirm the significance of the material, but suggest that the date of the site requires re-appraisal as the pottery assemblage appears to date from the middle Iron Age (*c* 4th-2nd century BC) without residual material from other periods, and largely undisturbed by later activity. The human remains archive includes remains of at least 16 individuals and an assemblage of metal-work including a group of weapons (especially spearheads) and personal items (Hurst and Jackson 2006).

A further possible hillfort, The Knolls Camp, lies some 9km south of Conderton Camp at 190m aOD. Middle Iron Age pottery has been recovered from the site (Dunning 1933), though not from a well-stratified deposit, but this site was not considered to be a hillfort in the RCHM survey of the Gloucestershire Cotswolds (RCHM 1976).

An extensive Iron Age settlement, thought to date from *c* 400-100 BC was excavated at Beckford in 1972-1979 on the lower lying ground to the south of Bredon Hill, on a gravel plain beside the Carrant Brook. The settlement included some 50 roundhouses, demonstrating that major Iron Age occupation in this area was not confined to the hillforts (Dinn and Evans 1990; Wills 2004). A number of other Iron Age settlements have been excavated in the Carrant Valley and published more recently.

Roman

Evidence for Roman rural settlement is extensive in the vicinity of the northern part of the pipeline, mainly concentrated on the lower-lying ground around the southern and western slopes of Bredon Hill. As in the Bronze Age the evidence is mainly concentrated on the gravel terraces of the Avon and Carrant Brook.

Four late Iron Age and Roman sites were excavated along the Carrant Brook and River Isbourne, and on both sides of the county boundary, in advance of the Wormington to Tirley Pipeline in 2000 (Walker *et al.* 2004). The broad conclusions

drawn from these sites suggest that substantial settlement enclosures were constructed from the middle Iron Age onwards and remained in use to the end of the 1st century AD, when an increased level of activity saw some enlarged and others abandoned and replaced. All four sites are considered to be typical of low status Iron Age and Roman rural settlement in southern England, and all were abandoned by the 4th century AD, although some evidence for later Anglo-Saxon and medieval activity was encountered on the same sites (Walker *et al.* 2004).

A range of other Roman farmstead sites have been excavated at Kemerton, Aston Mill, Beckford and Ashton-under-Hill (WHEAS HER; Dinn and Evans 1990). A wealthy farmstead (possibly a villa) and other nearby sites at Nettlebeds, Elmont Field and Overbury Wood, form a settlement cluster in Conderton and Overbury. Probable archaeological remains of the later prehistoric and Roman period have been identified to the south of Strensham Waterworks, and to the south-west and south of Bredon's Norton. Two enclosures lie to the west of Kemerton and further cropmarks were recorded in the fields to the south. Gravel quarrying in the area north-east of Aston-on-Carrant has removed a large area of Iron Age to Roman field systems, trackways and settlements on the north side of the Carrant Brook (WHEAS, HER).

No confirmed Roman villa sites were known in the Carrant Valley area prior to the excavations reported here. The most convincing potential villa site in the area is identified in Nettlebed Field, Beckford, on the south-eastern side of Bredon Hill, on the basis of surface finds of Roman brick, tile and possible hypocaust pilae (Bishop 2009). A substantial Roman settlement (*c* 10–12ha in extent) was investigated beneath the Oldbury district of Tewkesbury (Hannan 1993) alongside the Worcester-Gloucester Roman Road, close to the point where it crosses the River Avon. It has been interpreted as a large rural settlement or a series of farmsteads (Hannan 1997, 222–3) although others suggest that a roadside settlement is more likely (Walker *et al.* 2004). The excavations produced brick mortar, painted plaster and roofing tiles, suggesting the presence of buildings in the Roman style. To the south of Tewkesbury, and 5km west of the pipeline, two other potential high status Roman sites are suggested by surface artefact scatters, both of which occupied low gravel-topped hills. These have not been excavated, but surface finds suggest the presence of masonry/brick structures (Walker *et al.* 2004). At Tewkesbury Park, Roman roofing tile and brick tesserae were associated with 2nd- to 3rd-century pottery (Rawes 1973), while at Southwick Park finds, including brick tesserae and 2nd- to 4th-century pottery, suggest a settlement covering *c* 1ha (Marshall 1976).

It remains an open question whether the high density of archaeological features apparent on the River Terrace gravels in the late prehistoric and

Roman periods extends into other geological zones, which can only be answered by survey and/or excavation in non-gravel areas. A preference for building settlements on gravel rather than clay geology, in this and earlier periods, seems clear on present evidence, but as excavations on the Tewkesbury Eastern Relief Road have shown, it is not a universal pattern and may be less marked in some periods than others (Walker *et al.* 2004). This series of sites is particularly informative as a counter to the concentration of investigations on the River Terrace gravels in the Carrant Brook area, and provides a broader context for the Iron Age and Roman Gloucester SoS pipeline sites at Pamington and Fiddington, which are both located on the clay. The two sites on the relief road route which produced evidence for Bronze Age activity also contained the extensive traces of late Iron Age to Roman settlements (with very limited evidence for activity in the intervening Iron Age). The settlements, which were found on clay soils, comprised complex and varied sequences of roughly recti-linear enclosures, associated with a small number of roundhouses and scattered pits. The associated material culture was limited in its range and sophis-tication, and was considered typical of low status rural settlements in the region. The chronology of these sites is not well-defined, the pottery being broadly dated regional wares for the most part, but appears to be focussed mainly in the 2nd and 3rd centuries AD, with limited evidence (from coin finds) for activity in the 4th century AD at one site. Limited environmental evidence from the Roman sites suggests that crop-processing was undertaken on these sites, as well as animal husbandry (Walker *et al.* 2004).

Post-Roman

Evidence for post-Roman settlement is much less common but is clearly present in the Bredon Hill area, again with a strong focus on the gravel soils in the river and stream valleys. Two cemeteries which apparently dated from the late 5th to mid 6th century AD were excavated at Beckford, in the valley of the Carrant Brook, in the mid-1950s (Evison and Hill 1996). On the basis of the finds assemblage the population appeared to have an entirely Anglo-Saxon material culture with no trace of residual Roman material. Grave finds included spears, shields, brooches and beads, but there were few high status artefacts and the authors argue that the community was isolated (Evison and Hill 1996). Anglo-Saxon settlement features, in the form of sunken-featured buildings, have been recorded at Kemerton Water Treatment Works and Aston Mill Quarry (Dinn and Evans 1990; WHEAS, HER). Anglo-Saxon artefacts were reportedly found in Bredon's Norton in the mid-19th century, possibly during construction of the Birmingham and Gloucester Railway (Page 1913).

Medieval

Bredon's Norton is first mentioned by name in the Domesday Survey of 1086 as a relatively minor estate of two hides. By the 13th century, it was the largest of several outlying hamlets, and the most important of three chapelries, associated with the parish of Bredon. The parish lies at the southern edge of the County of Worcestershire, and is bounded on the west by the River Avon and the south by the Carrant Brook. Bredon's Norton forms the north-eastern extent of the parish, and encom-passes a diverse landscape which extends from the floodplain of the River Avon to the summit of Bredon Hill, the hamlet and 12th century church being located on a gravel terrace close to the spring line about midway up the hill. The main settlement at Bredon is located on a plain beside the River Avon, at the base of the hill, and was clearly the centre of an important estate in the mid-Saxon period, first mentioned in relation to a land grant by Ethelbald of Mercia to his kinsman Eanulf to found a monastery there, between AD 715 and 717 (VCH, Page 1913, 279-292; Hooke 1990, 26). In a charter of S116 A.D. 780 (Brentford, Middx, 22 Sept.), Offa, king of Mercia, granted to St Peter's Minster, Bredon 5 hides (manentes) at Teddington, 10 hides (cassati) at Little Washbourne, 10 hides (mansiones) at Cutsdean, all in Gloucs., and 10 hides (manentes) at Bredons Norton, Worcs. Latin, Worcester (http://www.esawyerorg.uk).

According to the VCH for Worcestershire, in 1913 Bredon as a whole covered 5853 acres, of which Bredon's Norton accounted for 1106 acres, including 317 acres of arable, 612 acres of perma-nent grass and 24 acres of wood. From the extensive remains of ridge and furrow it seems that open field agriculture was practised here prior to the 19th century (an Inclosure Act was passed for Bredon in 1808 and Bredon's Norton in 1814) (Page 1913).

Pamington and Fiddington are first recorded in documentary sources in AD 969 and AD 1004 respectively and were subsidiary 'Tithings' (town-ships) within the parish and manor of Tewkesbury at the time of the Domesday Survey (after the Dissolution the estate became Ashchurch parish). The Carrant Brook formed the northern boundary of this very large estate. The medieval landscape to the south of the Carrant Brook was predominantly one of heavy clay soils and appears to have been fairly sparsely inhabited, characterised by open field agriculture, and dispersed settlement divided between the various hamlets and scattered farmsteads. In 1327 there were 89 taxpayers in the whole parish (4284 acres), evenly divided between the main hamlets of Aston, Northway, Pamington and Fiddington, with Natton having a much smaller number than the rest. The landscape was later enclosed – partly in the 16th/17th century and partly in the 19th century (Elrington 1968).

Prior to establishment of this field pattern the lower-lying areas adjacent to the River Avon and

Carrant Brook were open fields, while the higher ground around Bredon Hill was devoted to pasture (Phase Site Investigations 2009a and 2009b; Page 1913; Elrington 1968). Traces of ridge and furrow were found along most of the pipeline route during the evaluation and excavations. Although rarely surviving as recognisable earthworks, the ridges and furrows are particularly clear on the geophysical survey plots (see below). Ploughing has clearly had a detrimental effect on the preservation of archaeological features at all three of the excavated sites.

GEOPHYSICAL SURVEYS CARRIED OUT PRIOR TO EXCAVATION

Magnetic Gradiometer survey

Phase Site Investigations Ltd was commissioned by Mr Glyn Davies of ARCUS to carry out an archaeological geophysical survey along the proposed Gloucester security of supply scheme water pipeline route. The proposed route was approximately 17km long and ran from Coombe Hill, Gloucestershire in the south (NGR S0 892 269) to Strensham Water Treatment Works, Worcestershire in the north (approximate NGR S0 914 395). The work was carried out in March and April 2009.

A 30m wide strip was surveyed along all parts of the route which were accessible and amenable for survey. Of the original 17km route, approximately 2.3km could not be surveyed because of ploughing, high vegetation or were excluded due to gravel extraction. An additional 4.6ha was surveyed beyond the corridor to cover proposed pipe drop off areas.

Bartington Grad601-02 magnetic gradiometers were used for the magnetic survey. The instruments were balanced on site in magnetically uniform areas within each field or group of fields and regularly checked for instrument drift during the course of the survey. Data was collected at 0.25m intervals over profiles spaced 1m apart and stored in the instrument for download at the end of the survey.

A 30m by 30m survey grid system was used for the majority of the survey. The survey grids were established on site using a Leica GX1230 SmartRover RTK GPS system. The GPS system was set to the OSGB36 co-ordinate system. Points were only set out if the positional error was better than 0.05m. Generally most points were set-out at between 0.02m and 0.03m accuracy.

The gradiometer data was downloaded and gridded in Archaeosurveyor 2.4.0 (DW Consulting). Where required the data was destriped and destaggered to remove errors caused by instrument drift and heading errors. Greyscale and X-Y trace plots were produced from this adjusted data. The data for the greyscale plots was clipped at -2nT to 2nT and the Grad. Shade (smoothing option) was selected. The data for the X-Y plots was clipped at -10nT to 10nT and set to a scale equivalent to 12nT/cm. The data was exported from Archaeosurveyor as raster images (PNG files).

The results of the work were presented in three volumes (Phase Site Investigations 2009, Volumes A-C). The data quality across the majority of the survey area is very good allowing the data to be viewed at a narrow range of readings to better identify weak anomalies. Only greyscale images of the three sites chosen for Strip Map and Sample excavation are included in this report (Figs 2.1, 2.6 and 2.14).

A gradiometer survey of the two fields at Bredon's Norton crossed by the pipeline, and covering about 2ha., was carried out in 2006 by an amateur geophysicist Richard Hart, and a greyscale plot supplied to the Worcestershire HER (see Fig. 2.14). The survey was undertaken using a Geoscan 256 gradiometer, using traverses 1m apart, and taking 8 readings per metre, with a resolution of 0.01 nt.

As a result of this survey, it was clear that the pipeline cut diagonally across an area of dense archaeological activity. The survey plot however includes numerous short lengths of ditch that, although closely in alignment with one another, do not quite join up. This may genuinely reflect the nature of the underlying features, but more likely indicates problems in matching the data from all of the grids. It gives a somewhat blurred appearance to the survey plot, making it difficult to be certain about the details of the settlement layout in places. The results of the later geophysical survey transect along the line of the pipeline by Phase Investigations largely agrees with the results of the 2006 survey, giving added confidence to the results of the 2006 survey outside this area.

The 2006 survey suggests that there was a series of curvilinear (circular or oval) enclosures running SSW-NNE along the east side of the surveyed area, possibly flanked on the west by a series of curving longer ditches in the northern part of the area. West of these were two main rectilinear enclosures with a gap between them that possibly represents a trackway entering the heart of the settlement from the west. On the west, north and south sides there were parallel boundaries, suggesting either successive phases of boundary or double ditched enclosures. The curvilinear enclosures lie within the larger area of the rectilinear enclosures, although towards the east linear ditches appeared to cross some of the curvilinear ones, perhaps indicating several phases of settlement rather than contemporary subdivisions. No trace of the masonry building was evident from the gradiometer surveys.

Earth Resistance Survey

Once the Roman building at Bredon's Norton had been discovered, Stratascan were commissioned by Oxford Archaeology to carry out an earth resistance survey of the Bredon's Norton site. In March 2010 a pilot area 60m by 30m was scanned, and a larger survey covering approaching 2ha. was then surveyed in January 2011. Grids were set out using a Leica 705auto Total Station and referenced to suitable topographic features around the perimeter of the site.

The resistance meter used was an RM15 manufactured by Geoscan Research incorporating a mobile Twin Probe Array. The Twin Probes are separated by 0.5m and the associated remote probes were positioned approximately 15m outside the grid. The instrument uses an automatic data logger which permits the data to be recorded as the survey progresses for later downloading to a computer for processing and presentation. Though the values being logged are actually resistances in ohms they are directly proportional to earth resistance (ohm-metres) as the same probe configuration was used through-out.

Readings were taken at 1.0m centres along traverses 1.0m apart. This equates to 900 sampling points in a full 30m x 30m grid. All traverses were surveyed in a 'zigzag' mode. The 0.5m probe spacing of a twin probe array has a typical depth of penetration of 0.5m to 1.0m. The collection of data at 1m centres with a 1m probe spacing provides an optimum resolution for the task.

The processing was carried out using specialist software known as Geoplot 3 and involved the 'despiking' of high contact resistance readings and the passing of the data though a high pass filter. This has the effect of removing the larger variations in the data often associated with geological features. The nett effect is aimed at enhancing the archaeological or man-made anomalies contained in the data.

The following schedule shows the processing carried out on the processed resistance plots.

Despike   *X radius = 1*
              Y radius = 1
              Spike replacement

An interpolation process was applied to the processed data using the following parameters.

Interpolation x2 linear x & y

The data for the site was presented in a report (Smalley 2011), and comprised a print-out of the minimally processed data as a grey scale plot, together with a grey scale plot of the processed data. Anomalies were identified and plotted onto the 'Abstraction and Interpretation of Anomalies' drawing. A greyscale plot of the results is presented in Figure 5.3.

STRUCTURE OF THE REPORT

The report first provides a summary of the methods and results of the geophysical surveys. It then describes the three sites in the order 2, 1 and 3, proceeding chronologically rather than geographically, and uses a chronological framework for description within each site. The geophysical survey data for each site is illustrated to provide a wider context for the features exposed within the relatively narrow transect stripped for construction of the pipeline. Where the Cotswold evaluation trenches fall within the limits of the stripped areas, or lie immediately alongside, these are also illustrated and summarily described in the narrative. Finds and environmental reports for all sites follow, and are organised by category of find or environmental remains, again treating the material from each site separately.

RADIOCARBON DATES

All radiocarbon dates cited in the text are those for the 95% confidence level (2 sigma).

ARCHIVE

The archives for Pamington and Fiddington will be deposited at Cheltenham Museum under accession number 2011.55, and the archive for Bredon's Norton with Worcestershire Museums under the code WSM 67179.

Chapter 2

Archaeological description

by Kate Brady and Tim Allen

PAMINGTON

Introduction

This site was just over 120m long, and ran north-east to south-west across an open field, ending at the B4079 (Fig. 2.1). In this area the easement was generally only 10m wide, increasing at the south-west end to nearly 12.5m wide. The total area excavated was 0.1517 ha. It occupies fairly level ground at a height of just over 24m aOD, the ground sloping down very gradually northwards into the valley of the Tirle Brook, which runs westwards only a few hundred metres north of the site.

The underlying geology is the Charmouth Mudstone Formation (BGS Geology of Britain Viewer 2014), and this lies below a truncated ploughsoil, surviving mainly within the furrows of medieval or post-medieval ridge-and-furrow cultivation (layer 2001). This was in turn overlain by the topsoil (layer 2000), which was generally 0.3m thick (Fig. 2.2).

The furrows crossed the site on a north-south orientation, and were spaced *c* 9m apart (centre to centre). In the northern part of the site some of these were removed during the machine stripping, but in the southern part their fills were not removed, so that the plan of the earlier features is masked at periodic intervals.

Middle-late Iron Age and early Roman (*c* 400 BC–*c* AD 50) (Fig. 2.3)

The principal archaeological features were concentrated in the southern part of the site, comprising a pair of adjacent small sub-rectangular ditched enclosures, which were very clearly defined by the geophysical survey (Figs 2.1 and 2.2). Dating evidence was scarce, but appears to indicate construction in the middle-late Iron Age and abandonment by the end of the 1st century AD.

Enclosure 2077

The more southerly, enclosure 2077, measured 17.5m north-south by up to 13.5m east-west, increasing from 11.5m wide from south to north. Located 3m north-east of 2077 was a roughly east-

west aligned enclosure, 2015, which measured 18m long and 11.5m wide. Neither enclosure was fully exposed on its west side within the easement, and both had been truncated by later plough furrows. No gaps for entrances were found within the excavation area, but there were gaps in the continuations of the ditches indicated in the geophysical survey plot that may indicate entrances.

Enclosure 2077 was investigated by cuts 2076, 2083, 2106, 2066, 2041 and 2057, and on the east side was also excavated in the Cotswold Archaeology (hereafter CAT) evaluation Trench 82, where it was numbered 82013. The ditch was generally 1.7m wide. The depth increased from only 0.6m on the north to 1.2m on the south-east, decreasing again to just under 1m on the south (Fig. 2.4). The profile was a sloping V on the north (Section 2012), but steepened on the east, where it included an ankle-breaker slot at the base in the CAT evaluation trench and in interventions 2106 and 2076 (Fig. 2.3; Fig. 2.4 Sections E-E and 2026; Plate 2.1). Both the depth and profile, however, varied around the east and south-east within short distances along the enclosure (compare Sections E-E, 2018 and 2026). The possibility was considered that the cuts with ankle-breaker slots belonged to an earlier phase of enclosure ditch, perhaps dug in segments, but no clear recuts were found either in plan or section in the cross-sections that were excavated. It is possible that the deeper lengths were due to gang-excavation, some individuals digging more deeply than others, or to the desire to have deeper sumps at intervals around the enclosure.

The fills also varied from only two to four, and again there was no obvious correspondence with depth or position around the enclosure. The shallowest cut on the north (2057), for example, contained at least three fills. The fills were varying colours of clayey silt, generally indicative of gradual natural silting. Typically they included charcoal flecks and contained small quantities of Iron Age pottery and some animal bone (see Fig. 3.1. Nos 1 and 2). The evaluation report noted a small Malvernian rock-tempered (CFTS 3) rim sherd from ditch fill 82015, which exhibits impressed decoration characteristic of middle Iron Age vessels in this ware type (Cotswold Archaeology 2009; Peacock 1968).

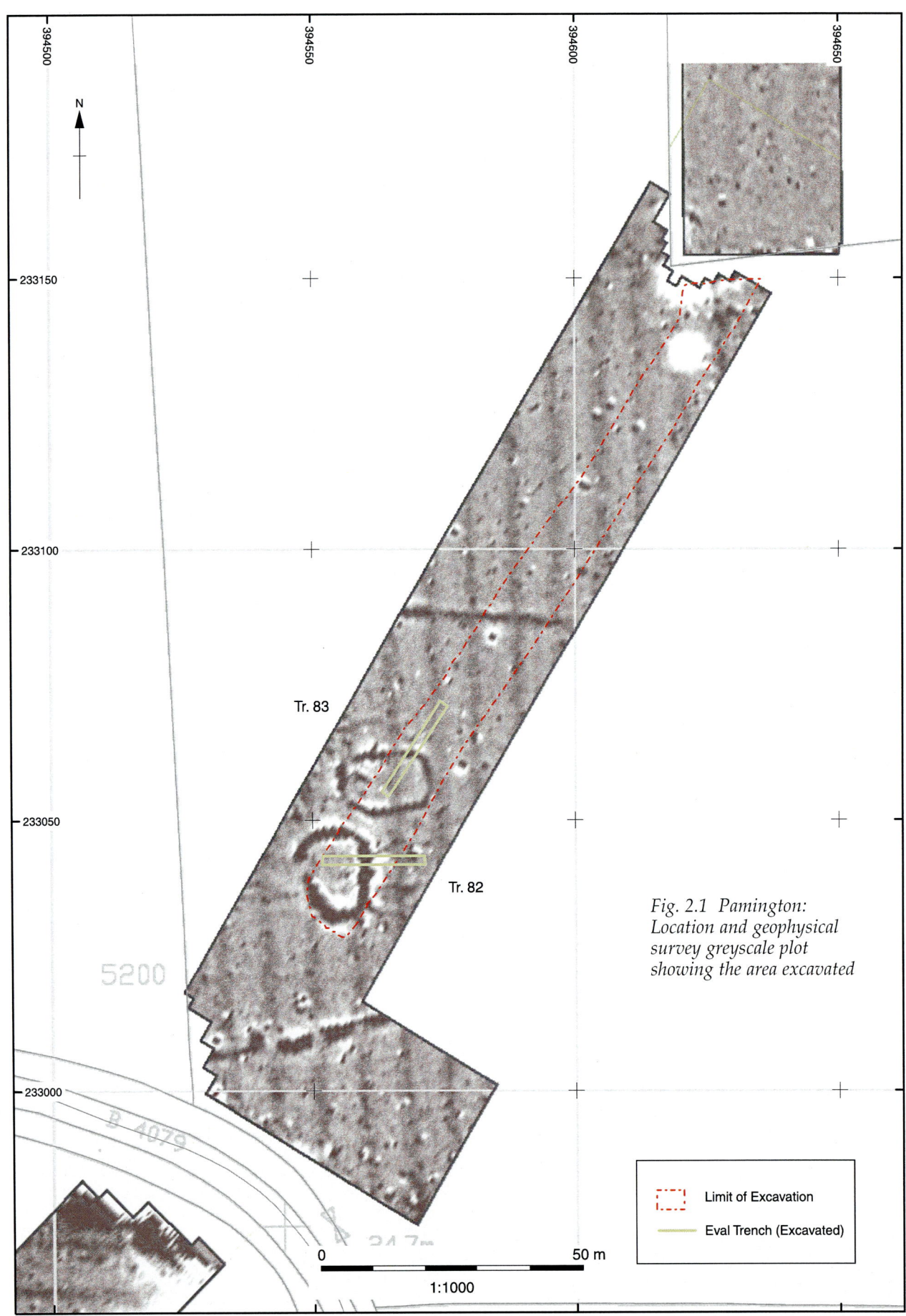

Fig. 2.1 Pamington: Location and geophysical survey greyscale plot showing the area excavated

Tr. 83

Tr. 82

Limit of Excavation

Eval Trench (Excavated)

0   50 m

1:1000

Fig. 2.2 Pamington:
Overall phased site plan
overlaid on the geophysical
greyscale survey plot

Middle/late Iron Age

No dating evidence

Medieval/post-medieval furrows

0   50 m

1:800

Plate 2.1 Enclosure 2077, S.2026

In intervention 2106 on the south-eastern side, the uppermost fill of the ditch (2095) contained 18 sherds of pottery (221g), together with bone and stone, and this has been interpreted as a deliberate dump. This group of pottery has been tentatively dated to AD50-100, providing an early Roman date for the last phase of use of this enclosure ditch.

On the east side the enclosure ditch apparently cut two features. In evaluation trench 82 the ditch is stated to have cut feature 82005 (Section E-E), interpreted in their report as an earlier ditch forming part of a sub-rectangular enclosure faintly visible on the geophysical survey plot (Figs 2.1 and 2.3). This had two fills, from the upper of which eight sherds of middle to late Iron Age pottery were recovered. Just south of this, cut 2066 truncated a shallow pit on the east side, pit 2068 (Fig. 2.4 Section 2018). Pit 2068 measured 1.2m east-west by 0.6m and was 0.2m deep. Its charcoal-flecked silty clay fill (2067) yielded bone and burnt stone.

Further south the enclosure ditch was truncated by two later features. At the south-east corner, the end of an east-west aligned ditch or pit (2104), 0.9m wide and 0.4m deep, clipped the edge of the ditch, cutting its uppermost fill 2103, but did not continue over or beyond it. The single dark greyish brown silty fill (2105) contained two sherds of Malverian ware pottery and bone and may have derived from a mixture of natural silting and deposition of refuse. Some 3m further north, another east-west aligned feature (2107) also clipped the outer edge of the ditch (Section 2026). This appeared to be very irregular in profile, but its light brown clay fill did include occasional fragments of charcoal and comminuted fragments of pottery.

Three undated features were found in the interior of enclosure 2077. Gully or slot 2019 was aligned east-west within the southern part of the enclosure, and was 4.25m long, but was only 0.45-0.55m wide and up to 0.12m deep, with sloping or steeply sloping sides and a rounded base. Its single greyish-brown silty clay fill was characteristic of natural silting. This was in line with feature 2107, but their fills were dissimilar. Two small pits or postholes (2072 and 2074), both sub-circular, up to 0.6m across and surviving only 0.12m deep, were located in the north-west of the interior some 2m apart (centre to centre). Both had a single fill of dark brown silty clay without finds, that of 2074 including two small stones. None of these features showed on the geophysical survey plot.

The geophysical survey plot shows that the north side of the enclosure ditch continued westwards without a break, and had a rounded north-west corner (similar to that on the north-east). It returned southwards for *c* 5m. Beyond this there was an apparent break 3m wide before the ditch began again, just north of the edge of the excavation. Within the excavation area the west side of the enclosure was masked by a later furrow running south-north, but although this was not removed, the geophysical survey shows the continuation of its south-west side running obliquely to the furrow.

Enclosure 2015

As exposed, enclosure 2015 was 14m wide by at least 15m long. It was investigated by cuts 2004, 2011, 2043, 2054, 2032, 2018, 2014 and 2023 (Fig. 2.3;

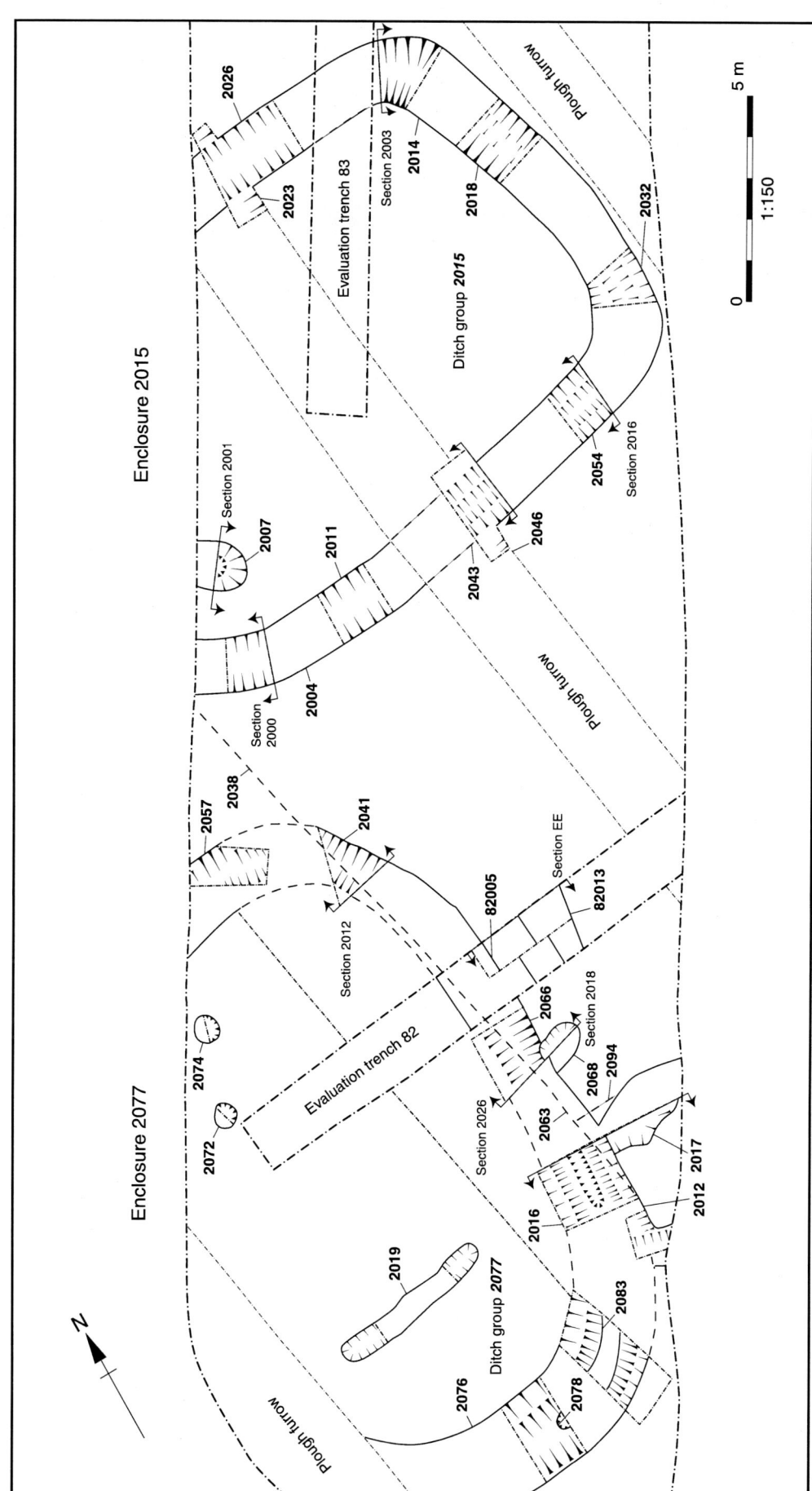

Fig. 2.3 Pamington: Detailed plan of enclosures 2015 and 2077

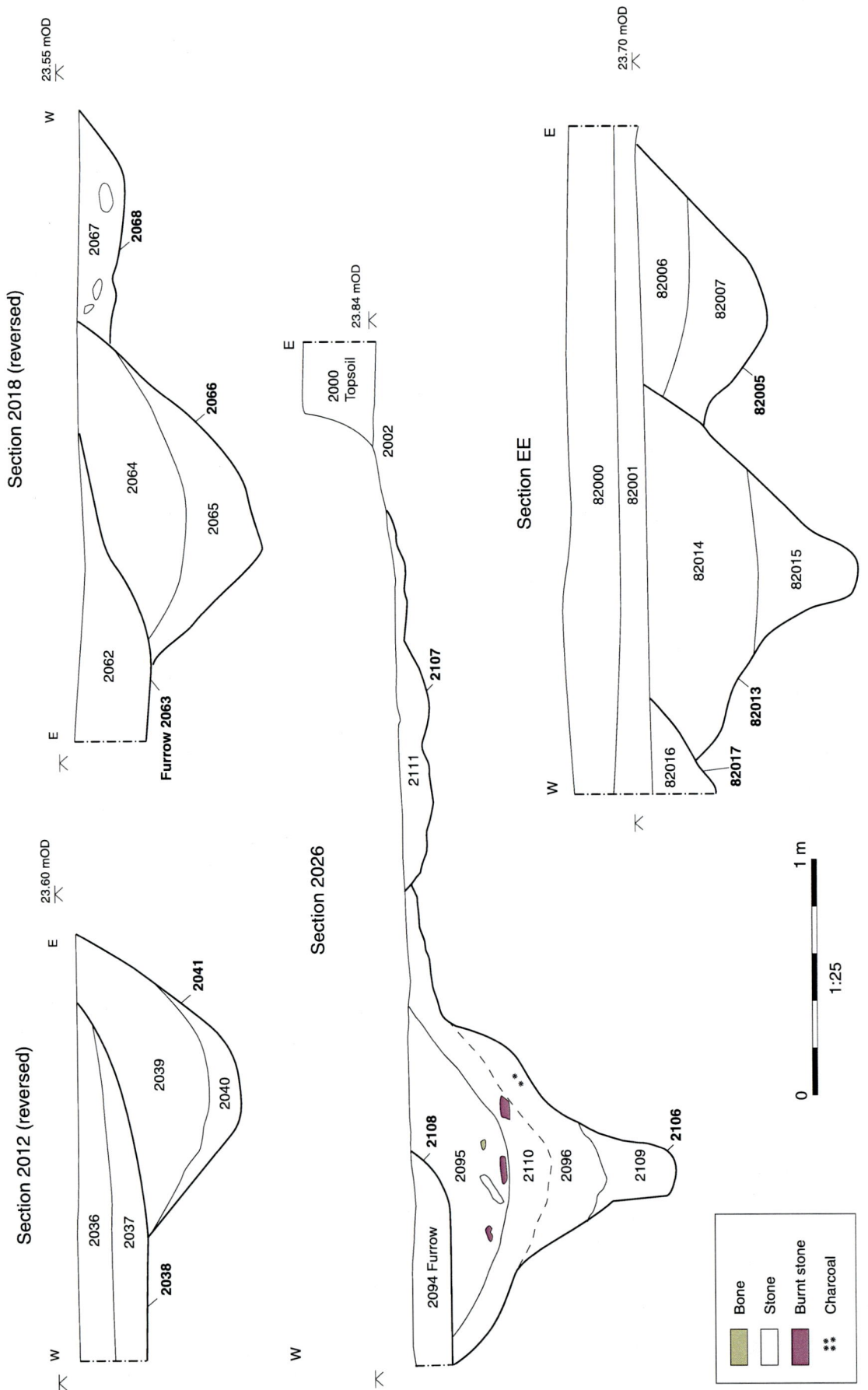

Fig. 2.4 Pamington: Sections of enclosure 2077 and associated features

Plate 2.2). The ditch measured 1.4-1.7m wide and was up to 0.55m deep, with a flat or gently cupped base and sides sloping at around 45 degrees, the outer side sometimes slightly steeper than the inner (Fig. 2.5). All of the slots through the ditch revealed a sequence of gradual natural silting (Plate 2.3), comprising 2 or 3 silty fills that yielded finds of small amounts of bone and pottery, mostly Malvernian ware. Part of the northern side of the enclosure ditch was also identified in the evaluation (Cotswold Archaeology 2009) in trench 83 and recorded as feature 83006. Two sherds of late prehistoric pottery and a single sheep bone and a piece of fired clay were recovered from the ditch during the evaluation.

A single feature, (2007), lay within the south-west corner of the enclosure beside the western baulk of the trench. This measured 1.2m in length, 0.9m in width and 0.5m in depth (Fig. 2.5 Section 2001), but the geophysical survey plot suggests that it was at least twice this long, and may have been associated with another similar feature visible on the survey plot just outside the excavation to the north.

The north-western part of the enclosure beyond the limit of excavation was traced by the geophysical survey. This indicated that the total length of the enclosure east-west was just over 18m. Both the west and north sides show as very strong responses, but there appear to be gaps at the south-west and north-west corners, that at the south-west being some 4m wide, that on the north-west only 2m wide. These may represent entrances.

Discussion including geophysical survey evidence

The pair of enclosures at Pamington are very similar in shape and size. Their internal areas (as surviving) were 9 x 13m = 117 sq.m and 9 x 15m = 135sq.m. Within the excavation area, no features were found within 2 m of the edges of the enclosure ditches, so it is possible that spoil was piled on the inner edge of the ditch to make a bank. This would however have reduced the usable interior area to 5m by 9.5m or 13m, or 45sq m and 65sq m. Alternatively, spoil might have been piled outside the enclosures.

The only evidence of entrances for either enclosure lay outside the excavated area. While the strength of the geophysical responses marking the continuations of the enclosure ditches was strong, the gaps might still not be genuine, so that the presence of entrances is not certain. Taking the survey information at face value, however, there may have been a single entrance to enclosure 2077 midway along the western side, and one or two

Plate 2.2 Enclosure 2015 looking north-west

Plate 2.3 Enclosure 2015, S.2010, looking south-west

entrances to enclosure 2075, the larger at the south-west corner, the smaller at the north-east one. What is immediately clear is that the entrances to the two enclosures were not placed to face one another, nor did they provide access to the area partly surrounded by the two enclosures at right angles.

Other Iron Age features

Some 28m to the north-east of enclosure 2015, an east-west boundary ditch was found. It was investigated on the west by cut 2084 and to the east by cut 2097. The ditch was V-shaped in profile, 1.9-2.1m wide and 0.78-0.85m deep (Fig. 2.5). It contained three yellowish-brown or greyish-brown fills derived from natural silting and yielded small amounts of animal bone and a single sherd of middle Iron Age pottery. (Fig. 3.1.3) The geophysical survey plot shows that the ditch continued in a straight line to the east and west, and was at least 35 m long.

Twenty-five metres north of ditch 2084/2097 was an oval pit (2027) with a flat base, 1.8m long, 1.4m wide and 0.29m deep, with steeply sloping sides and a flat base. It had three silty clay fills, the uppermost of which, 2030, contained a dump of charcoal and burnt clay, but there were no other finds recovered.

In the north-east corner of the site was an oval pit (2048) of probable Iron Age date. It was 1.1m long, 0.7m wide and up to 0.4m deep, with a steep side on the south and sides in the northern half shelving gradually to a cupped base (Fig. 2.5, Section 2015). It had two silty clay fills, the upper of which contained three small fragments of Malvernian pottery, much charcoal and some burnt animal bone, probably dumped from a fire. It was truncated on the north by irregular feature 2051, which had two fills, the lower similar to the basal fill of pit 2048, the upper very like the surrounding natural. This is interpreted as a tree-throw hole.

Medieval

Furrows from medieval ridge and furrow cultivation were found right across the area. These features were on a north-south alignment, and were spaced 9m apart (centre to centre).

FIDDINGTON (Site 1) (Figs 2.6-2.13)

Introduction

The excavation at Fiddington lay just east of the railway line that runs north-south to the east of the village, and skirted a small triangular copse adjacent to the railway line. It covered a length of 400m, crossing three fields in a north-east to south-westerly direction, clipping the north-western corner of the middle field just south-east of the triangular copse, and ending at the railway line. The total area excavated was 0.4999 ha.

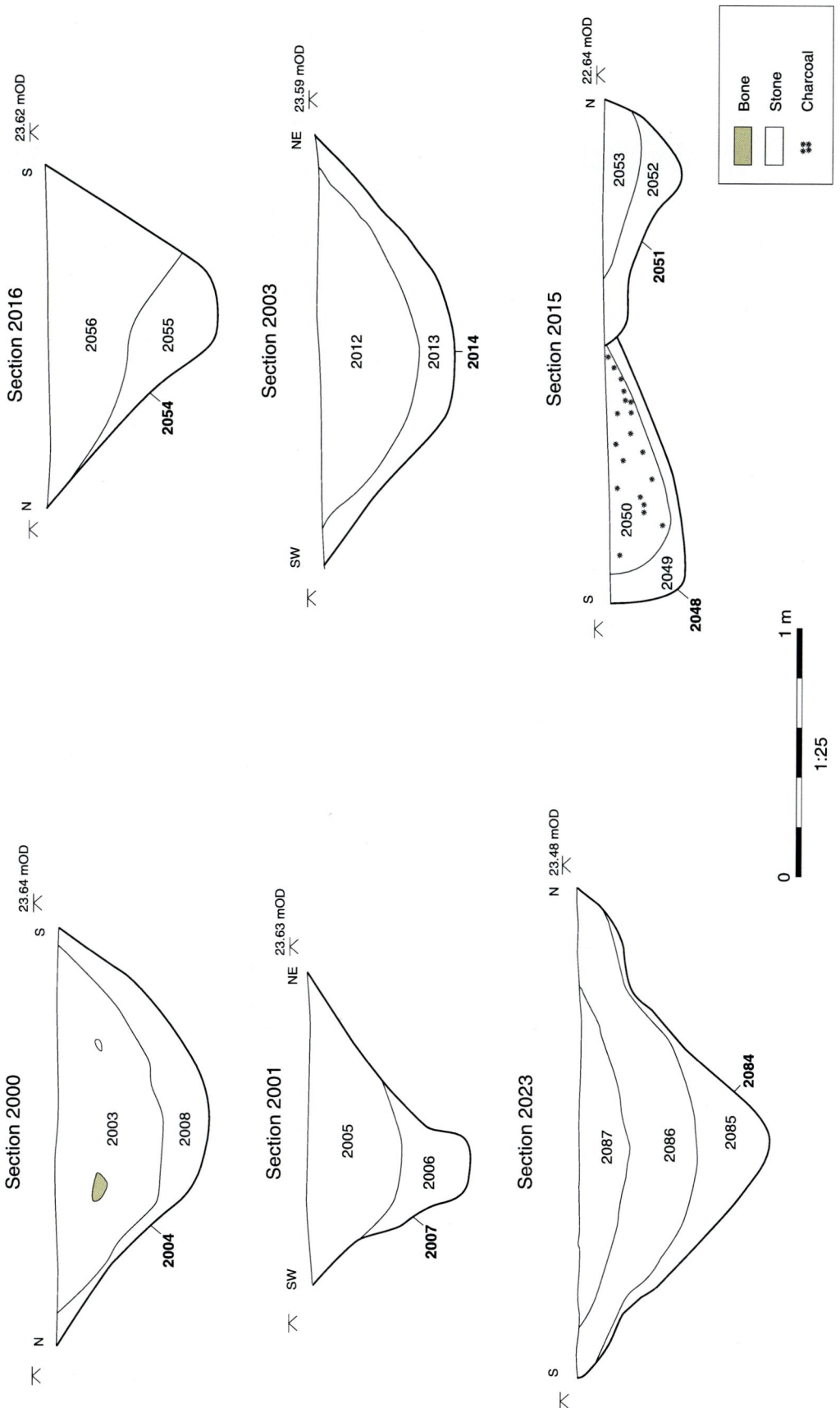

Fig. 2.5 Pamington: Sections of enclosure 2015 and other features

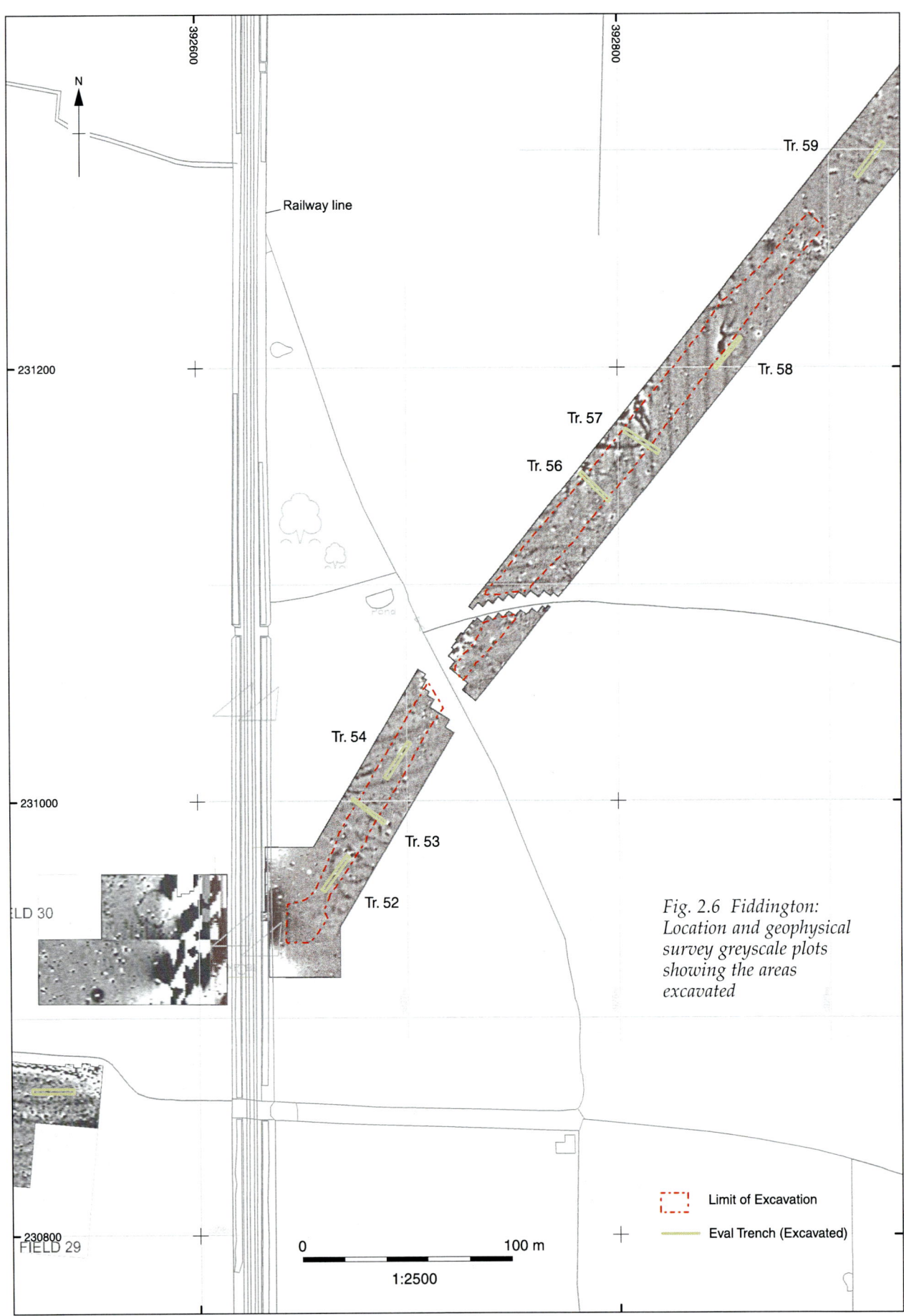

Railway line

Tr. 59

Tr. 58

Tr. 57

Tr. 56

Tr. 54

Tr. 53

Tr. 52

FIELD 30

FIELD 29

*Fig. 2.6 Fiddington:
Location and geophysical
survey greyscale plots
showing the areas
excavated*

Limit of Excavation

Eval Trench (Excavated)

0   100 m

1:2500

The underlying geology is weathered clay of the Charmouth Mudstone Formation (BGS Geology of Britain Viewer 2014), overlain in places by patchy spreads of dark brown silty clay. These were thought to indicate that the site had been boggy at some time in the past. These deposits were cut by the archaeological features, which were sealed by a truncated medieval or post-medieval ploughsoil (1002), probably the same as that filling regularly-spaced furrows of ridge-and-furrow cultivation. This soil was up to 0.2m deep. Layer 1002 was overlain by the modern ploughsoil (1001), a topsoil between 0.2m and 0.4m deep.

The site lay at around 24m aOD, the ground sloping gradually down to the north-east and the west. The nearest watercourse is the Hyde Brook just over 1km to the south-west, which runs north-west to join the River Swillgate, eventually meeting the River Severn.

The width of the pipeline easement was stripped of topsoil, and this gave an excavation area varying in width from 8-15m, generally 10-15m wide. The site was covered with the furrows of medieval or post-medieval ridge-and-furrow cultivation. Although the ridges have now been ploughed out, aerial photographs show that the furrows ran east-west in the southern two fields, but north-south in the third and largest field. Regular north-south furrows were picked up in the northern field, spaced just over 9m apart (centre to centre), and at the north end the change in alignment corresponds to an east-west headland that is faintly visible on aerial views of the site (Google maps 2014). The change from north-south to east-west just north of the southern boundary of this field is very clear on the geophysical survey (Fig. 2.6). The northern limit of the east-west furrows corresponds to the southern edge of the wood just west of the site, perhaps indicating that the field boundary has shifted southwards, leaving a track along the headland at the edge of the northern field. In the more southerly fields the furrows, all of which have the sinuous reverse-S profile, are clear on the geophysical survey plot, but are less regular on the excavation plan; some are missing entirely, probably removed during mechanical stripping. The sinuous shape of the northern boundary of the southern field reflects that of the furrows, explaining the WSW alignment of some furrows. The furrows straighten again at the very west edge of the field on the south. In general the furrows were not emptied during the mechanical excavation, and so the plan of the earlier features is incomplete.

Prior to the excavation, a geophysical survey of a strip 30m wide incorporating the pipeline was carried out (Phase Site Investigations Limited 2009a and 2009b), which has assisted in the interpretation of some of the features cut across by the pipeline easement. Figure 2.6 shows the geophysical survey results within the pipeline route, and Figures 2.7-10 show the revealed archaeological features after stripping, with the survey plot to either side,

together with details of the survey results overlain by the plan of the features in specific areas.

Occupation at Fiddington appears to have been largely confined to the Roman period (although one possible Anglo-Saxon sherd has been identified), and is broadly characterised by small ditched enclosures and drainage and/or boundary ditches, with little evidence for structures. The finds were generally sparse, but localised dumps of material were found in some contexts, including pottery, animal bone and metal objects. The archaeological sequence is not clearly defined, being truncated by later ridge-and-furrow cultivation and obscured by localised thin patches of alluvium, suggesting that the area had been flooded at some time since the Roman occupation.

Early to Middle Roman

At the northern end of the site, (Fig. 2.8) an intercutting sequence of ditches was revealed. One of the earliest of these was an east-west aligned gully (1029), up to 0.5m wide and 0.18m deep, with a single fill from which two sherds (70g) of early Roman pottery was recovered (S. 1008).

Gully 1029 was cut on the east by a WNW–ESE orientated boundary ditch (1027/1106) which measured 2.94m in width and 1.08m in depth. This had steeply sloping sides and a flat base, but with a V-shaped cut in the middle of the base (Fig. 2.9, S. 1008). There were no finds from this, or from a similarly aligned feature just to the north (1006), although the latter, which was shallow and irregular in profile, may have been a remnant of ridge and furrow.

Enclosure A

In the west, gully 1029 and ditch 1027/1106 were cut by a penannular enclosure (1035/1127/1110, hereafter enclosure A), the south-eastern half of which was situated within the excavated area. This was 19m NE-SW, and a continuation of the southern side was visible on the geophysical survey, from which it is clear that the enclosure measured at least 12m NW-SE, the enclosed area being 10m NW-SE and probably *c* 12m NE-SW. There was probably an entrance on the north-west, although faint traces of a possible line around the north-west side make it unclear how wide this was.

The enclosure ditch was narrowest on the south side, measuring *c* 2m wide and around 0.8m deep, although a full cross-section was not excavated here. On the east side the profile in plan bulged westwards (inwards) to a width of over 5m. The west edge sloped gently downwards to the edge of a steeper-sided cut at the bottom of the ditch, which was of similar width and depth to that on the southern side, with a broad flat base (Plate 2.4). A slightly deeper narrow cut lay towards the inner side, increasing the depth to 0.92m. The outer edge of the enclosure ditch was steep. The primary silting

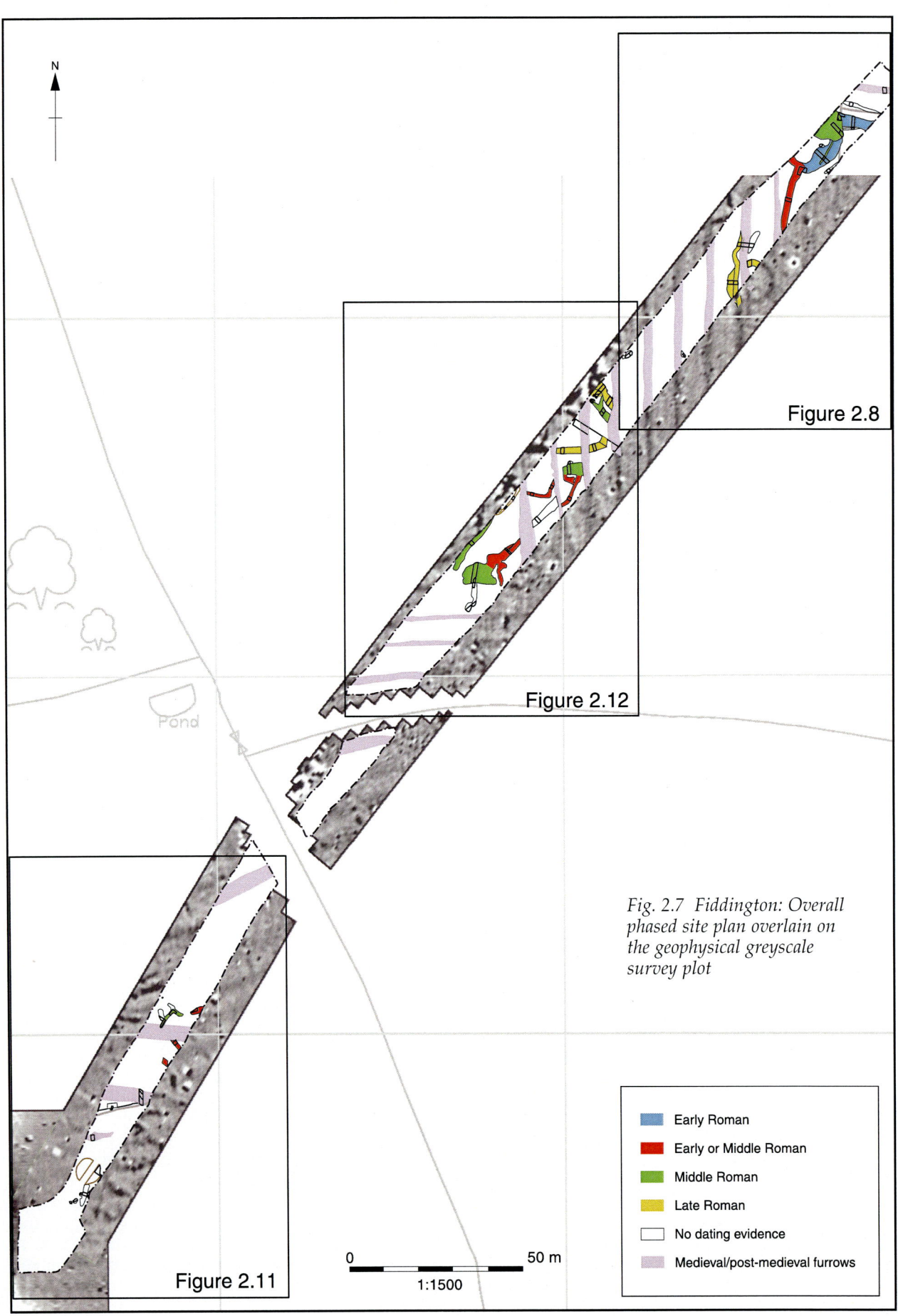

N

Figure 2.8

Figure 2.12

Figure 2.11

Pond

Fig. 2.7 Fiddington: Overall phased site plan overlain on the geophysical greyscale survey plot

Early Roman

Early or Middle Roman

Middle Roman

Late Roman

No dating evidence

Medieval/post-medieval furrows

0   50 m

1:1500

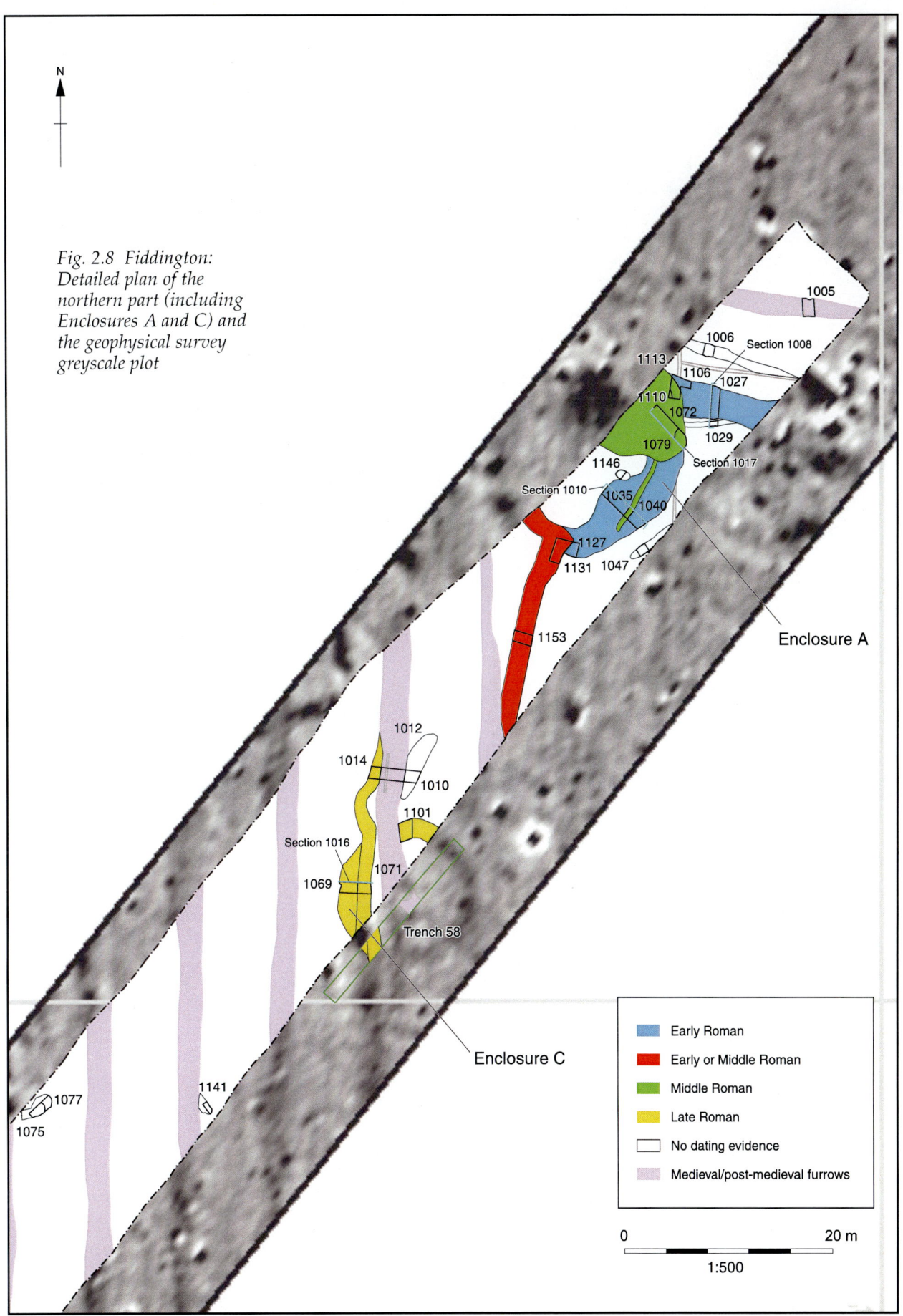

Fig. 2.8 Fiddington: Detailed plan of the northern part (including Enclosures A and C) and the geophysical survey greyscale plot

Enclosure A

Enclosure C

Trench 58

	Early Roman
	Early or Middle Roman
	Middle Roman
	Late Roman
	No dating evidence
	Medieval/post-medieval furrows

0   20 m

1:500

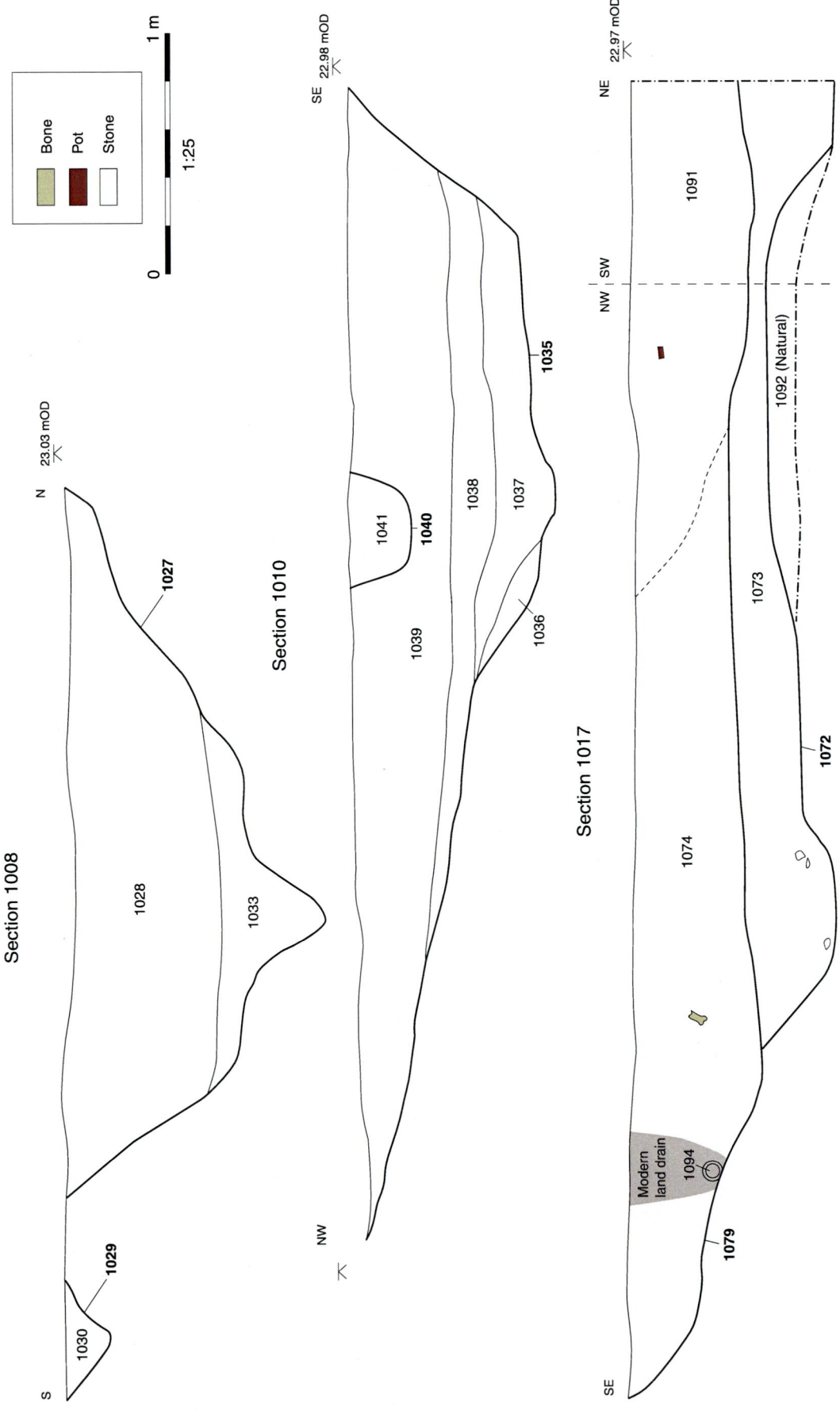

Fig. 2.9 Fiddington: Sections of Enclosure A and associated features

was eroded material from the inner side, and above this the base of the ditch was filled with a greyish-blue silty clay (1037), which contained one animal bone. Above this the upper silty clay fills (1038 and 1039) spread across the full width of the feature (Fig. 2.9, S. 1010).

This may indicate that the ditch was originally similar to that on the south, and was only widened when partially silted. As the outer edge of the ditch has an even profile all the way up, and despite being darker blue-grey than further south along the enclosure ditch no cut was visible in plan; it is unlikely that this represents a later feature altogether cutting across the ditch. The shelving slope may however indicate that this was an original feature of the enclosure, providing access to water in the base of the ditch for animals. Fills 1038 and 1104, the uppermost fill on the south, contained sherds of Malvernian ware pottery of 1st to 2nd century AD date, including a sherd from a club-rimmed bowl. An articulated hind leg of a horse was also recovered from the upper fill of the ditch on the south (1104) and may represent a ritual deposit.

Further to the north-east the ditch was truncated by a large shallow pit 1079=1113, and so is not visible in plan. Excavation at the intersection where this pit cut boundary ditch 1027 (Fig. 2.10, S. 1024) showed that the enclosure ditch survived below the pit. Here the ditch (1110) had a similar profile, with a steep (in some places vertical) outer side and a flat base with a narrow deeper cut in it. Fill 1112 is equivalent to 1038 further south, and the only finds were animal bones. It is probable that the enclosure ditch was of two phases here, as a second slot across pit 1079=1113 south of this showed the narrow cut

in the base of the enclosure ditch turning north-westwards (Fig. 2.9, S. 1017; S. 1021), rather than continuing north. The very varied colour of the natural in this slot meant that some was dug away as fill, so that the plan here is not complete. It is alternatively possible that the dip in the bottom of cut 1110 was simply due to digging into the softer fill of the earlier ditch.

Cutting the uppermost fill on the east side of 1039 was narrow gully 1040 (Fig. 2.9, S. 1010), whose fill contained sherds of Severn Valley ware. This ran north-east for 7.5m before being cut by pit 1079=1113. Some 3m to the east of the southern terminus of 1040 was the terminus of another gully 1047 running north-east into the baulk. It measured 0.82m wide and 0.23m deep and was filled by a mid yellowish grey silt. No artefacts were recovered from it, but it may have been associated with 1040.

To the west of 1140, and cutting the edge of layer 1039, was an oval feature 1146 aligned east-west, 1.4m long, 0.8m wide and up to 0.35m deep. This had a single very dark clay fill, possibly the residue of organic material, and no finds. The north edge was vertical and slightly undercut at the bottom, the south side sloped evenly down to meet it, and the profile suggests that this may have been a tree-throw hole.

Gully 1029, ditch 1027/1106 and the penannular enclosure ditch were cut by a large sub-circular pit (1079/1113), also visible beyond the limit of excavation on the geophysical survey (Figs 2.7 and 2.8). The south-east half lay within the excavation, and measured *c* 7m across (NE-SW). It was up to 0.55m deep, with a flattish base and moderately sloping concave sides (Fig. 2.10 S. 1024). It contained a

Plate 2.4 Enclosure A, east side, S1010 looking north

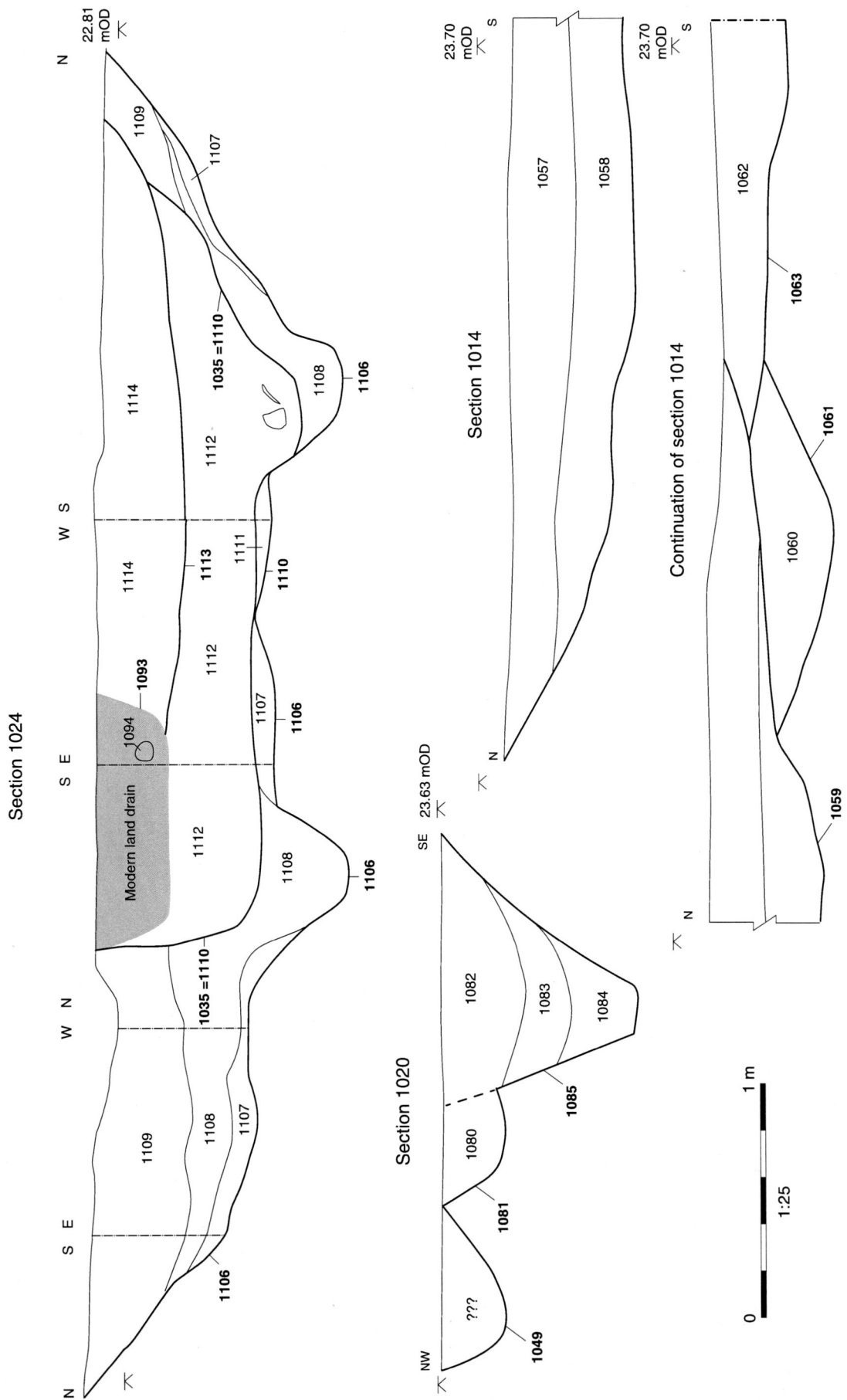

Fig. 2.10 Fiddington: Sections related to Enclosure A, and to ditches and hollows further south-west

single fill (numbered variously 1074/1091 and 1114) with further sherds of Severn Valley ware, along with animal bone, suggesting that at least part of the fill derived from domestic waste.

Extending up to the southern side of the penannular enclosure, cutting its fills and apparently recutting it to the west, was ditch 1131/1153. Where it cut the enclosure ditch, ditch 1131 had sloping sides and a broad flat base, similar to that of the enclosure, but just outside this, it had sloping sides and a narrow 'ankle-breaker' slot in the bottom. Further south the profile broadened, and was steep on the east but stepped on the west. The ditch was 1.8m wide and deepened as it approached the enclosure from 0.5m to 0.75m deep. The recutting of the enclosure ditch strongly suggests that the enclosure was still visible and in use, even though the ditch had largely silted up. The middle fill contained scraps of Malvernian pottery, the upper fill sherds of Severn Valley ware.

The ditch ran south for *c* 18m, disappearing beneath a furrow just before the edge of the site. Its terminus may be visible as a geophysical anomaly just beyond the line of the furrow, some 3m short of a second enclosure 1069/1101.

The southern area (Fig. 2.11)

Although there were a number of apparent curvilinear geophysical anomalies in the most south-westerly segment of the site (Fig. 2.10), most of these proved illusory, being found neither in evaluation nor after stripping for excavation. This area contained relatively few archaeological features, most of which were of uncertain character and were poorly dated. A group of features that may have been related included a 4m length of ditch aligned roughly east-west and projecting from the eastern side of the trench (1149). This ditch was U-shaped in profile, less than 1.4m wide and 0.3m deep. Its fill

contained a small pottery assemblage (9 sherds, 109g) of body sherds probably of early Roman date from a naturally accumulated silty fill. To the west of its terminus was a T-shaped ditch (1139/1098), which was 0.70m wide and 0.2m deep with a naturally silted single fill containing a tiny fragment of possible black-burnished ware. The 'stem' of the T, aligned north-east to south-west, cut an irregular feature (1096) that did not contain dating evidence. This was possibly a tree-throw hole. South-east of the stem of the T and partly masked by an east-west furrow was a 4m length of ditch (1138) alighted north-west to south-east. This was 1.1m wide and 0.48m deep, with a flat base and 45 degree sides. Its sole fill (1137) appeared to have been a result of natural silting and included bone and four small sherds of Malvernian pottery.

Some 17m south-west of this a slot through furrow 1087 revealed an undated ditch (1090) on a north-west alignment. This survived 0.8-1.0m wide and up to 0.32m deep, with gently sloping sides and a rounded base. The primary fill (1089) was an olive-grey silty clay derived from natural silting, overlain by (1088), a very dark grey-brown silty clay including charcoal, lumps of clay burnt red, lenses of redeposited clay and butchered animal bones, but no certainly diagnostic dating material (Plate 2.5), although a fragment of a possible triangular brick ('loomweight') may indicate a late Iron Age or early Roman date (see Poole, Chapter 3). This may correspond to an indistinct curvilinear feature on the geophysical survey plot.

South of this a number of other possible features (1120, 1122, 1124, 1134, 1144, 1145) were tested by hand-excavation, but most were irregular and did not produce any dating evidence. Feature 1120, which was traced on a north-south alignment to a southern terminus over a distance of 6m, and corresponded to an anomaly on the geophysical survey, may have been a shallow ditch with gently sloping

Plate 2.5 Ditch 1090 beneath furrow 1087, looking east

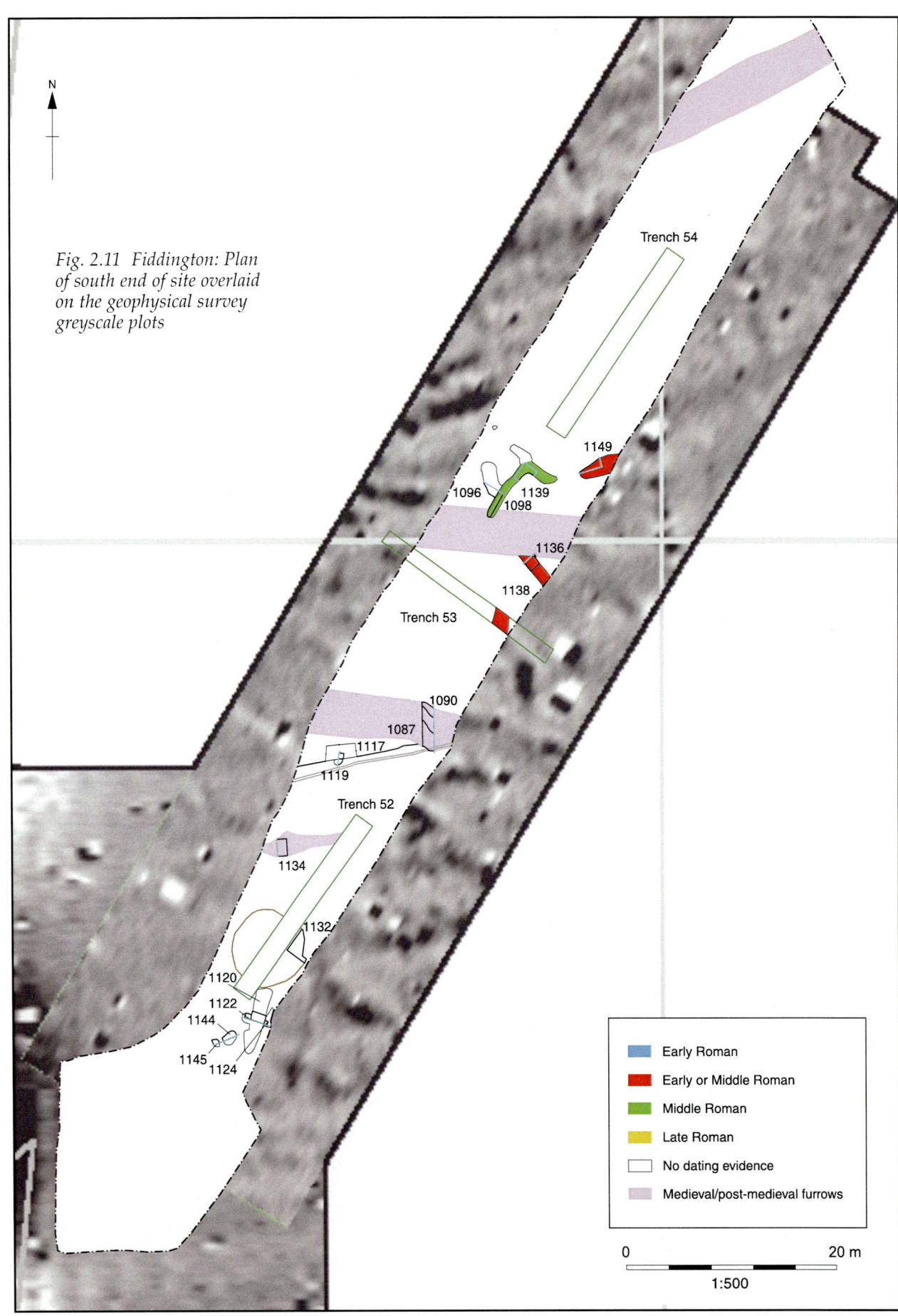

Fig. 2.11 Fiddington: Plan of south end of site overlaid on the geophysical survey greyscale plots

sides and a flat bottom, though it lay within an area of clays of different colours, which may all have been variations in the natural. These features, including a sub-circular feature (1132) *c* 7m across and 0.5m deep, were interpreted as natural hollows. The geophysics plan showed a circular ditch in this area (in the location of feature 1132) but it was not found in the excavation or in evaluation trench 52. Irregular oval pit 1144, measuring 1.4m by 1.1m across but only 0.08m deep, however had animal bone and a small fragment of fired clay in its fill.

One ditch (53003) was identified in evaluation trench 53 (Cotswold Archaeology 2009, 10 and Fig. 10), and contained a single sherd of late prehistoric pottery. This may correspond to a slightly curving anomaly on a north-east to south-west alignment, not plotted on the excavation plan, and lying 2-3m west of its position on the evaluation trench plan. There is a very poor correspondence between the discovered archaeological features and the geophysical survey in this part of the site, and it is possible that the geophysical survey is not plotted in the correct position here. A suggested realignment of the plan, which has a much closer correspondence to the excavated evidence, is shown in Figure 2.11 (inset).

The central area (Fig. 2.12)

Another focus of activity of the early to middle Roman period lay in the centre of the site, and was principally defined by a ditch running north-east to south-west (1025). This ditch was slightly sinuous in plan, and was traced for *c* 20m in a north easterly direction along the edge of the excavated area. Where sectioned it was 1.4m wide and 0.6m deep. It had a single greyish-brown silty clay fill (1026) that yielded a substantial pottery assemblage (56 sherds, 1497g) dated to the mid to late 2nd century (see Fig. 3.1.4-7). Its continuation beyond the site edge on the geophysical survey plot was uncertain, but a Cotswold evaluation trench (Fig. 2.12, Trench 156) was dug across the geophysical survey anomalies here, and identified a ditch of very similar dimensions on the same orientation (56002), although this contained only a handful of late prehistoric sherds (Cotswold Archaeology 2009, 10 and fig. 11). This appears from the geophysical survey to intersect with the continuation of ditch 1015, and to end just beyond it.

Immediately to the north-east of 1025 within the excavation area was a very shallow feature 1066, also on the geophysical survey and picked up by the evaluation (56007). It contained a little animal bone and fired clay, but nothing diagnostic of date. There was apparently no relationship with either 1025 to the south or 1015 to the north

Ditch 1015 ran just south of west-east into the excavation from the west, and cornered sharply before continuing NNE as ditch 1155. Where numbered 1015 the ditch was nearly 1m wide and 0.35m deep, but 1155 was only 0.16m deep, and

apparently ended below a medieval furrow. The geophysical survey however shows it continuing up to broad feature 1053, and the narrowness of the adjacent furrow in comparison to the others suggests that machining had removed the ditch here. Both ditches had a single brown silty clay fill containing a little Roman pottery. Feature 1053 was the number given to the cut for a spread of brown clay with orange-grey mottles (1054), which was 0.28m deep and contained Roman pottery (13 sherds, 372g) including black-burnished ware and central Gaulish samian of mid to late 2nd century date. This was sub-rectangular, orientated east-west, and was nearly 2.4m wide and around 5m long, with sloping sides curving in to a flattish base. It narrowed slightly at the west end, where there was an irregular soil spread to the south, which was not investigated. At the north-west corner it was cut by a slightly deeper oval pit 1055, whose fill did not contain any finds.

Also running into 1053 at its north end was ditch 1064, which was aligned SSE parallel to 1155. Where sectioned it was of similar depth to 1155, and had a similar single brown silty clay containing a little Roman pottery. This ditch turned south-westwards opposite the corner of 1015/1155, and beyond a medieval furrow continued as broader feature 1049 some 0.35m deep (equivalent to 56013 in evaluation trench 56), until obscured by a broader furrow. Beyond this several ditch cuts were evident continuing south-westwards. The two on the western side both had sloping sides and a cupped base, and were just under 0.3m deep, so may represent continuations of 1049. The relationship between them was uncertain. The third and easternmost ditch was 0.86m deep, with steep sides and a narrow flat base, and contained three fills, the middle one including scraps of Roman pottery (Fig. 2.10, S.1020). Although not excavated the terminus of this deep ditch is evident from the plan only 3m south of the cut across it, where these ditches ran into an extensive irregular area of clay.

A slot was cut across this towards the south end, opposite to the terminus of ditch 1025, where it consisted of pit or ditch terminus 1061 cut by ditch 1063 running due south, cut in its turn by broad saucer-profiled hollow 1059 (Plate 2.6), whose successive silty clay fills (1058 and 1057) contained Roman pottery, including a substantial part of a Severn Valley ware jar of 2nd to 3rd century date in the primary fill, along with an assemblage of 19 sherds (663g) of 2nd century date. The lower fill also contained many small limestone fragments. Feature 1059 was aligned east-west and was broadly sub-rectangular in plan, though somewhat irregular, and was up to 10m long and 5.5m wide (Fig. 2.10, S. 1014). It is just possible that 1061 represents the terminus of either ditch 1080 or 1049, as it lay on their projected alignment, but was interpreted on site as a tree-throw hole. Another tree-throw hole (1032) clipped the southern end of ditch 1034.

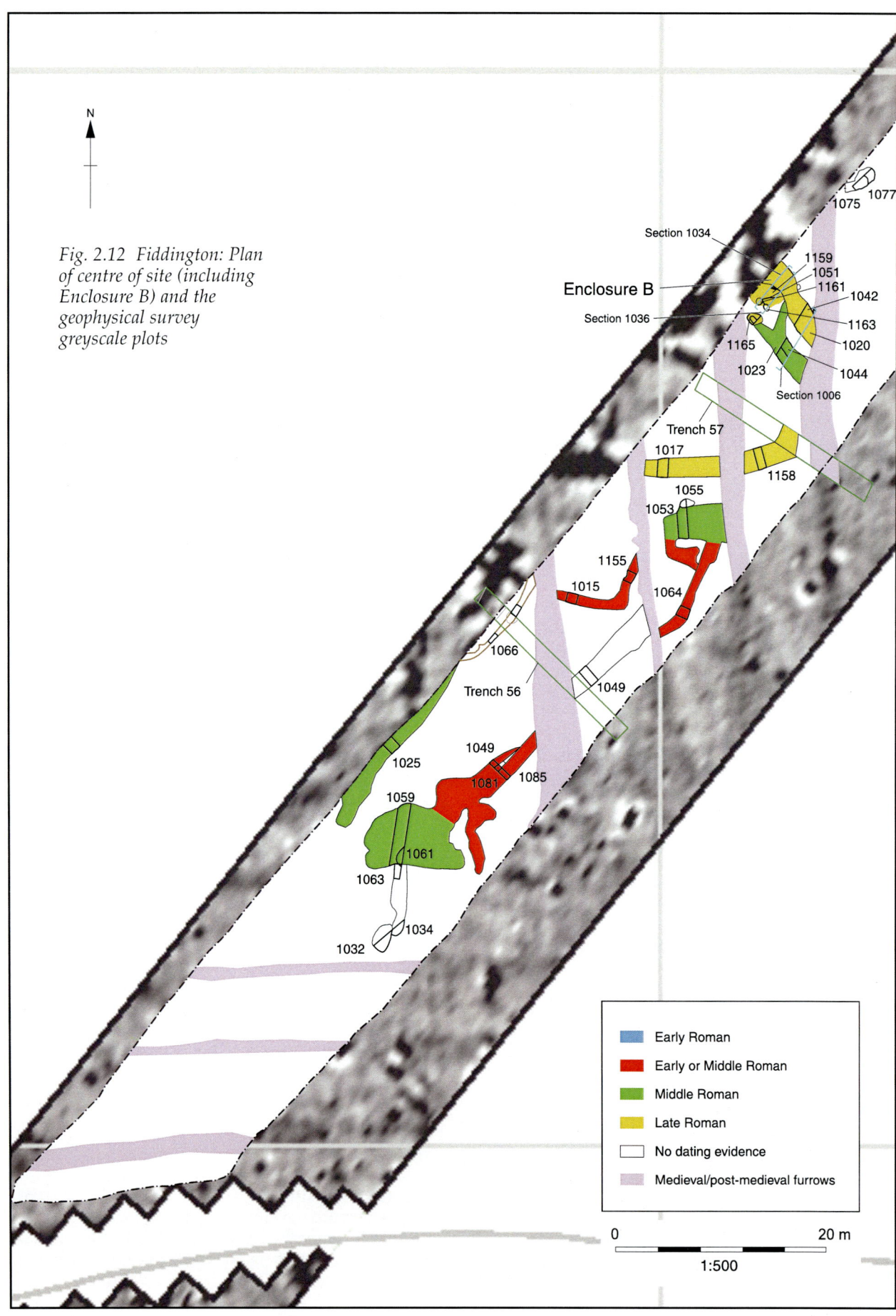

N

Fig. 2.12 Fiddington: Plan of centre of site (including Enclosure B) and the geophysical survey greyscale plots

1075
1077

Section 1034

1159
1051
1161
1042

Enclosure B

Section 1036

1163
1020
1165
1023
1044

Section 1006

Trench 57

1017
1158

1055
1053

1155
1015
1064

1066

Trench 56
1049

1049
1025
1081
1085

1059

1061

1063

1034
1032

Early Roman

Early or Middle Roman

Middle Roman

Late Roman

No dating evidence

Medieval/post-medieval furrows

0   20 m

1:500

Plate 2.6 Section showing 1059, 1061 and 1063, looking east

The interpretation of this complex of features is unclear. None of the features is diagnostically early Roman, and the whole complex could have belonged to the middle Roman period. Ditches 1015/1155 formed an L-shape, and appear to represent two sides of an enclosure approaching 10m north-south by at least 14m east-west, but no north side was evident on the geophysical survey, unless enclosure 1017/1158 was already in existence. If it was, these might represent small enclosures up against the south side of the larger enclosure, with an entrance on the north-east side. Ditches 1064, 1049 and 1081 may have formed part of one boundary belonging to a larger enclosed area attached to the enclosure to the north (as may ditch 1025 further west), parts of which were recut as more substantial lengths of ditch, but may also represent shorter and smaller ditches dug as occasion required for drainage around temporary pens or other working areas. The broad features at the north and south ends may represent dug features, or simply areas of trample close to entrances, with pottery (and in one case limestone) thrown in to help firm them up.

Middle Romano-British (Figs 2.12 and 2.13)

Two ditches orientated north-west to south-east, and running alongside one another, were uncovered on the west side in the central part of the site. Both ditches terminated within the site on the north-west, ditch 1023 having a straight terminus cut by pit 1165, ditch 1044 turning north-eastwards before being cut away by a later ditch 1020. Ditch 1044 had a V-shaped profile with a rounded base, and measured 0.95m wide and 0.56m deep; ditch 1023 had a broader V-shaped profile and measured 0.85m wide and 0.44m deep (Fig. 2.13, S.1006). Both ditches had a mid greyish-brown silty clay in the lower parts, so that which came first could not be determined (Plate 2.7). An assemblage of 17 sherds (151g) of pottery of probable 2nd century date was recovered from ditch 1044, and a group of 110 hobnails and further pottery from a decayed shoe from fill 1046 in ditch 1023 (Plate 2.8 ; Fig. 3.1. Nos 10, 13 and 15). The upper part of both ditches was filled with a mid greyish brown silty clay, from which 72 sherds (948g) of pottery dated to the late 2nd century or later was recovered. This suggests that both ditches were dug over a limited period of time, probably in the mid-late 2nd century.

Although the furrow that obscured these ditches at the south-east was not removed, the geophysical survey clearly shows that it masks two separate features curving southwards, the more northerly corresponding to the line of ditch 1020, the more southerly to a continuation of 1023/1044 (Fig. 2.12 inset). While it is possible that the former in fact marks the continuation of the medieval furrow, and that 1020 did not continue, the latter anomaly lies west of the line of the furrow, and must belong to one or both of ditches 1023/1044. Where the furrow crosses, there is a short linear anomaly running north-eastwards, which may be similar to the north-east end of ditch 1044. It is therefore possible that both ditches belong to a three-sided very small enclosure open on the north-east side. There is a distinct southward curve to the geophysical anomaly below the later furrow, which would make an acute angle at the south-east corner of this small enclosure; a similarly acute angle is visible at the junction of 1015 and 1155 25m further south. Alternatively, this curve may

Plate 2.7 Ditches 1044 and 1023 looking south-east

indicate that one of these ditches represents the original north-east side of the curvilinear enclosure (Enclosure B, see below) represented by 1158 and 1017, later recut and enlarged northwards as ditch 1020.

Plate 2.8 Close up of hob-nailed boot in ditch 1023

Late Romano-British

Pit 1165, which cut the end of ditch 1023, was oval in shape with an irregular profile and flat base. It measured 1.1m in diameter and 0.4m in depth and was partly filled by a deposit of large stones within a matrix of dark brown silt (Fig. 2.13, S. 1036). A large amount of pottery was recovered from this fill (45 x 433g), dated 2nd century or later, and suggesting a deliberate dump. Just over 1m to the north of pit 1165 ditch (1159) ran eastwards into the excavation area and terminated after 10m. It was cut away by ditch 1020, but the terminus survived east of this just north of ditch 1044. It measured 0.8m wide and 0.2m deep, and had a single olive-grey silty clay fill 1160. Like pit 1165 this also contained large stones, and is dated by pottery and a coin of Carausius (ruled in Britain from AD 286-293). The fills of both ditch 1159 and 1044 were sealed beneath a layer of grey brown silty clay with stone and charcoal inclusions (1051), which yielded another large assemblage of Roman pottery dating to the late 2nd century or later (see Fig. 3.1.8), along with bone and iron nails. The spread was cut by a pair of adjacent shallow postholes, 1161 and 1163, one of which (1161) contained four sherds (34g) of pottery dated mid 2nd century or later (Fig. 2.13, S.1034).

Enclosure B

Spread 1051 was cut by the north-eastern arm of a curvilinear enclosure ditch (1020/1158/1017, hereafter Enclosure B), which continued to the west on the geophysical survey plot. It defined an area at least 20m across north-east to south-west and greater than 10m north-west to south-east. The ditch

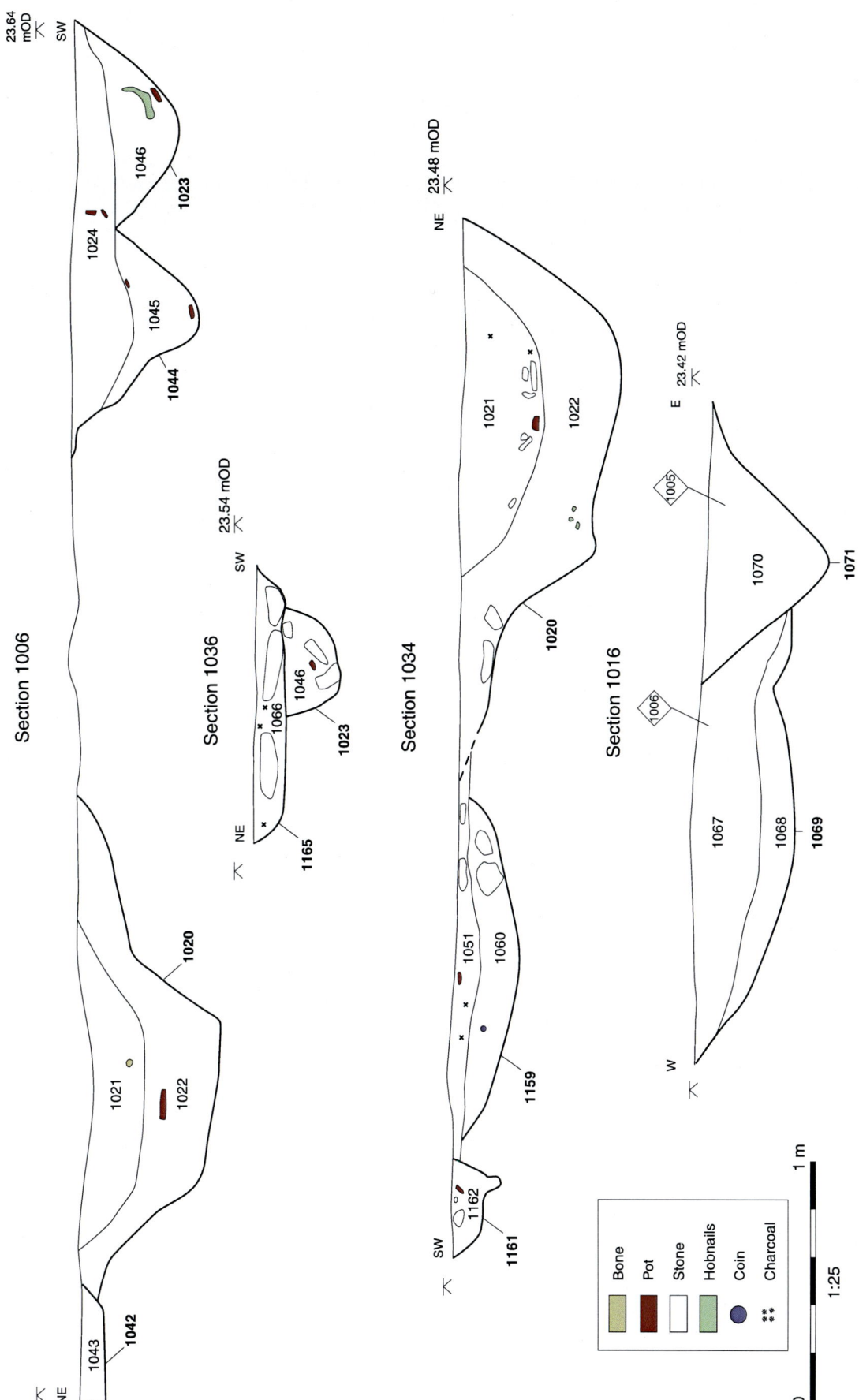

Fig. 2.13 Fiddington: Sections of features associated with Enclosures B and C

measured 2.1-2.3m wide and 0.6-0.7m deep, with a rounded profile containing two fills (Fig. 2.13, S.1034). Pottery from the three interventions (1017, 1020 and 1158) totalled 136 sherds (2154g) and indicates a 4th century, possibly later 4th century, date (see Fig. 3.1.11). A fourth intervention (Trench 57 feature 57003) was cut by CAT during evaluation (Cotswold Archaeology 2009, 11 and figs 11 and 20), but produced only 7 sherds of Severn Valley ware. Layer 1021, dark silty clay in the top of intervention 1020, was notably rich in pottery and also contained a moderately large assemblage of animal bone, suggesting a deliberate dump of domestic refuse here. The recovery of 50 hobnails from this fill suggests that a hobnailed shoe was also included in this dump. Finds from cleaning over layer 1051 and fills 1021-2 in ditch 1020 contained large sherds of Roman pottery of late 3rd to 4th century date and a single early Anglo-Saxon sherd.

Beyond the edge of the excavation the geophysical survey plot showed a complicated series of anomalies whose interpretation is not straightforward. There appears to be a blank north-south strip just west of the end of ditch 1023, perhaps indicating an entrance, but as this corresponds to the line of a medieval furrow it may instead represent interference.

Enclosure C

Some 50m further to the north-east was a sub-circular enclosure *c* 14.8m across east-west and 13.5m north-south, whose north-western half lay within the excavation (Figs 2.7 and 2.8, Enclosure C). The remainder was clearly visible on the geophys-

ical survey plot. Slots were cut across the north and western sides, and were numbered 1101 and 1069 respectively. Between these two areas the feature was truncated by a ditch (1014) and a medieval plough furrow, both aligned north-south. The furrow was not emptied. The enclosure ditch was 1.82m wide, and was 0.48m deep (Fig. 2.13, S.1016). It was filled with a dark grey to black silty clay, with much charred material on the west, possibly derived from a deliberate episode of backfilling with domestic waste. The fill on the north (1100) contained a large assemblage of animal bone, including an articulated horse hind leg, and a group of pottery possibly dating to the later 4th century. The western part (1069) contained a large group of pottery dated to the later 3rd or 4th century (possibly of 4th century date), fired clay oven fragments and a varied assemblage of charred remains (see Fig. 2.13, S. 1016; Fig. 3.1 Nos 9, 12 and 14). This was sampled (Sample 1006), and contained cereal remains, including seeds of spelt, emmer and probably free-threshing bread wheat, barley and possibly oats (see Hunter this volume). The presence of wild seeds, and of fragile chaff, suggested that crop-processing had been carried out close by.

The enclosure was cut by a sinuous broadly N-S aligned ditch (1071/1014) which was 1.20m in width and 0.48m in depth with a V-shaped profile (S. 1016; Plate 2.9). This ditch could be seen continuing to the south on the geophysical survey plot. Its grey silty clay fill contained only one sherd of Romano-British pottery, but included a fair quantity of charred material, and so was sampled for environmental remains (Sample 1005). The charred plant remains were similar to those in the enclosure

Plate 2.9 Section showing 1069 and 1071, looking north

Fig. 2.14 (opposite) Bredon's Norton: plan showing geophysical surveys and the location of the evaluation trenches and excavation area

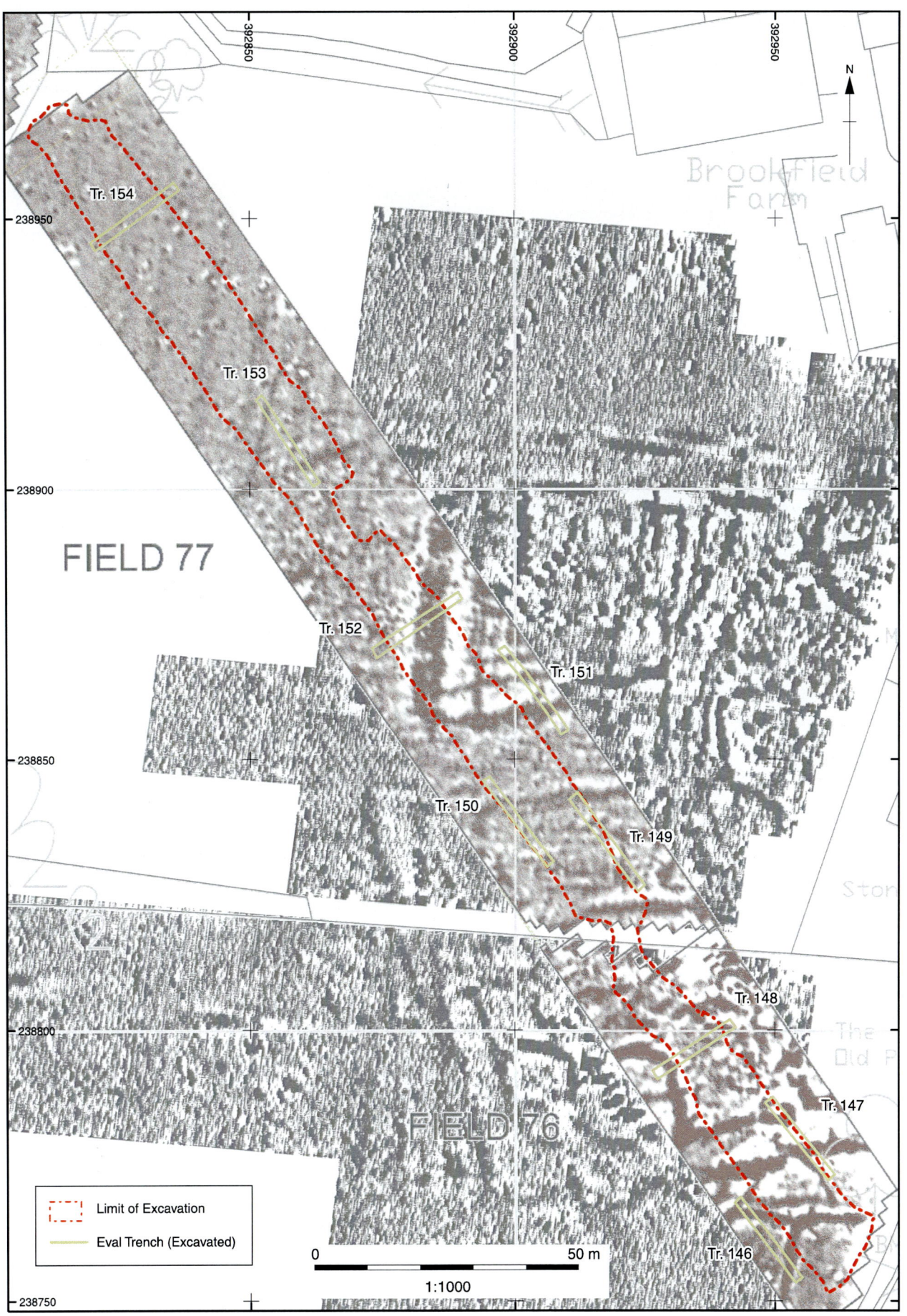

Tr. 154

Tr. 153

FIELD 77

Tr. 152

Tr. 151

Tr. 150

Tr. 149

Tr. 148

Tr. 147

FIELD 76

Tr. 146

Brookfield Farm

N

Limit of Excavation

Eval Trench (Excavated)

0   50 m

1:1000

ditch, and may have been redeposited from there. A shallow discrete feature just to the east of the sinuous ditch, numbered 1010, was not dated. Both were cut by medieval furrow 1012. The irregular shape of these features in plan originally led to their interpretation as the meanders of naturally-formed and shortlived watercourses crossing this area, but the excavated sections indicate that they were in part man-made.

CAT evaluation trench 58 also cut across the enclosure just east of the excavation (Fig. 2.6). Their excavated slot recorded the same sequence; the ditch of the enclosure on the south-west was numbered 58003, and was cut by the north-south ditch (here 58005) (Cotswold Archaeology 2009, figs 11, 19 and 20). The single fill of the latter contained an assemblage of later 3rd/4th century pottery and animal bone (ibid., 11). Further north, and within the interior of the sub-circular enclosure, they found a ditch (58012) running south-east, cut by a succession of pits (58010/58008). The geophysical survey plot does show a discrete anomaly that probably corresponds to the pits, and ditches running up to the enclosure from the south and south-east, the former of which may correspond to 58012. A few sherds of later 3rd or 4th century pottery also came from this ditch.

Medieval

The site was crossed by two sets of plough furrows which truncated many of the earlier features. In the northern part of the site these were on a N-S alignment, and in the southern part were aligned east-west. A section through one of the N-S aligned plough furrows (1012) showed a cut *c* 2.4m in width and 0.3m in depth.

Unphased

Some 12m north of enclosure 1020, on the western edge of the trench, a shallow straight-sided feature (1075) ran into the excavation from the west, and terminated after 2.3m (Fig. 2.12). It was filled with a silty clay (1076) containing flecks of fired clay, but there were otherwise no finds. At the terminus this was possibly cut by a shallower oval feature (1077) measuring 2.1m by 1.48m, and whose long axis was orientated north-east. This feature was filled with a heavily burnt and charcoal-rich deposit, and may represent the remains of an oven or fire pit. The charcoal was however broken up and not identifiable to species, and there were no associated finds.

BREDON'S NORTON (Site 3) (Figs 2.14-2.26)

Introduction

This site was first identified by a geophysical survey in 2006, commissioned by WHEAS and pre-dating

the pipeline works. Its existence, date and general extent were confirmed by further geophysical survey along the pipeline route and trial trenching (referenced in the WHEAS HER as WSM46889), although the masonry building crossed by the route was not identified (Phase Site Investigations 2009b; Cotswold Archaeology 2009; Fig. 2.14). The potential of the site was upgraded from low to high status (Wessex Archaeology 2010) following the reporting of tesserae (WHEAS pers. comm.) being found in the vicinity of the site. Strip map and sample excavation followed (reference number WSM 67179).

The site lies below the western edge of Bredon Hill at a height of around 30m aOD, and runs diagonally from north-west to south-east along the lower edge of an area of gently sloping ground at the base of the steep slope of the hill. From the site the ground slopes more steeply down to the west to the floodplain of the River Avon, which runs north-south some 160m from the site. Most of the site lies upon Head deposits overlying the Charmouth Mudstone formation, but the Head deposits peter out towards the south-east end, and here the archaeological features were cut directly into the Charmouth Mudstone (BGS Geology of Britain viewer 2014). The archaeological features were cut by the regular furrows of ridge-and-furrow cultivation of medieval or post-medieval date, and the truncated remains of the associated ploughsoil (numbered 3001=5001) survived up to 0.15m deep. This was overlain by the modern ploughsoil (3000=5000), a topsoil between 0.3m and 0.5m deep.

The strip, map and sample area comprised a single area with a maximum length of *c* 263m and a typical width of 12-13m, aligned roughly NNW-SSE. The total area excavated was 0.3139 ha. Despite being a continuous area the site was divided into two parts, Area 3B (contexts from 5000) lying north of a modern hedge, and Area 3A (contexts from 3000) to the south of it. Towards the southern end of the site part of the remains of a substantial masonry Roman building were revealed. The site saw activity from the middle Iron Age onwards. Features of late Iron Age to early 2nd century AD date (early Roman) and mid-2nd century to mid-3rd century date (middle Roman) were most widespread (Figs 2.15 and 2.16). Late Roman activity (late 3rd and 4th century) concentrated in the vicinity of the masonry building, with a small number of boundary ditches, a corndryer and just possibly a few burials also of this phase.

Middle-late Iron Age (*c* 400 BC–AD 43)

Evidence for activity during this period was focused in the southern half of the site (Figs 2.16-17), and although limited demonstrated the earliest land division on the site, a burial and several pits.

Fig. 2.15 (opposite) Bredon's Norton phased plan and geophysical surveys.

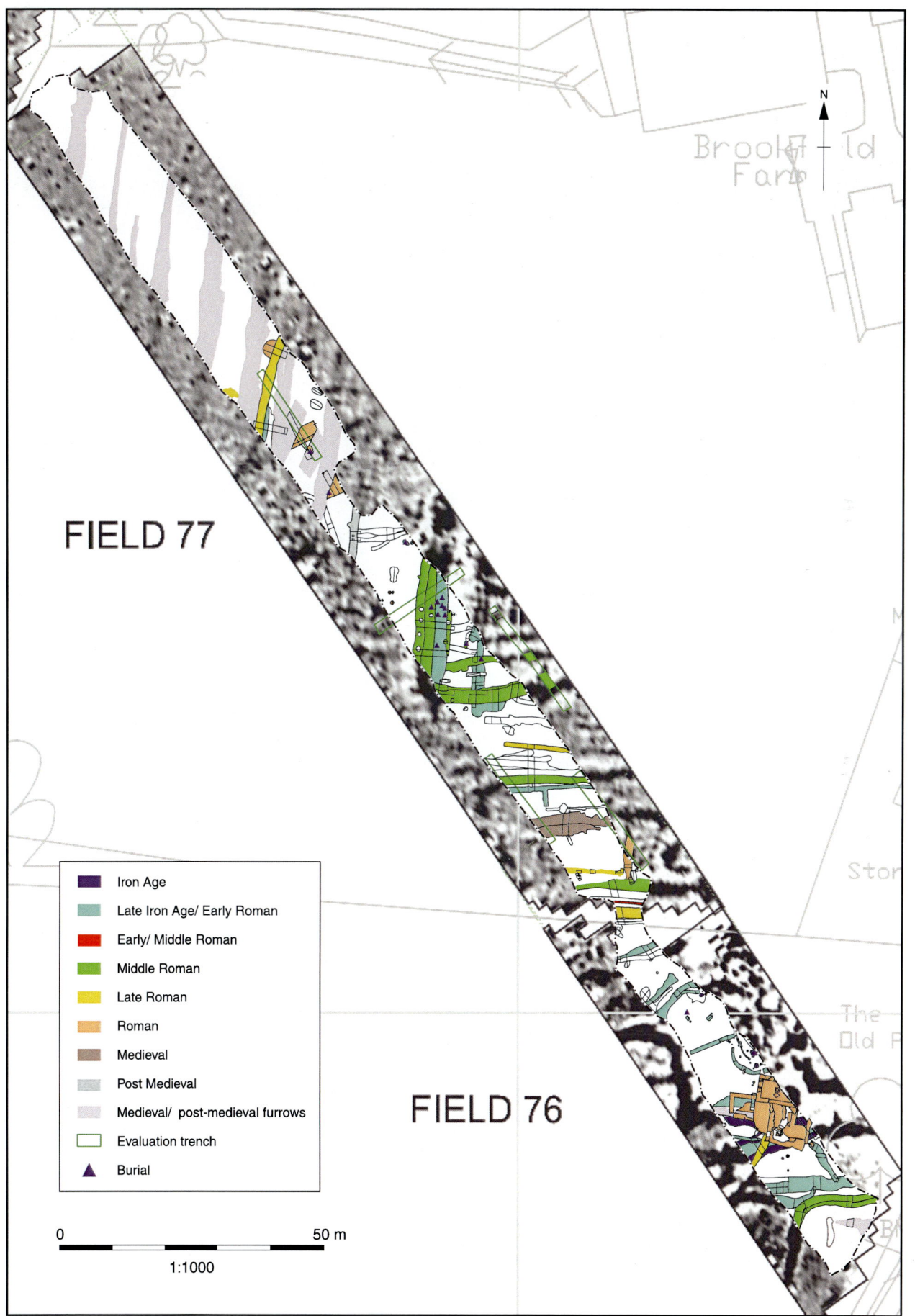

FIELD 77

FIELD 76

Iron Age
Late Iron Age/ Early Roman
Early/ Middle Roman
Middle Roman
Late Roman
Roman
Medieval
Post Medieval
Medieval/ post-medieval furrows
Evaluation trench
▲ Burial

0   50 m
1:1000

Brook field
Farm

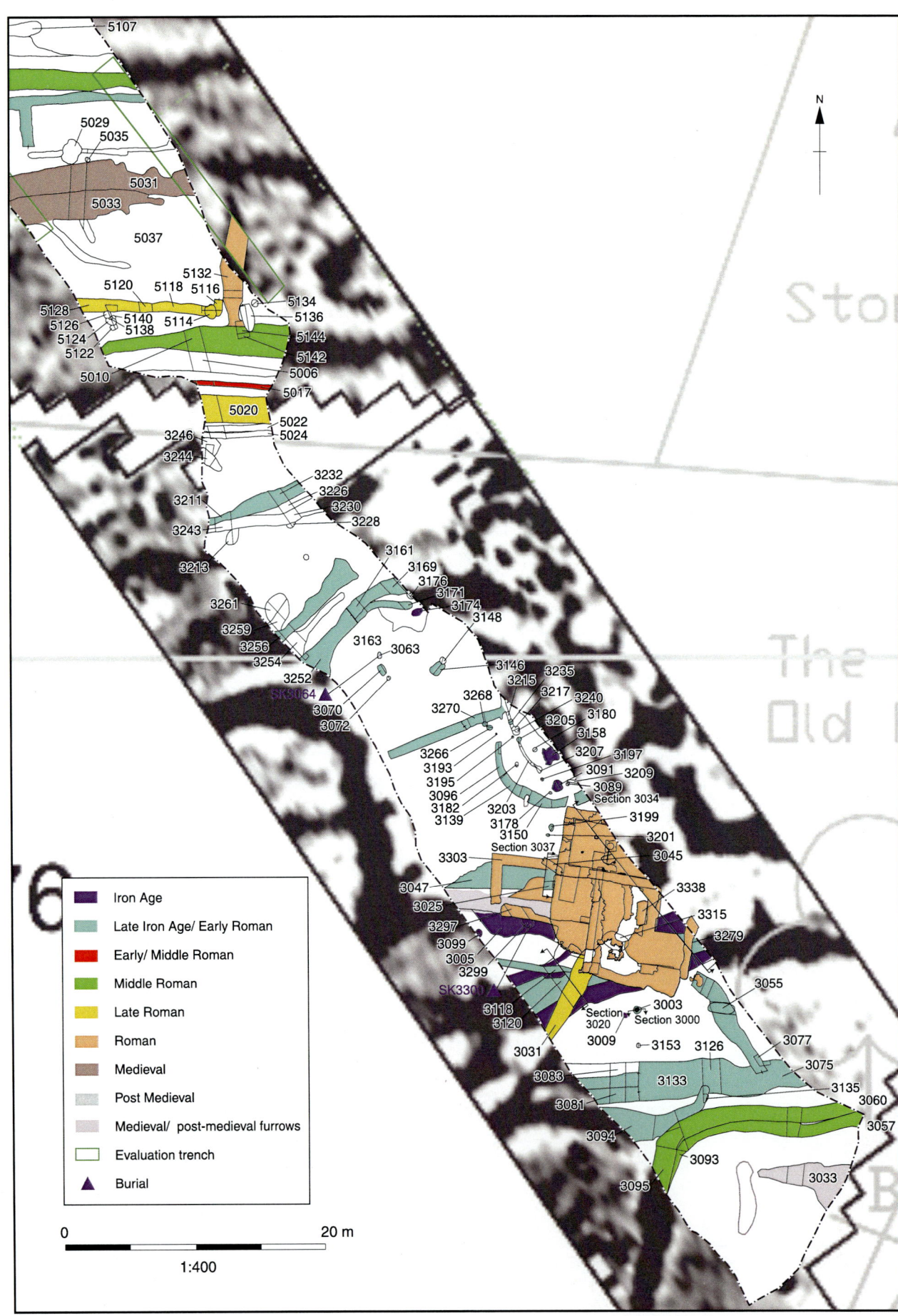

Land Division

In area 3A, evidence for land division was identified in the form of a substantial boundary ditch (3279), partly truncated by a later Roman building (Fig. 2.16). The ditch was aligned ENE-WSW and its full size was recorded in a section close to the eastern edge of the excavated area, where it was 3.7m wide, had sloping sides and was in excess of 1.3m deep (Fig. 2.17). The fills were an alternating sequence of blue-grey clays, probably waterlain, and dumps containing pottery and animal bone, suggesting that domestic rubbish was deposited here, more typically from the north-west side. Small amounts of pottery recovered from four of the lower fills were consistently of middle Iron Age and mid to late Iron Age type. Upper fill 3286, which contained a fair proportion of stones, also included a fragment of fired clay from a wattle structure. Above this the uppermost fill contained Malvernian wares of late Iron Age date. This ditch was also sectioned in CAT evaluation trench 147, where it was numbered 147002, and the fill 147003 (presumably only the uppermost fill, as it was only 0.57m deep) contained 9 sherds of late Iron Age or 1st century AD pottery. The sequence suggests that the ditch was dug in the middle to late Iron Age and infilled during the late Iron Age or very early Roman period.

Further west the terminus of another east-west ditch (3305) was found just west of the late Roman building. This ditch was 1.5m wide and 0.35m deep with a wide rounded V-shaped profile. Its two fills did not produce any datable finds but it was cut by grave 3299 containing skeleton 3300, which was radiocarbon-dated to 360-110 cal BC, so must have been middle Iron Age or earlier. Although north of the projected alignment of 3279, it is possible that this was a continuation of it, shallowing towards the west. The terminus of the ditch was not planned, but a stone-packed posthole (3099), whose fill also contained Iron Age pottery, was found just to the south-west, and the ditch was not planned here, nor was it visible on the geophysical survey plot, so it may have ended just before the west edge of the site.

Large ditch 3120 was planned south-west of ditch 3279 beyond the overlying Roman building, and was in direct alignment with it (Fig. 2.16). This ditch was 4.2m wide and at least 0.8m deep, but was not bottomed (Fig. 2.17). Here the lowest fill exposed (3121) contained only a little Iron Age pottery, a fragment of a firebar and a single human bone, but middle fill 3123, a sandy silt containing frequent limestones, may have been deliberate backfill. This contained pottery of 1st century AD date, either late Iron Age or early Roman. Above this the uppermost fill, numbered 3124 and 3125 to south and north

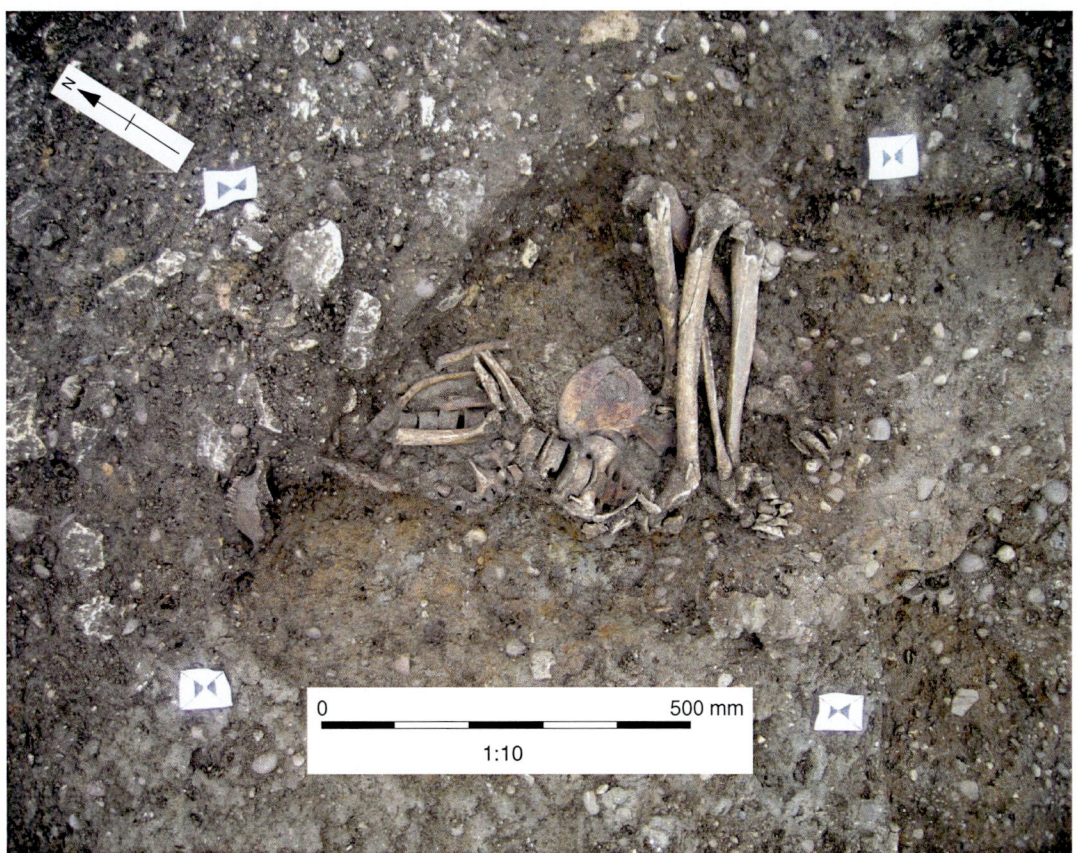

Plate 2.10 Skeleton 3300 in grave 3299, looking north

Fig. 2.16 (opposite) Bredon's Norton phased plan (S) with geophysical survey greyscale plots

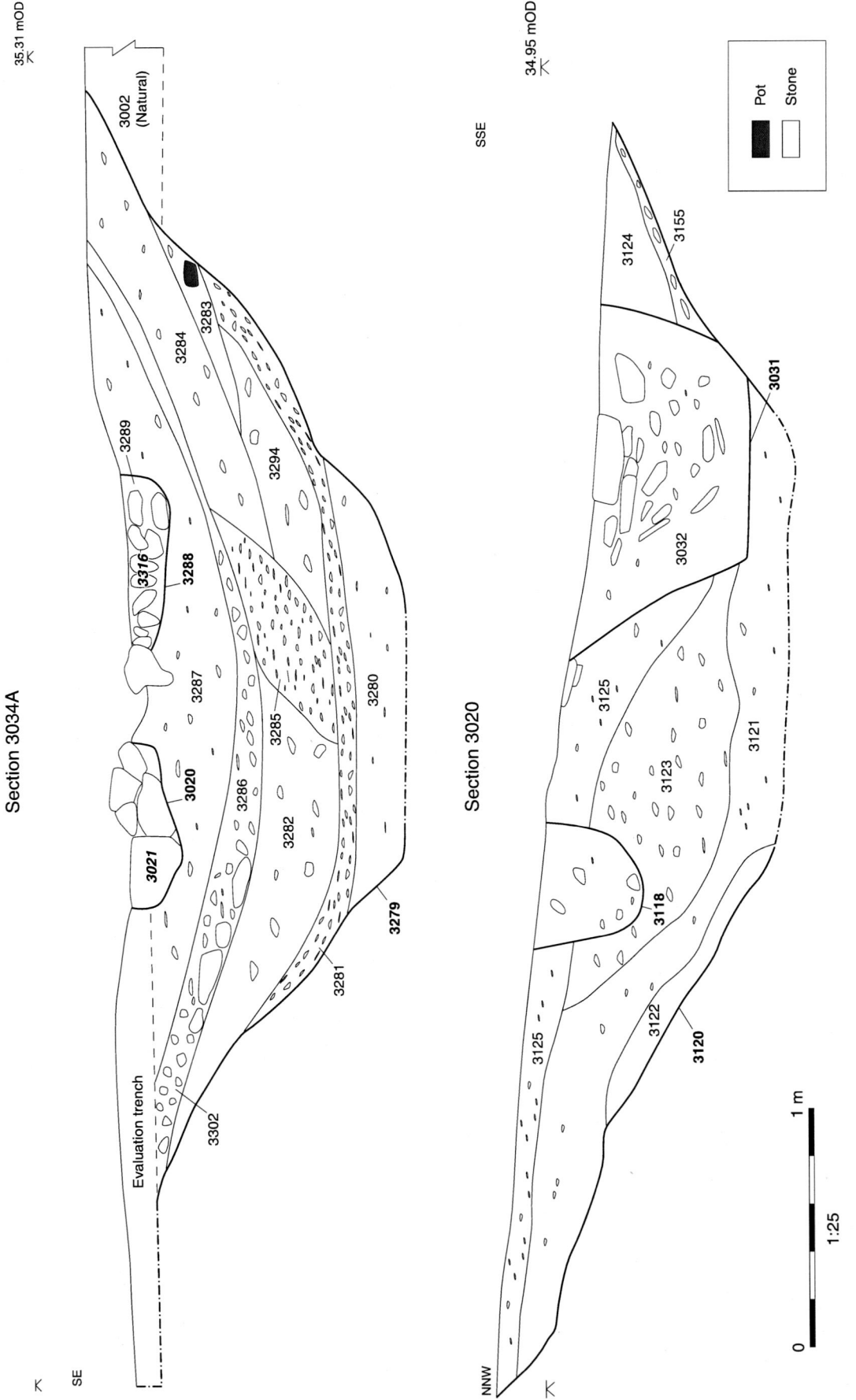

Fig. 2.17 Sections 3020 and 3034a showing ditch 3279

respectively, included early Roman pottery and a few large box flue tile and flat tile fragments. The northern limit of the ditch was not established at the west edge of the excavation, but the geophysical survey plot shows that this ditch continued westwards on a broadly east-west alignment, as did 3279 to the east. A slight misalignment is visible on the geophysical survey plot, perhaps indicating that ditches 3120 and 3279 were not one and the same, but this may be due to the masking effect of the overlying building.

Burials

An adult crouched burial (3300), aligned north-west to south-east and lying on its left side, had been cut into the upper fill of east-west Iron Age ditch 3305 (Plate 2.10). Its head would have been at the north-west end, but the upper half of the body had been removed by an east-west aligned robber cut 3297. The grave cut (3299) was oval in shape with moderate sides and a flat base and measured 0.7m x 0.9m and 0.18m in depth. Skeleton 3300 was an adult, *c* 26-35 years old, and probably male. The handle and a fragment of the blade of an iron saw (SF 3020) was found in the grave fill 3301 west of the spine behind

Plate 2.11 Skeleton 3300 showing iron saw handle and blade behind the spine at shoulder level.

Plate 2.12 Detail of iron saw showing wood mineralised on handle

the right shoulder (Fig. 3.10; Plates 2.11 and 2.12). This may originally have been complete, as it ended just where the robber trench cut across the grave. Two very small sherds of pottery recovered from the fill could not be dated. Bone from the right femur was submitted for radiocarbon dating, and produced a date range of 360-110 cal BC (SUERC-49694; 2167 ± 30 BP). An ulna from a bird of the corvid family was also found in 3301, though was not recognised as a grave offering during excavation.

Other features

Just south of ditch 3120 was sub-circular clay-lined pit 3003. The pit was 0.55m in diameter, with a slight shallow lip on the east side, and survived 0.25m deep, with very steep sides and a flat bottom (Fig 2.18). The base was covered with fired clay, by far the largest piece (SF 3011) having fingerprint impressions on the underside. This is interpreted as discarded oven lining (Poole Chapter 3). This was sealed by a greyish blue clay (3007) interpreted as a deliberate lining. Above this was a sandy clay (3004), upon which had been placed the base of a vessel (SF 3010). The vessel was in a Malvernian fabric, and the only other sherd of pottery of any size from 3004 was grog-tempered, suggesting a date in the first half of the 1st century AD. Burnt clay slab SF 3011, was a similar find to SF 3015, a piece recovered from Iron Age pit 3158 some 20m to the north-west (see below). Only 1m to the south-west of 3003 was another small pit 3009, 0.45m by 0.37m across, with steep sides and a flattish base. One small sherd of Iron Age pottery was recovered from its single fill.

Plate 2.13 Malvernian vessel in pit 3158

Around 15m north of ditch 3305 and burial 3300 were two features of probable late Iron Age date (Figs 2.16 and 2.22). Large pit 3158 was around 1.3m across and up to 0.43m deep, but was very irregular in shape and had been disturbed by animal burrowing. Its fill 3159 contained late Iron Age pottery including a large portion (48 sherds 1579g)

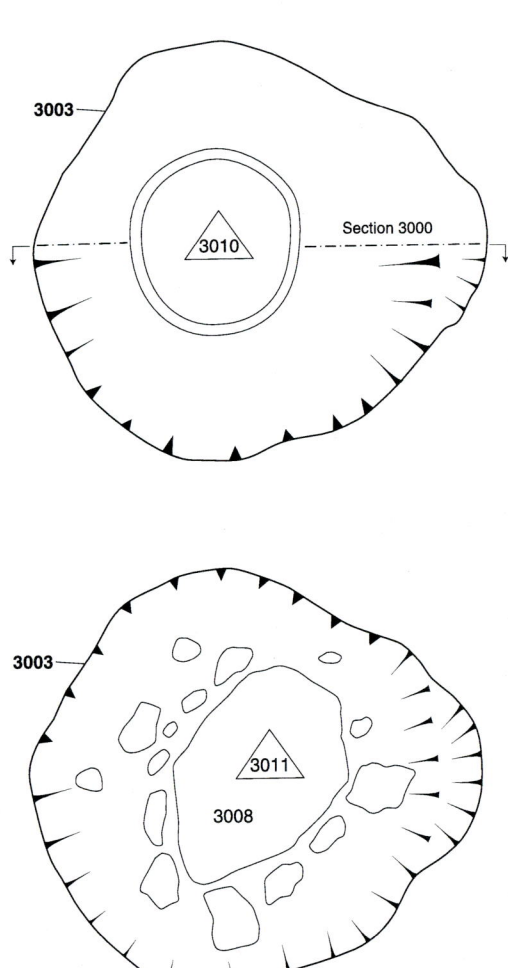

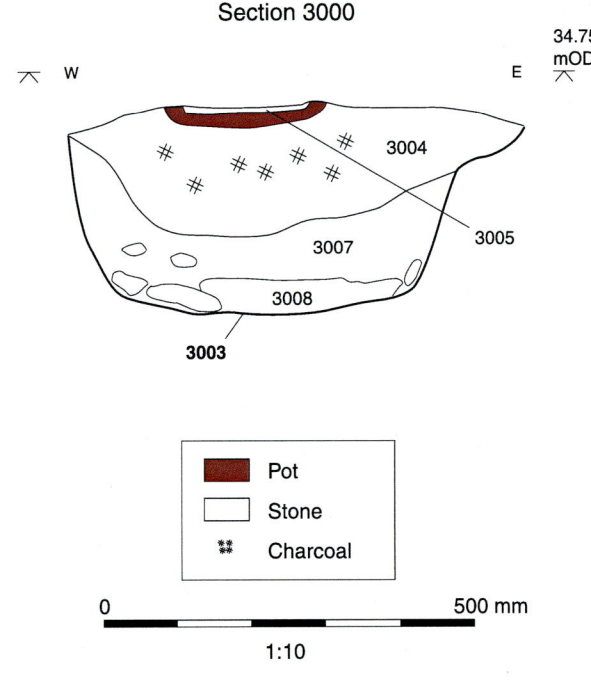

Fig. 2.18 Plans and section of pit 3003

Plate 2.14 Close up of stamped vessel as found

of a 'duck-stamped' Malvernian ware vessel (SF 3013; Fig. 3.3.40 and Plates 2.13 and 2.14). Also recovered was a fragmented whetstone, perhaps deliberately broken (SF 3014), and a large chunk of fired clay with visible finger impressions (Fig. 3.5.5; SF 3025). Fragments of Roman tile were also found within the fill, but were probably intrusive.

Just over 1m to the south, pit 3091 was an irregular oval 0.8m long, 0.65m wide and up to 0.18m deep, the base stepping down from the north to the south. Its fill 3092 contained a smaller late Iron Age assemblage (3x 48g) as well as some burnt stone, a fragment of fired clay oven structure and charcoal in its dark brown silty fill. The pottery included a sherd with stamped decoration (Fig. 3.2.17).

Another 15m further to the north-west was a probable pit 3174, which contained a group of eight Malvernian handmade sherds in its dark brown silty fill, suggesting a middle to late Iron Age date. This was overlain by a deposit of very similar silt (3173) filling a hollow approaching 5m north-west to south-east, and at least 2.5m south-west to north-east. Adjacent were gully 3254 and 3259, which may also have been Iron Age, but both were shallow with single fills that contained only fired clay and charcoal and animal bone respectively.

Late Iron Age to early Roman

Land Division

Land division was demonstrated by several perpendicular ditches (5195, 5073 and 5151=5168) in area 3B (Fig. 2.19). These were truncated by several similarly aligned ditches of later date, perhaps suggesting that the division of the landscape here began in the late Iron Age period.

Feature 5073 was aligned E-W and was V-shaped in profile. It measured 0.8m deep and was at least 1.8m wide, but was truncated by ditch 5070 (part of group 5288) on the north side (Fig. 2.20 S. 5012). The fills contained a small quantity of Malvernian pottery of middle to late Iron Age date (see Fig. 3.2.18), and a few disarticulated human bone fragments in top fill 5071. At right angles to it on the opposite side of 5288 (here numbered 5164), ditch 5148 (recut as 5151) probably represents a return running northwards (Fig. 20; Plate 2.15). Ditch 5148 deepened from 0.6m to 0.8m or more as it ran south, and had two fills. The recut (5151= 5168) measured 1.61m in width and also deepened to the south, from 0.82m to 0.96m deep. Datable material was not recovered from the earlier ditch, but its western side was aligned with the western terminus of ditch 5073, and although no recut was observed in ditch 5073, in profile ditches 5073 and recut 5151 are very similar. Ditch cut 5151 contained one Iron Age sherd, a fired clay fragment possibly from the perforation of a triangular brick or loomweight and a small quantity of Malvernian pottery of Iron Age or early Roman date from the uppermost fill. It is very probable that these features were contemporary. Together these ditch alignments appear to form the corner of an enclosure or field to the north-east.

Ditch 5151 was cut by another east-west ditch 5187 after only 7m. In plan the ditch was narrowing at this point, so one of the cuts may have ended below 5187, but one probably continued north of this as ditch 5193, which contained a small amount

Plate 2.15 Late Iron Age ditches 5148/5151

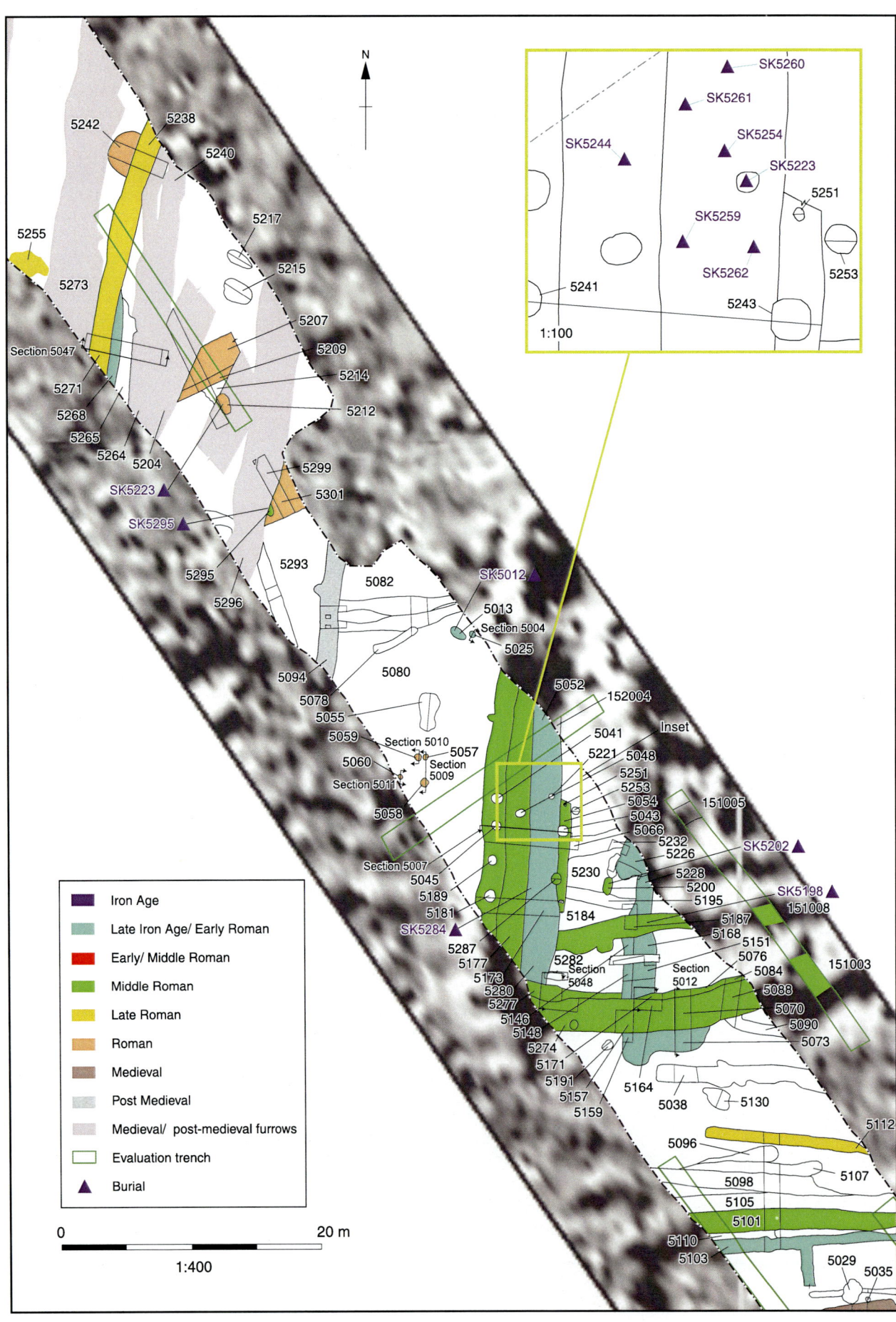

N

Inset 1:100

SK5260
SK5261
SK5254
SK5244
SK5223
5251
SK5259
SK5262
5253
5241
5243

5242
5238
5240
5217
5215
5255
5273
5207
Section 5047
5209
5271
5214
5268
5212
5265
5264
5204
5299
SK5223
5301
SK5295
5295
5293
5082
5296
SK5012
5013
Section 5004
5025
5094
5080
5078
5055
5059
Section 5010
5057
5060
Section 5009
Section 5011
5058
5052
152004
5041
Inset
5221
5048
5251
5253
5054
151005
5043
5066
5232
5226
SK5202
Section 5007
5228
5045
5230
5200
5189
5195
5181
5184
5187
SK5284
5168
5151
SK5198
151008
5076
5287
5177
5282
Section
5048
Section
5012
5084
151003
5173
5280
5088
5277
5070
5146
5090
5148
5073
5274
5171
5191
5164
5157
5038
5130
5159
5112
5096
5098
5107
5105
5101
5110
5103
5029
5035

■ Iron Age	
■ Late Iron Age/ Early Roman	
■ Early/ Middle Roman	
■ Middle Roman	
■ Late Roman	
■ Roman	
■ Medieval	
■ Post Medieval	
■ Medieval/ post-medieval furrows	
□ Evaluation trench	
▲ Burial	

0   20 m

1:400

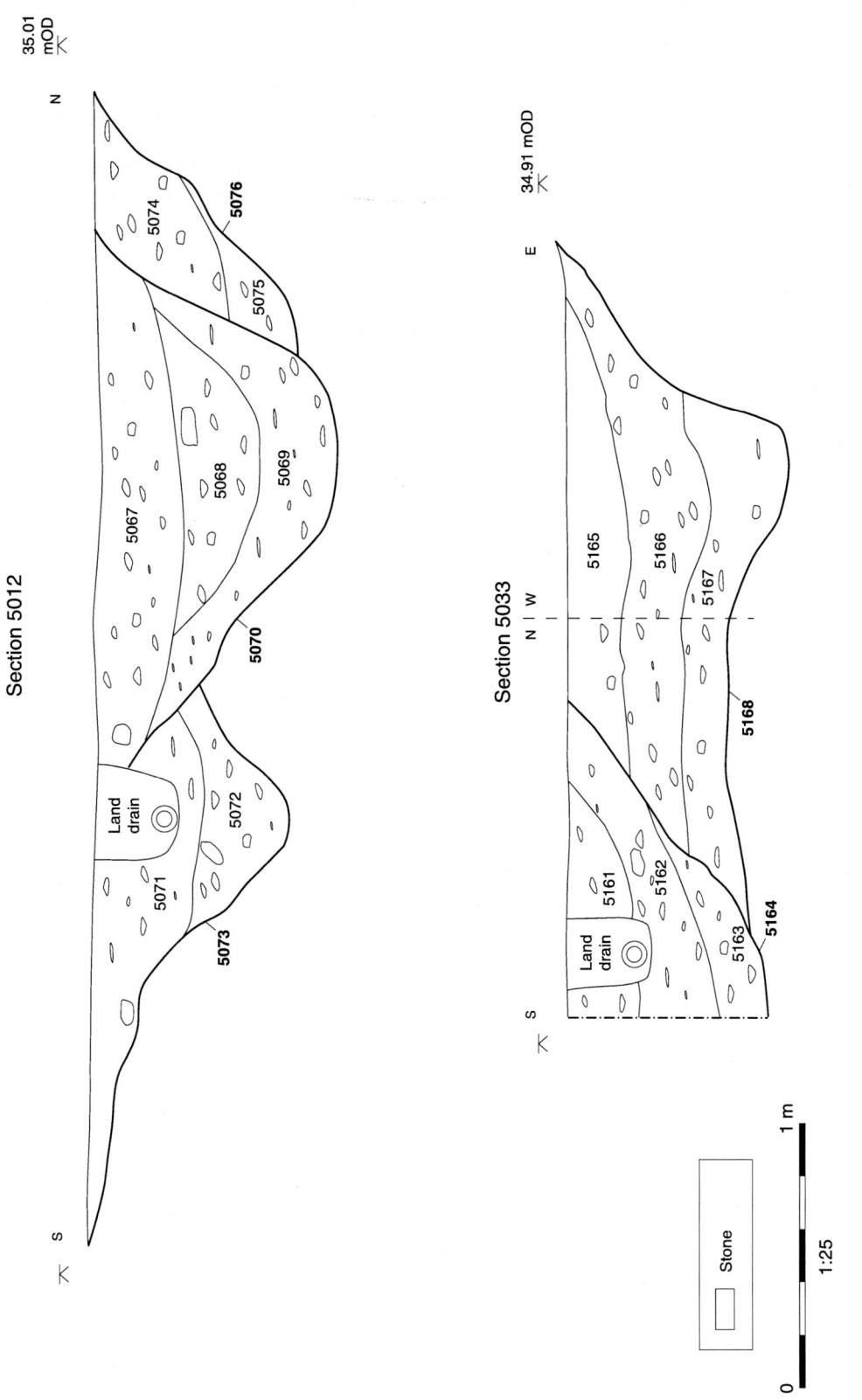

Section 5012

Section 5033

Stone

0   1:25   1 m

Fig. 2.20 Sections 5012 and 5033

Fig. 2.19 (opposite) Bredon's Norton phased plan (N) with geophysical survey greyscale plots

of late Iron Age to early Roman pottery. This ditch cut a very shallow east-west ditch 5195 on its west side. Ditch 5195 consisted only of a short length, being truncated after only 5m by another north-south ditch 5054.

There were no finds from its grey-brown clayey silt fill 5196. Ditch 5193/5228 was itself cut a few metres further north by pit 5226, whose single fill contained only early Roman pottery. Beyond this the continuation of the ditch to the north could be seen on the geophysical survey plan, but the E-W ditch appears only to continue for *c* 7m to the east.

The ditches contained a fairly small assemblage of pottery of late Iron Age to early Roman date from their two silty fills, but 10 of these sherds from the N-S return (fills 5165 and 5166) were definitely late Iron Age (see Fig. 3.2.38), perhaps indicating that they were infilled in the late Iron Age rather than the Roman period.

Parallel to ditch 5073 on the south side was E-W ditch 5038, which continued to the east beyond the excavated area on the geophysical survey plot (Fig. 2.19). It measured 1.52m wide but was only 0.12m deep with a single fill. Its alignment and similar width to N-S ditch 5151 make it tempting to suggest that this ditch belongs to the same Late Iron Age phase of activity, the western terminal perhaps forming an enclosure entrance with the south end of ditches 5148 or recut 5151. However its very shallow depth and lack of any finds makes this

spatial link less plausible, and it may instead have been a medieval furrow.

Just south of this ditch was an oval pit 5130, its long axis WNW-ESE. This was only 0.2m deep, with gently sloping sides and a flat base, and contained early Roman pottery. Its outline was somewhat irregular, and it may have been a tree-throw hole rather than a pit.

Some 14m south of ditch 5073 were east-west ditches 5110 cut by 5103. Ditch 5110 had a wide shallow profile, although it had been largely truncated by 5103 and by later ditch 5101 on the north. No pottery was recovered from its fill, but ditch 5103=15005 which cut it contained two sherds of late Iron Age/early Roman pottery (1st century AD), so 5110 was probably late Iron Age or very early Roman.

Burials

Some 35m north-west of ditch 5073 was inhumation grave 5013, orientated north-west to south-east and sub-oval in shape. It measured 1.35m in length, 0.72m in width and 0.6m in depth with steep sides and a flat base. The very well-preserved skeleton (5012) was of a mature adult aged 35-40 years, and was probably male The skeleton was in a crouched position on its left side with the head towards north (Plate 2.16). No finds were recovered from the grave, but bone from the right femur of the skeleton

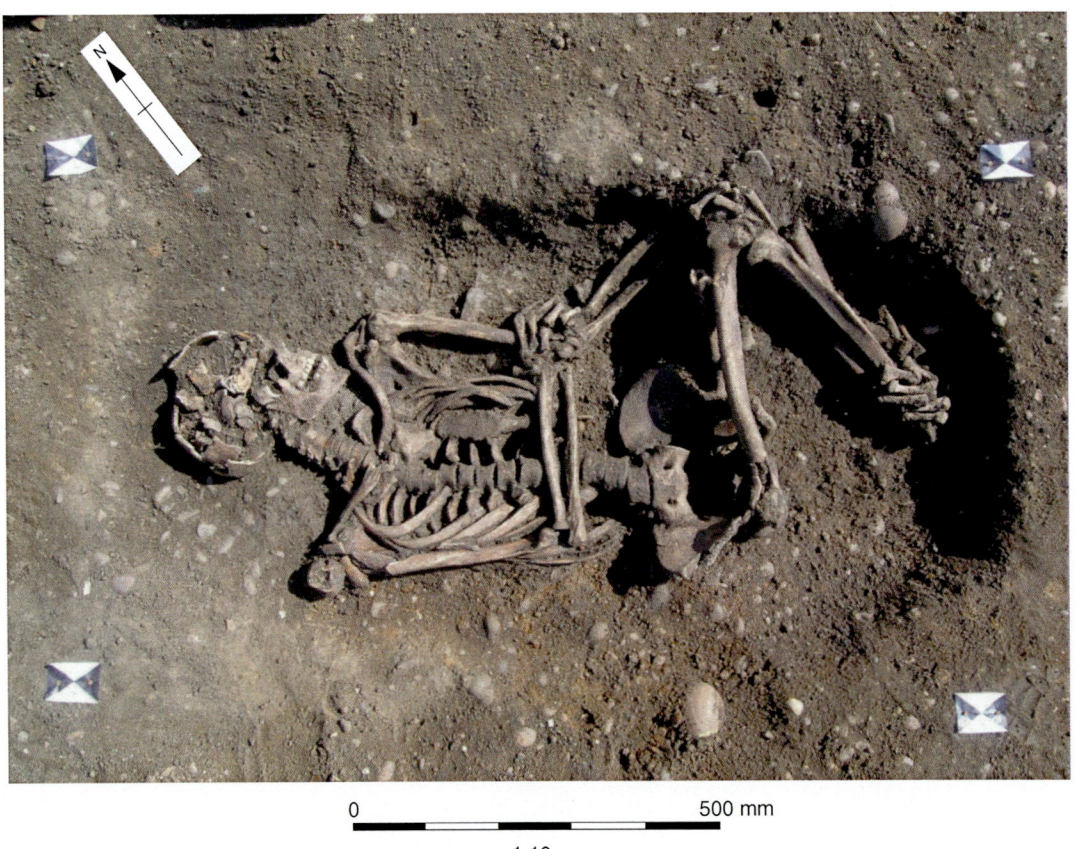

0   500 mm

1:10

Plate 2.16 Skeleton 5012 from above, with head to the north-west

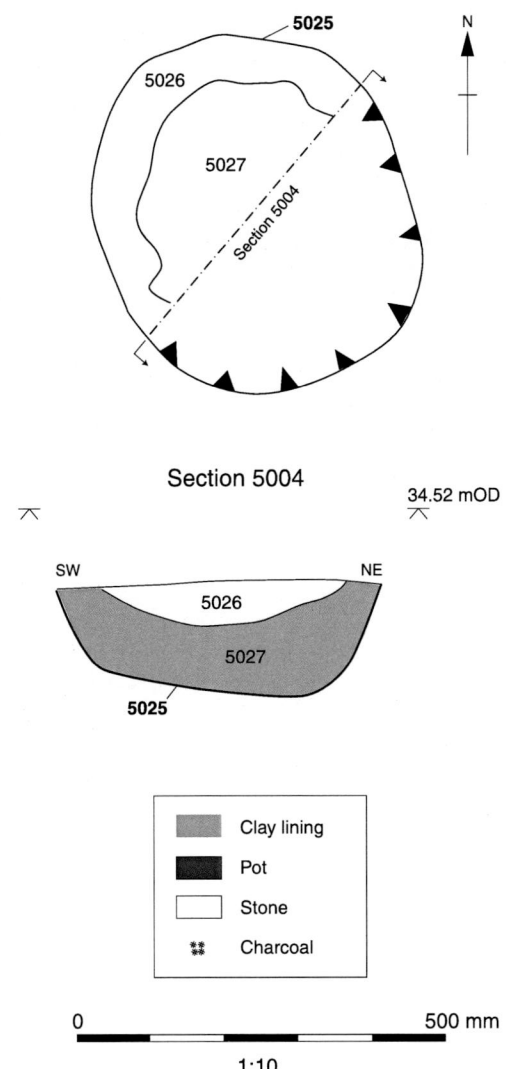

Section 5004

34.52 mOD

SW   NE

Clay lining

Pot

Stone

Charcoal

0   500 mm

1:10

Fig. 2.21 Plan and section of 5025

was submitted for radiocarbon dating, and gave a date range of 50 cal BC to 80 cal AD (SUERC 49695; 1983 ± 30 BP). This is therefore either a late Iron Age or very early Roman burial.

Immediately adjacent on the east side was a small circular clay-lined pit 5025, whose shallow dark brown silt fill (5027) inside the lining was sampled for environmental remains, and contained charred plant remains including wheat and oat grains, charcoal and small bones (Fig. 2.21). Two sherds of Malvernian ware suggest that this was also late Iron Age or early Roman in date.

Settlement in the southern part of the site

Some 20m north of ditch 3270, shallow ditches, 3259, 3256, 3252/3161/3169 and 3163/3171 had a broadly north-east to south-west alignment. Ditches 3169 and 3171 cut Iron Age hollow 3173, as did pit 3176 just south of, and cut by, 3169.

The earliest ditches or gullies were 3259 and 3254, which may have been middle to late Iron Age. Pit

3261 cut ditch 3259, was 0.3m deep with gently sloping sides and a flat base, but there were no finds in its single silt fill. Ditch 3256 however, which cut the ditches to either side, was 0.65m deep with a V-profile, and a single small sherd of late Iron Age or early Roman pottery came from its upper fill.

South of 3254, and cutting it, ditch 3161=3169= 3252 had steeply sloping sides and a slightly concave flattish base, and measured 0.95m wide and up to 0.38m deep. The western cut was only partial, and did not produce any finds. In the central cut across it the ditch was shallower and the base was undulating, due to there being two cuts, the more southerly of which was a narrower curving gully 3163=3171. This was just over 0.4m wide and 0.28m deep. No relationship between them was visible, both ditches containing the same silty fill 3162, from which 7 sherds (1002g) from two large jars or cauldrons in Malvernian ware dating to the 1st century AD were recovered (Fig. 3.3 Nos 48 and 49). The terminus of this gully also contained a large quantity of oven floor fragments, almost certainly of late Iron Age date, and reddened stone (which may also have derived from an oven). A fragment of oven wall or decorated hearth was also found in cut 3169 of the adjacent ditch, and there was also a fragment of hearth in pit 3176, whose north edge the ditch cut, and which contained early Roman pottery (Fig. 3.2.16). The large sherds and hearth fragments suggest that there was settlement activity taking place nearby.

Both 3161 and 3163 were curving, 3163 terminating on the east within the trench, 3161 continuing south-eastwards as a geophysical anomaly. The geophysical survey plot may indicate that there were two phases within 3161 in addition to 3163, as there were possibly two further terminals within the surveyed area. On the west, 3161 was broadening close to the edge of the excavation, and its south edge was turning southwards. The geophysical survey plot makes clear that both 3161 and 3163 ended just beyond the edge of the excavation at a terminus with a similar curve to that of the east end of 3163. Both features appear to have stopped short of a large curvilinear enclosure ditch on the west, to which they presumably formed an annexe of some sort.

On the east, another geophysical anomaly was plotted running south-east just beyond the limits of the excavation, south west of the end of 3161 and along the approximate line of gully 3163=3171. This was sectioned by CAT evaluation trench 148, where it was numbered 148003, was 1.17m wide and 0.15m deep, and produced one sherd of late Iron Age or 1st century AD early Roman pottery.

In the area partly enclosed by these ditches and gullies was a scattering of discrete features. Small cremation pit (3063) was egg-shaped in plan, with vertical sides at the narrower, northern end but sloping sides on the south. The base was flat and sub-circular, some 0.23m across, and the pit was 0.16m deep with a single black clayey silt fill 3064 containing charcoal and cremated bone from a juvenile. The edges of the pit itself were not burnt. Fill 3064 was recovered in its entirety (Sample 3005), as was natural clay 3069 into which pit 3063 was cut (Sample 3006), as some charcoal and bone had percolated into this through root action. There were however no finds. Less than half a metre to the south was a sub-rectangular shallow pit 3070. This measured 0.84m in length, 0.54m in width and was 0.19m deep, with very steep sides and a flat base. Its single clayey silt fill contained small amount of charcoal, late Iron Age/early Roman pottery, animal bone, fired clay fragments and burnt stone. Immediately south-east of 3070, and in line with its long axis, was circular posthole 3072, which was 0.3m in diameter and 0.2m deep. This contained several limestones, probably used as packing and possibly as a post-pad at the base, and a little charcoal in its clayey silt fill, but no dating evidence. All three features were probably of broadly similar date.

Early Roman period

Land division

This phase of activity is characterised by the establishment of a more extensive series of enclosures, probably in part representing the expansion of developments described above. The majority of features were east-west and north-south aligned boundary ditches, but other alignments were also represented. Geophysical survey of a wider area shows complex arrangements of both curvilinear and rectilinear features to which the excavated features were connected (Figs 2.14 and 2.15).

In the northern part of the site (Fig. 2.19), where the hillside slopes down to the west, the north-western limit of activity was poorly defined by ditches, although heavily truncated ditch 5268 may define a boundary. This was at least 1m wide but only 0.26m deep, and on the west it was obliterated by a late Roman ditch on the same alignment (5271). It was traced for 7m, but to the south was obscured and largely truncated by a group of later furrows. Only a single Malvernian ware body sherd was recovered from its fill, which could date anywhere from the late Iron Age to the 2nd century AD.

Pit 5242 was situated due north of ditch 5268 at the north-western limit of Roman activity within the excavation. It measured 3m in diameter and was 0.15m deep with a shallow concave profile. The fill contained only two sherds of broadly Roman date, but it too was cut by north-south late Roman ditch 5238.

Just south of ditch 5268 an ENE-WSW ditch (5209) crossed the excavation. It was 1.7m wide and 0.7m deep, and had been recut as ditch 5207, which was 1.9m wide and 0.45m deep. Both ditches contained small amounts of pottery of broad Roman date in their silted fills. The intersection of ditches 5268 and 5209 was masked by north-south aligned

furrows of probable late medieval/post-medieval date, which were not removed. Some 8m to the south-east was a further ditch (5301) on a similar alignment, which measured 3.2m wide and 0.2m deep, and from which a single sherd of Roman pottery was recovered. The spacing of these features would be consistent with their use as trackway ditches, but given their very different depths this is very speculative.

Nearly 65m to the south-east ditch 5110 was recut as ditch 5103, which was V-shaped in profile and measured 1m wide and 0.4m deep. It contained two silty fills, which contained only a single pottery sherd of late Iron Age/early Roman date (1st century AD). Ditch 5103 was also sectioned by CAT evaluation trench 150, where 5103 corresponded to 150005. This also produced a single sherd of late Iron Age or early Roman pottery and a Roman tile fragment.

Ditch 5103 had a spur running south at right angles, which appeared to stop just short of an east-west gully 5029. This feature was also identified in evaluation trench 149 to the east, where it was numbered 149007. It was only 0.06m deep, with sloping sides and a flat base, and there were no finds in its single fill. It was believed to have been associated with medieval furrows 5031 and 5033 to the south, with a similar grey-brown silty clay fill, but may have been earlier. To judge from the changes in width along its length, this may have consisted of two separate lengths, later joined up.

Some 30m further south was another group of ditches numbered as 3238 and 3239, a sequence of fairly shallow cuts and re-cuts, all between 0.9m and 1.2m wide and around 0.4m deep. There were three cuts on the east, where the soilmark was broader, the middle one (3226) being the earliest, cut on both the north and south sides (Fig. 2.16). The southernmost cut (3230) ran approximately east-west, the northernmost (3232) was aligned north-east to south-west. The recuts ran together on the west, becoming visible only as slightly deeper depressions within a cut (3211=3243) with an apparent single fill. The southernmost cut (3230=3243) truncated two earlier pits, 3213 and 3228, neither of which contained any finds. The northernmost ditch had a stepped profile on the north side, and was the only ditch to contain any datable finds, a couple of sherds of 1st century AD date and a box flue tile fragment. It is likely that all these cuts were cut in the late Iron Age or early Roman period.

Enclosure 3150

In Area 3a to the south, and approximately 10m north of ditch 3279, the south-western half of a small curvilinear enclosure (ditch 3150) lay within the east side of the site (Figs 2.16 and 2.22; Plate 2.17). The enclosure ditch was up to 0.8m wide and 0.4m deep and had a broadly V-shaped profile. It had a straight-ended terminus 3096 in the north-west, with a possible entrance north of this. The geophysics plan shows a probable continuation of the enclosure around the north-west side, and a short continuation on the south-east, but there were other anomalies giving a much stronger response beyond this, so that it is unclear whether it continued on the east and north-east. It measured approximately 11m north-south and 8m east-west, and surrounded late Iron Age pits 3158 and 3091; pit 3158 was at the approximate centre, so the enclosure may have been positioned deliberately in relation to it. The ditch contained two fills, the lower of which contained very little pottery, though it did include a small fragment of Roman black-burnished ware (BB1). The upper fill contained a mixture of pottery types, mainly Malvernian wares of late Iron Age or early Roman date, but including a dumped fill (3097) containing pottery of late 1st or 2nd century date and a scrap of flat tile at the north-west terminus.

After the ditch had partially silted, a number of stakes were driven into the fill, and into the surrounding area (see Fig, 2.22). One lay within posthole 3207, and probably cut this, although the relationship was only recorded on plan. At least two parallel lines of half a dozen stakes were evident on an east-west alignment, but otherwise it was very difficult to discern any structure to the stakeholes, which were scattered across the area of the former interior of the enclosure, its ditch and (on the south) also outside the ditch. The stakeholes were visible in three of the sections through the ditch (Fig. 2.23 sections 3025 and 3028), sealed by the later fill of the ditch, indicating that they had been driven in before the enclosure ditch had entirely silted up. The stakeholes were no more than 0.1m in diameter, and did not reach the base of the ditch. No finds were recovered.

Features within the enclosure were mostly poorly dated. Four postholes (3195, 3182, 3197 and 3089), spaced roughly 2m apart, formed an arc concentric with the enclosure ditch and 0.8-1.0m inside it. All but the first were substantial, with vertical sides and flat bases, but did not contain any finds. Posthole 3195 was smaller and only survived 0.06m deep, but contained scraps of early Roman pottery. Inside this arc, but forming a shallower curve, was a series of lengths of gully 3215, 3203 and 3209. They ranged in width from 0.2-0.34m, and all were shallow (0.06-0.08m deep). Each had a single fill with charcoal flecks, and fired clay oven lining and a fragment of Roman tile was recovered from 3216, and animal bone from this and from 3204. To the north gully

Plate 2.17 Working shot of curvilinear enclosure 3150, looking west

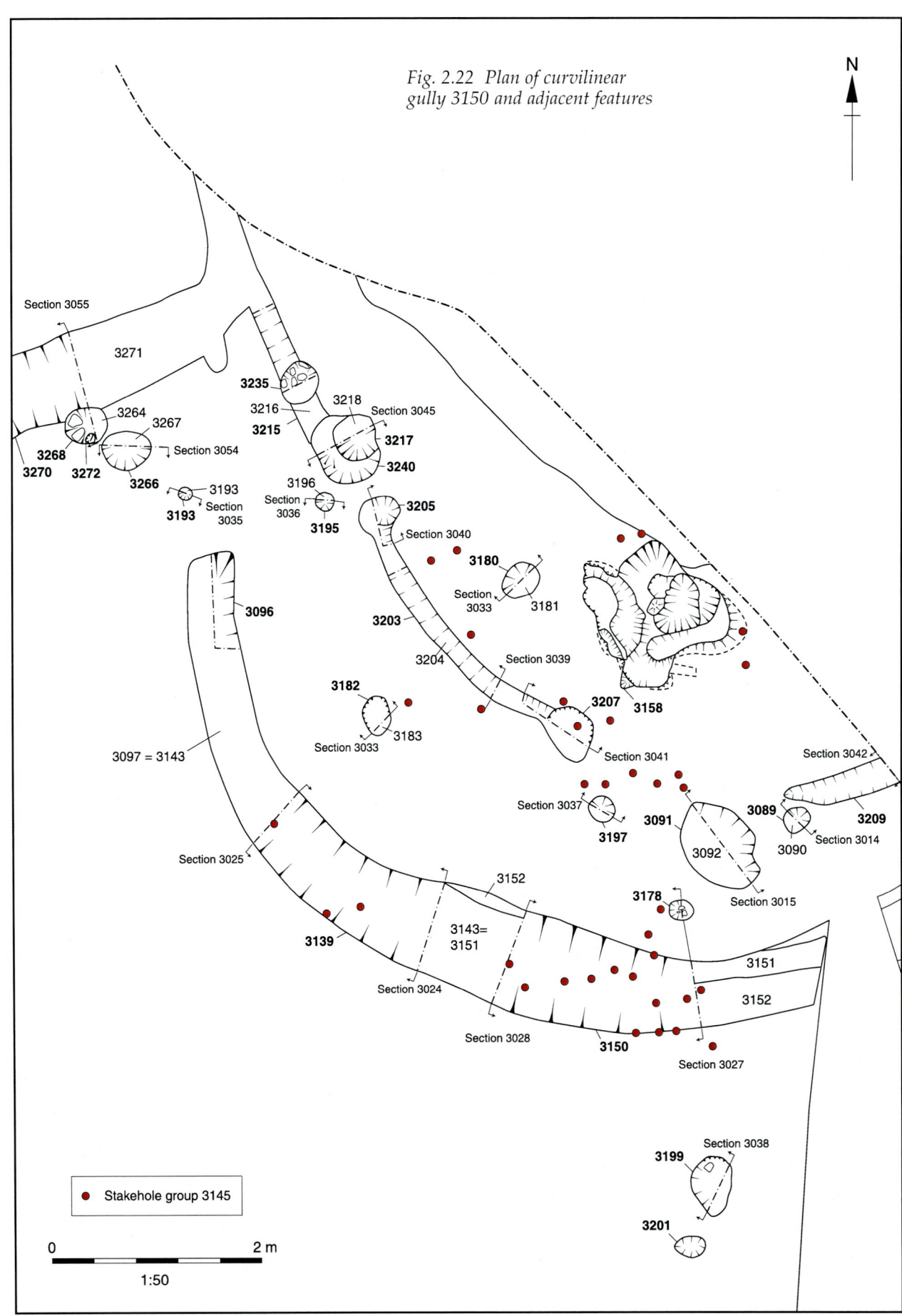

Fig. 2.22 Plan of curvilinear gully 3150 and adjacent features

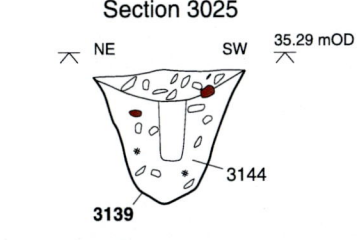

Section 3025

NE   SW   35.29 mOD

3144

3139

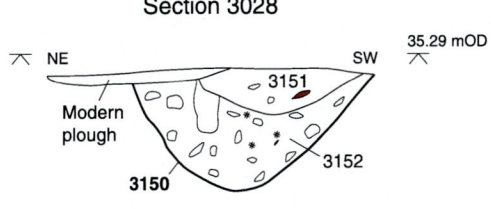

Section 3028

NE   SW   35.29 mOD

3151

Modern
plough

3152

3150

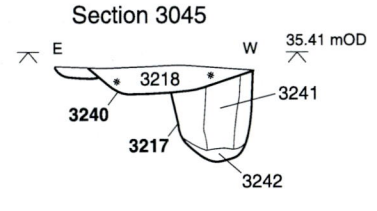

Section 3045

E   W   35.41 mOD

3218

3241

3240

3217

3242

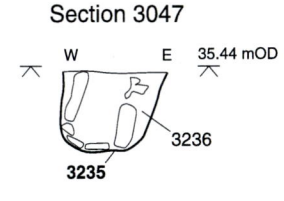

Section 3047

W   E   35.44 mOD

3236

3235

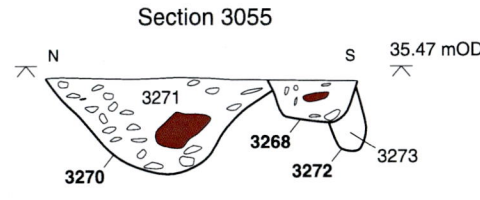

Section 3055

N   S   35.47 mOD

3271

3268

3273

3270   **3272**

Pot

Stone

Charcoal

0   1 m

1:25

Fig. 2.23 Sections 3025, 3028, 3045, 3047, 3055

3215 continued up to the baulk, but also ran into a wider ditch 3270 approaching from the west. No relationship was visible in plan, and this was not further investigated, although the narrow width of the soilmark continuing north perhaps indicates that both features were originally separate, and the gap later dug through to link them.

Ditch 3270 was of similar width and profile to enclosure ditch 3139/3150, though where sectioned it was only 0.3m deep (Fig. 2.23 S. 3055). It contained a small assemblage of 1st or early 2nd century pottery (see Fig. 3.2.38), and an iron T-shaped brooch of late 1st century manufacture (Fig. 3.9 SF 3019), plus a few fragments of Roman tile. The similar character and date of these two features suggests that they may have been part of one enclosure system, with an entrance 1.6m wide between them. At the point where 3270 turned north to meet gully 3215, it cut a posthole or gully terminus on the south side. If it was a gully terminus, it lay opposite to the end of enclosure ditch 3150, although it was much narrower, and more akin to gully 3215, of which it may represent another phase. On the west this ditch ran into an area of very varied natural, and was difficult to discern, but appeared to continue in a straight line westwards, terminating within the site. This was only a few metres short of a large curvilinear enclosure shown on the geophysical survey plot just west of the easement, with which the ditch was probably associated.

Both ends of gully 3203 were cut by postholes, 3207 on the south-east, 3205 on the north-west. These were of similar diameter, but were only 0.19m and 0.10m deep respectively. Posthole 3205 contained early Roman pottery and burnt limestone packing, while large pebbles in 3207 probably performed the same function, although neither had surviving traces of a post-pipe. A more substantial posthole, 3217, which was 0.32m deep, lay immediately adjacent to the terminus of gully 3215 on the east side, and this contained a post-pipe 3241 packed around with clay, but no finds (Fig. 2.23 S.3045). Any relationship between the gully and the posthole had been removed by a shallow pit or hollow 3240, whose fill was also without finds. Just north of this stone- and tile-packed posthole 3235 cut across gully 3215, and was one of a pair of very similar postholes, the other (3268) cutting ditch 3270 some 2m to the west (Fig. 2.23 S. 3047; S.3055). Posthole 3235 contained fragments of a Severn valley ware tankard (Plate 2.18). Both were of similar diameter, and both contained limestone packing and early Roman pottery. Posthole 3235 was 0.28m deep, posthole 3268 only 0.14m deep, but its fill overlay 3272, the ghost of a post- or stake-pipe 0.10m across and 0.20m deep. This could have been a stakehole cut by the posthole, and associated with the others further south, but alternatively it could perhaps have been a post-position within the posthole. Scraps of fired clay came from its fill. A small posthole (3193) was found midway between 3268 and the terminus of

Plate 2.18 Posthole 3235 half-sectioned, looking south

enclosure ditch 3096, and its fill contained a scrap of early Roman pottery.

Around 5m north-west of ditch 3270 was a pair of intercutting pits. The larger and earlier pit (3146) was oval in shape with steep sides and a flat base, and measured 1.8m in length, 0.46m in width and 0.1m in depth. It contained three sherds of pottery of early Roman date including a high-shouldered jar (Fig. 3.2.30). Pit 3146 was cut by 3148, a small oval pit that did not contain any dateable material. These pits were also uncovered by CAT evaluation trench 148, where they were numbered 148005. One sherd of early Roman pottery and three sherds of later prehistoric pottery were recovered from the surface.

South of the curvilinear enclosure 3150 smaller oval features (3201 and 3199) contained some animal bone and one or two Malvernian ware body sherds, and 3199 also contained Roman tile. Both were probably postholes of early Roman date.

Ditches at the south end of the site

At the far south-eastern end of the site a series of intercutting ditches dated to this phase (Fig. 2.16). Ditch 3081=3126 was aligned approximately east-west, and was one of the earliest ditches in the sequence. It was 2.52m wide and 0.8m deep. It contained three fills, the middle one containing fragments of box flue tile, the uppermost further tile fragments and a small assemblage of pottery of early Roman (1st or early 2nd century) date. From the geophysical magnetometer survey it appears

that this ditch continued westwards for *c* 7m, and then either terminated or turned to the south. This was probably an enclosure ditch.

Ditch 3346=3055 cut into ditch 3081 close to the eastern side of the site, terminating within it, and ran north-westwards up to and beneath the later Roman building. Halfway along it was cut across by a shallow elongated pit 3038 with vertical sides and a flat base, which was packed with large limestone blocks, possibly to create a firm crossing over the infilled ditch. The ditch must have met ditch 3279 just before the corner of the building, but this relationship was not investigated. Ditch 3346=3055 was concave in profile and deepened as it ran south-east, measuring 1.3m wide and 0.5m deep where it cut 3081. Two sherds of pottery manufactured from the late 1st century onwards were recovered from the primary fill here, and further Malvernian sherds from further north.

Ditch 3094 (Fig. 2.27 section 3018) ran into the site from the west parallel to ditch 3081 and just to its south, but turned northwards and narrowed at the terminus, cutting the south edge of ditch 3081 and ending within it. Ditch 3094 yielded a fairly large amount of 1st century pottery from its upper two fills (3062 and 3107), including a largely complete Malvernian ware jar (SF3012) from 3062 (Fig. 3.3.47; Plate 2.19), with the assemblage from the upper fill more closely dated to the late 1st century (Fig. 3.2. 32 and 3.3.42). Ditches 3081 and 3094 were also sectioned further west in CAT evaluation trench 146, where they were jointly numbered 146010, and yielded 21 sherds of early Roman pottery.

Plate 2.19 SF3012 pot profile in ditch 3094

Just north of ditch 3081 was a single undated posthole 3153, 0.35m in diameter, with one very steep and one steep side and a flattish base. No finds were recovered from its backfill, but it may have been associated.

Burials

A grave (5224) slightly to the south of ditch 5209 was aligned north-south and contained skeletons 5223 and 153006. Burial 153006 was identified during the evaluation in Trench 153 (Cotswold Archaeology 2009), where it was recorded as cut by the ditch, and was partly excavated. The bones were described as disarticulated, and no finds were recovered. The cut left for excavation by OA had steep sides and a concave base and measured, 1.6m in length, 0.6m in width and 0.4m in depth. Its fill contained a single sherd of pottery of Roman date and part of the skeleton of an adult. The sex could not be determined. Bone from the skeleton was submitted for radiocarbon dating, but there was too little collagen.

Only 8m further to the SSE, and also on the same orientation, pit 5296 containing cremation burial (5295) cut the top of ditch 5301. The pit was an oval, concave cut 1.1m long, 0.6m wide and only 0.15m deep. Cremated remains recovered from the fill (Sample 5015) weighed 767.8g and were of a mature adult aged 35-39 years. Also recovered were 4 hobnails, confirming a Roman date, and six nails, indicating either the former presence of a box in the grave, or the reuse of old timber on the pyre.

Middle Roman

Large enclosure 5288-5292

Late Iron Age or very early Roman ditches 5073 and 5151 (discussed above) were overlain by a more complex and substantial sequence of ditches on the same north-south and east-west alignments during this phase, representing the development of a more widespread field or enclosure system that can be seen beyond the limits of excavation on the geophysics plan.

The south-west corner of a large rectangular enclosure was formed by ditch groups 5290, 5291, 5292 and 5288 (Fig. 2.19). The area within the corner of this enclosure contained several roughly east-west aligned ditches, all of which were cut by 5054, the easternmost recut of the north-south arm of the main enclosure. Ditch 5195 has already been described. Ditch 5066/5232 (also identified in evaluation as 151005) was also very shallow, and did not contain datable material, but must have either predated or run into the earliest of the north-south enclosure ditches. The southernmost ditch, 5187, measured 1.65m in width and 0.56m in depth and contained a small amount of pottery of 2nd century or later date, along with charcoal and disarticulated human bone (Sk 5198) including skull fragments, perhaps suggesting that an earlier burial had been disturbed by the cutting of the ditch. This ditch was also sectioned further east in CAT evaluation trench 151, where it was numbered 151007, and contained 3 sherds each of later prehistoric and

Roman pottery, and was recut by a ditch containing late medieval or early post-medieval pottery at the top. To the west, ditch 5187 was planned as being cut by the uppermost fill of the easternmost (and earliest) of the north-south ditches, 5292.

The sequence of evolution of the enclosure is not precisely clear, as most of the south-west ditch intersection itself lay beyond the limit of excavation. The sequence on both the west and south sides was of cuts moving progressively outwards, or in the case of the north-south ditches, in a westerly direction, and in the case of the east-west ditches, in a southerly direction. The geophysical survey plot appears to indicate that the earliest north-south ditch extended beyond the east-west pair of ditches, and terminated around 3m further south, parallel to the corner formed by ditches 5151 and 5073 (Fig. 2.19).

Although the earliest of these north-south ditches truncated east-west ditch 5187, the upper fill of which dated to the 2nd century or later (on the basis of only a small number of diagnostic forms), it is likely that the earliest N-S boundary was dug before this, and that the very top of all the ditches (which were the only fills to contain later pottery) remained as depressions formed as the earlier fills settled, into which later material accumulated. The earliest ditch cut, towards the inner eastern side, was group 5292, comprising 5052, 5173 and 5280 (Figs 2.19 and 2.24-26). This substantial ditch measured 2.8m in width and 1.2m in depth and had 45 degree sides and a flattish base (Figs 2.25 and 2.26). The middle fill of this ditch contained pottery of late Iron Age date

and the upper fill contained an assemblage of largely mid to late 2nd century date (Fig. 3.2.37), together with some tile. This upper fill however also contained several sherds dated to the late 3rd to 4th century, although as suggested above it is likely that these sherds were deposited later in the sequence of development. Upper fill 5176 also contained a dog tooth pendant (Fig. 3.9.5), possibly associated with one of the associated cremation burials (see below).

This ditch was then cut along its western side by ditch group 5291, made up of cuts 5048 and 5177 (Figs 2.24-5; Plate 2.20). This was another substantial ditch, measuring 2.9m in width and 0.9m in depth with a wide 'V' shaped profile, and is likely to have been constructed in the mid to late 2nd century. It contained two dark silty fills, the upper of which was dated by pottery to the 2nd century (Fig. 3.2.19). It also contained a fragment of box flue tile, and flat tiles in its top. A further recut (ditch group 5290 comprising cuts 5181 and 5045) was cut along the western side of ditch 5291 (Plate 2.21). This ditch was much narrower and shallower than the earlier two and contained much pottery, the assemblage also being dated to the 2nd century (see Fig. 3.2. Nos 21, 26, 28, 39; Fig. 3.3.45). Fill 5044 also contained roof and floor tiles, and a fragment of a decorated bone knife handle (Fig. 3.9.6). An environmental sample [5019] from the primary fill 5182 produced charred wheat and barley remains. A short length of ditch of similar proportions, 5054, was cut along the east edge of the earliest cut 5292, and cut ditch 5187 to the east. This may have had a posthole (numbered

Plate 2.20 Ditches 5045 and 5048 with posthole 5041 and gravel spread to east

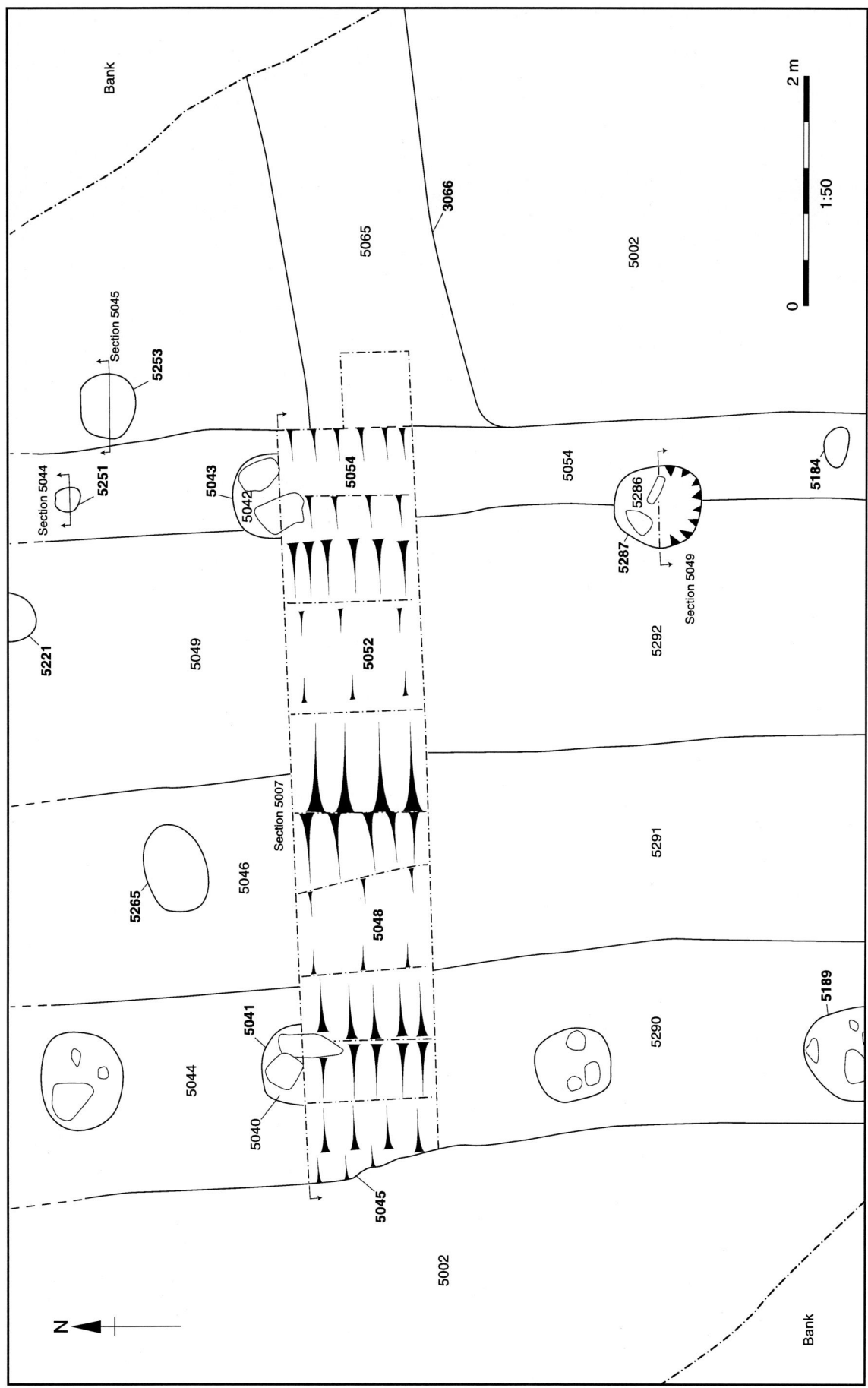

Fig. 2.24 Plan of ditch groups 5290-5292 and 5054, with posthole structure 5189

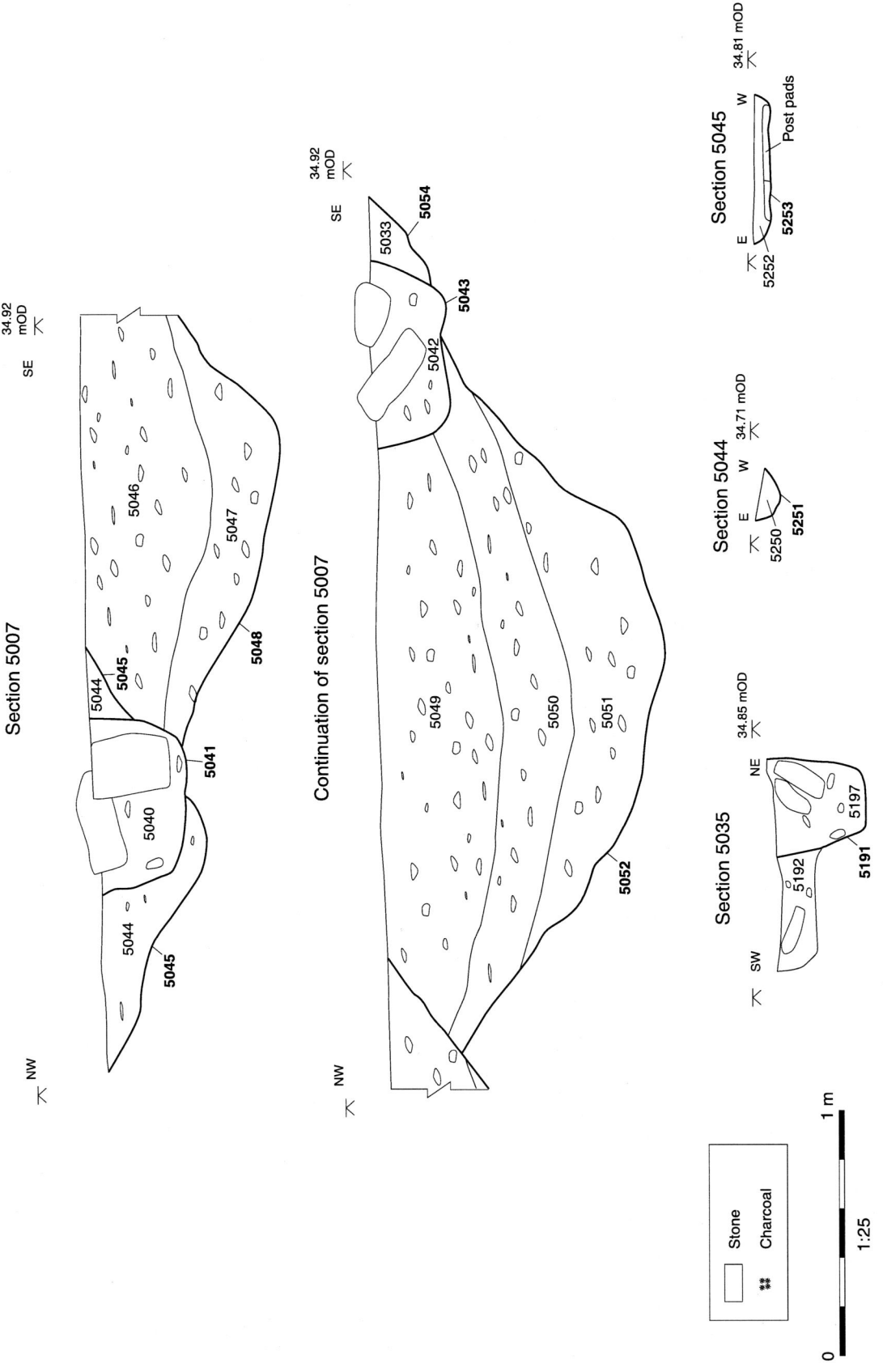

Fig. 2.25 Sections of ditch groups 5291/5292 and postholes cut into them (S. 5007, S5035, S. 5044-5).

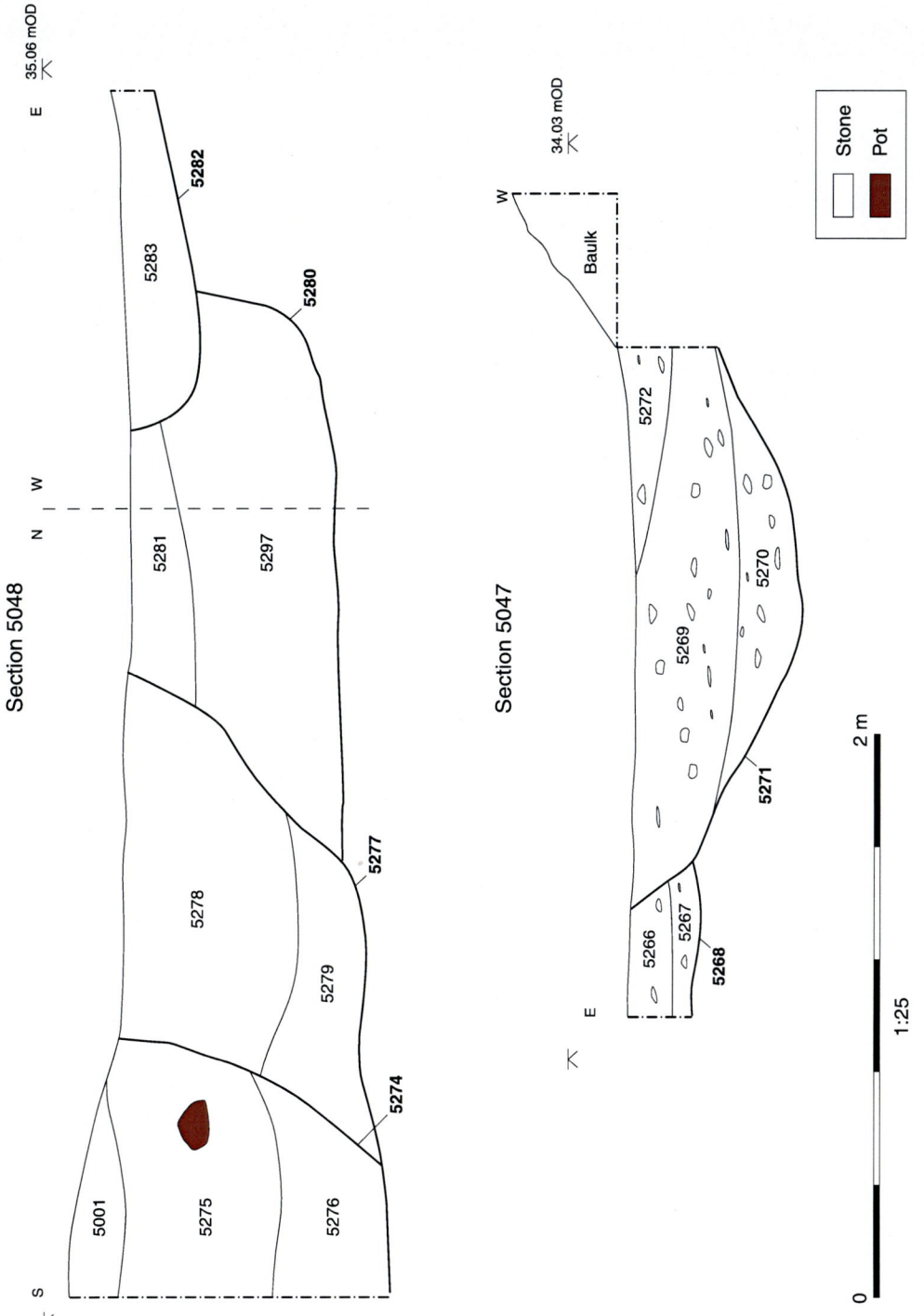

Fig. 2.26 *Sections of ditch group 5288, postholes 5057–60 and ditch 5271*

Plate 2.21 Ditches 5048 and 5052 with posthole 5043 and possible gravel spread

5184) cut into it east of posthole 5189 (see Fig. 2.24), due to a concentration of stone packing (and tile) at this point, but this was only noticed in section.

The east-west aligned southern arm of the main enclosure only comprised two cuts 5289 and 5288 (Fig. 2.19; Figs 2.20 and 2.26), both of which cut the fills of ditch 5292, suggesting that an earlier cut corresponding to ditch 5292 had not survived later recutting, or perhaps that no east-west corresponding boundary existed until later in the sequence of development. The earliest surviving ditch 5289 consisted of cuts 5277, 5171, 5076 and 5084, but had been largely removed by recut 5288 (Fig. 2.26). Recut 5288 comprised cuts 5274, 5164, 5070 and 5088, and measured 2.4m wide and 0.9m deep. Scraps of tile came from all the fills, and a tessera and flat tile from middle fill 5276. Pottery from the lowest fill 5069 and that from the middle fill 5086 suggests a late 2nd century date for its infill (Fig. 3.2. Nos 22, 25, 33 and 36). Sherds of the same vessel (Fig. 5.2.39) came both from fill 5069 and from fill 5044 in N-S ditch 5045 (part of group 5290), supporting their probable contemporaneity.

Burials

Just 3m east of ditch group 5292 (Fig. 2.19) was an oval grave 5200, orientated north-south and measuring 1.3m x 0.66m x 0.2m deep with steep sides and a flattish base. This contained skeleton 5202 buried in a crouched posture, a young adult of 20-25 years, possibly female (Plate 2.22). The grave fill contained 17 pottery sherds (111g) probably of 2nd century date, and a scrap of tile. This grave is probably middle Roman, though it may lie at the end of the early Roman phase.

The disarticulated remains of another burial, skeleton 5198, were found in ditch 5187 only 3m south of 5200, and suggest that there had been a pair of burials in this location either contemporary with the earliest phase of this enclosure, or possibly predating its construction.

The upper fill of the ditch group 5292, silt deposit 5049, contained a total of seven neonate skeletons (5259, 5260, 5261, 5262, 5254, 5220 and 5284) and a further neonate (5244) was recovered from the upper fill (5046) of the adjacent recut, group 5291(Fig. 2.19; Plates 2.23 and 2.24). All of these would appear to have been placed in the ditches whilst the silting process was occurring rather than being cut into the deposits after the ditches had fully filled. Bone from skeletons 5244 and 5262 was submitted for radiocarbon dating, and returned dates of 60-230 cal AD and 80-240 cal AD respectively (SUERC-49693, 1876 ± 30 BP; SUERC-49696, 1853 ± 30 BP).

Timber structure 5189 and adjacent postholes

Finally, after the latest ditches in the sequence had been infilled, the north-south and east-west boundaries appear to have been redefined by a timber

Plate 2.23 SK 5244 from above, with head to the north

Plate 2.22 Skeleton 5202 in grave 5200 from above, with head to the north

structure (Group 5189), represented by large postholes cut into the upper fills of the ditches. These were arranged in two rows along the north-south boundary, with two (5043 and 5286) along the eastern edge and four (5041 and 5189 and two not numbered) along the western side of the boundary (Figs 2.24 and 2.25; Plates 2.20 and 2.21). The postholes were all of a similar size, all measuring 0.8m in diameter and surviving between 0.25m and 0.4m deep. Within the fills were large limestone blocks used as packing that appeared to be still *in situ*, their positions suggesting that the posts had been rectangular in cross section. The only one of these postholes to contain finds was 5287, whose fill 5286 contained sherds of middle Roman date and scraps of tile. The postholes were between 2.5m and 3.5m apart.

Photographs of the ditch top show a thin layer of gravel, apparently confined to the area between the rows of postholes (Plates 2.20 and 2.21). Although very thin, this may perhaps represent an associated

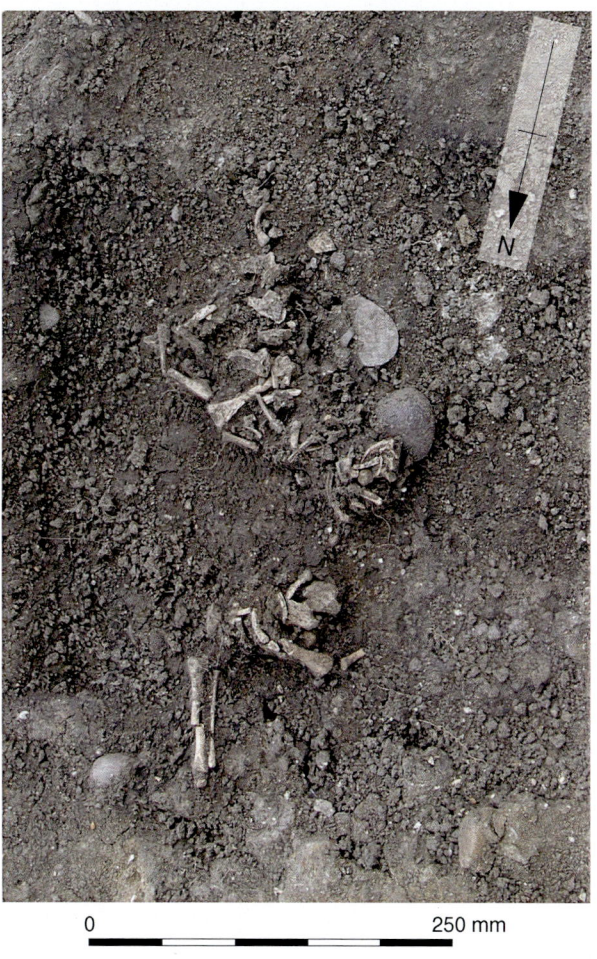

Plate 2.24 SK 5284 from above, with head to the south

surface. The pair of postholes in the eastern row did not however exactly correspond to the spacing of the four in the western row, and there were several other postholes in the vicinity that might have been associated, particularly 5253 just east of the ditch and two further south, one cutting the top of east-west ditch 5288 and another (5191) south-east of that. The postholes do not appear to have been associated with the burials in the ditch top, as the majority of the burials were north of the northernmost postholes in the group. Another possible posthole was planned protruding from the western edge of ditch 5291 some 6m further north (see Fig. 2.19), but this was of smaller dimensions than the main south-north line, so was probably not associated.

There was also a group of four postholes (5057-5060) to the west of the north-south arm of the enclosure, and also an oval patch of burnt soil and stones between the two rows, 5285, that might have been the base of another (Fig. 2.19). It is therefore possible that there were a variety of alignments and structures represented in this area, but only the six first-mentioned were all of similar size and depth. Posthole 5253 had a stone pad on its base, while posthole 5191 had a deep post-pipe and shallower surround, but both were undated. Postholes 5057-60 were all circular and shallow, and contained undiagnostic sherds of Roman pottery (Fig. 2.26). Posthole 5060 had a stepped base, and the dark brown silt fills of this and of 5058 contained limestones, presumably packing. An environmental sample (5012) from 5064, the fill of 5060, produced charred remains of oat, wheat and barley.

Less than 2m north of postholes 5057-5060 was a figure-of-eight shaped pit or hollow (5055), which was shallow, with gently sloping sides and a base sloping down northwards to a maximum depth of 0.28m. Its fill was a dark brown silt like that of the postholes, perhaps suggesting an association between them, and the fill contained a little charcoal, Roman pottery and animal bone.

Other ditches

North-west of the enclosure just described and south of ditch 5301 was a pair of parallel ditches (5082 and 5080) aligned east-west. They were both up to 1.25m wide but only respectively 0.12m and 0.18m deep, with flat bases and shelving sides. Ditch 5080 was believed to have cut 5082, but neither produced any finds. Ditch 5080 was cut on the south edge by ditch 5078, which was only 3.7m long with rounded ends, and was aligned ENE-WSW. This was 0.6m wide and up to 0.26m deep, with a wide V-shaped profile. The western termini of 5082 and 5080 were cut by a N-S aligned plough furrow.

Some 15m to the south-east of the enclosure ditch early Roman boundary ditch 5103 was replaced by ditch 5101 just to the north. Ditch 5101 measured 1.9m in width and 0.72m in depth, and like 5103 contained two silty fills, from which came a small assemblage of pottery no earlier than the 2nd century, and a fragment of tegula. This ditch was also sectioned by CAT evaluation trench 150, where it was numbered 15003, and contained 10 sherds of 2nd century or later Roman pottery and animal bones.

Immediately south of this was a possible circular posthole 5035, 0.26m in diameter and surviving 0.1m deep, but with sloping sides to a flat base. This had a single sterile silty clay fill. On the south side of medieval furrow 5033, and cut by it, was a short length of gully or slot 5037, 0.5m wide and 0.25m deep, with very steep sides and a flat base. This was undated, but was perhaps a Roman slot or gully. Another longer curving gully of similar width lay to the west, but this was not investigated.

A further 15m south of ditch 5103 was another ditch (5010=5142) on a roughly east-west alignment, continuing the pattern of E-W ditch alignments *c* 15m apart. Where completely sectioned, this had sloping sides and a wide flattish base (a wide 'V' shaped profile) and measured 3.4m wide and 1m deep. The primary fill (5011), which was found only down the north edge, was redeposited natural, perhaps indicating slipped upcast from a bank on this side (S. 5003). Its three silty fills contained a pottery assemblage (21 sherds, 979g) dated to the mid to late 2nd century (Fig. 3.2.24), plus Roman tile. This cut the south end of ditch 5144=5132 (also called 149003 in evaluation) running north at right angles (Fig. 2.19).

Ditch 5144 was 0.8m deep, of very similar depth to 5142 at their intersection. A single sherd of Roman pottery was found in the fill in the evaluation. Ditch 5142 also cut a sub-circular pit 5136 east of ditch 5144, which was shallow with shelving sides. There were no finds from its dark silty clay fill, but it included numerous pebbles and some larger limestones. A smaller circular pit 5134 lay adjacent on the north-east, and this had sloping sides to a narrow flat base at the centre, upon which there was a stone. Further limestones in its silty clay fill suggest an association with 5136, although this pit too was undated.

Towards the west edge of site a sequence of inter-cutting undated pits and postholes lay just north of the ditch (Fig. 2.19). The earliest (5122) was on the south, was subrectangular and was the deepest of the group at 0.2m. Pit 5124 which cut it was oval, and its fill 5123 contained animal bone and a tile tessera, but no pottery. This was probably Roman, and was cut, again on the north side, by pit 5126, like 5122 without finds. On the north-east edge of pit 5124 was an even shallower small pit or posthole 5140, not noticed initially. Both 5124 and 5126 were cut by deep oval posthole 5138, 0.29 by 0.23m across and 0.32m deep, whose fill was without finds.

To the south the sequence of east-west features continued with three gullies, 5017, 5022 and 5024. All were less than 1m in width and 0.25m or less in depth. They were all aligned with the present field boundary hedgerow. Of these only 5017 produced dating evidence, a small pottery assemblage dated to the 1st-2nd century and a tile scrap.

Ditches of late Iron Age and early Roman date beneath and just to the south of the Roman building have been discussed above. West of the building ditch the top fill of ditch 3120 was cut by an east-west aligned gully (3118) that extended beyond the western limit of excavation. Its eastern end was truncated by later ditch 3031 and by later Roman building 3184. It had vertical sides and a concave base, measuring 0.5m in width and 0.45m in depth. Its dark grey sandy silt fill contained a single sherd of pottery of 1st to 2nd century date (Fig. 2.17).

Ditches at the south end of the site

Parallel to east-west early Roman ditch 3081, and on the same line as early Roman ditch 3094 to the east, was ditch 3093=3057 (Fig. 2.16; Fig. 2.27). This turned southwards just before it met 3094, suggesting that ditch 3094 was still extant when it was dug, and possibly defined the north and west sides of a rectilinear enclosure. This ditch measured 1.15m in width and 0.6m in depth and contained pottery of the 2nd century date in its two fills, including Central Gaulish samian, indicating a date after *c* 125 AD. This is therefore middle Roman, and later than 3094. It also contained a tile tessera and a large imbrex fragment. This ditch was recut (3060=3095) on the outer (west and north) side, and this recut truncated ditch 3094. Ditch 3095 itself consisted of two phases, the earlier (and more westerly) a ditch of similar dimensions to 3081. This was shallowing just before its intersection with 3081. Ditch 3095 was recut as a shallower but steeper-sided cut, and where it ran east had near-vertical sides and a flat base. The first phase of 3095 was larger than ditch 3093, being nearly 1.5m wide and 0.75m deep. Its five fills were a mixture of silting fills and dumps with a greenish tinge. Pottery from the upper fills 3112 and 3113 comprised a large group of mid 2nd century or later date (Fig. 3.2. Nos 20, 34 and 35; 3.3.41) and a few fragments of tile.

Within the enclosure defined by ditches 3093 and 3095, a short irregular linear feature aligned north-south was planned but not excavated. An east-west feature to the east of this (3033) was investigated, but proved to be a medieval furrow. A bulge on the south side of this probably represented another archaeological feature, perhaps a pit, but this was not investigated.

North of ditch 3305, and also sealed by the late Roman building, was ditch 3037=3310. This was only observed below the western room, where it was running WSW. It was only sectioned in one place, and here it was 2.3m wide and 0.9m deep, with sloping sides and a profile varying from V-profile to rounded (Fig. 2.29). There were four fills, of which only the third (3043) contained any pottery, a small group of Malvernian sherds of early Roman date (Fig. 3.3.46). The ditch was cut by the construction trench (3047) for the westernmost room of the Roman building, and by the construction cut for 3025 for the hypocaust.

Late Roman (*c* AD 250–410)

This phase was characterised by the construction of a substantial building, the most prominent feature of which was a sunken-floored room, well-preserved due to the fact that it had been terraced into the hillside (Figs 2.16 and 2.28). Several adjoining rooms, constructed conventionally at ground level, were less well- preserved, having suffered from truncation by post-Roman ploughing. A few linear features were of this date, indicating the maintenance of parts of the enclosure system established in the early Roman period. It is worth noting, however, that while evidence for the later use of the building and its destruction is consistently of later 3rd-late 4th century date, there is effectively no close date for its construction, and the limited evidence from the underlying ditches would certainly permit a construction date as early as the mid 2nd century AD.

Corndryer 5255

At the north-west end of the site, nearly 80m north-west of the masonry building, were the truncated lower courses of an east-west aligned corndryer or

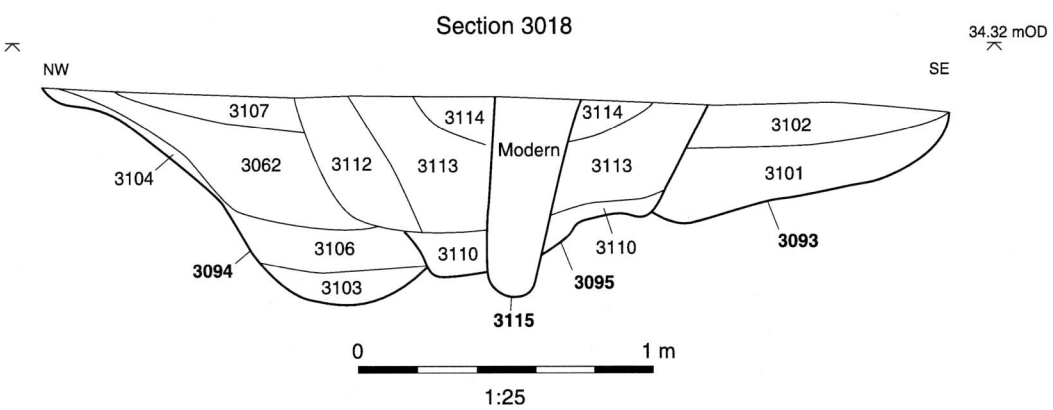

Fig. 2.27 Section 3018 showing ditches at the south end of the site.

Plate 2.25 Corndryer 5225 excavated, looking west

malting oven, structure 5225, which measured 3.5m (surviving) by 1.2m and was 0.4m deep (Fig. 2.19; Plate 2.25). This was the westernmost pre-medieval feature uncovered within the site. The structure consisted of two parallel unmortared walls of limestone blocks, two to three courses high, with a base of fire-cracked stone at the lower, eastern end. This presumably formed the fire pit or stokehole at one end of the flue formed by the parallel walls; the drying chamber to the west had been removed by later agricultural activity. There were three silty clay fills (5247-9), 5249 being reddened by burning at the stokehole end. Fill 5247 contained a nail, and 5249 a single Roman pottery sherd that could not be more closely dated. Charred plant remains including wheat and possibly barley grains were found in samples from 5247 and 5249. A charred grain from 5249 gave a radiocarbon date range of 230-390 cal AD (SUERC -49697; 1736 ± 29 BP).

Boundary ditches

Some 5m east of the corndryer ditch 5271/5238 was dug, offset slightly to the west of north-south earlier boundary ditch 5268, and on a slightly more ENE-WSW alignment (Fig. 2.19). This ditch measured 2.2m wide and 0.7m deep, with gently sloping sides and a cupped base (Fig. 2.26). Its two dark clayey silt fills contained small pottery groups of late 3rd-4th century date (see Fig. 3.3.50). A probable medieval furrow 5273, which ran on the same alignment down the west side of the ditch, contained box flue tile fragments probably derived from the ditch.

There is no firm indication of continued use of the middle Roman enclosure defined by ditch groups 5289-5292. A little to the south of this enclosure an east-west gully (5112) with a shallow concave profile terminated within the excavated area. Its fill contained a tiny sherd of possible Oxford colour-coated ware and may therefore have been of late Roman date. Some 22m further south (Fig. 2.19), east-west ditch 5120 measured 0.8m in width and 0.12m in depth. It ran broadly parallel and adjacent to earlier Roman ditch 5010, and then turned north. Pottery and tile came from cuts 5120 and 5128, and included a late Roman flanged bowl but also a small post-medieval sherd. Close to the eastern end of ditch 5120 a sub-circular pit (5114) cut through the ditch (here numbered 5118). It had a concave profile, measured 0.81m across and 0.52m deep, and contained animal bone. No pottery was recovered from its dark brown clayey sand fill, but its stratigraphic position confirms that it is late Roman or later in date. Beyond pit 5114 was a ditch at right angles, 5116. This was deeper than 5118, but had exactly the same dark clayey sand fill, and may have been a return running north. A probable continuation of this return was excavated in CAT evaluation trench 149, and was numbered 149003. This was 0.3m deep, and contained one sherd of Roman pottery and cow, sheep and dog bones.

About 7m south of ditch 5120 was a more substantial east-west ditch, 5020. This ditch was a wide 'V' shape in profile, 2.4m wide and 0.75m deep, with two fills, a silty clay (5019) overlain by clayey silt (5018). Both contained pottery and animal bone, that from 5019 including an Oxford colour-coated sherd indicating a late Roman date. Fill 5018 also included tile fragments. Just south of this were two parallel narrow gullies 5022 and 5024, neither of which contained any finds.

The Roman building

The sunken room 3184

Structure 3184, the northernmost part of the Roman building, had been constructed within a terrace/construction cut (3224) which measured more than 8m east-west by 5.1m north-south and was cut into the natural clay/gravels to a depth of 0.65-0.7m, at about 34.32m aOD. The western part of the room was exposed within the easement and the eastern part lay beneath the eastern limit of the excavation (Figs 2.16, 2.28 and 2.29).

All of the western wall and substantial parts of the southern and northern walls of the room were revealed within the excavation (Plate 2.26). The western (3249) and northern (3185) walls appeared to have been constructed up against the edge of the construction cut, and like the southern wall (3012), had been built upon a foundation (3293) some 0.8m wide. This consisted of limestone blocks laid with straight edges and a rubble core. On the north side of the room this foundation was 0.3m thick and without apparent bonding, whereas to the west and south yellow/orange sandy mortar was encountered between the stones (Plate 2.27). The walls themselves were around 0.7m wide, and were constructed of irregular limestone blocks, typically <400 x 200 x 120mm, which were laid with straight edges on the faces, and were bonded with lime mortar. They followed the outer edge of the foundation, and survived up to 0.6m above foundation level. Traces of mortar and wall plaster were still attached on the inner faces (Plates 2.28 and 2.29), as was a quarter-round moulding of pinkish plaster (3222) at the north-west corner and along the north side (Plate 2.30), sealing the junction between wall 3185 and the flagged floor (3187). No mortar surfacing was found on the south side of wall 3012 (Plate 2.31), indicating that this was not intended to be visible.

Almost all of the west side, and the west end of the south side, had been robbed out almost to the bottom of the foundations, and 1m on the west had been removed altogether (Plate 2.32). The northern end of the west wall 3249 survived up to 4 courses and 0.0.74m high above foundation level, the northern wall 3185 also up to 4 courses, but only 0.6m high. The southern wall 3012 also survived to a height of 4 courses in places, but only to 0.5m high above floor level.

Inside the foundations, a layer of construction debris (3291), probably formed by trimming foundation/wall stones to shape, overlay the natural clay in the bottom of the construction (cut 3224). Above this, redeposited clay (3292) was laid as a levelling deposit up to 0.2m deep, and probably also acted as a waterproofing or damp proofing layer for the overlying limestone flagged floor 3187 (Plate 2.33). The flagstones of the floor were mostly approximately rectangular, and were laid upon the clay and fitted tightly against one another; the largest exposed was 1.2m long and up to 0.9m wide, though most were much smaller (Fig. 2.28; Plate 2.34). The observed thicknesses ranged from 40-80mm. There was no mortar between or beneath the flagstones.

Before this floor was laid, however, a 0.75m deep, limestone-lined cistern or tank (3248), 0.6m in diameter, was constructed centrally between the north and south walls (Plate 2.35). The cistern, whose base was a single slab of limestone, was cylindrical, consisting of nine courses of unmortared limestones. Just under 0.5m above the floor, a pair of sockets, carved into opposite sides of the interior of the cistern, may have supported a timber cross-bar (Plate 2.36). The overlying flagstone floor (3187) overlapped the edge of the tank, but had a 0.5m diameter aperture for access to it.

The flagstone floor was not exactly level, being slightly higher on the east (34.59m aOD) than on the west (34.50m aOD), but it clearly sloped downwards towards the cistern in the centre of the room at 34.40m aOD (Fig. 2.29, S. 3034). When first uncovered during excavation, water collected over the cistern, the rest of the floor being dry (Plate 2.37). This shows that water was clearly intended to drain into it.

At some point during the building's life a V-profiled groove up to 60mm wide and 40mm deep was chiselled into the two flagstones south of the tank (Fig. 28; Plate 2.38), running from the southern edge of the cistern for 1.2m towards the southern wall 3012, where a hole gave access to a stone-built drain (3167) aligned north-south (Plate 2.39). Drain 3167 was built within a trench up to 0.4m deep and 0.5m wide, and consisted of a limestone slab floor with block-built walls and a slab capping, numbered 3191 to the north and 3192 to the south (Plate 2.40; Fig. 2.30). The internal dimensions of the drain were therefore no more than 0.3m across and 0.25m deep. Only a limited number of levels were taken on the base of the drain, and these did not indicate an even fall to the south, but sufficient to drain from the interior of the building. This drain ran southwards below the pitched stone floor of the adjacent room for 6.5m, and then probably drained into ditch 3031, which ran south-west away from the building complex (Figs 2.16 and 2.17). Ditch 3031 contained a reasonably substantial group of pottery dated to the 4th century, and a mixture of box tile, roof tile and floor tile, indicating that it was during this time that the drainage system silted up, and at least part of the building was demolished.

Between the groove and the hole in the wall there was an L-shaped gap (3333) in the flagstone floor 3187, some 0.12m deep (Plate 2.41). This may simply be where some flagstones had been removed, and the gap patched with a mixture of stone roof tiles, small stones, tile fragments and mortar (3332). It was suggested during the excavation that it represented the position of a trough or basin up to 2m in length and 0.45m in width, from which water would have drained into stone drain 3167. This is, however, unlikely, as the base of the groove in the flagstones was less than 100mm above the surface upon which a trough would have stood, making it unable to hold any depth of water. Even a wooden structure would not have held a significant depth of water. The end of the drain under the south wall of the building 3012, and immediately to the south, had no silt in it, and had been deliberately infilled with gravel 3340, which was abutted and sealed by layer 3332, showing that the removal of the flagstones here may have been to ensure that the drain was blocked, probably indicating a change of use. Fill 3332 included eight stone tesserae, and 3340, the backfill of drain 3167 adjacent, contained another seven, showing that the infilling included either robbed or surplus material from another room. Layer 3332 also contained a few sherds of pottery, a variety of metal finds and three sherds of late Roman vessel glass.

Plate 2.26 *Rectified photograph of Romano-British building*

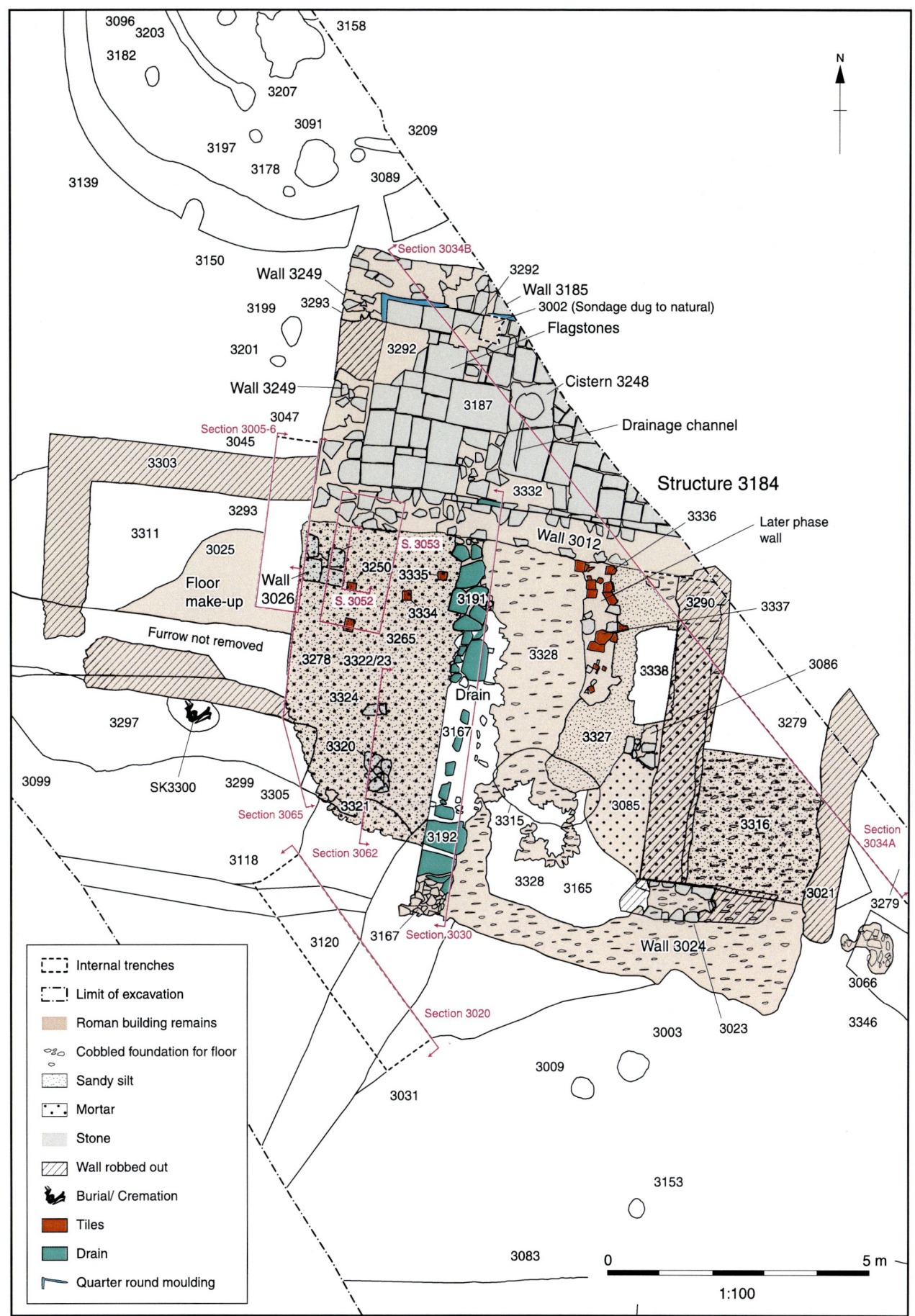

Fig. 2.28 Plan of Romano-British building

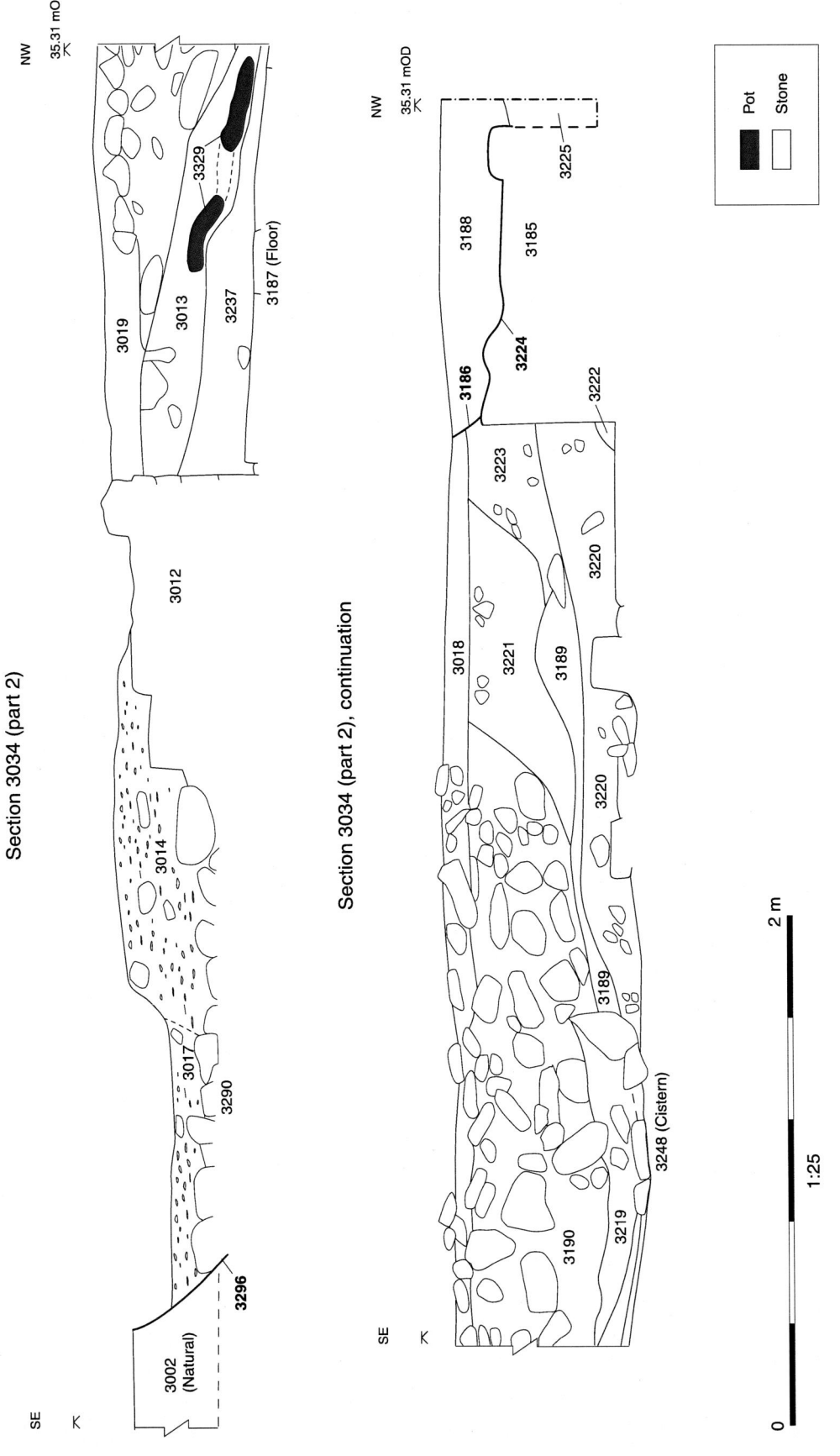

Section 3034 (part 2)

Section 3034 (part 2), continuation

Fig. 2.29 Section 3034b across sunken room 3184

Plate 2.27 View of floor abutting foundation on the N, with wall offset and burnt layer directly overlaying offset foundation up to the wall face

Plate 2.28 Mortar on north face of wall 3012, looking south

Plate 2.29 Red stripe on white background in situ on the north side of wall 3012

Plate 2.30 NW corner of room 3814, showing floor, wall and quarter-round moulding, looking NW

Plate 2.31 Unpointed south face of wall 3012, looking north

Unusually, the stones of the lowest courses of wall 3012 appeared to have been robbed just to the east of the drain, but the wall was virtually continuous above this (Plate 2.41). This suggests selective robbing of stone, though for what purpose is not clear. The hole was not carefully finished off, and there was no corresponding hole on the south side of the wall, so this was not another phase of drain. It is possible that some decorated piece of stone had originally been included into the wall here, and that this was removed before the building was demolished, but why such a feature should have existed at this point in the wall is not easy to explain. One possibility is that there had originally been a set of steps down into the sunken room at this point, and that these had been keyed into the wall, so that their removal, which created feature 3333, had also left holes in the wall. There must have been steps down from the surrounding area, but where these had been remains uncertain, and this suggestion can only be speculative.

The function of the cistern/tank and adjacent drain is not entirely clear, but the groove cut to the south was clearly only for a small volume of water. It suggests that the cistern may have been fed by groundwater from the sides, and that on occasions it overflowed, threatening to make all of the floor wet, and that the overflow was then channelled southwards into the drain.

The southern rooms

An area lying immediately to the south of structure 3184, measuring approximately 7m north-south by 8m east-west, had been also been terraced out of the hillside down to around 34.65m aOD, so was cut between 0.35m and 0.4m into the natural as surviving (Figs 2.28, 2.29 and 2.31). On the west the cut, here numbered 3025, was overlain by a thin layer of light brown clay 3053, overlain by 3052, a layer of silty sand and flat angular stones 60-100mm across and 60mm deep (Fig. 2.31 S.3005). This layer was part of a pitched limestone floor (Plate 2.42) numbered variously 3322, 3328, 3024 and 3290,

Plate 2.32 Room 3184 with west half fully excavated, looking east

Plate 2.33 Section through flagged floor showing clay and mortar bedding layers, plus quarter-round moulding between foundation and wall 3012, looking east

Plate 2.34 Flagstone floor largely exposed, looking west

which further east had been rammed into the natural clay base of the cut without intervening make-up layers. Excavation of the construction cut was slightly deeper where the cut truncated earlier ditches, and this explains the presence of levelling up layers.

The stones of the floor were generally rectangular (Plate 2.43), and measured 100-400mm long, 60-200 mm wide and 60-140mm deep. Most were 200-300mm long. The stone floor formed a broadly level surface filling the cut west to east, with straight west and east sides, ending on the west just beyond masonry 3026, and on the east beyond robber cut

3338, where it was numbered 3290. The pitched stone surface ran right up to the south edge of wall 3012, overlapping the capstones of drain 3167, and although no section recorded the relationship of the floor to the construction trench of the wall, it seems clear that the floor was laid after the wall had been constructed. It also partly overlay capstones 3191 and 3192 of drain 3167.

In between the stones and overlying them on the west was a thin layer of sandy silt with mortar flecks 3323 (equivalent to 3052), probably laid to fill gaps and level the floor. Where recorded the layer was from 10-60mm thick, generally 20-30mm, and it covered the whole of that part of the stone floor numbered 3322. This layer contained a small quantity of pottery of late 3rd or 4th century date, including a Harrold shell-tempered dish that probably dates to after AD 350, a stone tessera and a few animal bones. Although it incorporated some finds, it seems most likely that this was a deliberate levelling layer to even the stone surface here, rather than an occupation deposit. It was overlain in much of its area by layer 3265, a yellowish-brown mortar, sand and gravel up to 40mm thick. In places these two layers were

Plate 2.35 Cistern emptied in centre of floor

Plate 2.36 Detail of hole in wall of cistern

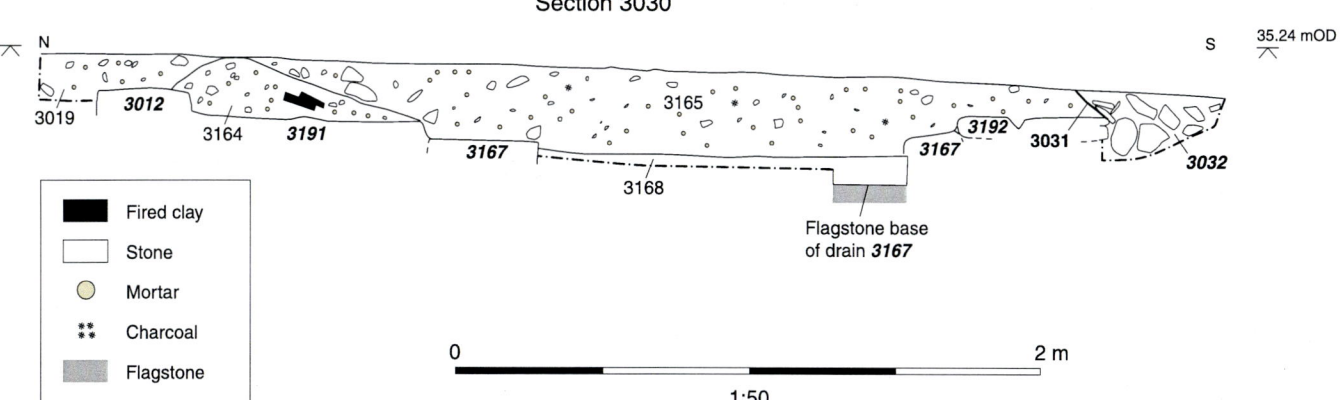

Fig. 2.30 Section 3030 showing long north-south section of drain 3167

Plate 2.37 *Floor in centre of trench showing standing water over central cistern*

Plate 2.38 *Flagstone floor showing groove cut running south from cistern, looking north*

described as if they were the same, suggesting that 3265 was a surfacing for 3323 beneath. Layer 3265 did not contain any finds, and was directly overlain by fragments of wall 3026, 3320, 3324 and 3086, and by pilae stacks 3250, 3278, 3334 and 3335.

East of the drain, where the floor was numbered 3328, it was overlain in part by a compact orange sandy silt (3327), which ran east up to a surviving wall fragment 3086, at which point it gave way to layer 3085, a rammed surface of limestones and sandy mortar (Fig. 2.28). A layer including much

Plate 2.39 Room 3814 looking south, showing groove crossing flags and drain running under wall 3012

Plate 2.40 Drain 3167 with cobbled floor either side and capstones above, looking south

mortar and pebbles 3017 overlay 3290 further north, and may perhaps have been equivalent, but this was recorded on site as a destruction layer. Layer 3085 continued until it disappeared below east-west wall fragment 3023. Further limestones (layer 3024), but without a mortar surface, continued south beyond wall 3023, and extended eastwards over ditch fill 3287 along the projected line of wall 3023, which sat directly upon 3024=3085. Layer 3024 ended at the edge of wall foundation 3021, which ran north-south, ending in line with wall 3023, but layer 3024 continued south along the same line for another 1.6m before making a sharp corner and returning westwards.

Within the area enclosed by walls 3021 and 3023 was a similar cobbled limestone floor (3316), sitting within a cut up to 0.25m deep, but this was packed with mortar and pebbles 3289, and formed a square, limited by 3085 on the west and ending at a sloping cut 3288 some 3.1m short of wall 3012 on the north (Fig. 28). There was no apparent surface to the north of this, layers 3287 and 3286, the top fills of ditch 3279 into which 3288 was cut, being visible here. The stones may have been laid as a form of foundation raft over the soft fills of the earlier underlying ditches, although their apparent absence north of cut 3288 may indicate otherwise.

On the south there was a large irregular area between the west edge of wall 3023 and drain capstones 3192 where the limestone floor was

Plate 2.41 *Floor gap against wall 3012 with roof slates in it, showing drain opening in wall, looking south*

Plate 2.42 *Cobbled floor 3290 and wall 3012, looking south-west*

apparently missing, and where the fills of ditch 3279 were directly overlain by destruction layers 3315 and 3165. A decorated fragment of early Roman pottery came from here, presumably derived from the ditch (Fig. 3.2.17). The southern part of this area could have been removed when wall 3023 was robbed out, but there is no obvious reason for the rest of this robbing.

Wall and other masonry fragments

Towards the north-west corner of the cobbled area, a fragment of probable wall 3026 was constructed directly upon layer 3265 (Figs 2.31 and 2.32). This lay at the very west edge of the platform, in line with wall 3249 of room 3184 to the north. At the south it consisted of two large cuboid limestone blocks, both

Section 3005+6

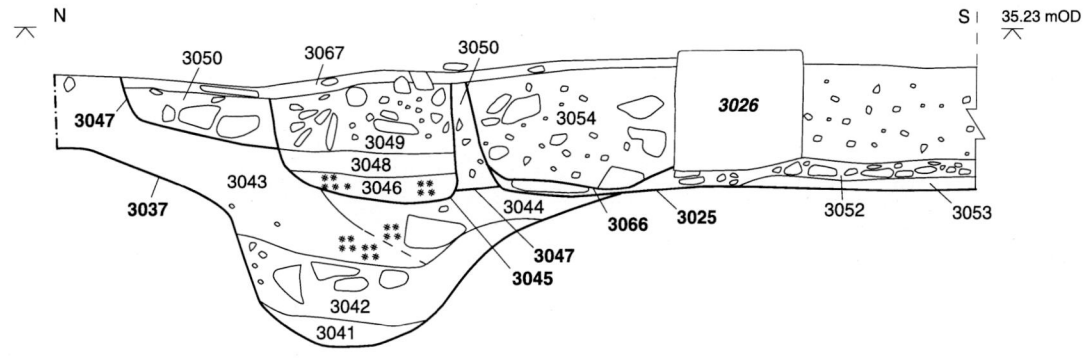

Continuation of section 3005+6

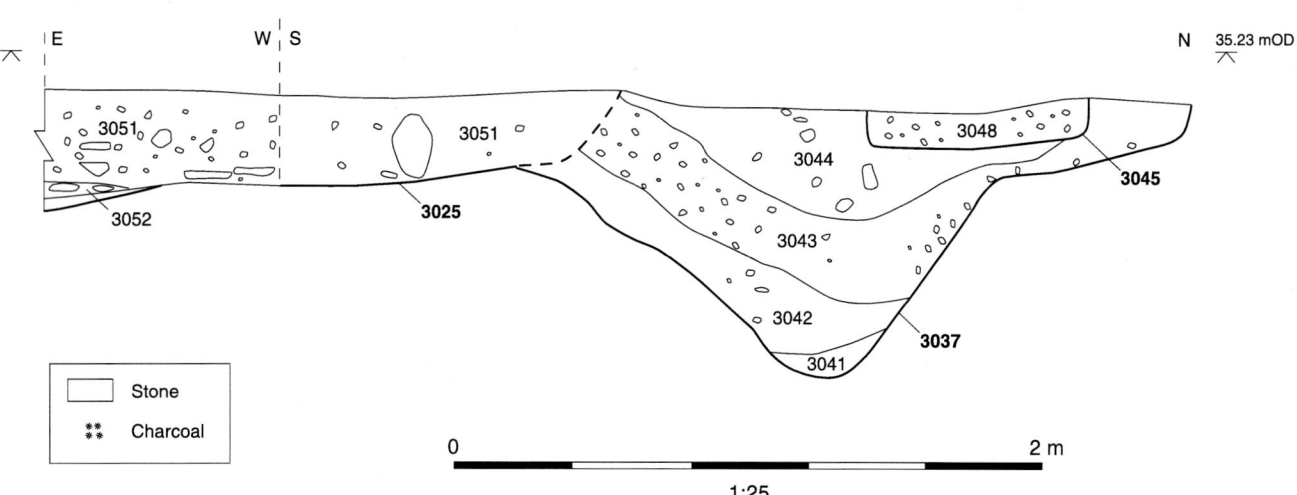

Stone

Charcoal

0   2 m

1:25

Fig. 2.31 Sections 3005-6

very carefully-dressed and up to 450mm long and high, forming a straight edge on the south side parallel to wall 3012 of room 3184. Together the blocks were of the same width (0.76m) as wall 3249 to the north. North of the blocks were several more roughly dressed limestone blocks, giving a surviving length of 0.88m, but with a ragged north edge indicating that the masonry had continued northwards (Fig. 2.32, S. 3052 and S. 3053). The robber trench of this continuation (numbered 3066) was seen in section (S. 3005) north of the masonry extending almost as far as the edge of the robbing of wall 3012), but not to the south. It seems likely that this was part of the west wall of a room, and the carefully dressed blocks suggest that there may have been an opening immediately to the south.

To the south-west, masonry 3320 was built upon layer 3323 some 0.8m in from the southern edge of the terrace cut, and consisted of two courses of limestone blocks bonded with a lime mortar, surviving up to 0.24m high (Figs 2.28 and 2.33; Plate 2.44). The north and south faces appeared to be intact, giving a probable width of 0.65-68m, the west

and east edges were irregular, and only up to 0.5m of masonry survived in this dimension. About 0.65m north of this another fragment of possible wall (numbered 3324) was also constructed upon layer 3323, but this consisted only of a pair of super-imposed limestone blocks to a similar height to 3320. A layer of small limestone chips and fragments in a matrix of grey silty clay (3326) abutted masonry 3320 on the south side, and extended as far as the edge of 3318, the cut for the building (Fig. 2.33). This was overlain on the south by 3319, a dark grey-brown sandy silt with occasional limestone fragments that lay against the side of the cut, and sloped down northwards from it. This is likely to be eroded material from the side of the cut higher up, accumulating while the hypocaust in this room was under construction. A couple of sherds of Severn Valley ware came from this layer, and were probably derived from ditch fill 3317, into which the cut for the platform had been excavated.

North-south aligned masonry fragment 3086 lay towards the east edge of the cobbled platform, but nearly 1m to the west of it. It survived as a single

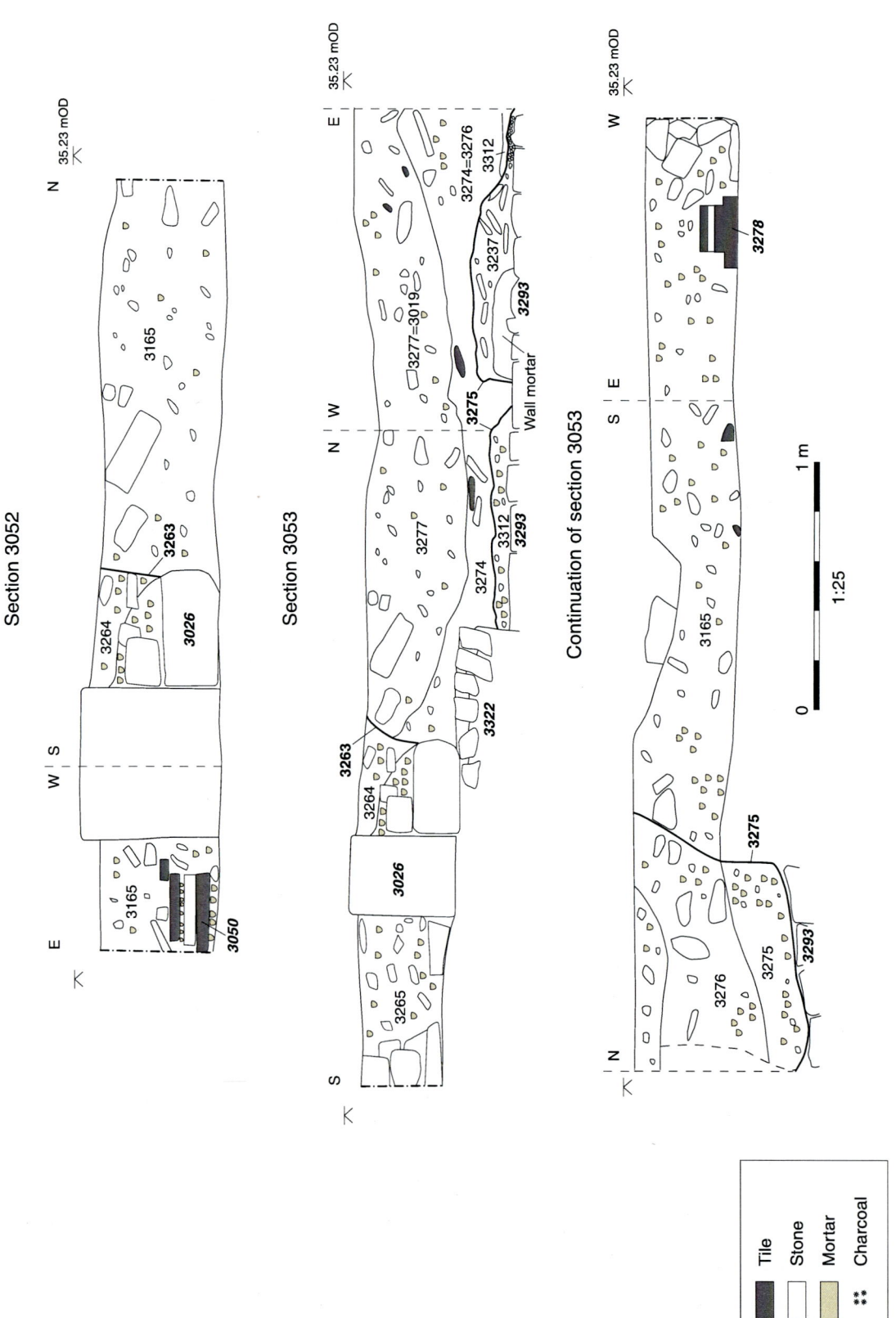

Fig. 2.32 Sections 3052 and 3053 of masonry 3026 and pilae 3250 and 3278

Section 3062

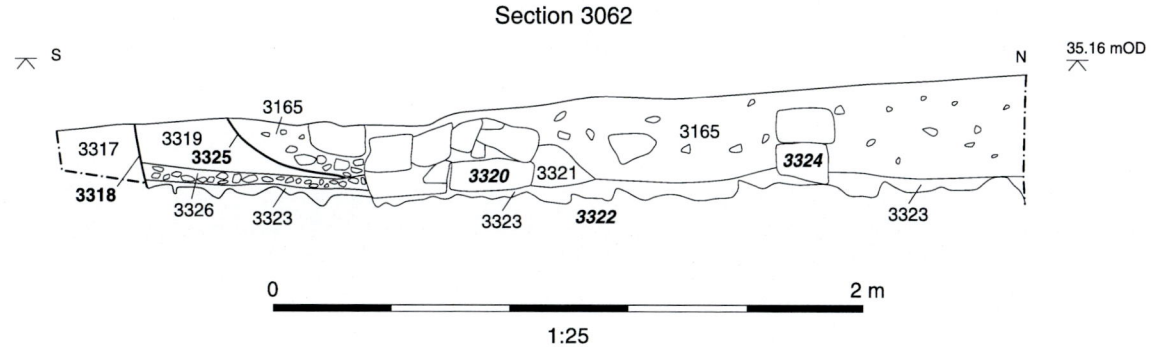

Fig. 2.33 Section 3062 showing the cut for the southern room and masonry 3320 and 3324 within it

course of limestone blocks up to 0.8m long sitting upon surface 3085, with one intact facing block on the west (Fig. 2.28). The surviving masonry was up to 0.64m wide, but there were no well-dressed blocks on the east, so the masonry was probably wider. A shallow linear trench (3338) some 0.8m wide continued its approximate line to the north for at least 1.8m, cutting up to 0.16m deep through the mortar layer beneath and partially removing the cobbled floor 3328 below this. This was probably a robber trench, which ended at layer 3014, a demolition deposit that overlapped wall 3012 (Fig. 2.29). Whether this was a wall or a support for the hypocaust floor is discussed further below (see Collapse and Demolition).

South-east of wall 3086 was wall 3023, which was aligned east-west, was 0.7m wide and survived 1.3m long and consisted of a single course of limestones bonded with mortar, edged with larger blocks with straight edges and with smaller limestones in the core (Fig. 2.28; Plate 2.26). This wall was built directly upon layers 3085 and 3024, and was at right angles to wall segment 3086 and parallel to wall 3012.

It is unclear whether this wall was contemporary with 3086 or was added at a later date, as it ended on the west just before the projected intersection with 3086. The western edge was ragged, perhaps suggesting that it had not abutted 3086, but the evidence is not conclusive. Wall 3023 lay along the

Plate 2.43 General view across cobbled area, looking south-west

Plate 2.44 Drain 3167, cobbled limestone floor, masonry fragments 3320, 3324 and 3025 and pilae, looking west

Plate 2.45 Ditch 3279, floor 3316 and wall foundation 3021, looking south-west

south edge of rammed floor/yard surface 3316, which sat within its own construction cut (3288) on the north, and abutted floor 3085 to the west. The straight edge of 3290/3085 continued southwards all the way to wall 3024, but did not reappear to the south of it, suggesting that this was the original limit of the limestone platform, to which 3316 was added. Surface 3316 was bounded by stone foundation 3021 along its eastern side to form a surface 2.5m square.

Foundation 3021 was traced northwards as a robber trench for 4.6m, continuing beyond surface 3316 and beyond the limits of the site (Plate 2.45). The foundation trench bottomed at the same level as the base of the stone platform adjacent, and survived at most 0.25m deep. This had a fairly straight east edge, but as planned varied in width from as little as 0.55m to 0.8m, though it was generally 0.6m or more wide. It seems likely that the foundation, which was not further investigated except at the north edge of the site, was originally 0.7m wide all the way along, but had been unevenly robbed. The fact that 3021 continued north of 3316 shows that the area between it and platform 3290 was enclosed at some stage.

To the south of wall 3023, the unmortared pitched stone surface 3024 may have served as a rough path or as a base for one whose flags had been removed.

The hypocaust

Within the north-west of this range, five pilae (3250, 3278, 3334, 3335 and 3336) were found upon layer 3265 (Plate 2.46). The first two of these were constructed with a larger flat tile (*pedalis*) at the base, and up to 3 smaller tiles (*bessalis*) surviving above this, with a combined height of 0.15m (Figs 2.31 and 2.32). An oval mortar ring found on the top of these may indicate that they were topped by a box flue tile filled with clay and tile (Plate 2.47; see L Allen, Chapter 3). A third (3336) was found up against wall 3012 further east, incorporated within the construction of later wall 3337 (Plate 2.48). This pila consisted of 3 stacked *bessalis* tiles, and also had a mortar ring on top, but does not appear to have sat upon a pedalis tile. The other two did not have a larger tile at the base either, and consisted of only two superimposed bessalis tiles, the upper of which lacked the mortar ring. The two pilae that consisted of only smaller tiles may have been displaced during demolition, rather than being *in situ*. It is not clear whether pila 3336 was displaced or *in situ*. On the analogy of hypocausts where pilae of this type survive to full height (Darenth in Kent, for example), it is probable that the pilae would have been approaching 0.5m high, not counting the larger bricks that would have straddled them, or the floor surfacing above. The floor in this room is therefore likely to have been at a height of at least 35.35m aOD, and thus at least 0.75m above the internal floor of structure 3184. No evidence of scorch marks/burning was found in relation to these pilae.

Plate 2.46 Pilae *bases on mortared stone floor, wall 3025 and robber trench 3293, west room robber trench 3047 and reddening to south, looking west*

A mixture of floor/pilae tiles and general rubble, bonded with a yellowish-white sandy mortar and incorporating *pilae* stack 3336, formed a crude dividing wall (3337) aligned north-south, which abutted what remained of wall 3012 (Plate 2.48). This appears to have been constructed from the same level as the original walls and *pilae* stacks, so could represent a modification to the supports for

the raised floor during construction. The incorporation of numerous other *pila* tiles however suggests that this was a later modification, perhaps necessitated due to the collapse of a small part of the floor, which was then shored up with a cruder wall.

The remains of a further room or walled area 3303 were observed as a robber cut which formed three sides of a rectangle against the western edge of the range (Fig. 2.28; Plate 2.26). The cut (3297 on the south, 3047 on the north) was flat-bottomed with vertical sides and measured up to 0.9m wide and 0.3m deep (Figs 2.31 and 2.34). The two robber trenches did not quite meet at the south-west corner, and had probably been truncated, rather than indicating a genuine gap, as this was only 0.25m wide. Its fill 3298=3050 contained much mortar and limestone rubble in a matrix of grey silty clay, but there were no finds. On the south the wall had bottomed on the surface of layer 3323, at the same level from which wall 3026 was built (Fig. 2.33), but on the north the robber trench (and the wall) appears to have been some 0.1m higher (Fig. 2.31). The southern robber trench met the platform at the southern limit of its straight north-south edge, south of which the platform began to turn south-eastwards; the northern trench was not in line with wall 3012, but offset some 0.3m northwards, and the robber trench appears to have been cut by the robbing of 3012 (cut 3045). The internal dimensions of the area enclosed were 4m (east-west) by 3m.

Plate 2.47 Pilae stack 3250 showing mortar where box flue tiles were attached above, north to left

Plate 2.48 Wall 3337 incorporating pila 3336 over floor 3328, looking west

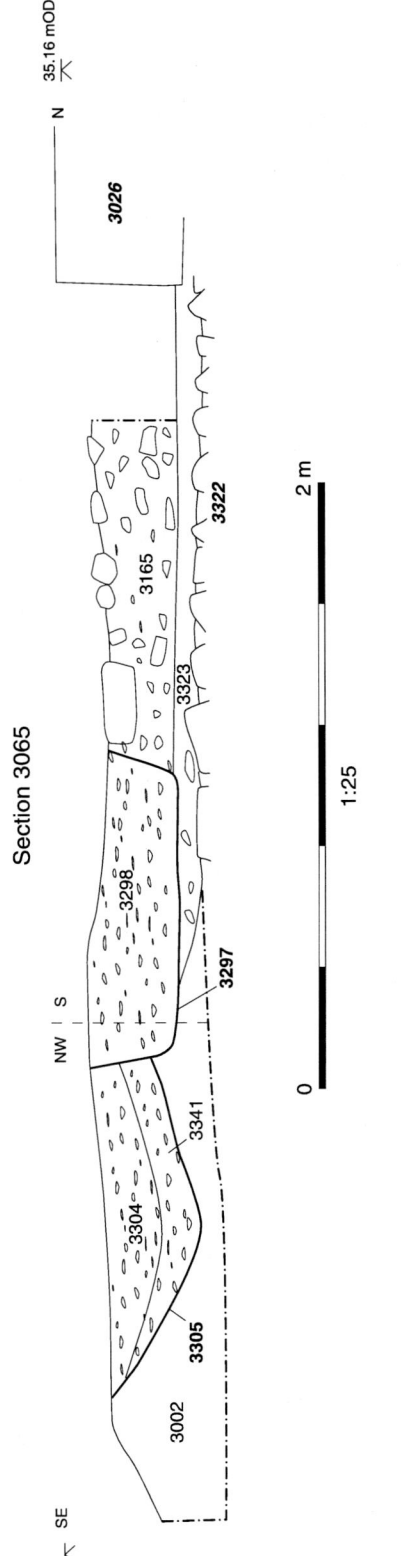

Section 3065

35.16 mOD

N

3026

3322

3165

3323

3298

3297

3341

3304

3305

3002

NW | S

SE

2 m

1:25

0

Fig. 2.34 Section 3065 showing the robber trench of the south wall of the western building extension

Within the area surrounded by these walls the original platform cut (3025) had apparently extended westwards, and was filled with 3051, a mid-greyish-brown sandy silt and frequent limestones that included a few sherds of Roman pottery, one dated 2nd century or later. This layer is likely to be part of the destruction deposits, as it was also recorded abutting masonry 3026 to the east. The extent of cut 3025 was not clearly recorded, but clearly did not cover the whole of the interior of 3303. It probably corresponds to a curve visible on the north side that extended some 2.2m west of 3026, but was obscured by a medieval furrow on the south that was not removed (Fig. 2.28). This may have been connected with the opening in the wall adjacent, possibly even the stokehole from which the hypocaust was heated; although no trace of burning was recorded in the excavated slot across it, the photographs show reddening of the soils at the edge of cut 3025 within the east end of the room at the appropriate level (Plate 2.46; Fig. 2.31).

There is no firm evidence to determine whether this room was earlier than 3814 and the platform or had been added against them. The southern arm of 3297 was in line with the two superimposed limestone blocks (3324) within the pitched stone area to the east, and it is possible that these represented a continuation of the wall line; there was however no robber cut visible in section here (Fig. 2.33 S. 3062), and the stones may instead relate to the pilae of the hypocaust.

Secondary use of Room 3184 in the late Roman period

It seems likely that the sunken room 3184 had a secondary phase of use towards the very end of the Roman period.

A layer of charred material, numbered variously 3220, 3237, 3345 and 3331, immediately overlay the floor and the cistern (Fig. 2.29 S. 3034; Plate 2.49). When removed, many of the flagstones were either cracked or flaked on the surface, and this is likely to have been the result of contact with the charred material while still hot (Plate 2.34). The layer was thickest at the edges, thinning out towards the centre of the room. Charred grain in large quantities was clearly evident (Plate 2.50) and following the inspection of initial samples, and in order to understand the composition of the deposit, the spatial distribution of the grain and how it might have been stored prior to burning, a sampling grid was set up (see Fig. 4.4). Analysis of selected samples from this deposit (particularly that element numbered 3345) showed that the deposit consisted mostly of abundant charred spelt grains, suggesting that one type of grain had been stored within this part of the building. A variety of burnt bones of small animals was also found, including field vole, field mouse and shrews, as well as a puppy.

Towards the top of the deposit, layer 3331 contained recognisable linear bands of charcoal

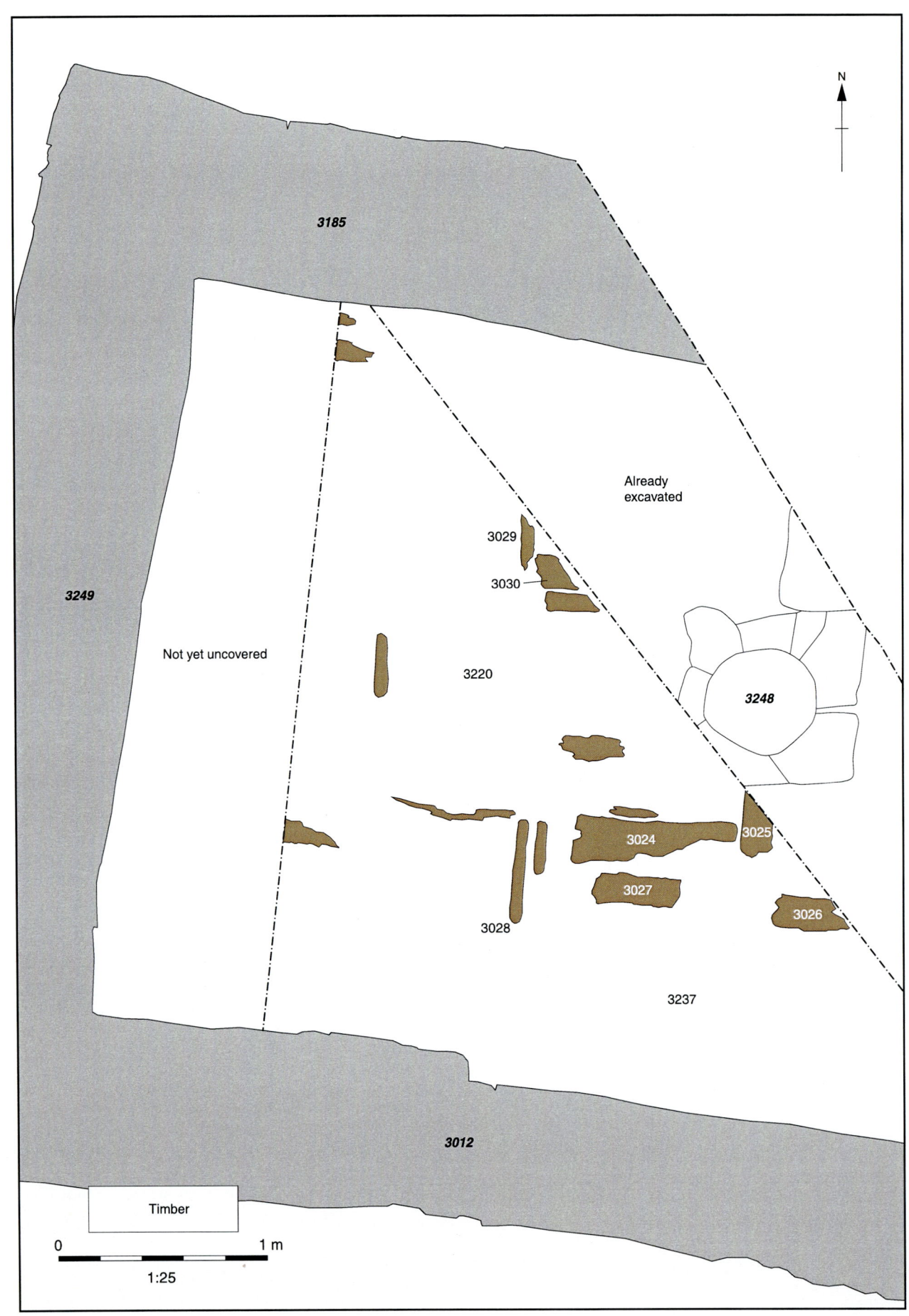

Plate 2.49 Burnt deposit upon the flagstone floor within room 3481, overlain by plaster, looking west

Plate 2.50 Detail of charred grain

representing joists/beams running north-south (Fig. 2.35; Plate 2.51), with thinner east-west aligned charcoal deposits suggesting battens/laths or perhaps floor boards and planks (Plate 2.52), together with a number of iron nails (particularly in contexts 3037 and 3331). Such a framework of timber is likely to derive from either collapsed ceiling or from the roof.

The cistern was filled with a loose greyish black sandy silt (3247) containing large fragments of a straight-sided pottery dish (Fig. 3.3.54), common fragments of limestone roof tile, nails, wall plaster,

ceramic building material, horse and bird bone and mussel and oyster shells. A sample from this (sample 3010) showed that it contained the same ash and burnt grain as in the spread across the floor, although the records state that the fill was overlain by the burnt grain deposit 3237. It is possible that the cistern had been loosely backfilled with debris from another building on the site before the fire occurred. It is however more likely that the cistern was still in use, so contained only water, when the fire occurred, and that charred material fell into it, followed by debris from the collapse of the walls and roof, which was all mixed together in the water. Continuing burning, or simply the suspension of the light charred material on the surface of the water, may have resulted in a layer of burnt material apparently overlying the other, heavier materials.

Collapse and demolition

The charcoal was overlain by a deposit of ash that incorporated powdery mortar, roof tile fragments, stone roof tiles/slates and fallen painted wall plaster (Fig. 2.29, layer 3013; Plates 2.51, 2.53 and 2.54). Layer 3013 extended from the south wall (3012) into the centre of 3184. On the north side of the room the equivalent ashy deposit was 3189, which formed before collapse of this side of the building. In 3013 the painted plaster had green/yellow and white base pigments and broad bands of deep red colour (see Biddulph Chapter 3). The roof

Fig. 2.35 (opposite) Plan showing charred timbers in the burnt deposit in Building 3184

Plate 2.51 Charred beams within the charred deposit on the floor of room 3184 (scale 200mm)

Plate 2.52 Charred plank overlying the charred deposit on the floor of room 3184 (scale 200mm)

slates/tiles recovered were in two colours (see Shaffrey Chapter 3). The smothering effect of overlying rubble/mortar deposits such as 3190 had starved the underlying timbers of oxygen, resulting in the survival of charcoal and charred grain rather than ash below. Much of the surface of the wall plaster was burnt and blackened, indicating direct contact with a fire. Together with the evidence of the flaking and cracking of the flagstones, it is likely that the burning event that resulted in the charring of grain, and of wall or roof timbers, was a significant fire that resulted in the destruction of this part of the building.

The possibility that the structure had dwarf walls of masonry topped by timber and plaster upper walls is suggested by the evidence of some of the large fragments of plaster recovered from deposit 3013. Slab 3329, approximately one metre square, consisted of three distinct layers with a total thickness of over 180mm, and had the impressions of wattling at the back (see Biddulph Chapter 3). This appears to indicate a wattle and plaster freestanding wall rather than a wall facing.

On the north side, layer 3189 was followed by loose silty sands and limestone fragments 3323 and 3321, possibly discarded stone and mortar from the robbing of wall 3185. A straight-sided bowl with a flanged rim from 3321 is illustrated (Fig. 3.3.53).

The overlying deposit (3190) was a sandy silt containing much limestone rubble, some of it burnt.

Plate 2.53 Room 3184 showing collapsed plaster, looking west (trim)

This extended across most of the interior of structure 3184. This most probably derived from collapse and further robbing of the walls, as did the overlying fill 3019=3314, a beige sand, mortar and limestone rubble layer, which also included one stone tessera. Robber trenches 3047 removed the west end of wall 3012, robber trench 3275 the west wall 3249 and part of the south wall, and robber trench 3186 the north wall 3185. Part of robber trenches 3045 and 3275 are visible in section (Figs 2.31 and 2.32; see also Fig. 3.3.51).

Room 3184 and the hypocaust to the south were clearly robbed at the same time. Deposit 3164=3014, which abutted the south of wall 3012, and was the first deposit upon the sub-floor of the hypocaust and the drain covering slabs at the north end, also overlapped the southern edge of the robbed wall (Fig. 2.30, S. 3030) and the remains of crude wall 3337. This contained much ceramic building material, particularly box flue tile, as did a further discrete dump of demolition material 3315 (see Fig. 3.3.52). At the west edge of the platform section 3053 showed the robbing of 3249 (the west wall of 3012) continuing south as far as 3026, indicating that they were robbed at the same time. S. 3005 (Fig. 2.31) suggested that the robbing of 3021 and 3012 were separate, and that the shallow western extension to the range of buildings, group 3303, was robbed out before the robbing of

Plate 2.54 Fallen plaster against S wall

south-west end of wall 3012 (cut 3045), but in the light of S. 3053, this may not be correct.

Across the southern room, walls 3086, 3023, 3320, 3324 and 3026 had been heavily robbed out, leaving short lengths of wall only one or two courses high. The north-south aligned drain 3167 was robbed by cut 3342, removing most of the covering slabs, and was backfilled with 3343, a dark greyish-brown clayey silt containing stones and mortar fragments. The clayey element may indicate the reincorporation of original clayey silt from the drain in the backfill. Deposit 3164, the robbed drain and all of the cut for the cobbled floor south of wall 3012 was then infilled by deposit 3165=3117, a fairly homogeneous sandy silt with frequent mortar flecks and rubble, including most of the ceramic building material found on the site, small pieces of limestone rubble, three lumps of tufa, two stone tessera and two stone discs (Fig. 3.1 4 and 5). This deposit overlay truncated masonry 3320 and 3324 (Fig. 2.33 S. 3062). A very large assemblage of pottery of mid to late 4th century date (82 sherds, 1991g) was recovered from this layer (see Fig. 3.4).

At the east edge of the platform the first demolition deposit, directly overlying 3316, was 3035, very similar to layers 3117=3165, which overlay the west edge of foundation 3021. Overlying this, and extending further to the west, was 3040, a dark grey sandy silt with much charcoal. On the west this ended at a straight edge corresponding to the edge of the underlying platform, due to a robber trench 3016 running north-south along the edge of the platform (Fig. 2.28). This robber trench extended from wall 3012 on the north to wall 3023 on the south, and was 0.9m wide, stopping at the surviving edge of masonry 3086 on the west. A section was drawn was at the very north end (Fig. 2.29), where the bottom was filled with 3017, which directly overlay the cobbled platform 3290. Above this the main part of the trench was filled by layer 3018, a dark grey/black sandy silt with common charcoal, mortar and limestone fragments. The wall therefore bottomed either directly upon the platform, or upon 3085, which was noted on site as rammed, probably in fact the result of lying beneath a wall.

Masonry 3086 lay immediately west of the robber trench, and the absence of clear facing stones on its east side was either due to robbing by trench 3016, or may indicate that this masonry was integral with the robbed wall. North of 3086 was a robber cut 3338, and this was filled by layer 3088, a dark brownish-grey clayey silt with common sand and limestone fragments. This was visible in the top of layer 3165-3117, but was cut by 3016, strongly suggesting that masonry 3086 had extended further north, and had survived the general levelling, and was robbed subsequently, but before the wall to the east was robbed. To the south of 3086 a very similar deposit (3087) continued south as far as wall 3023, and may represent the continuation of the robbing, although it spread further west than 3088. If so, then 3086 may have been part of a stone structure along most of the length of the room, perhaps acting as a platform to support the floor.

The robbing of the structure was finally sealed by a levelling deposit (3019) containing two sherds of pottery of 4th century date and a stone ring (Fig. 3.11.6). Some of the truncation of structural elements was probably the result of post-Roman ploughing, but there are no clear indications that stone robbing was taking place much later, for example in the medieval or post-medieval periods.

Post-Roman

The destruction of the building clearly occurred either right at the end of the Roman period, or shortly afterwards. The stone discs and ring found in the destruction layers of the building, neither of which were materials likely to have been used in the destruction, suggest that activity may have still been continuing elsewhere on site at this stage, but for how long activity continued, and of what character, is unclear.

After the destruction, the only significant evidence of post-Roman activity consisted of plough furrows. These features were aligned north-south in the northern part of the site and east-west further south. Dating evidence was extremely scarce. Although the furrows are likely to have been medieval in origin their use may have continued into the post-medieval period and the transformation of the landscape by enclosure.

Chapter 3

Finds reports

THE IRON AGE AND ROMAN POTTERY
by Paul Booth

Introduction

Some 2399 sherds (49.909kg, 37.82 REs) of later prehistoric and Roman pottery, and including a single early Anglo-Saxon sherd, were recovered during the fieldwork. The material derived mainly from excavation but includes 57 sherds (743g) which were surface finds, mainly from Fields 31 and 33. These are quantified by fabric in Table 3.2 but are not considered otherwise. A small amount of additional material recovered from sieved soil sample residues was not quantified or examined; a very rapid scan suggested that it added nothing of significance to the recorded dataset. Pottery was recovered from each of the three main excavated sites, with 1446 sherds from Bredon's Norton, 822 sherds from Fiddington and only 69 sherds from Pamington. The pottery was recorded using codes set out in the OA later prehistoric and Roman recording system (Booth 2011), and was cross-referenced to the Worcestershire type series (http://www.worcestershireceramics.org), which has fabric details and photographic sections. Quantification was by sherd count, weight and rim equivalents (REs) with an additional more subjective count of vessels based on individual rim sherds. Details of rim, base, handle, spout and decorative types and other characteristics were recorded where present. The full record of the pottery (on an Excel spreadsheet) is contained in the project archive.

The pottery was in moderate to good condition; the overall mean sherd weight, 20.8g, was quite high, potentially indicating a relatively low level of redeposition for much of the assemblage, although the mean sherd weights for each of the three sites were quite different (see below). The surface condition of sherds was also variable. Burnished surfaces were recorded quite commonly on fabrics such as Severn Valley ware, but even so were not as common as would have been expected had the sherds been in consistently good condition. Slightly acidic soil conditions were probably the principal cause of poor surface preservation, though taphonomic processes such as redeposition may have been a contributory factor in some cases. This factor would certainly have been relevant in connection with the mean sherd weight, particularly at Pamington. Nevertheless, very few sherds were noted as heavily worn.

A small proportion of the total assemblage was of exclusively middle Iron Age character, but as a proportion of site assemblages was only significant in the small group from Pamington. The remainder of the pottery was assigned to the late Iron Age and Roman periods, but this date bracket included a significant component of Malvernian wares, an indeterminate proportion of which seems certain to have been of pre-Conquest date. The date range of the Roman pottery extended well into the later 4th century, particularly at Bredon's Norton. All these aspects are discussed further below.

Fabrics and wares

'Later prehistoric'

Iron Age fabrics were defined in terms of (usually) their two most common inclusion types and an indicator of fineness on a sliding scale of 1 (very fine) to 5 (very coarse). The definition of fabrics using this system does not necessarily serve to identify production sources, since these are generally unknown for Iron Age material within the region. Nor does it automatically follow that identically coded sherds were from the same (unknown) source, merely that their makers exploited very similar clay and tempering resources, indicating a uniformity of potting tradition. Quantification of the material by individual fabric is shown in Table 3.2, where equivalences with the Worcestershire online reference series are noted (in bold) as far as possible. The identifying letters of the inclusion types present are as follows:

A   quartz sand
C   Calcareous grit
G   Grog (crushed ceramic)
L   Limestone
N   None visible
P   clay Pellets
S   Shell
V   Vegetable/organic (sometimes voids)
Z   indeterminate voids

The fabrics are all handmade. Two main broad traditions are apparent. The first is tempered principally with medium sand grains, either with no discernible secondary inclusion type (fabric AN) or occurring with shell (AS, and in one case also clay pellets) or organic inclusions/voids (AV or AZ). The second broad tradition comprises shell-tempered fabrics, typically coarser than the sand-tempered ones. Most commonly the shell is dominant and unaccompanied by other inclusions (SN4 and SN5), but it was occasionally found with quartz sand or 'calcareous grit' – rounded limestone inclusions. The latter were occasionally a dominant inclusion type, occurring in one instance as large inclusions alone (fabric CN5) and in another as rather finer inclusions with shell (fabric CS3). The calcareous grits are superficially reminiscent of the Malvernian Palaeozoic limestone fabric (see also fabric C22 below), but do not seem to be the same.

Only three small rim sherds were present in these fabrics, all in variants of the sand-tempered tradition. All were from basic jar forms with simple slightly insloping rims, two rounded and one slightly squared. These forms are middle Iron Age in character but are not otherwise diagnostic. Overall the quantities of these fabrics are such that characterisation of significant traditions is impossible.

'Later Iron Age and Roman'

Late Iron Age and Roman fabrics were assigned to major ware groups, defined on the basis of significant common characteristics. The ware groups can be combined to constitute two main classes of material, fine and specialist wares on the one hand, and on the other the rest of the coarse wares (cf Booth 2004). The fine and specialist ware groups represented in the present assemblage (identified by the initial letter of the fabric code) are: samian ware (S), fine wares – colour-coated, lead glazed, mica coated etc – (F), amphorae (A), mortaria (M), white wares – other than mortaria – (W), and white-slipped (Q) wares – only a single sherd here . The remaining coarse ware groups are: 'Belgic type' (broadly in the sense of Thompson 1982, 4-5), usually grog-tempered, fabrics (E), 'Romanised' oxidised coarse wares (O), 'Romanised' reduced coarse wares (R), black-burnished wares (B), and shell-tempered wares (C). A separate ware category for 'coarse gritted' wares (G) is used for Malvernian fabrics, and for present purposes this group includes the limestone-tempered fabric C22 as well as 'G' fabrics.

Within these classes are hierarchically arranged subgroups, usually defined on the basis of inclusion type, and individual fabrics/wares are then indicated at a third level of precision, both levels of subdivision being expressed by numeric codes. Thus O40 is a general code for oxidised Severn Valley wares, while O41 is a particular organic-tempered Severn Valley ware. For the bulk of the present assemblage, however, fabric identification

was at the intermediate level of precision, particularly since specific sources are not known for most of the coarse wares. Only summary fabric descriptions are given here (in Table 3.1), but where appropriate these are cross-referred to codes in the National Roman Fabric Reference Collection (Tomber and Dore 1998), placed in brackets in bold type. Cross references to the Worcestershire County Council fabric codes are also given. More complete descriptions are contained within the project archive. Quantification of the pottery by fabric/ware is set out in Table 3.2, where it is broken down by site.

Overall the assemblage is dominated by Severn Valley and Malvernian wares, which together constitute 78.8% of all sherds from the project. This collective domination is seen at all three sites, although in different ways. At Pamington this contribution (84% of sherds) consists almost entirely of Malvernian wares (with most of the rest of this small assemblage of 'middle Iron Age' date). At Fiddington the Severn Valley wares are particularly prominent (63.6% of sherds) with Malvernian products bringing the combined figure up to 80.4% of the site total, while at Bredon's Norton the total of 78.2% comprises roughly one third Malvernian wares and two thirds Severn Valley ware (26.8% and 51.4% of sherd count). These figures include the minor contribution of reduced Severn Valley ware (fabrics R49 and probably R60), identified sherds of which amounted to just 1.8% of the combined sites sherd total. No attempt was made to subdivide the main group of Severn Valley wares (O40), except to separate out organic-tempered variants, which are usually of early Roman date (eg Timby 1990, 249), but not exclusively so (Bryant and Evans 2004a, 278). Fabric O41 is often characterised by quite large voids. In the present assemblages a consistently finer version of O41 has also been identified and distinguished from the other material as fabric O41F. Fabrics O41 and O41F were present in roughly equal amounts at Bredon's Norton, but at Fiddington the finer version was much more common. Its representation there was boosted by the occurrence of a large number of sherds from a single jar in context (1057), but other vessels were also present there. The evidence from Bredon's Norton shows that this fabric was used for almost as wide a range of vessel forms (carinated bowls and tankards as well as jars) as was present in the general fabric O40. Fabrics other than Severn Valley ware in the O ware group were numerically insignificant but not without interest; sherds assigned to the O30 group might have comprised products of the North Wiltshire industry, while fabric O81 can be identified with confidence as pink grogged ware, with a production centre at Stowe in Buckinghamshire. At the present sites these sherds are close to the western margin of the distribution of the fabric.

The Malvernian wares form a mixed group. At Pamington the limestone-tempered fabric G25 was the most important, being twice as common as

Table 3.1 Summary description of later prehistoric and Roman pottery fabrics

Ware/fabric code	Summary description	Worcs CC code
Samian ware		
S20	South Gaulish samian ware (LGF SA)	43.1
S30	Central Gaulish samian ware, (including LEZ SA 2)	43.2
S30B	Central Gaulish samian ware – black surfaces	
Fine wares		
F50	red colour-coated fabrics, possibly Oxfordshire	
F51	Oxfordshire red colour-coated fabric (OXF RS)	29
F52	Nene Valley colour-coated ware (LNV CC)	28
F60	fine sandy oxidised, red-brown colour-coat, sources uncertain	
F61	'South western brown slipped ware' (Cirencester fabric 105)	
Amphorae		
A10	Buff amphora fabric, source uncertain	
A30	Coarse oxidised amphora fabrics, source uncertain	
Mortaria		
M22	Oxfordshire white mortarium fabric (OXF WH)	33.1
M31	Oxfordshire white-slipped mortarium fabric (OXF WS)	33.2
M41	Oxfordshire red colour-coated mortarium fabric (OXF RS)	33.3
White wares		
W10	fairly fine white fabric(s), source uncertain	incl 38
W23	Oxfordshire burnt white ware	39
W30	fine sandy white fabrics	
White-slipped wares		
Q20	oxidised white-slipped fabric, source uncertain	20
'Belgic-type' coarse wares		
E10	'Belgic-type' organic-tempered fabrics	
E20	'Belgic type' fine sand-tempered fabrics	
E80	'Belgic type' grog tempered fabrics (SOB GT)	
Oxidised coarse wares		
O20	coarse sandy oxidised wares	13
O30	common fine/medium sand-tempered coarse wares	13
O40	Severn valley ware (includes SVW OX 1 and SVW OX 2)	12
O41	organic tempered Severn Valley ware	12.2
O41F	fine organic tempered Severn Valley ware	12.2
O81	pink grogged ware (PNK GT)	17
Reduced coarse wares		
R10	fine (slightly sandy) reduced coarse wares, various sources	14
R20	coarse sandy reduced wares, various sources	15
R30	medium sandy reduced wares, various sources	
R49	reduced Severn Valley ware	12.1
R60	reduced coarse ware with organic inclusions	12.3
R85	micaceous 'south-western' reduced ware	
R90	coarse grog- and sand-tempered reduced wares	
R95	Savernake ware	
Black-burnished wares		
B11	Dorset BB1 fabric (DOR BB 1).	22
B30	wheel thrown imitation black-burnished type fabrics	
Shell-tempered wares		
C10	shell-tempered wares, uncertain source(s)	
C11	shell-tempered wares, include Harrold (HAR SH)	23
Malvernian and related wares		
C22	Palaeozoic limestone, fabric ?Malvernian	4.2
G20	Malvernian fabrics, general	
G21	Malvern igneous rock fabric (MAL REA)	3 and 3.2
G22	Malvern 'Romanised' reduced fabric	within 3.1, 19
G25	Malvern limestone fabric (Peacock 1968, fabric B1)	4.1
G26	Malvern sandstone fabric (Peacock 1968, fabric C)	5.2
G31	Clee Hills dolerite fabric (Gelling and Peacock 1970)	

Table 3.2 Summary quantification of Iron Age and Roman pottery fabrics by site (column percentages)

Ware/fabric code	Unstratified			Fiddington			Pamington			Bredon's Norton		
	Nosh	Wt	RE	Nosh	Wt	RE	Nosh	Wt	RE	Nosh	Wt	RE
AN3 5.1				0.2	+		5.8	9.3	2.1			
AS3 (AS2, ASP3) 4.4						1.4	0.3		0.3	0.1	0.1	6
AV3 (AZ3)							1.4	0.3		0.3	0.1	0.1
CN5				0.1	+							
CS3 4.5										0.1	0.1	
GZ3/4							1.4	0.6				
LA4 4.6										0.1	+	
SA4							1.4	0.3				
SC4							1.4	0.6				
SL4							1.4	0.3				
SN4 4.3							1.4	0.8		0.1	+	
SN5 4.3	1.8	1.2		0.2	0.3							
ZA3										0.1	+	
Subtotal	1.8	1.2		0.6	0.3		15.9	12.4	2.1	1.0	0.3	0.3
S20										0.1	+	
S30	7.0	3.9		0.7	0.2	1.6				0.6	0.1	0.2
S30B				0.1	+							
S subtotal	7.0	3.9		0.9	0.2	1.6				0.7	0.2	0.2
F50										0.2	+	
F51				0.7	0.2	0.3				2.1	1.7	4.1
F52										0.1	+	
F60				0.4	0.1							
F61										0.1	+	1.9
F subtotal				1.1	0.3	0.3				2.5	1.8	6.1
A10										0.1	5	
A30										0.1	1.4	
A subtotal										0.2	1.4	
M22				0.1	+					0.4	0.9	1.5
M31										0.1	0.2	0.4
M41										0.8	0.9	2.1
M subtotal				0.1	+					1.2	2.0	4.0
W10	1.8	2.2								0.1	+	
W23										0.1	+	
W30										0.1	0.1	
W subtotal	1.8	2.2								0.2	0.1	
Q20 subtotal										0.1	+	
Fine & specialist subtotal	**8.8**	**6.1**		**2.1**	**0.6**	**1.9**				**4.9**	**5.6**	**10.2**
E10										0.1	+	
E20										0.1	+	
E80										0.7	0.6	0.5
E subtotal										0.9	0.6	0.5

Nosh	%	Total Wt	%	RE	%
6	0.3	73	0.1	0.01	+
	0.3	45	0.1	0.03	0.1
5	0.2	22	+	0.04	0.1
1	+	3	+		
1	+	38	0.1		
1	+	4	+		
1	+	5	+		
1	+	2	+		
1	+	4	+		
1	+	2	+		
3	0.1	8	+		
3	0.1	43	0.1		
1	+	2	+		
31	1.3	251	0.5	0.08	0.2
1	+	15	+		
19	0.8	96	0.2	0.20	0.5
1	+	6	+		
21	0.9	117	0.2	0.20	0.5
3	0.1	15	+		
37	1.5	634	1.3	1.18	3.1
1	+	12	+		
3	0.1	12	+		
1	+	9	+	0.53	1.4
45	1.9	682	1.4	1.71	4.5
1	+	5	+		
2	0.1	52	0.1		
4	0.2	499	1.0		
7	0.3	331	0.7	0.42	1.1
1	+	61	0.1	0.10	0.3
11	0.5	329	0.7	0.58	1.5
19	0.8	721	1.5	1.10	2.9
2	0.1	28	0.1		
1	+	4	+		
1	+	22	+		
4	0.2	54	0.1		
1	+	8	+		
94	**3.9**	**2081**	**4.2**	**3.01**	**8.0**
2	0.1	4	+		
1	+	6	+		
10	0.4	218	0.4	0.15	0.4
13	0.5	228	0.5	0.15	0.4

fabric G21, which is consistent with the evidence that G25 was predominantly of Iron Age date. It was present at both Fiddington and Bredon's Norton, but at these sites was outnumbered (in terms of sherd count, but not weight) by the igneous rock fabric G21. The latter, too, was produced during the Iron Age, but its use continued through the early Roman period well into the 2nd century AD. Inevitably the vessels in all these fabrics were mostly jars, but the G21 range included a dish (Fig. 3.3.45), while lids occurred in fabric G22 (eg Fig. 3.1.15). The G25 repertoire included occasional examples of large bowls of 'cauldron' type (Fig. 3.3.48-9). A further element in the Malvernian range was the 'Romanised' reduced fabric G22. This was particularly well-represented at Fiddington where it was the most common Malvernian fabric by sherd count and totalled 21.8% of that assemblage by weight. It should be noted, however, that some of these sherds were almost certainly from prefabricated ovens of a type being increasingly recognised in the region, particularly at Worcester (Jane Evans pers. comm.; for fragments see eg McSloy 2008a, fig. 16, nos 36 and 37; for earlier discussion see Bryant and Evans 2004b), but distinguishing between small pieces of such ovens and sherds of large jars in the same fabric is effectively impossible, and an added complication is that the upper opening of ovens of this type can have a rolled rim very like one from a large storage jar (Fig. 3.1.14; cf eg Peacock 1967, 23-4, no. 88). It is not clear if any of the G22 sherds from Bredon's Norton were also of this type. Minor components of this general fabric group were two sherds of Malvernian sandstone-tempered fabric (G26) from Bredon's Norton and (arbitrarily placed here) a single sherd of Clee Hills dolerite ware from Fiddington. Both fabrics should be of later prehistoric date.

The dominance of Severn Valley wares means that reduced coarse wares, typically forming the principal coarse ware group in lowland British sites, were of relatively minor significance here, amounting to only 4.9% of all sherds if the reduced Severn Valley ware fabrics are excluded (6.7% with these), and were indeed outnumbered by black-burnished wares in the assemblage as a whole. None of the components of the reduced coarse ware group can be assigned to a known source – the generic characteristics of R10 (sparse quartz sand-tempered) and R30 (moderate quartz sand-tempered) sub groups, for example, do not permit close identification. Sherds in both groups could include Oxford products, for example, though it is more than likely that they did not. Occasional R30 sherds were perhaps from North Wiltshire, paralleling the occurrence of O30 sherds and the presence of two sherds assigned to the Savernake industry (R95), but this is not certain. More local but unidentified sources are likely to have supplied most if not all of this material, although a few sherds (only from Bredon's Norton) were assigned to fabric R85, with parallels in a probable south-

Table 3.2 (continued)

Ware/fabric code	Unstratified			Fiddington			Pamington			Bredon's Norton		
	Nosh	Wt	RE	Nosh	Wt	RE	Nosh	Wt	RE	Nosh	Wt	RE
O20				0.6	0.3	1.8				0.2	0.1	
O30										0.1	+	
O40	63.2	68.5	80.0	49.6	42.0	47.6	1.4	1.7	27.1	40.9	37.8	45.5
O41	1.8	4.2		0.7	0.7	1.1				3.3	4.4	1.2
O41F	7.0	6.5		11.3	8.0	12.4				3.5	5.2	1.4
O81				0.2	4.4					0.3	0.4	
O subtotal	71.9	79.1	80.0	62.5	55.3	62.8	1.4	1.7	27.1	48.3	48.0	48.1
R10				0.5	0.6					2.0	1.4	3.7
R20				0.2	0.2	0.9				0.3	0.1	0.1
R30				3.8	3.7	4.1				2.2	1.2	1.8
R49				0.2	0.2					1.2	1.0	2.0
R60				0.9	0.9					1.9	1.0	0.8
R85										0.3	0.3	
R90				0.1	0.2					0.5	0.6	
R95										0.1	0.2	0.5
R subtotal				5.7	5.7	5.0				8.6	5.7	8.8
B11	7.0	4.4	11.7	10.2	5.6	10.2				6.0	5.7	9.0
B30				0.2	0.8	0.6				1.5	2.0	2.8
B (subtotal)	7.0	4.4	11.7	10.4	6.4	10.8				7.5	7.7	11.8
C10										0.1	0.1	
C11				1.8	2.6	3.5				1.9	1.5	3.6
C subtotal				1.8	2.6	3.5				2.1	1.6	3.6
C22										0.3	0.1	
G20										0.1	0.1	
G21	7.0	6.5	8.3	6.5	3.5	2.6	24.6	23.6	25.0	14.9	14.0	9.9
G22	3.5	2.7		7.4	21.8	11.2	1.4	1.8		1.4	1.2	1.3
G25				2.8	3.7	2.2	56.5	60.5	45.8	9.9	15.0	5.4
G26										0.1	0.2	
G31				0.1	+							
G (Malvern & related) subtotal	10.5	9.2	8.3	16.8	29.1	16.0	82.6	86.0	70.8	26.8	30.5	16.6
Z10				0.1	+							
Overall Total	57	743	0.60	822	13262	8.98	69	719	0.48	1446	34670	27.76
%	2.4	1.5	1.6	34.3	26.8	23.7	2.9	1.5	1.3	60.4	70.2	73.4

Iron Age fabric code equivalents in Worcestershire series (http://www.worcestershireceramics.org/) are shown in bold

western micaceous ware tradition (eg Timby 2000, 137, fabrics 55a-d). Black-burnished ware consisted mainly of Dorset BB1 (fabric B11), but a distinctive wheelthrown imitation (B30), of unknown origin but identified regularly (if in modest quantities) in the Upper Thames region, for example, was also present, amounting to a fifth of all black-burnished ware sherds at Bredon's Norton (eg Fig. 3.4.68 and 79). The occurrence of Dorset BB1 at Fiddington and Bredon's Norton was at broadly similar levels – although the fabric was more common at Fiddington in terms of sherd count, quantities were very similar by other measures.

Other coarse ware categories were of minor significance. A very few sherds, all from Bredon's Norton, were assigned to the E ('Belgic type') ware

Nosh	%	Total Wt	%	RE	%
8	0.3	84	0.2	0.16	0.4
1	–	2	+		
1038	43.3	19377	38.9	17.50	46.3
55	2.3	1670	3.3	0.43	1.1
148	6.2	2926	5.9	1.50	4.0
7	0.3	639	1.3		
1257	52.4	24798	49.7	19.59	51.8
33	1.4	563	1.1	1.04	2.7
7	0.3	74	0.1	0.10	0.3
63	2.6	904	1.8	0.87	2.3
19	0.8	366	0.7	0.55	1.5
25	1.0	464	0.9	0.21	0.6
4	0.2	98	0.2		
8	0.3	239	0.5		
2	0.1	55	0.1	0.15	0.4
161	6.7	2763	5.5	2.92	7.7
175	7.3	2766	5.5	3.48	9.2
23	1.0	812	1.6	0.83	2.2
198	8.3	3578	7.2	4.31	11.4
2	0.1	18	+		
43	1.8	877	1.8	1.31	3.5
45	1.9	895	1.8	1.31	3.5
4	0.2	36	0.1		
2	0.1	19	+		
291	12.1	5600	11.2	3.16	8.4
84	3.5	3349	6.7	1.38	3.6
205	8.5	6191	12.4	1.91	5.1
2	0.1	57	0.1		
1	+	5			
589	24.6	15257	30.6	6.45	17.1
1	+	6	+		
2399		49855		37.82	

Bredon's Norton assemblages. In effect only a single fabric, C11, was identified, though it is possible that sherds assigned to this fabric derived from more than one source even if no meaningful distinction amongst the material was achieved. The majority of forms present were jars with rim forms consistent with (but not necessarily exclusive to) products of the industry at Harrold, Bedfordshire (Brown 1994), such as Fig. 3.4.71. Single examples of a flanged bowl (Fig. 3.4.72) and a dish in fabric C11 (both from Bredon's Norton), however, are particularly distinctive; the association of these forms with Harrold supports the suggestion that many if not all of the C11 jars were probably from the same source. If so, this material provides a useful indicator of late Roman activity (see further below), as it is unlikely to have reached the area before about the middle of the 4th century AD – the date suggested for its earliest certain appearance at Cirencester (Cooper 1998, 341; Holbrook 2013, 33) and at sites such as Alcester, Warwickshire (eg Evans 1994, 146-7).

Fine and specialist wares amounted to only 3.9% of the total sherds from the project, although it is notable that they were twice as common in terms of REs. Unsurprisingly completely absent from Pamington, these wares were respectively just above and below 2% of sherd count and REs at Fiddington, but more common at Bredon's Norton: 4.9% of sherd count and 10.2% of REs. Samian ware formed a relatively small proportion of this overall group, with only a single sherd of South Gaulish samian ware and no East Gaulish sherds identified with confidence. Central Gaulish material was present at both Fiddington and Bredon's Norton; much the most striking piece was a single small sherd of black Central Gaulish samian ware, probably from a beaker of Déchelette form 74, from Fiddington. Samian ware excepted, early Roman fine and specialist wares were scarce. Amphorae, white and white-slipped fabrics were completely absent at Fiddington and only a single mortarium sherd was recovered there. The fine wares from that site were six small sherds (25g) of Oxfordshire colour-coated ware and three small sherds (12g), probably from a jar, in fabric F60, with an orange-red slip – perhaps a Severn Valley ware variant. This is not closely dated but occurred in a late Roman context (1067).

Bredon's Norton produced a (slightly) wider range of fine and specialist wares, though little of this material was remarkable. Four amphora sherds were undiagnostic, as were white wares and a single white-slipped sherd. The latter might perhaps have been an Oxford product (Young's (1977) fabric WC), as might both W10 sherds and the one sherd of fabric W23, identified (albeit tentatively) as Oxford burnt white ware. Definite Oxford products dominated fine ware and mortarium categories; the latter consisted exclusively of Oxford material, with all three main fabrics of that industry present. Oxford colour-coated ware amounted to 31 out of 35

category. These can be dated to the 1st century AD and are consistent with other evidence for activity potentially spanning the Conquest period. Such pottery is uncommon in the region, but is known at nearby sites such as Beckford. Grog-tempered (E80) fabrics were the most important amongst this small group. Shell-tempered pottery, distinct from the earlier tradition seen at Pamington, amounted to 1.9% of the overall sherd total, forming almost identical proportions of both Fiddington and fine ware sherds and all but one of the fine ware vessel rims, the single exception being a relatively substantial (in proportional terms) flagon fragment in 'south-western brown slipped ware' (F61).

Anglo-Saxon

A single Anglo-Saxon sherd weighing 6g was recovered from context 1052 at Fiddington. This was in a black hand-made fabric with medium organic inclusions and voids and with subrounded quartz sand as a secondary inclusion type. There was no evidence for surface treatment. The general fabric type has numerous regional parallels and cannot be dated closely.

Vessel types

Vessel types were grouped in classes relating to their general shape. The classes are defined by commonly used labels (jar, bowl, dish, etc) with a perceived relationship to the function of the vessels, although the latter association has to be treated with caution. The class codes used, ordered in a sequence roughly from closed narrow forms to wide open ones, are B (flagons and jugs), C (jars), D (jars/bowls), E (beakers), G (tankards), G/H (tankards/bowls), H (bowls), I (bowls/dishes), J (dishes), K (mortaria), L (lids), M (miscellaneous) and Z (unclassified). In those cases where distinction between broad classes, such as jars and bowls or bowls and dishes, is dependent upon the ratio of the vessel height to its rim diameter (Webster, G, 1976, 17-19), intermediate categories are sometime employed for vessels where there is significant doubt about the likely height:diameter ratio. Class D therefore comprises uncertain jars/bowls, and class I comprises uncertain bowls/dishes. A further composite class, G/H, consists of a fairly small number of upright rims in Severn Valley ware which could have come either from early tankards or upright sided carinated bowls. Classes A (amphorae) and F (cups) were not represented by rims at all and are therefore omitted from the tables. Most of the major classes in the present system are divided into subclasses, and further definition is provided by a detailed coding system for rim type, while reference was also made to detailed typologies such as those for samian ware (eg Webster 1996) and that of Young (1977) for the Oxford industry. This level of detail is not used extensively here, but the data are available in the project archive. The breakdown of

broad vessel classes by site is shown in Table 3.3 and the correlation of these classes with individual fabrics for Fiddington and Bredon's Norton is given in Tables 3.4 and 3.5, which show the composition of vessel classes for each fabric, using RE data.

All the assemblages were dominated by jars, but to very varying degrees. The early site of Pamington might plausibly have produced nothing but jars, and the 0.35 jar REs from the site were indeed from ten different vessels (all in Malvernian wares (Fig. 3.1.1-3) except for a single tiny rim in fabric AN3), but this very small assemblage is skewed by the presence of a single Severn Valley ware rim either from a tankard or a carinated bowl, with the result that the representation of jars was reduced to 72.9% of REs. At Fiddington jars amounted to 69% of the assemblage, a still significant figure, with possible jars (class D) adding a further 2.4%. Tankards (eg Fig. 3.1.6) were the next most numerous single vessel class after jars, at 7%, followed by bowls, dishes (Fig. 3.1.10, in black-burnished ware, iks notable) and intermediate forms, all at around 6% and giving a combined total of 18% for these open forms. Minor components of the assemblage were lids and beakers, the latter a single example in Severn Valley ware. Although small, the breakdown of the Fiddington assemblage in terms of vessel classes presents a coherent picture of the range of vessels in use in a rural context in this area.

The pattern of Bredon's Norton vessel classes is broadly similar, but this larger assemblage contained a greater variety of vessels (some 242 vessels were represented by rim sherds), even if only in small amounts, with the result that jars, while still dominant, were reduced in importance (to 51.9%). Interestingly, tankards were more common here than at Fiddington, and if the uncertain tankard/bowl value is added the combined figure for these vessels (14.9%) is almost exactly twice that at Fiddington. The combined value for open forms (bowls and dishes – 23.2%) was also greater than at Fiddington, although the difference was less marked; indeterminate bowls/dishes were almost absent here. Mortaria formed 4% of the Bredon's Norton assemblage by REs. Minor types included flagons (but only a single vessel represented by a rim), beakers (more common than at Fiddington but still very scarce) and one 'miscellaneous' form, a colander in Severn Valley ware (Fig. 3.2.29).

The size of the Fiddington assemblage is such that detailed analysis of vessel types in terms of

Table 3.3 Percentage of major pottery vessel classes (RE) by site

						Vessel Class							
Site	*B*	*C*	*D*	*E*	*G*	*G/H*	*H*	*I*	*J*	*K*	*L*	*M*	*Z*
Pamington		72.9				27.1							
Fiddington		69.0	2.4	0.8	7.0		5.9	5.8	6.3		2.2		0.4
Bredon's Norton	1.9	51.9	1.3	1.7	12.6	2.3	16.0	0.7	6.5	4.0	+	0.9	

Table 3.4 Fiddington. Vessel type by fabric – percentages (RE) (row %)

Ware/fabric code	B	C	D	E	G	G/H	H	I	J	K	L	M	Z	Total	%
S30 (subtotal)									100					0.14	1.6
F51(subtotal)									100					0.03	0.3
Fine & specialist subtotal									100					0.17	1.9
O20								100						0.16	1.8
O40		68.9	4.7	1.6	14.8		2.8	2.8	3.5				0.9	4.27	47.6
O41							100							0.10	1.1
O41F		100												1.11	12.4
O subtotal		71.8	3.5	1.2	11.2		3.9	5.0	2.7				0.7	5.64	62.8
R20							100							0.08	0.9
R30		75.7					5.4	18.9						0.37	4.1
R subtotal		62.2					22.2	15.6						0.45	5.0
B11		42.4					17.4	13.0	27.2					0.92	10.2
B30								100						0.05	0.6
B subtotal		40.2					16.5	17.5	25.8					0.97	10.8
C11(subtotal)		100												0.31	3.5
G21		91.3	8.7											0.23	2.6
G22		80.2									19.8			1.01	11.2
G25		75.0					25.0							0.20	2.2
G (Malvern & related) subtotal		81.3	1.4				3.5				13.9			1.44	16.0
Overall total		6.20	0.22	0.07	0.63		0.53	0.52	0.57		0.20		0.04	8.98	
%		69.0	2.4	0.8	7.0		5.9	5.8	6.3		2.2		0.4		

individual fabrics is not likely to generate statistically robust patterns in the data (Table 3.4). In broad terms, however, the dominant vessel class, jars, is represented in oxidised (almost entirely Severn Valley) wares at a level corresponding to the overall site figure and is particularly common in Malvernian and shell-tempered fabrics (respectively 81.3% and 100% of vessels in these fabrics). Lids, usually associated with cooking vessels, formed a complementary 13.9% of the Malvernian repertoire (and occurred exclusively in fabric G22, both here and at Bredon's Norton). Jars were less prominent in the reduced coarse ware and black-burnished ware ranges, though they still amounted to 62.2% of the former. Black-burnished ware was the only coarse ware category in which jars were a minority component; almost 60% of vessels in these fabrics were bowls and dishes, forms which together made up almost 38% of the reduced coarse ware range but only amounted to 11.5% of vessels in oxidised wares. Dishes were the only vessel class represented in fine and specialist

wares, with three examples in samian ware (all of Drag 18/31 or 31) and an effectively identical form (Young 1977 type C45) in Oxford colour-coated ware. Examples of other vessels classes – beakers and tankards, occurred exclusively in Severn Valley ware, comprising 1.6% and 14.8% of the generic O40 repertoire by REs (one and six rim sherds respectively).

As already mentioned, the Bredon's Norton assemblage shows greater diversity of vessel types. It is interesting that the smaller proportion of the assemblage made up of jars, compared to Fiddington, is reflected closely in the Severn Valley ware component, in which jars (including uncertain jar/bowl types) comprise almost exactly half of all vessels (Fig. 3.2.20-22, 30-31). Jars form a very similar proportion of vessels in black-burnished ware, although it is notable that they are more numerous in Dorset BB1 (eg Fig. 3.2.36), whereas the not insignificant element of black-burnished wares formed by fabric B30 seems to have been used entirely for bowls and dishes (Fig. 3.4.68-70).

Jars amounted to 57.5% of vessels in reduced coarse wares, a similar percentage to that at Fiddington, though with a wider range of fabrics. As with black-burnished ware, however, there was some variation in vessel type representation within what was only a relatively minor component of the assemblage (vessels in reduced fabrics totalling only 8.9% of REs); jars formed at least 70% of vessels in all reduced fabrics except the fine R10, in which bowls (eg Fig. 3.2.33, Fig. 3.3.53) were the dominant type. Jars were thus well-represented in reduced Severn Valley (fabric R49, Fig. 3.2.34), as they were in the early vesicular/organic-tempered oxidised Severn Valley wares (fabrics O41 and O41F, eg Fig. 3.2.30-31). Organic-tempered sherds recorded as fabric R60 were also probably reduced Severn Valley wares. Jars were again prominent here (but the numbers involved were very small), while the only other vessel in this fabric was of the indeterminate tankard/carinated bowl (G/H) class, characteristic of Severn Valley ware.

As at Fiddington, the shell-tempered and Malvernian fabric groups were dominated by jars, with occasional bowls and dishes, which in the case of the shell-tempered fabric C11 were of distinctive late Roman types (eg Fig. 3.4 72). The 'bowls', amounting to almost 10% of vessels in Malvernian fabric G25, were large vessels of 'cauldron' type (amongst many parallels eg Willis 2012, fig. 4.3 nos 9-11). In total there were fragments of five such vessels, one recorded as a very large jar. It may be significant that two of these (Fig. 3.3 Nos 48 and 49 below) were from one context (3162; the others were from 3001, 3056 and 3058). Inevitably the Severn Valley repertoire again included the widest range of vessel types. These included all the coarseware beakers in the assemblage – 83% of all beakers by REs, with the only fine ware example being in fabric F51 – and a strong showing of tankards (Fig. 3.1.6, 3.2.24-25 and perhaps 26), which comprised 12.6% of all the vessels from the site, amounting to 26.2% of all oxidised Severn Valley ware vessels. Where readily possible, tankards were assigned to the broad types in Peter Webster's (1976) typology as an aid to clarification of chronological trends. Out of 31 tankard rims (6 from Fiddington and 25 from Bredon's Norton), 17 (only one from Fiddington) were assigned to type, as follows: type 39 (2), type 40 cf approximately Fig. 3.1.6, though this example lacks decoration), type 43 (10) and type 44 (4). The ten examples of type 43 (eg Fig. 3.2.25) accounted for 75% of the REs of these 17 vessels, underlining the middle Roman emphasis of much of the Bredon's Norton assemblage. The O40 range also included a single example of a colander, this vessel being a 'second' as it had a distinctly warped rim (Fig. 3.2.29).

Vessels in fine and specialist wares totalled just over 10% of the Bredon's Norton RE assemblage, almost 80% of which consisted of Oxfordshire products. The largest component (38.7% of all fine and specialist ware REs) was formed by mortaria,

closely followed by bowls. These were entirely Oxfordshire products; colour-coated ware bowl and dish types (Young 1977) represented by rims were C48, C51 (3), C70, C72 (Fig. 3.4.55), C81 (2, eg Fig. 3.4.56), C85 (Fig. 3.4.57) and C117, while mortarium types present were M18, M20, M22 (3, eg Fig. 3.4.58), WC4 (Fig. 3.4.59), C97 and C100 (2, Fig. 3.4 60-61). The chronological implications of this list are discussed below. The only other fine and specialist ware vessels were a single flagon in possible 'south-western brown-slipped ware' (fabric F61) and two rims from Central Gaulish samian ware dishes of Drag form 18/31 or 31. Samian ware forms not represented by rims included a Central Gaulish Drag 27 and possibly a Drag 18 dish, the latter South Gaulish. There was not a single sherd of decorated samian ware from any of the pipeline sites.

Use and reuse

There was limited evidence for these aspects of the assemblage. Most sherds were slightly or moderately worn (see above), and heavy wear was only noted in three cases, one from each of the three sites. The Severn Valley ware colander (Fig. 3.2.29) recorded as a 'second' (and otherwise in good condition) has been noted above, and a further sherd from Bredon's Norton, a base fragment in fabric R10, was also recorded as a (distorted) 'second'. Evidence of use was indicated most clearly by the presence of soot and related deposits on vessels likely to have been used for cooking. External soot deposits were noted on 5 sherds from Fiddington and 68 from Bredon's Norton. A range of fabrics was represented; the Fiddington sherds included three from a jar in fabric C11 (Fig. 3.1.11), one from a cooking pot in fabric G22 (Fig. 3.1.13) and one from a flanged dish in B11 (fig. 3.1.10). The use of black-burnished ware bowls and dishes for cooking (perhaps as a 'casserole' unit as suggested by Gillam (1976, 76)) is also demonstrated at Bredon's Norton, where a further bowl or dish in B11 and two dishes and a base sherd in B30 also had soot deposits; the apparent absence of sooting on 'cooking pot type' jars in B11 is notable, but their use for cooking is indicated by the presence of internal limescale deposits, noted on ten sherds of B11 (and one of B30). Exterior sooting was also recorded on fabrics C11 (7 sherds), G21 (41 sherds – 28 from one vessel, including Fig. 3.3.40, 42 and 44-45, this last a dish), G22 (2 sherds – one a lid), G25 (13 sherds), O40 (2 small sherds) and R30 and R90 (1 sherd each). Internal deposits, potentially indicative of burnt food remains, were recorded on 30 sherds in fabrics C11 (9 sherds – 6 from Fiddington), G21 (15 sherds, eg Fig. 3.2.41), G25 (3 sherds, eg Fig. 3.3.47) and O40, while limescale deposits were recorded on 19 sherds in addition to the instances on black-burnished ware already mentioned. It is notable that the majority of these (16) were on Severn Valley ware, including a sherd of reduced

Table 3.5 Bredons Norton. Vessel type by fabric – percentages (RE) (row %)

Ware/fabric code	B	C	D	E	G	G/H	H	I	J	K	L	M	Z	Total	%
AS3 (AS2, ASP3)		100												0.03	0.1
AV3 (AZ3)		100												0.04	0.1
Subtotal		100												0.07	0.3
S30 (subtotal)									100					0.06	0.2
F51				7.0			87.8		5.2					1.15	4.1
F61	100													0.53	1.9
F subtotal	31.5			4.8			60.1		3.6					1.68	6.1
M22										100				0.42	1.5
M31										100				0.10	0.4
M41										100				0.58	2.1
M subtotal										100				1.10	4.0
Fine & specialist subtotal	**18.7**			**2.8**			**35.6**		**4.2**	**38.7**				**2.84**	**10.2**
E80 (subtotal)							100							0.15	0.5
O40		45.4	2.7	3.1	27.2	5.0	13.6	0.1	0.9			2.0		12.62	45.5
O41		100												0.33	1.2
O41F		64.1			15.4	7.7	12.8							0.39	1.4
O subtotal		47.3	2.5	2.9	26.2	4.9	13.3	0.1	0.8			1.9		13.34	48.1
R10		29.8					70.2							1.04	3.7
R20		100												0.02	0.1
R30		74.0					26.0							0.50	1.9
R49		76.4	1.8				21.8							0.55	2.0
R60		71.4				28.6								0.21	0.8
R95		100												0.15	0.5
R subtotal		47.5	0.4			2.4	39.7							2.47	8.9
B11		63.5					4.8	6.8	24.9					2.49	9.0
B30							28.2		71.8					0.78	2.8
B subtotal		48.3					10.4	5.2	36.1					3.27	9.1
C11 (subtotal)		*86.0*					*5.0*		*9.0*					*1.00*	*3.6*
G21		89.1							10.9					2.76	9.9
G22		97.3									2.7			0.37	1.3
G25		90.6					9.4*							1.49	5.4
G (Malvern & related) subtotal		90.3					3.0		6.5		0.2			4.62	16.6
Overall total	**0.53**	**14.41**	**0.35**	**0.47**	**3.49**	**0.72**	**4.44**	**0.19**	**1.80**	**1.10**	**0.01**	**0.25**		**27.76**	
	1.9	51.9	1.3	1.7	12.6	2.3	16.0	0.7	6.5	4.0	+	0.9			

fabric R49, with only single instances in fabrics G21 (two sherds from the same vessel) and R20. In addition, internal and external burnt deposits occurred on one sherd of G21, and sooting and limescale deposits together on one sherd of fabric B11 and two sherds of C11. These figures suggest fairly clear differences in the patterns of use of particular fabrics. The association of Malvernian vessels and sherds in fabric C11 with burnt deposits is unsurprising, but what is more notable is the association of BB1 'cooking pot type' jars and Severn Valley ware vessels with the boiling – or perhaps, in the case of the Severn Valley ware vessels, with 'extended storage' (McSloy 2008b, 95) – of water. Unfortunately there is no indication of which Severn Valley ware vessel types were associated with this activity as all the relevant evidence was on undiagnostic body sherds.

'Simple' burning was recorded on 29 sherds in total. Its significance is less clear than in the case of sooting as it could easily have occurred in secondary contexts (soot could also have accumulated on sherds in such contexts, but on the whole is thought less likely to have been deposited on sherd surfaces post use). Burning is seen much more easily on oxidised than on reduced fabrics and it is therefore no surprise that 25 of the burnt sherds were of Severn Valley ware and one was of samian ware. All but one of these were from Bredon's Norton, which also produced a burnt sherd in fabric R10, perhaps significantly from a flanged bowl (Fig. 3.3.53). Burnt sherds at Fiddington comprised one of Severn Valley ware and three in fabric G22.

Evidence of repair and reuse was more restricted. Clear indication of repair at Fiddington consisted of a Central Gaulish samian ware body sherd in context 1022 which had a rivet hole, consistent with the view that samian ware is more likely to have been curated than other types of pottery. At Bredon's Norton, however, a sherd from the base angle of a large jar in fabric O81 from context 5269 had a hole *c* 6mm in diameter. This is likely to indicate a repair since vessels in this fabric also seem to have been favoured for this treatment (eg Booth forthcoming). Two sherds at Bredon's Norton had been reused; one each of black-burnished ware and Severn Valley ware (contexts 3006 and 3036 respectively) had wear on one edge caused by repeated rubbing, but the purpose of this is unclear.

Phasing and chronology

A breakdown of quantities of fabrics by phase is given for Fiddington and Bredon's Norton to clarify some aspects of the evolution of these assemblages over time. The Fiddington assemblage was only divided into two main phases, early-middle and late Roman (a very small quantity of pottery from unphased or post-Roman contexts (21 sherds, mostly of Severn Valley ware) is not presented separately in Table 3.6 but is included in the overall totals column). Consequently only broad trends can

be discerned; moreover some of the context groups assigned to the early-middle Roman phase were dated on ceramic criteria to the late 2nd century at the earliest, so this phase is of extended duration. In broad terms, however, the clearest trend is a decline in the proportion of Severn Valley ware through time, with corresponding increases in black-burnished and shell-tempered wares and a very small rise in the collective representation of fine and specialist wares. Malvernian wares show a more complex pattern. Collectively they remain consistently important as measured by sherd count, while their representation by weight and REs increases substantially. In reality the late Iron Age-early Roman fabrics G21 and G25 decline dramatically in importance – and are probably entirely residual in the late Roman phase. By contrast, the 'Romanised' version of MAL RE A, fabric G22, already present in the later assemblages of the early-middle Roman phase, provides the great bulk of Malvernian material in the late Roman phase, but is almost certainly over-represented here as a number of the larger fragments of this fabric are from a prefabricated oven or ovens (see above).

The comparative data for Bredon's Norton show some similarities to the Fiddington pattern, but also some differences (Table 3.7) (as with Fiddington, sherds from post-Roman contexts and those of uncertain phase are included in the fabric totals but not presented otherwise, this material totalled 66 sherds with a weight of 1152g). More phase groups were defined at this site, but some of them are small and may not necessarily provide reliable indications of the evolution of the assemblage. The earliest phase group, notionally of middle-late Iron Age date, is one such. Although dominated by Malvernian fabrics, as would be expected, these amount to less than half of the group by weight, by which measure Severn Valley ware is particularly well-represented, while a variety of reduced coarse wares also makes a significant contribution. It is likely that at least some context groups assigned to this phase were contaminated with later pottery, or that the phase as a whole should be dated to the late Iron Age-early Roman period; both scenarios are probably relevant here. The subsequent phase assemblage incorporates context groups which probably range in date from the mid-late 1st century to the early-mid 3rd. Malvernian fabrics continued to be well-represented, occurring at much the same level as previously (by weight) but significantly reduced in importance by other measures. The apparently inflated weight figure is explained by the presence of fragments of large cauldron-like vessels in fabric G25. Severn Valley wares, nevertheless, dominate, accounting for a little over half of all sherds (including reduced Severn Valley wares), almost exactly half of the pottery by weight and nearly 65% of REs in this phase. Black-burnished ware is consistently present, although in small quantities.

The later Roman phase groups are rather different in character, but the significance of some of

Table 3.6 Fiddington. Summary quantification of Roman pottery fabrics by phase – column %

Ware/fabric code	Early-Middle Roman			Late Roman			Total		
	Nosh	Wt	RE	Nosh	Wt	RE	Nosh	Wt	RE
AN3	0.2	+					2	6	
CN5	0.2	+					1	3	
SN5				0.6	0.4		2	34	
Subtotal	0.4	0.1		0.6	0.4		5	43	
S30	0.4	0.2	1.8	1.3	0.2	1.3	6	26	0.14
S30B				0.3	0.1		1	6	
S subtotal	0.4	0.2	1.8	1.6	0.3	1.3	7	32	0.14
F51				1.9	0.4	0.8	6	25	0.03
F60				1.0	0.2		3	12	
F subtotal				2.9	0.5	0.8	9	37	0.03
M22	0.2	0.1					1	4	
M subtotal	0.2	0.1					1	4	
Fine & specialist subtotal	**0.6**	**0.2**	**1.8**	**4.5**	**0.8**	**2.1**	**17**	**73**	**0.17**
O20	0.8	0.6	2.3	0.3	0.1	1.1	5	42	0.16
O40	48.8	50.5	50.2	49.8	33.8	43.8	410	5632	4.27
O41	0.8	0.9	2.0	0.3	0.4		6	88	0.10
O41F	18.1	16.0	19.5	1.3	0.7	2.9	93	1056	1.11
O81				0.6	8.6		2	586	
O subtotal	68.5	68.0	74.0	52.4	43.6	47.8	516	7404	5.64
R10	0.8	1.2					4	77	
R20				0.6	0.4	2.1	2	28	0.08
R30	3.3	4.5	6.8	4.8	3.0	0.5	31	488	0.37
R49	0.2	0.2		0.3	0.2		2	25	
R60	0.8	1.2		0.6	0.6		7	115	
R90				0.3	0.4		1	29	
R subtotal	5.1	7.2	6.8	6.7	4.5	2.6	47	762	0.45
B11	8.7	3.8	8.2	13.1	7.3	13.2	84	744	0.92
B30	0.2	1.4		0.3	0.2	1.3	2	101	0.05
B (subtotal)	4.9	5.2	8.2	13.4	7.5	14.5	86	845	0.97
C10									
C11				4.8	5.0	8.2	15	342	0.31
C subtotal				4.8	5.0	8.2	15	342	0.31
G21	9.3	6.1	4.1	2.6	1.0	0.5	54	465	0.23
G22	3.0	6.0	2.7	14.7	36.9	23.0	61	2896	1.01
G25	3.9	7.2	2.3	0.6	0.3	1.3	23	495	0.20
G31	0.2	0.1					1	5	
G (Malvern & 16.5 related) subtotal	19.3	9.2	17.9	38.4	24.8		139	3861	1.44
Z10				0.3	0.1		1	6	
Overall total	**492**	**6286**	**5.12**	**313**	**6890**	**3.79**	**826**	**13335**	**8.98**

the changes apparent in the group defined as generically late Roman is unclear because this is quite small. A subset of the late Roman phase group, here defined as phase LR2 (see further below) has several similar characteristics, however, which reinforce aspects of the general late Roman pattern. Consistent characteristics of these groups are very significantly reduced quantities of Malvernian fabrics, by now largely if not entirely residual, and increases in quantities of black-burnished wares and fine and specialist wares. The general late Roman group provides contradictory indications of the importance of Severn Valley and reduced coarse wares. The former are well-represented by sherd count and weight, maintaining the levels present in early-middle Roman period, but decline in impor-

Table 3.7 Bredons Norton quantification of Roman pottery fabrics by phase – column %

Ware/ fabric code	LIA-ERB			E-MRB			LR			LR2			Total incl post Roman, US etc	
	Nosh	Wt	RE	Nosh	Wt	RE	Nosh	Wt	RE	Nosh	Wt	RE	Nosh	Wt
AS3 (AS2, ASP3)	2.8	1.9		0.1	+	0.2							5	43
AV3 (AZ3)	0.9	0.2		0.4	0.1	0.3							4	20
CS3				0.1	0.2								1	38
LA4				0.1	+								1	5
SN4				0.2	+								2	2
ZA3				0.1	+								1	2
Subtotal	3.7	2.2		1.1	0.3	0.4							14	110
S20				0.1	0.1								1	15
S30				0.9	0.2		0.8	0.2		0.3	+		9	41
S subtotal				1.0	0.2		0.8	0.2		0.3	+		10	56
F50				0.1	+		0.8	0.2		0.3	0.1		3	15
F51							9.2	8.4	5.7	5.8	4.3	13.4	31	609
F52							0.8	0.4					1	12
F60														
F61							0.8	0.3	14.3				1	9
F subtotal				0.1	+		11.5	9.2	20.0	6.1	4.4	13.4	36	645
A10										0.3	0.1		1	5
A30				0.1	0.1					0.6	6.1		3	494
A subtotal				0.1	0.1					0.9	6.2		4	499
M22							0.8	1.1	1.4	1.5	3.8	5.3	6	327
M31										0.3	0.8	1.4	1	61
M41							1.5	2.1	1.1	2.8	3.4	7.7	11	329
M subtotal							2.3	3.2	2.4	4.6	7.9	14.4	18	717
W10				0.1	0.1								1	12
W23										0.3	0.1		1	4
W30				0.1	0.1								1	22
W subtotal				0.2	0.2					0.3	0.1		3	38
Q20 subtotal				0.1	+								1	8
Fine & specialist subtotal				1.6	0.3		14.5	12.5	22.4	12.2	18.5	27.8	71	1963
E10	0.9	0.1		0.1	+								2	4
E20				0.1	+								1	6

tance in terms of REs for reasons that are not clear. The position of reduced coarse wares is relatively consistent, although the RE value is inflated in the general late Roman phase; this, however, is largely caused by the presence of a single large flanged bowl sherd in fabric R10.

Phase group LR2 has been extracted somewhat arbitrarily from the wider late Roman assemblage on the basis of the presence of fabric C11 and the presumption, discussed above, that this is likely to indicate a date after AD 350 for associated groups. In many respects these are not radically different in character from groups assigned to the general late Roman phase, but some of the trends suggested there seem to be developed even further, although rather different pictures are suggested by the relative

Table 3.7 (continued)

Ware/ fabric code	LIA-ERB			E-MRB			LR			LR2			Total incl post Roman, US etc	
	Nosh	Wt	RE	Nosh	Wt	RE	Nosh	Wt	RE	Nosh	Wt	RE	Nosh	Wt
E80	3.7	5.6		0.7	0.6								10	218
E subtotal	4.6	5.5		1.0	0.7								13	228
O20				0.1	+		0.8	0.8		0.3	0.1		3	42
O30				0.1	+								1	2
O40	9.3	10.6		41.2	37.7	57.1	50.4	38.4	37.0	42.5	44.1	28.7	591	13278
O41	4.6	22.7		3.9	3.8	1.6	3.1	3.9		1.8	1.9	1.0	48	1551
O41F	5.6	6.3		3.7	5.8	2.3	5	6.5		2.4	3.2	0.4	51	1822
O81							3.1	2.9					5	53
O subtotal	19.4	39.6		49.1	47.3	61.0	61.1	52.4	37.0	47.1	49.4	30.1	699	16742
R10				1.7	0.6	2.2	3.1	7.1	15.4	3.4	1.5	1.9	29	486
R20	0.9	0.2		0.2	0.1	0.1				0.1	0.2		5	46
R30	6.5	2.5		0.4	0.1		3.1	3.4	3.2	5.2	3.0	5.4	32	416
R49	1.9	0.7		1.4	1.1	2.6	0.8	0.1					17	341
R60				3.0	1.3	1.3				1.2	0.9		28	349
R85				0.2	0.3					0.6	0.4		4	98
R90	1.9	3.0		0.5	0.5					0.3	0.6		7	210
R95	*0.9*	*1.6*	*17.2*										*2*	*55*
R subtotal	12.0	8.0	17.2	7.4	4.0	6.2	6.9	10.7	18.6	11.0	6.7	7.3	124	2001
B11				4.2	4.0	8.1	9.2	14.8	17.0	12.2	8.3	8.6	87	1989
B30				0.1	0.3		0.8	1.3		5.8	7.7	11.1	21	711
B (subtotal)				4.1	4.3	8.0	9.9	16.1	17.0	18.0	16.0	19.7	108	2700
C10				0.1	+		0.8	0.5					2	18
C11										8.6	6.9	14.3	28	535
C subtotal				0.1	+		0.8	0.5		8.6	6.9	14.3	30	553
C22				0.5	0.2								4	36
G20				0.1	+								2	19
G21	23.1	17.4	20.7	22.2	21.1	15.9	1.5	0.6		1.2	1.1	0.6	216	4917
G22				0.7	0.4		5	2.3	4.9	0.6	1.1		20	420
G25	37.0	27.3	44.8	12.0	21.1	6.8				0.3	0.2	0.3	143	5261
G26							1.5	1.7					2	57
G (Malvern & related) subtotal	60.2	44.7	65.5	35.6	42.8	22.7	6.9	4.7	4.9	3.1	2.4	0.9	387	10710
Overall total	108	1625	0.87	815	21287	15.70	131	3295	3.70	327	7743	7.01	1447	35112

proportions of fabrics indicated by different measures. RE data present the most 'developed' view of the latest Roman assemblage. In these terms the representation of Malvernian wares is minimal and Severn Valley wares have declined to about 30% of the assemblage. The new component in the coarse wares, shell-tempered ware, accounts for 14.3% of REs, while black-burnished ware accounts for almost 20%. Dorset BB1 might be expected to fall out of use within the compass of a phase of activity spanning the second half of the 4th century, and this may indeed have been the case since the majority of the black-burnished ware group (by REs) consisted of the 'imitation' fabric B30, which was used for characteristic late Roman straight-sided dishes and flanged bowls. Over a quarter of the LR2 assemblage consisted of fine and specialist wares – specifically Oxford colour-coated wares and mortaria discussed above. It must be said that the distinctive character of this group emerges with less clarity from the sherd count data. While these demonstrate the minimal importance of Malvernian products they suggest that the dominant role of Severn Valley ware in the assemblage was maintained, with reduced coarse wares also relatively important and certainly more so than shell-tempered wares. The increase in fine and specialist ware representation, is not seen by this measure, though it is clearly marked in the data for weight and REs. Despite these differences a distinct late Roman ceramic phase is apparent.

A summary of the site assemblages

Pamington

The small assemblage from Pamington is very simple in character and comprises relatively well fragmented material with a mean sherd weight of only 10.4g. Fifty-seven of the 69 sherds from this site are in Malvernian fabrics, while all but one of the rest are in a range of handmade fabrics of broad later prehistoric character. A single Severn Valley ware rim sherd from an early Roman tankard or carinated bowl in context 2095 might have been intrusive, but some of the Malvernian pottery could have belonged to a late Iron Age/early Roman component in the assemblage, although this is not demonstrable. The Malvernian material included 7 rim sherds, 4 of which had stamped or tooled decoration (Fig. 3.1.1-3). Overall it is likely that the majority of the activity represented by the pottery was of middle-late Iron Age date, with only a very small component assignable to the post-conquest period. Close absolute dates cannot be assigned on ceramic criteria.

Fiddington

The assemblage from Fiddington contrasts with that from Pamington in having no meaningful Iron Age component, and had a rather higher mean sherd weight (16.1g). Some 139 sherds (16.8% of sherd count but 29.1% of weight) were in Malvernian fabrics, but the majority by weight were in the 'Romanised' Malvernian fabric G22. Some of the material in fabrics G21 and G25 could have been of later Iron Age date, but this cannot be proven. Distinctive pieces such as rims with stamped decoration on the shoulder (as seen at Pamington) were not noted. Overall, the earlier Roman groups were dominated by Severn Valley wares. Later Roman groups, including one (1052) which produced a single early Anglo-Saxon sherd, accounted for just over half of the assemblage by weight. A slight later Roman emphasis might be indicated in these terms, but the proportion is rather less in terms of sherd count and REs and the material came from a noticeably smaller number of contexts than the earlier pottery. A substantial part of the weight of the later Roman phase group is provided by fabric G22, but includes at least some fragments from ovens. Only one later Roman context contained Oxford colour-coated ware (F51) – this was from a dish of Young (1977) type C45, a type dated AD 270-400 by Young (ibid., 158) but probably to be dated AD 240-400 and apparently most common in the later 3rd century (Booth *et al.* 1993, 167). Other late context dates are assigned on the basis of the presence of probable Harrold shell-tempered wares in four cases, and of late black-burnished and Severn Valley ware types in others. A single sherd of pink grogged ware was also present in one of these groups and is consistent with a late Roman date, though not itself closely dated. An apparent scarcity of very late Roman groups (in contrast to Bredon's Norton) makes the appearance of the single early Anglo-Saxon sherd the more surprising, but it is impossible to judge if the association of this sherd with late Roman pottery here is anything more than fortuitous.

Bredon's Norton

The Bredon's Norton assemblage is the largest of the three in terms of sherd count and is also notable for a particularly high mean sherd weight (24.3 g). The assemblage includes a modest but significant Iron Age component (perhaps at least *c* 10% of sherds), but this figure is boosted by the presence of two largely complete Malvernian vessels, a tall jar with stamped decoration just below the slightly-expanded rim (SF 3013 from context 3159; Fig. 3.3.40) and most of a burnished jar with a short slightly everted rim from context 3062 (SF 3012; Fig. 3.3.47). Some 1st century material, to which the vessel from 3062 should perhaps be added, suggests potential continuity of activity from the late Iron Age through into the early Roman period. As at Fiddington, context groups dated to the early Roman period (mid 1st-2nd century and early-late 2nd century) were considerably more numerous than later groups. Here, moreover, they also contained a significantly higher proportion of the material by both sherd count and weight than the later Roman groups

In slight contrast to Fiddington, however, there were more groups at Bredon's Norton specifically assigned to the 4th century, including several datable to the second half of the century on the basis of the presence of diagnostic late vessel types. The most notable of these is an Oxford colour-coated ware handled bowl of Young (1977) type C85 (Fig. 3.4.57) from context 3165, a group which also contained two examples each of types C81 and C11 as well as white-slipped and white ware Oxford mortaria and two late shell-tempered jars (overall, Fig. 3.4.Nos 56, 57, 59-61, 63, 64, 66-68, 70 and 71). Such a group could date very late in the 4th century.

Bredon's Norton produced all the Oxford products recorded from the scheme, with the exceptions of the Oxford C45 bowl from Fiddington noted above, and a single fragment of white ware mortarium (fabric M22) from the same site. Apart from this later Roman material, however, (supplemented by single sherds of colour-coated fabrics F52 and F61) there is relatively little to suggest that this was a high status site. More samian ware sherds, for example, came from the smaller Fiddington assemblage than from Bredon's Norton. In ceramic terms it is only the latest Roman groups that perhaps indicate a distinctive character for the site.

Discussion

The three sites present overlapping stages of a continuous sequence of pottery assemblage development from the middle Iron Age to the end of the Roman period, and in broad terms conform well to established regional patterns. Malvernian products dominate assemblages in this area after the earlier part of the middle Iron Age (eg McSloy 2006, 56). This dominance is maintained into the early Roman period, with the result that it is impossible to be certain if sites with predominantly Malvernian assemblages, such as Pamington, where occupation almost certainly ended within the 1st century AD, survived after the conquest period. Such survival is likely in the case of Pamington, although the great majority of the assemblage is of middle-late Iron Age date. Bredon's Norton includes a number of Malvernian dominated groups for which a late Iron Age date seems quite likely; such groups are not present at Fiddington. Jane Timby has noted variation in the relative proportions of Malvernian A and B fabrics in a number of local assemblages (Timby 2010, 26, 29; see also Hancocks 1999, 115, table 13) and suggests that the limestone-tempered B fabrics are significantly more numerous at sites likely to be of higher status in the early Roman period, whereas at 'other more rural sites' such as Longdon Marsh the rock-tempered A fabric tends to predominate (Timby 2010, 29). This may be so, but it seems at least as likely that chronological factors are important. In the earliest, admittedly small but surely 'low status', assemblage from Pamington limestone-tempered fabric G25 is more than twice as common as fabric G21 in terms of both weight and sherd count. At

Bredon's Norton, with (as suggested above) some evidence for a late Iron Age phase as well as abundant later activity, the representation of fabrics G21 and G25 is similar in terms of weight, but G21 is more numerous by sherd count and (more importantly) by REs (2.76 as opposed to 1.49 for G25). At Fiddington, with no discernible late Iron Age phase, the sherd count for G21 is more than twice that for G25, but by other measures the representation of these fabrics is more or less the same (see Table 3.2). Here, as noted above, the 'romanised' version of the rock-tempered fabric (G22) is dominant, but includes certain and probable oven fragments. If the contributions of G21 and G22 are combined the result might support Timby's hypothesis, but at Fiddington fabric G22 sherds occur mostly in later Roman (mid 3rd century or later) contexts, by which time most occurrences of G21 and G25 will have been residual, so G22 was probably irrelevant to the discussion of relative proportions of rock- and limestone-tempered Malvernian fabrics.

By the later 1st century all rural assemblages in the region were dominated by Severn Valley wares. This situation then prevailed throughout much of the rest of the Roman period, but perhaps changed in the later 4th century; for example the group from context 3165, one of the latest from Bredon's Norton, contains about one third Severn Valley wares by sherd count and weight, but rather less by REs. This group may be exceptional in some respects but the decline in Severn Valley wares here is suggestive. The higher proportion of Severn Valley wares at Fiddington as opposed to Bredon's Norton (see above) might reflect, amongst other things, subtle variations in site chronology, including more intensive activity in the middle of the Roman period, and in particular a relative absence of later Roman features, especially ones dated to the 4th century (although at least four contexts here may be of later 4th century date based on the presence of late shell-tempered ware).

As has been commented upon quite regularly, assemblages from the region tend to be 'dominated by a small range of wares from industries with a long time span' (Timby 2010, 26). The two main elements of this trend have been discussed above. It is notable that both are regional industries which cannot be considered immediately local to the present sites, the nearest located Severn Valley ware production site, at Great Malvern, lying some 16km north-west (Evans *et al.* 2000). It is possible that Severn Valley production sites remain to be found closer to hand, but the 'second' from Bredon's Norton was an unusual form otherwise in good condition and need not imply local production. The pattern of provision based on regional rather than local sources appears to have been widespread and suggests that local pottery production of any kind was on a small scale at best. Despite the dominance of Malvern and Severn Valley ware products, therefore, there was scope for the acquisition of other types of pottery (and not just fine and specialist wares) from extra-regional sources. Black-burnished ware was the most widely occurring of these wares; Dorset BB1 occurred consistently at Fiddington and Bredon's Norton and was supplemented in the late Roman period by material from an unsourced but perhaps more local industry (fabric B30), characteristic products of which (bowls and dishes) were present at both sites. North Wiltshire (including the Savernake industry) and perhaps another south-western British source (of fabric R85) were contributors, but only of very small quantities of pottery, while extra-regional sources to the east included the pink grogged ware and shell-tempered industries. The contribution of the latter pottery was relatively small scale but is significant as providing diagnostic evidence of later 4th century activity. As elsewhere in the region pink grogged ware occurred as large storage jars in contexts of 3rd-4th century date (eg Bryant and Evans 2004a 264, but note that fig. 165 no. 14 there is not a pink grogged ware form), with a western limit to the distribution broadly along the line of the River Severn (Taylor 2004, 63-5, fig. 3, to which Worcester should be added). The question of whether they served as transport vessels with specific contents remains unresolved.

A lack of fine and specialist wares, and in particular of imported vessels, is another characteristic of rural settlement sites in the region – particularly in the absence of good evidence from villa sites. (It is clear that fine and specialist wares were plentiful in the late Roman site at Bays Meadow, Droitwich (eg contributions in Barfield 2006, 154-7), which makes the lack of usable quantified data from this site particularly unfortunate). The miserable quantities of samian ware and the few small amphora

fragments from the present sites (the latter only from late contexts at Bredon's Norton) underline this point. Identifiable fine and specialist wares are therefore very largely from a single source just outside the region, the Oxford industry. By definition the fine wares from this industry would not have reached the region before the middle of the 3rd century at the earliest, but it is notable that at Bredon's Norton none of the (five) white ware mortaria are of types dated earlier than AD 240, although the single sherd from Fiddington is from a context assigned to the early Roman phase. In total, of nine Oxford mortarium rims (in all fabrics) from Bredon's Norton three are of types dated AD 240–300, four have a date range of 240–400 and two are entirely 4th century. Mortaria from other industries occasionally encountered in the region (although usually in earlier periods), such as the Severn Valley and Mancetter-Hartshill, are completely absent here. The situation with regard to the date of Oxford colour-coated wares is if anything more striking, given that many types in this fabric only have a broad date range of AD 240–400. Of ten vessels at Bredon's Norton represented by rims only three have a start date of AD 240, one is dated 270–400 and the rest are exclusively 4th century types, including C85 which is dated after AD 350.

The number of more closely dated types rather suggests that much of this material might not have arrived at the site before the 4th century, although the stamped vessel (Fig. 3.3 No. 50), of which only the base survived, is more likely to have been of later 3rd century than later date on the basis that the relatively limited practice of 'name' stamping in this industry is most likely to have been practised at a time when aspects of the ancestral samian ware

Table 3.8 Selected comparative pottery data from a range of Worcestershire and Gloucestershire sites

Site	Total pottery Nosh/Wt (g)	Date range	MAL REA	MAL REB
Worcester Deansway Period 3**	2195/44768	45-120	7%/	
Worcester Deansway Period 4**	5957/113211	120-240	3%/	
Worcester Deansway Period 5**	5173/97498	240-410	-	
Worcester 14-24 The Butts CP1	1675/33331	Mostly 2-3C	10%/7%	
Worcester 14-24 The Butts CP2	1463/30446	Mostly 4C	<1%/<1%	
Dymock, Sewage Works	2865/67647	Mostly 1-2C	3%/1%	1%/<1%
Dymock, Rectory	339/3607	1-2C	4%/6%	-
Dymock, Stallards Place	435/6173	1-2C?	7%/12%	
Longdon Marsh (Worcs)	2424/35916	LIA-(most) RB (3C)	23%/30%	13%/6%
Ripple (Worcs)	2361/60568	MIA-RB (most LIA-early 3C)	34%/40%	4%/1%
Beckford, Elm Farm (Worcs)	1013/10970	1-4C, mostly 1-2C	15%/12%	23%/24%
Dumbleton, Bank Farm	130/1157	Mostly 1-2C	12%/7%	20%/34%
Dumbleton, College Farm	560/7493	Mostly 2-early 3C	12.5%/9%	2%/<1%
Aston Somerville, Wormington Farm (Worcs)	122/1666	Early-mid 2C	6%//7%	49%/27%
Tewkesbury, Walton Cardiff	5838/81941	LIA-4C	13%/8%	11%/4%
incl C100	8/329? incl M22, @	3%/2%	McSloy 2008a	
Tewksbury	/169700 + samian ware	1-3C		
Tewksbury Site I	1030/9978	1-3C?	<1%/<1%	

tradition were still relatively well understood. This point is underlined by the close correlation between name stamps and the dish form C45 (eg Booth *et al.* 1993, 172-4). The single Oxford colour-coated ware vessel at Fiddington was of this type, considered to be more common in the later 3rd century than later (see above). These associations support the suggestion that 4th century activity at Fiddington, although clearly occurring, was at a low level. At Bredon's Norton, by contrast, while the number of later 4th century pottery groups is not large they provide a significant assemblage of that date.

A comparison of the groups from the two site containing fabric C11 (used as a marker of later 4th century date) is informative. The four groups of this type at Fiddington contain 99 sherds (1912g, 1.21 REs), together a not inconsiderable proportion of the site assemblage as a whole. Fifteen of these sherds are of fabric C11, but what is of interest is the representation of fine and specialist wares, which comprise 4% of sherd count, 1.1% of weight and 2.5% of REs. At Bredon's Norton the corresponding (phase LR2) groups total 327 sherds (7743g, 7.01 REs), of which only 28 are in fabric C11, but the fine and specialist ware component is substantially different, amounting to 12.2% of these groups by sherd count, 18.5% by weight and a substantial 27.8% of REs. These figures suggest a significant difference in the character of the two sites in their latest Roman phases. This is of course underlined by the structural evidence at Bredon's Norton.

The key questions are, when does this change of ceramic character occur, and can it be correlated directly with events such as the construction of the stone building? It should be noted that there is no meaningful pottery evidence for the date of construction of the building. In this regard it is unfortunate that the relationship of the small 'general late Roman' phase group to the LR2 group is unclear – does the former represent activity through the whole of the period from the mid 3rd to the mid 4th century, as a broad reading of the dating evidence might suggest, or do these context groups relate to a shorter phase of activity more closely related to that assigned to phase LR2? Pottery from LR contexts related to the demolition and robbing of the building, and therefore probably to be associated with material assigned to ceramic phase LR2, contains a significant component of fine and specialist wares, including all but one of the rim sherds in these wares in all late Roman contexts, with the net result that pottery from contexts associated with the demolition of the building and related deposits has a fine and specialist ware RE value of 29.2% (of 9.45 REs). Nevertheless, this material still only amounts to 13.4% of sherds in these contexts, and while the fine and specialist ware RE value from the remnant of the LR phase group is minimal, by sherd count these fabrics still amount to 10.3%. The overall impression, therefore, is of a potentially significant change in pottery assemblage character in the late Roman period, but at a date still undefined. Moreover, while a direct association with the construction of the stone building is plausible, it is not demonstrable.

Interpretation of the pottery associated with demolition and robbing and related contexts is equally problematic. Does the high proportion of this material consisting of fine and specialist wares reflect what was in use in and around the building at the point at which it fell out of use, the material simply being disposed of as rubbish, or did it relate to some subsequent phase of activity with no clear structural correlates within the excavated area?

Other MAL	Severn Valley	Black-burnished ware all	Oxford colour-coated	Oxford mortaria	Total fine and specialist wares; comments	Reference
<1% /	75% /	-			9% / **	Bryant and Evans 2004
4% /	67% /	4% /		5 /, @	12% / **	Bryant and Evans 2004
2% /	87% /	4.5% /	29 /	14 /, @	4% / **	Bryant and Evans 2004
2% / 2%	69% / 78%	12% / 7%	9 / 48	3 / 69 @	4% / 2%	Evans *et al.* 2011
3% / 3%	56% / 45%	19% / 14%	116 / 1402	27 / 324	15% / 28%	Evans *et al.* 2011
<1% / <1%	67% / 81%	6% / 3%	6 / 30	1 / 24, @	4% / 5%	Timby 2007b
-	67% / 69%	3% / 3%		@	4% / 9%	Brown and Timby 2007
1% / 2%	50% / 52%	19% / 15%	-	- @	6% / 11%	Booth 2013
7% / 6%	50% / 52% incl reduced		-	1 / 83	<1% / <1%	Timby 2010
2% / 2%	48% / 49%	1% / 1%	1 / 4	1 / 39 @	4% / 3%	McSloy 2008c
-	44% / 51%	3% / 3%	14 / 89		3% / 2%; RB only	McSloy 2006
-	52% / 44%	1.5% / <1%	2 / 2		3% / 3%; RB only	McSloy 2006
<1% / <1%	65% / 64%	4% / 8%	7 / 137	-	8% / 8%	McSloy 2006
<1% / <1%	39% / 63%	<1% / <1%	-	-	<1% / <1%; RB only	McSloy 2006
10% / 18% *	46% / 58%	10% / 6%	66 / 211			
/ 15%	/ 52%	/ 9%	?	?	?	Hannan 1993
2% / 1%	71% / 72%	14% / 17%	-	- @	2% / 3%	Timby 2004

While it is possible that the most significant change in fine and specialist ware representation (and hence, wider assemblage character) is not seen until the second half of the 4th century, there are equally some indications of the presence of fine wares before this time, particularly if the chronological implications of pieces such as Fig. 3.3. No. 50 (see above) are valid. It is notable, however, that all the occurrences of late Roman fine wares apart from those associated with the stone building and the deposits succeeding it are at the northern end of the site at a considerable distance from the building. The extent to which there was chronological overlap between the activity in these two discrete locations is quite uncertain; it is possible, but not demonstrable, that there was no direct link between these activities at all.

The presence of reasonable quantities of late Roman pottery at Bredon's Norton, and to a lesser extent at Fiddington, distinguishes these sites from many others in the area, where late Roman activity is often absent or in significant decline from about the early 4th century onwards (eg McSloy 2006, 56; Holbrook 2008b, 73; see summaries of date ranges in Table 3.8). Where later 4th century activity is attested, as for example at St James's Railway Station, Cheltenham (McSloy 2008b, 95-6) and at Bishop's Cleeve, at Home Farm (Timby 1998) and, less certainly, at Church Road (Lovell *et al.* 2007, 101), the key components of the assemblage appear to be closely comparable to those at Bredon's Norton.

Some of the implications of variation in quantities of fine and specialist wares have been mentioned above. Such variation has been considered a potentially useful pointer to aspects of site socio-economic status in the adjacent regions of Warwickshire and the Upper Thames Valley in Oxfordshire and Gloucestershire (eg Booth 1991; 2004; 2007). Explicitly comparable work has not been carried out in this region, though implicit assumptions about site character are made on the basis of aspects of their pottery assemblages (eg McSloy 2006, 56; Timby 2010, 26). Quantification of some fabrics is given in Table 3.8, in which percentages are mostly rounded to the nearest whole number. In some cases the assemblage size is so small that percentages have little meaning, and for some categories the original quantification is retained rather than converted into percentages. Systematic collection of relevant comparative data beyond Fiddington and Bredon's Norton has not been attempted here, although total values for fine and specialist wares are shown in the table where the data are retrievable from the published sources.

In the absence of a regional frame of reference, the significance of these figures is not clear, but by comparison with both of the adjacent areas studied the overall fine and specialist ware figures seem low and, if the comparisons are valid, would appear to support the interpretation of most of the sites listed in Table 3.8, including both Fiddington and Bredon's Norton, as of relatively low status. It is likely that the 'Oxford effect' (Booth 2004, 42, 44) identified as a key factor increasing the base line representation of fine and specialist wares in the late Roman period (and thereby invalidating simple comparison between assemblages of early- and late-Roman date) applied in this region. It is seen fairly clearly at Droitwich Bays Meadow, for example (French 2006), and in a late group from The Butts at Worcester, but curiously, not in Period 5 at Worcester Deansway, where the lack of Oxford colour-coated ware in this period group is remarkable (Bryant and Evans 2004a, 280, table 49). The extent of the Oxford factor is therefore uncertain, and may have been variable across the region. As described above, it is seen in extreme form at Bredon's Norton although not to the extent of raising the overall fine and specialist ware value for the site significantly), but it is arguable that this is not just a result of a general increase in availability of Oxford products in the region in the later 4th century, but also reflects a significant change in some aspect of the character of the site, whether specifically at this time or a little earlier.

The regional context

The pipeline excavations provide further examples of assemblages which are in most respects typical of those from other rural sites in the region (see Table 3.8), characterised by a relatively limited range of fabrics with few exotica. These contrast with material from 'small town' sites in the region such as Worcester (roughly 18km NNW of Bredon's Norton), and other minor nucleated settlements such as Dymock (*c* 24km WSW), where a wider variety of fabrics, including modest quantities of imported wares, are present. The possibility of military activity at Dymock seems to have been discounted, with the settlement regarded as entirely civilian in character (Catchpole *et al.* 2007, 235). The range of fabrics is certainly indicative of more than simple rural settlement, and it is also notable that on the basis of the excavated samples occupation does not seem to have extended beyond the 2nd century.

A probably analogous site to Dymock lay much closer to the pipeline sites, at Tewkesbury, where it is likely that a minor nucleated settlement lay on the Roman road from Worcester to Gloucester (Hannan 1993). This settlement is not well-understood, but the quantity of pottery from the small Cinema site, excavated in 1972-4 (*c* 170kg plus an indeterminate amount of samian ware) indicates a density of deposition greatly in excess of what would be typical of a rural farmstead. Unfortunately there is no record of the range of fabrics beyond Malvernian products, Severn Valley and black-burnished wares. The dominance of the assemblage by these groups is consistent with the regional picture for most sites, whether rural or nucleated, but amphorae were present in small amounts and the quantities of samian ware, although noted as 'too small to make valid statistical deductions' (Wild 1993, 49) nevertheless amounted to 'about 325 vessels' (ibid., 48), of which *c* 16% were decorated (ibid., 49). The samian ware may have formed only a small proportion of a relatively large total site assemblage, but it appears remarkable by contrast with the material from the pipeline sites.

Clearly, however, assemblage size does have implications for diversity, as the relatively large group from the Tewkesbury Bypass Site II – roughly 58kg of pottery and therefore about one third the size of Hannan's assemblage by weight, produced a slightly wider range of fabrics than seen on the pipeline sites (eg Timby 2004, 68, table 4), even though the total weight of the latter assemblages was not much less. By sherd count, fine and specialist wares amounted to 3.2% of the Bypass Site II assemblage (and 2.3% of the smaller assemblage from Bypass Site I (Timby 2004, 67, table 3). The latter figure is very close to that for Fiddington, while the former is between the overall figures for Fiddington and Bredon's Norton. As discussed above, however, it is only in the late Roman period that fine and specialist wares formed a significant part of the Bredon's Norton assemblage, probably particularly at a date after the Bypass sites had fallen out of use.

The probable nucleated settlement at Tewkesbury may not even have lasted this long, the last significant phase of activity here (period 7) being dated *c* AD 200-250 (Hannan 1993), although the illustrated pottery from this period includes an Oxford mortarium which must date after AD 240 (ibid., 61, fig. 17 no. 40). The lack of significant late Roman occupation here recalls the situation at Dymock, though this absence is based only on a very localised sample. At Worcester there is also evidence for a reduction in the scale of activity at a number of sites in the late Roman period, but while important earlier, it is notable that these all lie towards the margins of the settlement and reduction in the scale of activity here may not reflect the situation closer to the focus. The most striking characteristic of the Deansway assemblage, noted above, is the marked decline in fine and specialist wares in the late Roman period, contrary to the trend that might have been expected, and indeed seems to be indicated elsewhere in the region (not least in the relatively adjacent assemblage from 14-24 The Butts), though rarely with great clarity as the number of sites with significant late Roman assemblages is small.

In all the assemblages in the region Severn Valley ware is the great constant, only totalling less than half of all sherds in those early groups where Malvernian fabrics are particularly important, and not infrequently amounting to more than two-thirds of all the pottery. The other constant is black-burnished ware, which was omnipresent from the 2nd century onwards, even in rural contexts, albeit

rarely in large quantities. The significance of variation in these quantities from site to site is not always clear; chronological factors will have played a part, as will location in relation to the main road network (Allen and Fulford 1996), though recent work in the Upper Thames Valley suggest that there may have been additional factors related to specific site character that might have complicated distribution patterns even further (Booth forthcoming). Nevertheless, the routine presence of black-burnished ware suggests at least a low level of integration of all rural communities with trade networks that allowed access to some non-local ceramics.

Catalogue of illustrated vessels

The illustrations show a representative selection of the vessels present as well as pieces of intrinsic interest. No attempt is made to show the comprehensive range of fabric/form combinations from all three sites. The vessels are arranged as far as possible by type sequence within ware group by site phase.

Pamington

Fig. 3.1.1. Fabric G21. Barrel shaped jar ('tubby cooking pot') with slightly angled rim. Stamps beneath rim are almost crescent shaped. Context 2071.

Fig. 3.1.2. Fabric G21. Barrel shaped jar ('tubby cooking pot') with slightly angled rim. 'Duck'/S-shaped stamps beneath rim. Context 2081.

Fig. 3.1.3. Fabric G25. Jar with slightly expanded rim with horizontal and oblique grooves beneath. Diameter uncertain. Context 2086.

Fiddington

Early Roman phase

Fig. 3.1.4. Fabric O40. Medium mouthed jar with thickened outcurving rim. Context 1026.

Fig. 3.1.5. Fabric O41F. Medium mouthed jar with hooked rim. Context 1026.

Fig. 3.1.6. Fabric O40. Tankard with slightly outsloping sides, beaded rim and concave base. Context 1026, fill of ditch 1025.

Fig. 3.1.7. Fabric G21. 'Tubby cooking pot' with slightly beaded rim. Burnished on rim and shoulder and with vertical burnished lines beneath. Context 1026.

Fig. 3.1.8. Fabric R30. 'Cooking pot type' jar with outcurving rim. Context 1051.

Late Roman phase

Fig. 3.1.9. Fabric O40. Large jar with thickened hooked rim. Context 1067.

Fig. 3.1.10. Fabric B11. Bead and flanged dish, the only example of this type in black-burnished ware from any of the pipeline sites. Exterior sooting. Context 1046.

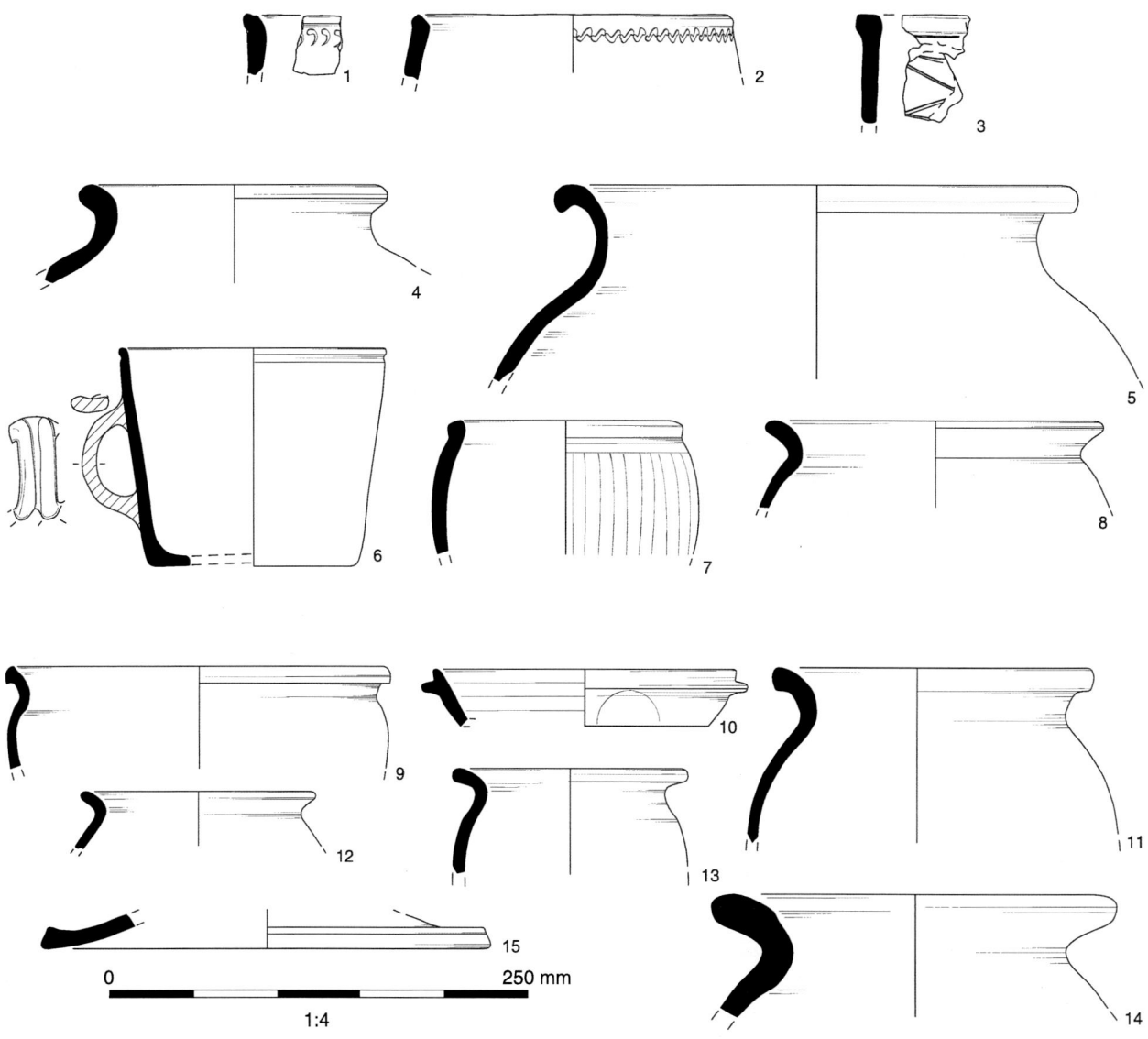

Fig. 3.1 Iron Age pottery from Pamington and early and late Roman pottery from Fiddington

Fig. 3.1.11. Fabric C11. Medium mouthed jar with thickened outcurving rim and rilled body (not shown). There is exterior sooting on the rim and burnt deposits on the internal surface of non-joining body sherds from the same vessel. Context 1157, ditch 3158.

Fig. 3.1.12. Fabric G22. 'Cooking pot type' jar with outcurving rim. Burnt. Context 1067.

Fig. 3.1.13. Fabric G22. 'Cooking pot type' jar with thickened outcurving rim. Exterior sooting. Context 1046 (late 3-4C)

Fig. 3.1.14. Fabric G22. Possible storage jar with thickened outcurving rim, burnt on exterior. It is possible that this is a fragment from the top of a prefabricated oven. Context 1068.

Fig. 3.1.15. Fabric G22. Lid with thickened, grooved rim. Context 1046.

Bredon's Norton

Late Iron Age/early Roman phase

Fig. 3.2.16. Fabric E80 (grog and sand-tempered). Carinated bowl with slightly beaded rim. Grooves at base of neck and girth and burnish on top of rim and shoulder. Context 3176.

Fig. 3.2.17. Fabric G21. Barrel shaped jar with thickened grooved rim. Stamped decoration below rim. Context 3092, pit 3091.

Fig. 3.2.18. Fabric G25. Barrel-shaped jar with expanded slightly beaded rim. Context 5071.

Early-middle Roman phase

Fig. 3.2.19. Fabric O40. Narrow mouthed jar with outcurving rim. Cordon at base of neck and overall burnish. Context 5180, ditch 5177.

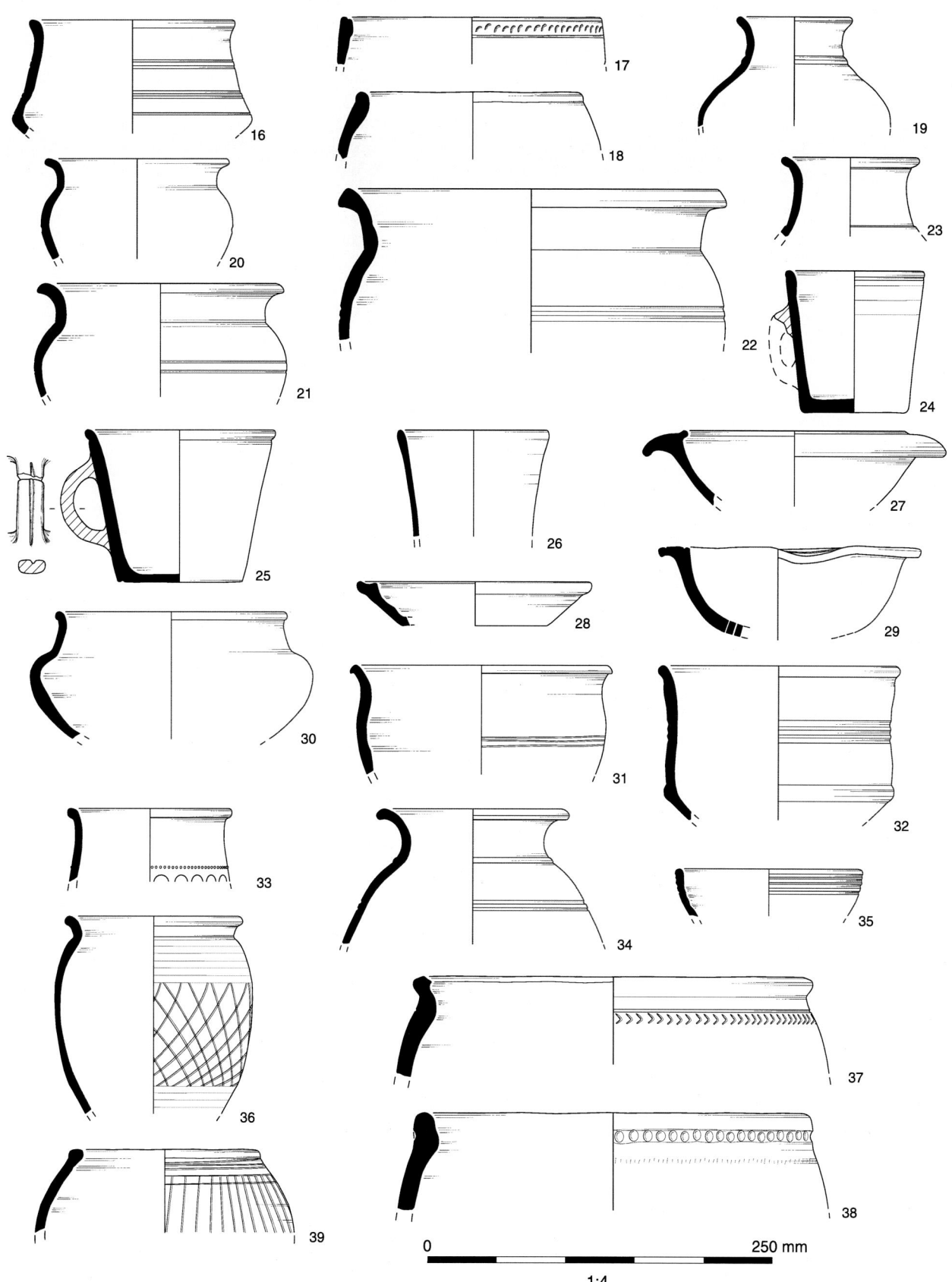

Fig. 3.2 Early and middle Roman pottery from Bredon's Norton (16-39)

Fig. 3.2.20. Fabric O40. Medium mouthed jar with outcurving rim. Grooves at base of rim and girth. Internal limescale deposit. Context 3113, ditch 3095.

Fig. 3.2.21. Fabric O40. Wide mouthed jar with thickened outcurving rim and girth grooves. Burnish on top of rim and shoulder. Context 5182.

Fig. 3.2.22. Fabric O40. Wide mouthed jar with thickened outcurving rim. Grooves at base of neck and girth. Context 5069.

Fig. 3.2.23. Fabric O40. Beaker with short angled everted rim. Context 5180.

Fig. 3.2.24. Fabric O40. Straight sided tankard with upright rim defined by groove. Burnt. Context 5009, ditch 5010.

Fig. 3.2.25. Fabric O40. Sloping-sided tankard with beaded rim and sagging base. Contexts 5275 and 5276.

Fig. 3.2.26. Fabric O40. Tankard (or possibly) carinated bowl with simple expanded rim. Context 5044, ditch 5045, group 5290.

Fig. 3.2.27. Fabric O40. Rounded bowl with slight bead above flanged rim. Context 5009.

Fig. 3.2.28. Fabric O40. Dish with recessed rim. Context 5044, ditch 5045, group 5290.

Fig. 3.2.29. Fabric O40. Colander with roughly flat-topped rim with grooves. The vessel is well-fired and the rim is distorted. Context 5180.

Fig. 3.2.30. Fabric O41. High shouldered jar with outcurving rim. Context 3146 (pit).

Fig. 3.2.31. Fabric O41F. Wide mouthed jar with outcurving rim with downturned tip. Girth grooves. Context 5180.

Fig. 3.2.32. Fabric O41F. Carinated bowl with simple bead rim. Grooves at base of neck and girth. Context 3107, ditch 3094.

Fig. 3.2.33. Fabric R10. Fine carinated bowl with thickened outcurving rim. The fragmentary barbotine decoration comprises a horizontal row of fine dots with ring(s) beneath. Context 5161, ditch 5164, group 5288.

Fig. 3.2.34. Fabric R49. Narrow mouthed jar with thickened overhanging rim. Cordon at base of neck and groove on shoulder, burnished on top of rim and shoulder. Context 3113, ditch 3095.

Fig. 3.2.35. Fabric R49. Small rounded bowl or possibly cup with simple slightly thickened rim. Context 3113, ditch 3095.

Fig. 3.2.36. Fabric B11. 'Cooking pot type' jar with outcurving rim. Burnish on top of rim and shoulder, and acute angle lattice decoration. Contexts 5086 and 5155, ditch 5088.

Fig. 3.2.37. Fabric G21. Barrel shaped jar with internally stepped rim. Stamped chevrons beneath a groove on the shoulder. Context 5050, ditch 5052, group 5292.

Fig. 3.2.38. Fabric G21. Large (diameter uncertain) ?barrel shaped jar with slightly expanded upright rim. There is a row of oval impressions beneath the rim, but these do not appear to be made with a fingertip. Context 5166, ditch 5168.

Fig. 3.2.39. Fabric G21. Barrel shaped jar with beaded rim. Irregular horizontal and vertical burnished line decoration. Contexts 5044 and 5069, ditch group 5290.

Fig. 3.3.40. Fabric G21. Tall jar, almost complete, with slightly stepped rim. Stamped decoration just below rim, and exterior sooting. Context 3159 Pit 3158, SF 3013.

Fig. 3.3.41. Fabric G21. Barrel shaped jar with thickened rim. Burnished on top of rim and shoulder, with vertical burnished line decoration below. Internal burnt deposit. Context 3112, ditch 3095.

Fig. 3.3.42. Fabric G21. Barrel shaped jar with slightly in-sloping thickened rim. Two rows of deep, irregular oval impressions just below rim. External sooting. Context 3143.

Fig. 3.3.43. Fabric G21. Barrel shaped jar with slightly in-sloping thickened rim and a line of S-shaped stamps below rim. Context 3143.

Fig. 3.3.44. Fabric G21. Barrel shaped jar with upright thickened rim. External sooting. Context 3062, ditch 3094.

Fig. 3.3.45. Fabric G21. Dish with slightly out-turned tip of sloping sides. Exterior sooting. Context 5182, ditch group 5290.

Fig. 3.3.46. Fabric G25. Jar with insloping beaded rim. Burnished overall. Context 3043.

Fig. 3.3.47. Fabric G25. Barrel shaped jar with slightly angled rim. Burnished on top of rim and shoulder, and with vertical burnished lines on the body. External sooting. Context 3062 ditch 3094, SF 3012.

Fig. 3.3.48. Fabric G25. Very large jar or 'cauldron'. Context 3162, ditches 3161 and 3163.

Fig. 3.3.49. Fabric G25. Large 'cauldron' with stepped rim. The diameter is uncertain but probably in excess of 450mm. Context 3162, ditches 3161 and 3163.

Late Roman phase

Fig. 3.3.50. Fabric F51. Base of dish, probably of Young (1977) type C45, with illiterate potter's stamp. Context 5236, ditch 5238.

Fig. 3.3.51. Fabric O40. Small carinated bowl with simple angled rim. Context 3275.

Fig. 3.3.52. Fabric O40. Large rounded bowl with outcurving rim. Context 3315.

Fig. 3.3.53. Fabric R10 with fine sand and undefined (possibly organic) voids. Straight-sided bowl with bead and flanged rim. Burnished on top of rim and shoulder, with horizontal burnished lines below. Burnt. Context 3321.

Fig. 3.3.54. Fabric B11. Straight-sided dish with simple upright rim. Burnished internally. Context 3247.

Phase LR2

Fig. 3.4.55. Fabric F51. Bowl of Young (1977) type C72. Context 3036.

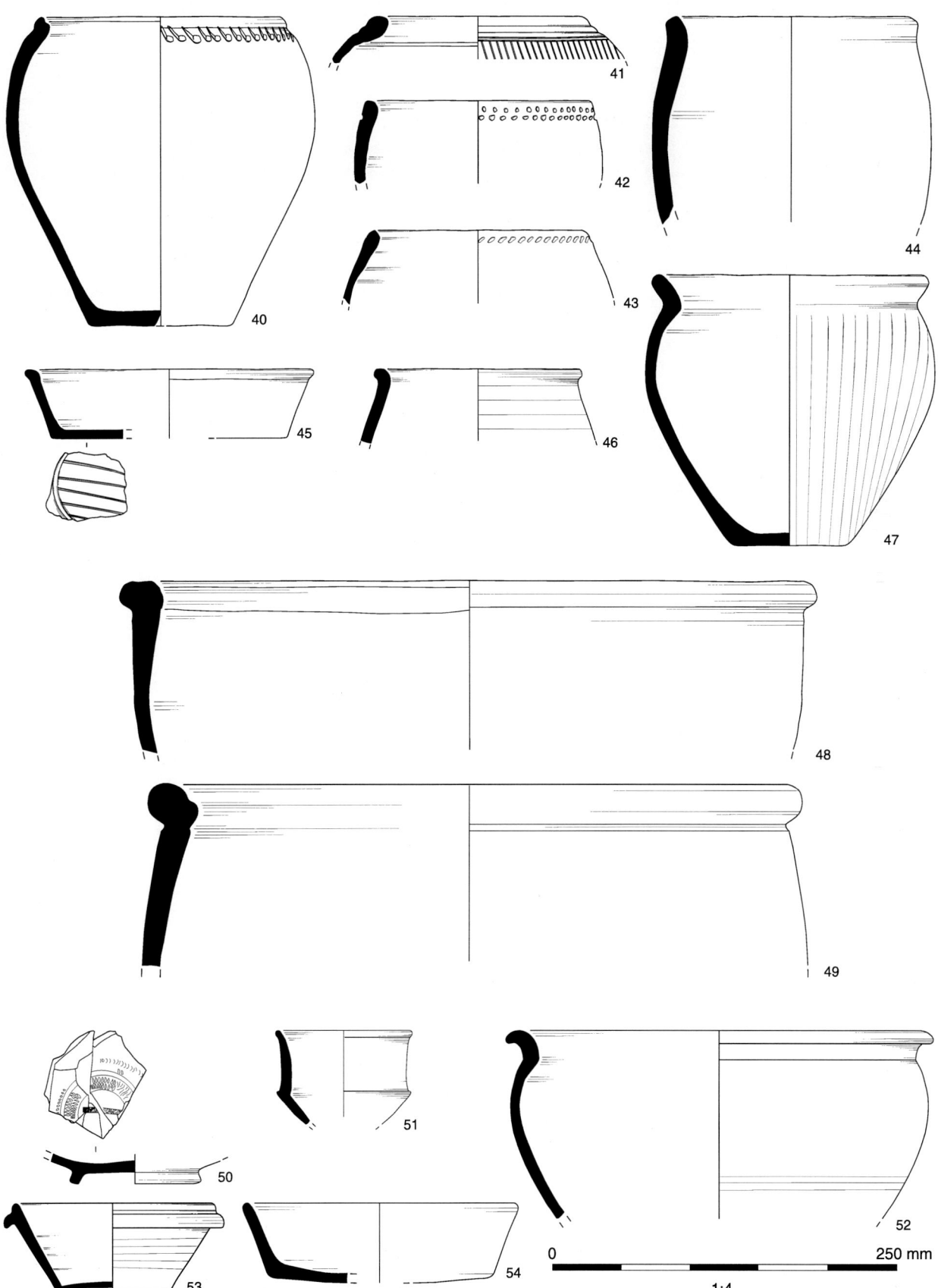

Fig. 3.3 Middle and late Roman pottery from Bredon's Norton (40-54)

Fig. 3.4.56. Fabric F51. Carinated bowl of Young (1977) type C81 with rows of rouletting. Context 3165.

Fig. 3.4.57. Fabric F51. Handled carinated bowl of Young (1977) type C85, with complex grooves on shoulder and multiple applications of demi-rosette stamps. Context 3165.

Fig. 3.4.58. Fabric M22. Mortarium of Young (1977) type M22. Context 3006.

Fig. 3.4.59. Fabric M31. Mortarium of Young 1977) type WC4. Context 3165.

Fig. 3.4.60. Fabric M41. Mortarium of Young (1977) type C100. Context 3165.

Fig. 3.4.61. Fabric M41. Mortarium of Young (1977) type C100. Context 3165.

Fig. 3.4.62. Fabric O40. Wide mouthed jar with thicked hooked rim. Burnished on shoulder. Context 3006.

Fig. 3.4.63. Fabric O40. Rounded bowl with outcurving rim. Fragmentary white paint decoration. Context 3165.

Fig. 3.4.64. Fabric O40. Rounded bowl with grooved flange rim. Context 3165.

Fig. 3.4.65. Fabric O40. Rounded bowl with simple slightly outsloping rim. Partly burnished on lower body. Context 3018.

Fig. 3.4.66. Fabric R30. 'Cooking pot type' jar with outcurving rim. Burnished on top of rim and shoulder. Context 3165.

Fig. 3.4.67. Fabric B11. Straight-sided bowl with bead and flanged rim. Burnished internally and on top of rim. Context 3165.

Fig. 3.4.68. Fabric B30. Straight sided bowl with bead and flanged rim. Burnished internally and on top of rim. Context 3165.

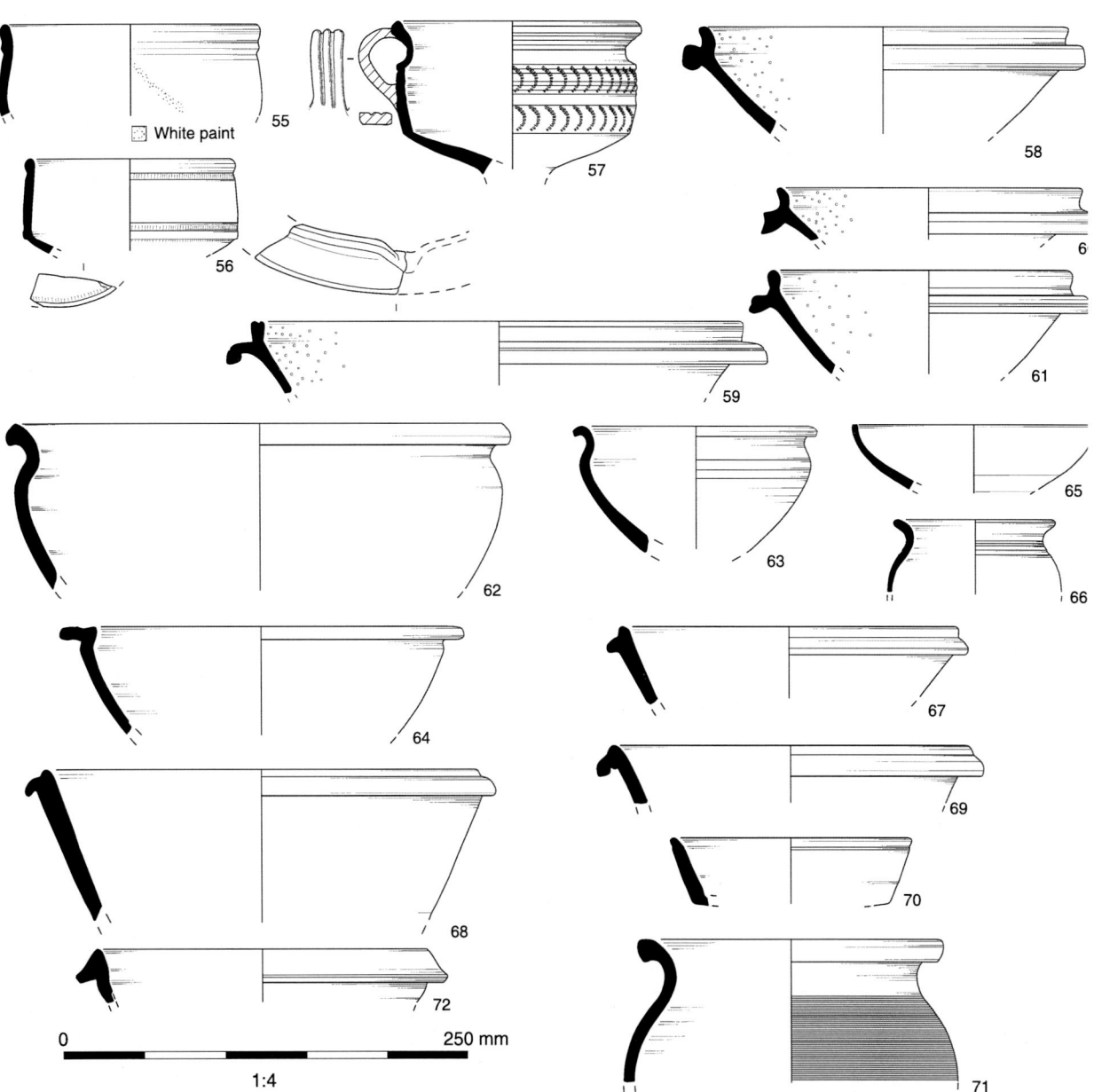

Fig. 3.4 Late Roman pottery from Bredon's Norton (55-72)

Fig. 3.4.69. Fabric B30. Straight-sided bowl with bead and flanged rim. Burnished on interior and on top of rim. Context 3006.

Fig. 3.4.70. Fabric B30. Straight sided dish, burnished internally. Context 3165.

Fig. 3.4.71. Fabric C11. Medium mouthed jar with thickened overhanging rim and rilled body. Exterior sooting. Context 3165.

Fig. 3.4.72. Fabric C11. Flanged bowl of late Roman type. Context 3189.

FIRED CLAY *by Cynthia Poole*

Area 1 – Fiddington

Introduction

A small assemblage of 64 fragments weighing 534g was recovered from the excavation at Fiddington. The material was studied in order to establish what types of structural or other material was represented, and thus to aid the interpretation of the archaeological structures from which it came. Preservation was generally poor with a mean fragment weight of 8g, though this rises to 12g if sieved samples are excluded. As a result diagnostic material formed a small proportion of the assemblage, which is interpreted as debris from domestic ovens or hearths. The assemblage has been recorded on an Excel spreadsheet that forms part of the site archive, and a summary of the quantities of fired clay by form and fabric is given in Table 3.9.

Fabrics

The fabrics were characterised on the basis of macroscopic features and inclusions visible in hand specimen and with the aid of x20 hand lens. The majority of the assemblage was made in the same sandy fabric Q. A few small fragments were assigned to a finer silty fabric A.

- Fabric Q: reddish yellow, red, brown and grey micaceous clay, sometimes laminated, containing variable quantities of medium-coarse rounded quartz sand. In some fragments there might also occur occasional coarser quartz grits 2–3 mm, red ferruginous clay or haematite grits 1-5 mm or calcareous grits/shell 1–3 mm, which are all likely to be naturally occurring in the clay. Only one example contained the void and impressions of deliberately added organic temper of fine chaff.

- Fabric A: reddish yellow, brown or grey fine silty smooth clay sometimes micaceous but containing no visible inclusions except occasionally red ferruginous/haematite grits 1-3mm. This clay is similar to the clay matrix of fabric Q.

The clay was probably sourced from locally available deposits close to or on the site, probably clay

Table 3.9 Fiddington: quantification of fired clay by form and fabric

| | | Fabric | | | |
Form		A	Q	QV	Total
Oven structure	Nos		12		12
Oven lining	Nos		1		1
Disc/plaque	Nos		15		15
TPB?	Nos			3	3
Utilised (single surface)	Nos	1	22		23
Indeterminate	Nos	4	6		10
Total	Nos	5	56	3	64
Oven structure	Wt (g)		139		139
Oven lining	Wt (g)		5		5
Disc/plaque	Wt (g)		263		263
TPB?	Wt (g)			20	20
Utilised (single surface)	Wt (g)	6	61		67
Indeterminate	Wt (g)	32	8		40
Total	Wt (g)	38	476	20	534

derived from weathering of the Charmouth mudstone formation.

Forms

Much of the fired clay was undiagnostic, having only evidence of a flat moulded surface or was otherwise amorphous. Two pieces from PH 1119 and ditch 1159 each had a single wattle or small stem impression measuring 9 and 14mm diameter on the reverse suggesting these may have formed part of a wattle supported structure, possibly the superstructure of an oven. Both examples were also noted as having the same mauvish pink colour perhaps indicating they originated from the same structure. Other pieces (ditch fills 1067, 1083), which may represent oven lining, had a flat roughly moulded surface with finger impressions and the back surface pressed over another material or surface. One piece had been pressed up against the surface of a tile suggesting it formed the internal render or bedding of a clay and tile oven. Most pieces interpreted as oven structure range from 9-26mm thick.

Oven or hearth furniture is represented by fragments from three discs or plaques from late Roman ditch fills 1021, 1046 and 1067. These took the form of flat slabs with smooth flat moulded surfaces on both sides, sometimes slightly rougher on the base, joined by a vertical flat edge with rounded angles. In some cases the edge was slightly thicker than the body of the disc creating a slightly hollowed top with shallow lip. Two of these were circular (or possibly oval): one measured 150mm diameter and 15-18mm thick and the other 380mm diameter and 19-24mm thick. The third example measured 16-21mm thick, but too little of the edge

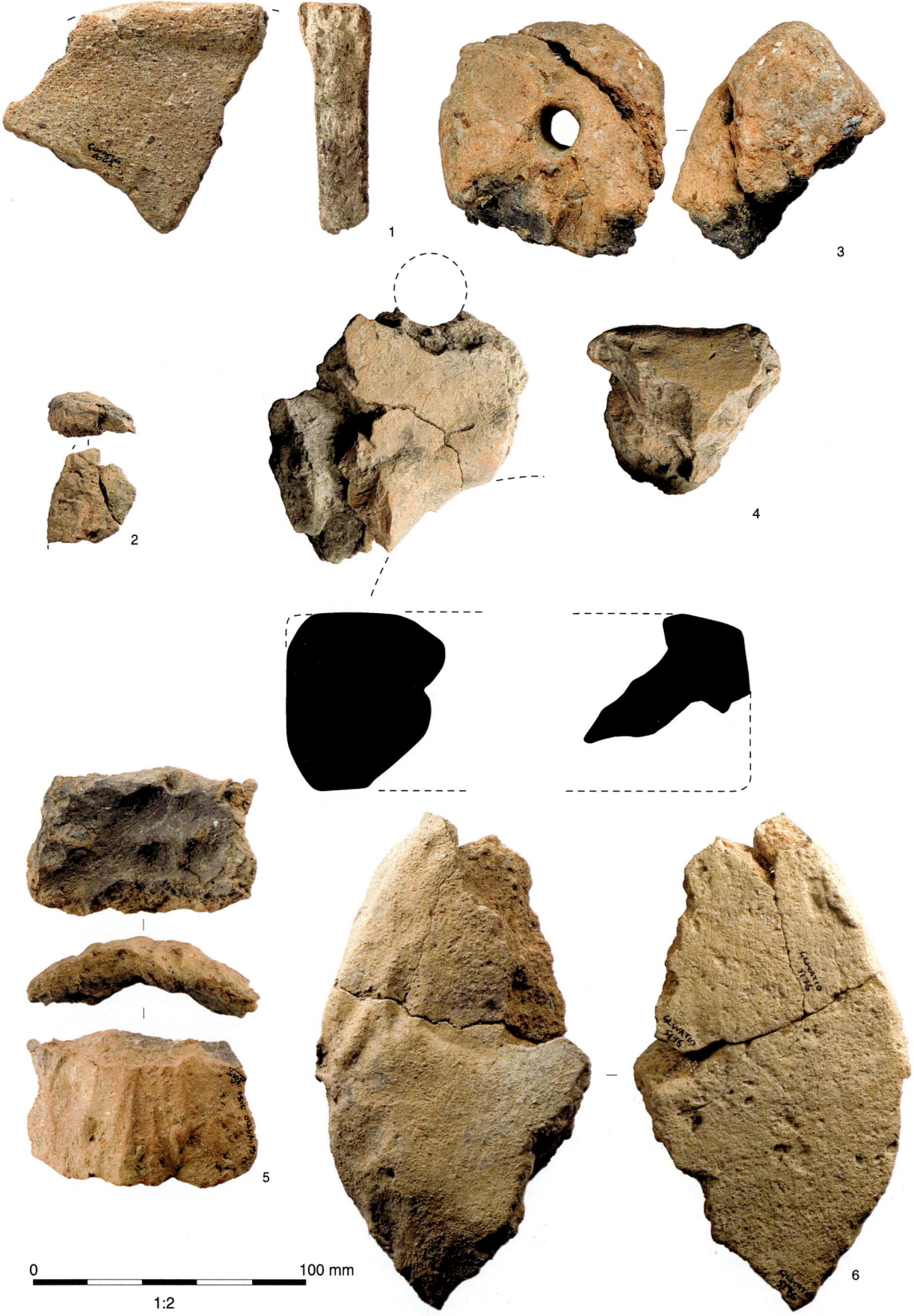

0   100 mm

1:2

Fig. 3.5 *Fired clay objects and structures*

survived to judge whether it was circular or some other shape. One had been fired to a black – greyish maroon colour on the base and another had differential firing on the base suggesting part of it was resting on a support or pedestal.

No definite supports were found, but the pieces in the chaff-tempered fabric (fill 1088 from ditch 1090) may have been the corner fragment of a triangular brick ('loomweight') though none of the diagnostic section with perforations survived to confirm the identification.

Discussion

Much fired clay is inherently undateable and is usually dependent on other dateable artefacts for its phasing. Most of the fired clay comes from contexts containing 2nd to 4th century Roman pottery, whilst some are associated with Iron Age or 1st century AD material. Oven structure – walls and lining produce little variation from one period to another, whilst some clue to function may be provided by intensity of firing. The main diagnostic pieces are the oven or hearth furniture. The clay discs are more typical of the later Iron Age and Roman period, and here belong to the later Roman period, whilst the triangular brick is typically Iron Age but is regularly found in Roman contexts, especially of the 1st – early 2nd centuries. Both items would appear to represent the continuation of native traditions in relation to the use of ovens and hearths.

Several of the contexts producing fired clay (1067, 1083, 1088, 1118, 1143) also contained charcoal and burnt debris suggesting that these were deposits of cinders raked out of ovens or hearths and included clay fragments broken from the structure or broken and discarded furniture. The general character and intensity of firing of the fired clay assemblage suggests that this represents structures for domestic use for cooking or baking, or for small scale crop processing.

Catalogue of illustrations

Fig. 3.5.1. Disc: edge fragment from circular disc. Surfaces are flat, smooth and well finished, joining to a very slightly curved vertical edge. The plaque thickens at the edge, resulting in a shallow lip to the upper surface. Differential firing on the base may indicate it was partly resting on a pedestal or support. Diameter: 380mm; thickness: 19-24mm. Wt: 159g. Fabric: Q. Late Roman. Ctx: 1067, ditch 1069.

Area 2 – Pamington: the structural fired clay

Introduction and objectives

A small assemblage of 95 fragments weighing 678g was recovered from the excavations at Pamington, all from ditch fills, in particular the enclosure ditches 2015 and 2077, except one small fragment from a shallow pit. The material was studied to

Table 3.10 Pamington: quantification of fired clay by form and fabric

Form		Fabric				
		A	AV	Q	QV	Total
Oven structure	Nos			15		15
Plaque	Nos		4	37		41
TPB	Nos			3		3
Utilised (single surface)	Nos			25		25
Vessel	Nos		1			1
Indeterminate	Nos	3			7	10
Total	Nos	3	5	80	7	95
Oven structure	Wt (g)			89		89
Plaque	Wt (g)		18	169		187
TPB	Wt (g)			223		223
Utilised (single surface)	Wt (g)			103		103
Vessel	Wt (g)		26			26
Indeterminate	Wt (g)	17			33	50
Total	Wt (g)	17	44	584	33	678

characterise it and help determine the use of the enclosures in whose ditches it was found. The poor preservation reflected in a mean fragment weight of 7g suggests the fired clay had been subject to breakage and attrition on floor surfaces or in middens for example, prior to deposition in the ditches. The fired clay comprises predominantly oven and hearth furniture and structure with a limited number of identifiable forms represented. The assemblage has been recorded on an Excel spread sheet that forms part of the site archive, and a summary of the quantities of fired clay by form and fabric is given in Table 3.10.

Fabrics

The fabrics were characterised on the basis of macroscopic characteristics and inclusions visible with the aid of x20 hand lens. The majority of the assemblage was made in the same sandy fabric Q with a small quantity assigned to a finer silty fabric A.

- Fabric Q: the fabric occurred in various shades and combinations of reddish yellow, red, brown and grey. The clay, sometimes laminated, contained variable quantities of medium-coarse rounded quartz sand and in some examples coarser stone and sandstone grits 2–18mm, red ferruginous/haematite grits 1–5 mm, shell fragments or rounded cream clay pellets 5–8mm. Most of the sparser inclusions are likely to be naturally occurring in the clay

- Fabric A: red, reddish yellow or brown fine silty smooth dense clay, but containing no visible inclusions except occasionally red ferruginous/haematite grits 1–5mm or sparse quartz sand. This clay is similar to the matrix of fabric Q.

A small quantity of both fabric types contained added organic temper (QV and AV) in the form of fine chaff inclusions surviving as voids and impressions. The clay was probably obtained from a local source, the most likely being clay weathered from the Charmouth mudstone formation, which forms the geological bedrock across the locality (British Geological Survey http://mapapps.bgs.ac.uk/geologyofbritain/home.html).

Forms

Diagnostic pieces and forms are poorly represented. Structural material included a small quantity of lining or repairs to oven walls. These had a single smooth moulded surface, a rougher opposite face, lentoid, wedge or lunate section and were up to 15mm thick. Thicker pieces with a flat or curving surface occasionally with finger marks and *c* 20–40mm thick are also likely to derive from oven walls or bases. Some of the thin flat slabs may have formed small plaques for use as oven furniture, but it is difficult to differentiate such objects from slabs of lining material.

Evidence of oven furniture is limited. An angular corner of a triangular perforated brick had even surfaces and was pierced by two perforations 16 mm in diameter. The two perforations start so close together that they are off-set in the side face. One is set 30mm from the corner and if the other is the same from the opposite corner, it suggests this was a fairly small example of triangular brick perhaps 90–100 mm or less long. It measured 74 mm thick. Triangular perforated bricks are a well known form of Iron Age-early Roman date. Though traditionally interpreted as loomweights, an association with oven debris was noted at Danebury, Hampshire (Poole 1995), and more recently evidence has been found for their use as pedestals in salt working on the Isle of Thanet, Kent (Poole 2015) and in association with pottery production in Essex (Poole 2010). They were probably multifunctional, being used as pedestals, oven or kiln lining (Lowther 1935) and possibly as hearth floors.

A fragment of flat slab 20–23mm thick with smooth moulded surfaces with fine striations from wiping may be part of a disc with thickened edge and lip. Discs of this form, somewhat more complete, have been found at Fiddington and Bredon's Norton.

Discussion

The fired clay derived from ditch contexts of Iron Age or early Roman date. The character of the assemblage and the few diagnostic pieces are consistent with such a date. The material is similar to the other fired clay assemblages from the project and is likely to derive from domestic activities of cooking or possibly small scale crop processing.

Catalogue of illustrations

Fig. 3.5.2. Oven lining: This piece has rough surfaces with one face smoother and undulating and a roughly moulded edge. This may have formed part of a small plaque for use in an oven, but is more probably a slab of inner render lining the oven superstructure. Thickness: 13mm; width: >35mm. Wt: 18g. Fabric: AV. Undated. Ctx: 2016, enclosure ditch 2015.

Fig. 3.5.3. Triangular perforated brick: Angular corner fragment with even surfaces and pierced laterally by two perforations 16 mm diameter. The two perforations start so close together that they are off-set. One is 30 mm from the corner and if the other is the same from the opposite corner, it suggests the brick was a fairly small example probably no more than 90-100 mm long. Length: >75mm; thickness: 74mm. Wt: 223g. Fabric: Q. IA-ERB. Ctx: 2088, enclosure ditch 2077.

Area 3 – Bredon's Norton: The structural fired clay

Introduction

This site produced the largest assemblage of fired clay amounting to a modest 197 fragments weighing 2.2kg. The material was studied to characterise the types of structure or object represented, and thus to assist in establishing the range of functions carried out on the site over time. Preservation was somewhat better than at the sites of Pamington and Fiddinton with an overall mean fragment weight (MFW) of 11g, which rises to a much higher MFW of 31.5g if sieved samples are excluded. By comparison with the other sites diagnostic material formed a higher proportion of the assemblage and included a wider range of forms. The assemblage has been recorded on an Excel spreadsheet that forms part of the site archive, and a summary of the quantities of fired clay by form and fabric is given in Table 3.11

Fabrics

The fabrics were characterised on the basis of macroscopic features and inclusions visible with the aid of x20 hand lens. The majority of the assemblage was made in the same sandy fabric Q with a small quantity assigned to a finer silty fabric A. A number of very small fragments from samples were not assigned to a fabric.

- Fabric Q: the fabric occurred in various shades and combinations of reddish yellow, red, pinkish red, brown, occasionally with black or grey core. The clay was generally micaceous

Table 3.11 Bredon's Norton: quantification of fired clay by form and fabric

Form		A	AV	Q	QC	QV	U	Total
Oven lining	Nos	80						80
	Wt (g)	484						484
Oven str	Nos		1	10		1		12
	Wt (g)		12	185		13		210
Oven/hearth floor	Nos	4		1				5
	Wt (g)	18		13				31
Oven cover	Nos			2				2
	Wt (g)			488				488
Oven furniture	Nos		1	1		1		3
	Wt (g)		14	78		22		114
Discs	Nos	1		9				10
	Wt (g)	37		507				544
TPB	Nos					1		1
	Wt (g)					15		15
Utilised	Nos	2		23		2	20	47
	Wt (g)	59		61		31	85	236
Indet	Nos	2	2	5	3		25	37
	Wt (g)	2	3	35	13		25	78
	Total Nos	89	4	51	3	5	45	197
	Total Wt (g)	600	29	1367	13	81	110	2200

and sometimes laminated with cream streaks. It contained variable quantities of medium-coarse rounded quartz sand and in some examples red ferruginous clay pellets 1–5 mm, mudstone, limestone and other rock grits. Three records also contained fine inclusions of chaff, broken straw or fine monocot stems.

- Fabric A: red, reddish yellow or brown fine silty smooth dense clay, but containing no visible inclusions except occasionally red ferruginous/haematite grits 1–5mm or sparse quartz sand. This clay is similar to the matrix of fabric Q. Two examples also contained deliberate additions of moderate-high density of fine-medium chaff inclusions surviving as voids and impressions.

The fabrics are essentially the same as those found at Fiddington and Pamington reflecting the same geology and clay deposits accessible to all three sites. All three sites produced a few fragments with a pinkish mauve or cherry tinge which is sometimes associated with salt production, but there is no reason in this location to link this to salt working and it may reflect minerals occurring naturally within the clay.

The forms

The fired clay forms can be divided into oven/hearth structure and furniture. The main elements of oven structure found were wall lining and oven cover. Oven lining was distinguished by a single moulded surface with clear finger marks pressed into the surface and a back that appears to have been daubed over another surface, probably the sides of the construction cut. Clay lining (3008) with typical smoothed outer surface with finger impressions and back bonding face was found lying face down across the base of a small pit 3003. Other fragments with a smooth moulded surface, but no other features are also likely to be oven wall surface or lining. One piece (context 3177) had a smooth flat moulded surface fired pale whitish grey, which is typical of hearth floor. Fragments with surface fired or burnt black (context 3216) are more likely to be the floor or lower wall surface of ovens.

A piece from ditch 3169 (3170) with a wedge shaped depression in the surface and finger marks on the opposite side may be part of an oven wall. The wedge shaped depression appears to have been made with the end of a pointed bladed implement. Similar impressions were found on fired clay at Cotswold Community in the upper Thames valley (Poole 2010, 139-40), where it was suggested they may be remains of decorated hearth or oven cover, though it may be a type of keying in preparation for a further surface of clay.

An example of oven cover from ditch 3095 (context 3113) in area 3a took the form of a flat plate pierced by a flue of 140mm diameter and one perforation 25mm diameter set 75mm from the flue. This type of oven cover is a distinctive known form, usually of Iron Age date, so may be residual as the ditch is dated to the 2nd century AD. This form consists of a flat or domed plate with a central circular hole *c* 150mm diameter encircled by 12-15 smaller perforations 15-25mm diameter (Cunliffe and Poole 1991, 149). Most comparable examples occur in Wessex, though a similar form has also been found in Essex at Orsett 'Cock' (Carter 1998). These plates probably formed the tops of cooking stoves, the large hole holding a pot whilst the small holes acted as vents to allow smoke to escape and maintain a flow of air through the fire.

Oven furniture included fragments of discs or small plates, a possible firebar and triangular perforated brick. The firebar fragment has a linear form and was made from a slab of clay 17mm thick curved into an almost semi-circular cross-section *c* 100-120mm wide, of unknown length of which only 50mm survives. It has longitudinal finger marks down the exterior surface and finger tip depressions on the interior surface. It was found in pit 3158, dated to the late Iron Age. A small fragment similar in character found in layer 3121 in ditch 3120, also of late Iron Age date, may derive from a second object of this form.

Parts of four discs or small plates were found in two features of 2nd century or later date. Three were from the boundary ditch 5173 (layer 5176) and one from a robber trench 3297. They took the form of a circular or oval disc usually with one smooth flat or slightly concave surface and one convex surface with a slightly rougher finish. The edges had either a vertical flat profile or rounded. One small fragment appeared to have a straight edge rather than curved suggesting it may be of rectangular or polygonal form. The fragments represent a range of plate sizes, which are summarised in Table 3.12. All were made in fabric Q, except one in fabric A. One had been burnt black or sooted on the edge and underside.

An oblong hand squeezed lump was found in a 4th century rubble layer (3088). It measured 30 by 25mm wide and over 46mm long and may have served as some sort of support within an oven. A fragment from the fill (5166) of an Iron Age ditch 5168=5151 may be part of a triangular perforated brick: all that survived was a small area of smooth concave surface which may be part of the perforation.

Discussion

This site produced the largest collection of fired clay from this group of sites. Most was found in contexts of Roman date (ranging from 1st to 4th century),

with a small number dated to the Iron Age, and the character of the fired clay is consistent with this. The majority of the fired clay was found discarded in ditches, with small quantities in gullies, postholes and pits. Spatially there were two main concentrations. In the southern area fired clay was concentrated in the vicinity of the curvilinear late Iron Age/early Roman enclosure 3150 and the Roman building 3184 immediately to its south. The second concentration was in the northern area in the corner of the rectangular enclosure defined by ditches 5288 and 5291/2.

One burnt structure, heavily truncated corndryer 5225, lay at the north-west extremity of the site. It produced only a few small fragments of clay lining, recovered from a sieved sample. A second feature that may have been a burnt structure lay at the opposite extreme of the site to the south of the Roman building 3184. This was a small circular pit 3003 measuring 0.55m in diameter, 0.25m deep with vertical sides and a flat bottom. It had a layer of clay lining (3008) across the base, which was lying face down, so must have either collapsed from part of the superstructure or been dumped from elsewhere. It was overlain by a thick layer of blue grey clay (3007), which could represent the outer unfired cladding of an oven structure. This in turn was covered by a further layer of clay flecked with charcoal (3004) and containing small pebbles up to 30mm size. Finally a pot base sat on the surface, interpreted on site as the truncated remains of a cremation, though the deposits are not typical of cremation burials. It is difficult to envisage how the clay lining may have been used in relation to the pit itself in the absence of any remaining *in situ* or other burning or structure, suggesting that this group of material represents some sort of structured deposit.

The oven cover found in ditch 3095, though similar to Iron Age pieces in its design, is thicker than Iron Age examples, and the lack of abrasion suggest there is no reason to dispute its use being contemporary with the 2nd century ditch in which it was found. The circular flat discs were all found in 2nd century contexts, indicating that this form, which first appears in the Iron Age, continued well into the Roman period. Examples were also found at Fiddington and Pamington, which with the Bredon's Norton examples represent some of the

Table 3.12 Bredon's Norton: Forms and sizes of fired clay discs or plates

Context	Shape	Thickness	Diameter/Size	Surface 1	Surface 2	Edge	Illustration
F3297 (3298)	Circular	19-22mm	*c* 360mm	Smooth flat	-	Flat vertical with rounded angles	
Ditch 5173 (5176)	Circular	18-26mm	240mm	Smooth flat	Convex, regular	Rounded	No.6
Ditch 5173 (5176)	Circular/oval	23mm+	550mm	Smooth concave	Convex, regular	Rounded	
Ditch 5173 (5176)	Rectangular/polygonal	17-19mm	>47mm	Smooth concave	Flat, even	Flat vertical with rounded angles	

most westerly examples of this form. Discs are consistently found along the Thames valley to the east, usually in late Iron Age or early Roman contexts, with examples from Watkins Farm (Allen 1990), Gravelly Guy (Barclay and Wait 2004, 384) and the Wittenhams (Poole 2010b, 166), as well further to the north and east at sites such as Stagsden, Bedforshire (Gentil and Slowikowski 2000, 92 and fig. 56).

The firebar, found in the pit (3158) at the centre of the curvilinear enclosure, is of an unusual form, either representing a local tradition or more likely an isolated one-off example. Wrapping clay around wattles to form firebars is known from both Roman (Swan 1984) and Saxon kilns (Musty 1984, 52) but in this case the piece was formed as a hollow tube and may have had some other structural use. Although some of the items are on occasions associated with artisan activities such as pottery production, there is no evidence to suggest that the assemblage represents anything more than domestic ovens or hearths, for cooking and heating, or possibly small scale crop processing for domestic needs.

Catalogue of illustrated items

Fig. 3.5.4. Oven cover: Two pieces from a thick flat or domed plate with part of circular vent 140mm diameter and pierced by a cylindrical perforation 25mm diameter centred 70mm from the vent edge, probably originally one of several encircling the vent. One surface is smooth and flat (?upper) and the other more irregular and undulating, though little survived. The vent edge was curving and rounded. The second piece has part of a flat smooth surface and undulating straight edge, joined by curving angle. It is similar in character to the vented piece suggesting it formed the outer edge of the cover indicating a rectangular shape. Thickness: 57-61mm; width: >75mm, length: >100mm. Wt: 488g. Fabric Q. IA. Ctx: 3113, ditch 3095.

Fig. 3.5.5. Firebar: Linear object with curved profile, probably semi-circular, rather than cylindrical with longitudinal finger grooves running along exterior convex surface and fingertip depressions on the interior from pressing into the clay. Thickness: 17mm; diameter: 120mm (interior *c* 80mm);

length: >50mm. Wt: 78g. Fabric Q. IA-RB Ctx: 3159, pit 3158.

Fig. 3.5.6. Disc: Approximately a quarter of a circular disc. One side is hand moulded, smooth and flat and the opposite face convex, but flat in centre pressed on a flat work surface curving up with evidence of finger marks from moulding to a narrow rounded edge. Thickness: 18-26mm diameter: 240mm. Wt: 397g. Fabric Q. Date: LIA-ERB Phase: M-LRB Ctx: 5176, enclosure ditch 5173.

CERAMIC BUILDING MATERIAL *by Leigh Allen*

Introduction

A total of 860 fragments of ceramic building material weighing 129624g was recovered from the three excavation areas along the route of the Gloucester Water Pipeline, Security of Supply (the assemblage is quantified in Table 3.13). Area 1 (Fiddington) and Area 2 (Pamington) produced only small quantities of tile, 833g and 166g respectively. The material from these areas was studied to determine the types of material and chronological periods represented. The site at Bredon's Norton (Area 3) produced the bulk of the assemblage, a total of 128625g of ceramic building material. The site was divided for excavation into two parts, south (3A) and north (3B). Only 57 fragments weighing 2980g came from the northern area (contexts from 5000 onwards), the remaining 125645g came from the southern area (contexts 3000-3399) mainly from contexts associated with the demolition of sunken-floored room 3184.

The material from this site was studied to establish the types of building material present, the proportions of different types represented and thus the character of the buildings from which they came, the sources of the materials and to examine changes in these over time, and how this might inform the development of the building and other structures on the site. It was also hoped to provide information for comparison with other Roman buildings in the region.

The majority of the ceramic building material assemblage (54%) comprises fragments of tile associated with a hypocaust system. These include

Table 3.13 All tile by form

Function	Tile type	Weight (g)	% by weight	Frag. count	% by frag. count
Roofing tile	*Imbrex* and *tegula*	9357	7.2%	49	5.7%
Hypocaust tiles	Box tile (*tubuli*)	35157	27.1%	277	32.2%
	Bessalis for *pilae*	35458	27.3%	104	12%
Flooring tiles	Large floor tile	35954	27.7%	58	6.7%
	Tesserae	243	0.18%	8	0.93%
Undiagnostic	Undiagnostic flat fragments	6508	5.02%	28	3.2%
	Misc/unknown	6947	5.3%	337	39.2%
Total		129,624	100%	860	100%

fragments from flat square tiles, bessalis, that were built up in stacks (*pilae*) to support the floor under which hot air flowed, and fragments from box tiles (tubuli) that would have carried warm air up and around the walls. Also recovered in large numbers were fragments from floor tiles (*pedalis* and *sesquipedalis*) that could have been used either as base bricks for pilae columns or to cap off the pilae forming a suspended floor (*suspensura*). The assemblage includes very few fragments of roofing material.

The condition of the assemblage is poor; the mean fragment weight is 150g, which is low for ceramic building material. There are only four examples of complete tiles, all *bessalis*, in the retained assemblage, although a further nine complete examples were recorded *in situ* but were not removed from site. There are a small number of tiles (59 fragments weighing 18477g) that have a single surviving intact dimension (other than thickness), in particular *tubuli*, which have most commonly been broken at the edges of a face, leaving a measurable fragment from the front, back or side panels.

The assemblage has been fully recorded on an Access database. Forms have been identified with reference to Brodribb 1987, and the fabrics have been characterised using a hand lens with x20 magnification, and on occasion with the aid of a microscope at x25 magnification.

Tile forms

The small assemblages from the excavations at Pamington and Fiddington contain very few fragments that are identifiable to form. At Fiddington a single fragment from a brick (fabric 3) is the only identifiable piece. The fragment has a thickness of 39mm and is probably from a pedalis, used as a capping or base tile for *pilae*. At Pamington the bulk of the fragments are again unidentifiable with the exception of two *imbrex* fragments recovered from modern topsoil. With these exceptions, all of the material described and discussed below is from Bredon's Norton.

Roofing tile

A total of 49 fragments of roofing material weighing 9357g was recovered from the excavations. This relatively small quantity consists almost entirely of fragments from imbrices; there were only four fragments from *tegulae* present in the assemblage. This is almost certainly because the original building/s had a stone roof (see Shaffrey Chapter 3) but possibly with ceramic tiles (imbrices) forming the ridge. The majority of the *imbrex* fragments have a thickness of between 15mm-19mm with fragments most commonly measuring 15mm-16mm. Only one context (3190) produced fragments that could be reconstructed to form a complete profile. This imbrex has a width measuring 161mm and a height of 82mm (external dimensions).

Tiles associated with a hypocaust system

Tubuli

A total of 277 fragments of *tubuli* weighing 35157g were recovered, and two distinct types are present in the assemblage. The first (56% of the total fragments) is a thin-walled form (*c* 11mm-15mm thick) made from a soft pinky/orange fabric (fabric 6). It has plain side panels that measure *c* 80mm in width (Fig. 3.6.1-2) and decorated (keyed) front and back panels *c* 140mm wide (Fig. 3.6.4-5). Only one surviving example has a complete length, and this measures *c* 293mm (Fig. 3.6.4). The outside corners of the *tubuli* are rounded but are more sharply angled on the inside. The vents in the side panels measure *c* 90mm in length and are *c* 30mm wide, often with knife cuts at the corners (Fig. 3.6.1-3). There are no complete examples surviving in the assemblage and in most cases the *tubuli* have broken at or near the corners. One further feature is that there is commonly a thickening of the walls at the base of the tile on the inside; sometimes this is quite crude, where the clay has been roughly pushed up or folded, in others it is a neat sub-rounded step (Fig. 3.6). This may have been formed when the *tubuli* were standing drying or in the kiln.

The second form of tubulus is a more robust, thicker-walled type (*c* 20-21mm thick) made from fabric 8, a harder-fired orange/red fabric. There are no examples in the assemblage of a complete width or length for this form.

Bessalis

A total of 104 fragments weighing 35458g possibly belonging to this type were recovered from site, including 4 complete examples. These small, plain, square tiles appear to vary very slightly in size; the complete examples measure between 170mm square and 192mm square, and are between *c* 24mm and 29mm thick (Fig. 3.6.7).

Five stacks of *bessalis* forming pillars (*pilae*) were recorded on site and were left *in situ*. The recorded dimensions roughly conform to the sizes recorded above, ranging from 170mm to 200mm square with a thickness of *c* 30mm. The predominant fabrics used for bessalis tiles were fabrics 12 and 13.

Large tiles/bricks

A total of 58 fragments from large floor tiles, that is fragments with a thickness of 35mm or more, and weighing 35954g, were recovered from the site. No complete examples were recorded in the retained assemblage, but the presence of some quite sizeable fragments indicate that a range of larger tile sizes was being used (e.g. Fig. 3.6.8).

Pedalis

A number of fragments have measurable thicknesses of between 35mm and 47mm and are probably from *pedalis* tiles. This type of tile was used as a capping or base tile for *pilae* and generally measures *c* 296mm square (equivalent to a Roman

Fig. 3.6 Ceramic building material: box flue tiles and their patterns, bessalis *and* sesquipedalis

123

pes or foot). Two examples recorded on site at the base of two pilae measured almost exactly 296mm square and had thicknesses of 35mm. One of these *in situ* examples has a simple key for plaster, consisting of sets of wide shallow grooves (finger width) running diagonally from corner to corner forming a cross on the upper face of the tile. This type of keying is seen on many of the *pedalis* fragments in the retained assemblage. The predominant fabric for this type of tile was fabric 3, a distinctive buff-coloured fabric that has a black core.

Sesquipedalis

A small number of fragments have a measurable thickness of 50mm or more, and these include one of the largest fragments recovered from site, measuring at least 350mm by more than 370mm (Fig. 3.6.8). This could be a fragment from a sesquipedalis, a type of tile used as a base for *pilae* or for flooring, equivalent to one and half Roman feet square (443mm). The predominant fabric is again fabric 3.

Tesserae

Six tile *tesserae* were recovered from the site, all roughly 20mm x 22mm.

Fabrics

Only those fragments with a measurable thickness, and therefore potentially identifiable to form, have had their fabric type recorded. There are 4 main fabric types:

Fabric 3 – a distinctive fabric with dull pink/buff surfaces and a heavy grey core. The fabric is soft but well fired. Inclusions are ill-sorted, set in a clean, compact and micaeous clay matrix. Abundant angular grains of light orange or light grey grog dominate, while limestone, quartz and dark red-brown or black iron rich grains are normally present with occasional fragments of flint (Fig.3.7.2 detail). I am grateful to Paul Booth (OA) for identifying this fabric as identical to pink-grogged ware, a fabric used for pottery manufacture and originating from Buckinghamshire. At Bredon's Norton this fabric is exclusively used to produce large floor tiles, pedalis and sesquipedalis.

Fabric 6 – a buff/pinky orange fabric with soft sandy feel. The inclusions are sparse set in a clean, well-mixed micaeous clay matrix. Very occasional quartz, grog and dark red-brown or black iron-rich grains are normally present. This fabric is almost exclusively used for the thin-walled type of box tile.

Fabric 8 – an orange/red fabric smooth to the touch and with frequent quartz and occasional dark red-brown or black iron-rich grains. Harder fired than fabric 6, this fabric is mainly used to make the thicker type of box tile.

Fabric 12/13 – having orange/red surfaces with a

Fig. 3.7 Ceramic building material: detail of grain impressions and of fabric 3

grey core, this fabric is hard-fired and has a hackly fracture. The clay matrix is micaceous with occasional quartz, dark red-brown or black iron-rich grains and limestone inclusions. At Bredon's Norton this fabric is used to make bessalis tiles.

Markings

The only deliberate markings found on the tiles were keying for plaster on tubuli and finger-applied signatures on the bessalis and the larger bricks. No tally marks, stamps or graffiti were seen. Accidentally-made marks are also rare; there are for instance no animal prints, and only one fragment that has finger-tip indentations in it where the tile was handled while the clay was still soft.

Keying

A total of 168 fragments of *tubuli* (23397g) have a key for plaster on them. In all cases the design was made using a comb; no examples of roller-printed relief patterns were seen. In most cases the fragments are too small to determine the full combed design to which they belong. There are however 52 fragments (11122g) that display enough of the key to classify the design.

Eight different combed designs were identified, six of which (designs 1, 3, 6, 7, 9 and 11) include a cross or crosses, with or without a frame and with horizontal or vertical bands. The other two patterns are a figure-of-eight within a frame (design 12, see Fig. 3.6.5) and overlapping semi-circles in a frame (design 5). All of these designs were recorded on *tubuli* made from fabric 6, but only designs 1, 6 and 7 appear on *tubuli* made from fabric 8.

Signatures

Only one design, the very simplest, was found on the *bessalis* and bricks. It consists of a band of 4 shallow finger-width grooves running from corner to corner, forming a simple cross. This form of signature was recorded on 31 fragments of *bessalis* (13015g) and 11 brick fragments (19634g).

Scoring

Two fairly thick fragments from *tubuli* (context 3165) have deeply-scored grooves across them, probably incised with a knife (Fig. 3.6.6). The straight grooves are in a lattice pattern producing rectangles. Scoring is much less common than combing, and cannot have provided a very good grip for keying; less sophisticated and efficient than combing, it might have been an earlier practice before the comb was developed (Brodribb 1987, 109).

Accidental marks

There are 3 fragments, all from context 3165, including the complete keyed face of a *tubulus* (Fig. 3.6.4), that have numerous small indentations in the clay made while it was still soft. In all three cases the indentations are over the key. It is possible that these are marks from the hobnails in the sole of a shoe where someone has stepped on the soft clay while it was drying.

There are two examples (context 3165) where the mark of the edge of a tile is impressed into the keying on another, where tiles rested against each other before firing.

Two fragments from the side panels of *tubuli* (contexts 3014 and 3164) have misshapen bases that appear to have been squashed, perhaps as a result of being dropped before firing (Fig. 3.6.8). Preserved in this squashed edge are the impressions of chaff from spelt wheat (Fig. 3.7.1), which must have been lying on the floor where the tile fell. I am grateful to Kath Hunter for the identification of the grain impressions.

Discussion

Source of the tiles

The fabric used for the larger floor tiles found in the hypocaust at Bredon's Norton is equivalent to the Roman pottery pink grogged ware fabric (Booth and Green 1989). This fabric, for which a source at Stowe in Buckinghamshire has been found (Taylor 2004), has a distribution that reaches almost as far as the Severn, but in very small quantities. The main focus of distribution of the pottery seems to have been to the north-west, probably up Watling Street, and thence to the valleys of the upper Ouse, Nene and Avon. Although outside the main distribution, a wider variety of wares is found in the Avon valley than elsewhere in the outer (peripheral) zone of distribution (ibid., 63). This may also have been the route by which the tiles were transported, although Booth now believes that the distribution is as likely to have been by road from Stowe to Alchester, and thence by road to Alcester and the surrounding area (Booth pers. comm.).

The date and distribution of ceramic building material of this fabric has not been studied in detail, but is known at a number of sites in the outer zone of the pottery distribution. At Dorchester-on-Thames, at Alchester and at Alcester, it has always been found in 4th century contexts (Booth pers. comm.), and thus appears to represent a late development of the use of this material.

The use of tile

Other than noting the presence of tile at Pamington and Fiddington, no further discussion of the material from these sites is possible. At Bredon's Norton, the bulk of the tile was recovered from contexts 3164 and 3165, rubble deposits associated with the secondary infilling and levelling of the Roman building south of sunken room 3184. The total quantity of tile recovered from these deposits is 110766g (628 fragments) constituting 85% of the total tile recovered from Bredon's Norton. The assemblage from the building comprises almost equal quantities of fragments (by weight) of *tubuli* (27.7%), *bessalis* tiles (29.7%) and larger bricks (28.4%), with only 4.9% being from roofing material (*imbrex* and *tegula* fragments).

It is evident that we are looking at the remains of a heated room; the five extant *pilae* stacks and the large quantity of hypocaust tiles are clear evidence of this. The *pilae* stacks found *in situ* indicate how the floor of the hypocaust was constructed. In two cases a large tile (*pedalis*) was placed on a mortar-rich levelling layer (3265) that had been used as surfacing for pitched stone surface 3322 (Plate 3.1). Smaller *bessalis* tiles were stacked up on top of the *pedalis*; *pilae* 3250 and 3278 each have three *bessalis* tiles still in place and in addition the top tile has a ring of mortar in the centre that is almost exactly the same dimensions as the base of a *tubulus* or box flue tile (140mm x 80mm). This suggests that the *pilae* were originally constructed from a combination of *pedales*, *bessales* and a *tubulus*. Another *pedalis* would probably have been placed on the top of the *tubulus* to form the capping tile and then an even larger tile or brick used to bridge the gap between the *pilae* and form the suspended floor. Three other *pilae* (3334,

Plate 3.1 Pilae *stack 3278 showing mortar where box flue tiles were attached above, north to left*

3335 and 3336) found to the east of 3250 each consist of two *bessales*, but they are not resting on a base tile. This would have made the *pilae* very unstable, and they are therefore probably part of stacks that were disturbed during the demolition of the hypocaust.

There are numerous examples in Britain of *pilae* being constructed from types of tile other than *bessalis*, and there are at least 15 sites (Brodribb 1987,

94) where *tubuli* have been used. At the villa at Darenth in Kent the floor of room 6 (section A) is constructed from 34 flue tiles with a large tile at the base and at the top. Although *tubuli* used in this way are often found filled with mortar (Brodribb 1987, 94), Payne writes that the *tubuli* (at Darenth) were filled with clay, pieces of chalk and tile to give them greater stability (Payne 1897, 54) and the accompanying photograph (Plate 3.2) shows the *tubuli* as being hollow. At Bredon's Norton none of the *tubulus* fragments had traces of mortar on the inside (although plenty survives on the external surfaces) and the ring of mortar on the tiles of the extant *pilae* would further suggest that the *tubuli* were not filled with mortar but could well have been packed with fragments of tile.

In his book *De Architectura*, Vitruvius states that in the building of hypocausts the *pilae* are to stand 2 feet (592mm) high (Brodribb 1987, 89-90), but the heights of *pilae* in extant hypocausts across Britain and beyond vary greatly. It all depends upon the thickness of the tiles used, the number of tiles in the pilae and the thickness of the mortar in between. The surviving pilae bases at Bredon's Norton measure *c* 150mm high, and with *tubuli* on top (293mm) and another *pedalis* on top of those the height would have been *c* 493mm, or a little under 2 Roman feet.

The presence of two *pilae* bases 3250 and 3278 *in situ* and in the same alignment means that we can attempt to calculate the size of the tiles that were being used to form the floor and bridge the gap between the stacks. The distance between the centre

Plate 3.2 Black and white photo showing box flue tiles uses as pilae *at Darenth (Payne 1897)*

of the mortar rings on the two uppermost *bessalis* is *c* 750mm. This however is too wide for any one type of Roman tile to span, as even the largest *bipedales* only tend to measure up to 610mm (Brodribb 1987, 42-43). Therefore there would probably have been another *pilae* situated between 3250 and 3278, halving the distance to be spanned to *c* 375mm, This is a little small for a sesquipedalis, which generally measure 1.5 Roman feet (444mm), but examples have been found (for example at Shakenoak, Oxfordshire) with dimensions as small as 350mm (Brodribb 1987, 41). The largest surviving fragment of a possible *sesquipedalis* from Bredon's Norton does not have any complete dimensions, but its surviving width and length (at least 350mm by at least 370mm) would fit with the hypothesis that these tiles were used for the floor of the heated room.

The *tubuli* would have been mortared vertically to the wall to form a continuous battery of flue tiles across the whole width and height of the wall. A room with an average ceiling height of 8ft (2.4m) would require a stack of 9 *tubuli* to reach from floor to ceiling (assuming all were round about 293mm, the length of the only complete example recovered), and allowing for half of a *tubulus* below the floor level so that the hot air can enter it from the hypocaust. Although no complete *tubuli* were recovered from the site we do have one complete face that allows us to estimate the total weight of one of these types of tile to be *c* 2500g. This would mean that the total assemblage of *tubuli* fragments recovered from the site are only equivalent to 14 complete tiles, or less than 1.5 stacks … a very small proportion of the total number of tiles required to furnish a room. This indicates that tile, as well as stone, was very extensively robbed from this building for reuse elsewhere.

PAINTED WALL PLASTER *by Edward Biddulph*

Location

Over 300 fragments of painted wall plaster were recovered from the site. All pieces were associated with structure 3184, a sunken-floored room with a limestone flag floor and cistern dated to the late Roman period. Wall plaster was recorded as fragments collected mainly from the surface of a charcoal-rich deposit (3227) that overlay the floor surface, and abutted the edge of wall 3012. In places there were still traces of mortar and plaster adhering *in situ* to the interior face of wall 3012, but most of the plaster comprised large and smaller slabs (labelled as plates during excavation and lifted in these units) either separated from wall 3012 but lying against it, or fallen face-down on top of the burnt deposit (layer 3013).

Objectives of the analysis

The material was studied to investigate the range of colours and designs present, whether these came from one or more phases of decoration, and where within Room 3184 these might have been found. It was also hoped that this would help establish the function of this room, and provide information for comparison with decorative schemes used in other Roman buildings in Roman Britain.

Construction

The large fallen slabs comprised three layers of mortar behind the painted surface (Plate 3.3). The background colour was applied to a relatively fine mortar layer (*intonaco* – Mora *et al.* 1984, 10) up to 20mm thick. This had been applied to two layers of thicker, coarser, mortar (*arriccio*), the layer behind the fine mortar layer being deep red and up to 80mm thick and comprising frequent amounts of sand, pebbles and rounded chalk/limestone fragments, with elongated voids from burnt-out organic material, and behind this in turn, a layer of mortar of similar thickness, but of medium coarseness. The back of this last layer often carried the impressions of wattle rods to which the mortar was fixed. Many fragments of mortar had broken along the join between the fine and coarse layers of mortar.

Paint colours and designs

The painted surfaces of many pieces were burnt or covered with charcoal. A range of colours was nevertheless recorded. These included light and dark grey, white, red, orange, cream or light yellow, and turquoise. Most pieces were white (or cream), suggesting that the walls were predominantly this colour. Borders or frames of panels are suggested by stripes of various colours. A plaster fragment from context 3251 was decorated with a red stripe *c* 50 mm thick on a white ground (Fig. 3.8.2). A red stripe was also seen on a fragment of plaster recorded *in situ* on wall 3012 (Plate 2.29). Grey stripes were also painted on white walls (Fig. 3.8.1). A group of joining pieces

Plate 3.3 Larger fragments of fallen wall plaster showing three layers of mortar

0   250 mm

1:4

0   100 mm

1:2

Fig. 3.8 Painted plaster

Discussion

The evidence suggests that the walls of structure 3184, or at least wall 3012 where the fragments were concentrated, were painted white or cream. The walls were divided into panels, whose frames were painted in red, orange or grey. A red or grey border or dado may also have been applied as broader stripes to the lower part of the walls; indeed, given its position close to the floor of the room, the red stripe shown in Plate 2.29 may well have been below the putative dado, possibly to form part of a series of low red-framed rectangular panels, as at Carisbrooke, Isle of Wight (Liversidge 1969, plate 4.3). There is a hint of the use of curvilinear, possibly floral, motifs. This basic scheme, though undoubtedly a simplification given the condition of the material, is likely to have been replicated widely across Roman Britain. Similar designs have been recorded at, for example, the legionary baths at Exeter (Bidwell 1979, 157-8) and Northfleet villa, Kent

was decorated with a grey stripe *c* 5 mm thick and a series of narrower lines that may have been applied with a comb or other toothed implement, although it is possible that these narrower lines were an accidental result of a finishing technique (Fig. 3.8.5). A piece from charcoal layer 3013 showed a grey stripe on a white ground (Fig. 3.8.1). Turquoise was used to cover areas of the wall or to outline a panel (Fig. 3.8.4). A curvilinear pattern, apparently using orange paint on a white ground, was seen on a piece from context 3330 (Fig. 3.8.3).

Table 3.14 Coin finds from Fiddington (Site 1) and Bredon's Norton (Site 3)

SF	Ctxt	Denomination	Est date	Rev	Mint	Obv
1002	1160	Antoninianus 19mm	286-293	PAX AUG ?		....CARAU]SIUS PF AUG
3001	5001	AE3 15mm	335-337	GLORIA EXERCITUS 1 standard	?TRS Trier	]IUNNOBC
3003	5001	AE2 18mm	351-353	VICTORIAE DD NN AUG ET CAE	?	DN MAGNEN] TIUS PFAUG
3017	5001	Antoninianus? 13-15mm	270-296	standing figure		radiate head r

(Biddulph 2011, fig. 139.3). Other examples have been found preserved *in situ* in rooms of the Roman villas at Witcombe, Gloucestershire, and Iwerne, Dorset, which comprised white walls and panels and borders marked by yellow, red, green, or grey stripes. The walls were otherwise plain, except for traces of a green leaf design recorded between the panels at Iwerne and a black candelabra motif between the panels at Witcombe (Liversidge 1969, 130, 143). Possible curvilinear motifs on plaster from structure 3184 may have been similarly placed. In addition, the room's turquoise pieces recall the blue panels framed by red stripes also recorded at Witcombe (Liversidge 1969, 146).

The simplicity and ubiquity of the decorative scheme do not suggest an obvious function for the room, although the range of colours and overall scheme hints at a public or social use. Nor does the evidence point to any specific school or centre of wall-painting tradition. However, urban centres such as Cirencester may well have accommodated guilds concerned with wall painting on similar lines to, say, the guild of craftsmen recorded on the Cogidubnus inscription from Chichester (RIB 91).

Catalogue of illustrated plaster

Fig. 3.8.1. Piece with grey stripe on white background, burnt layer 3013
Fig. 3.8.2. Red stripe on white background, context 3251
Fig. 3.8.3. Fragment with traces of orange paint on white background. Part of a slab of plaster (context 3330) within burnt layer 3013.
Fig. 3.8.4. Fragment with turquoise and yellow paint. Part of a slab of plaster (context 3330) within burnt layer 3013.
Fig. 3.8.5. Piece with combed pattern of thin grey stripes on white background. Part of a slab of plaster (context 3330) within burnt layer 3013.

ROMAN COINS *by Paul Booth*

Four late Roman copper alloy coins were recovered during the excavations, one from Fiddington and three, all unstratified, from Bredon's Norton. They are listed below in Table 3.14.

The Fiddington coin, of Carausius, is stratified in fill 1160 of ditch 1159, and is associated with pottery of late 3rd-4th century date. The coins from Bredon's Norton include a further antoninianus, almost certainly irregular and therefore not closely dated within the later 3rd century. The other two

coins, of AD 335–337 and 351–353, are typical 4th century issues consistent with other dating evidence for the later part of the occupation sequence of the site. As such they are unremarkable; the general absence of later Roman coinage at this site is more notable in view of the relatively high status character of the structures.

METAL FINDS *by Ian R Scott*

Introduction and methodology

The metal finds assemblage comprises 409 objects (485 fragments). Hereafter fragments will be abbreviated to frags; where the number of fragments is equivalent to the number of objects, it will not be repeated. There are 388 iron objects (418 frags), 18 copper alloy objects (42 frags) and 3 lead objects.

The provenance and descriptions of the finds have been recorded onto a database and where possible they have been identified and assigned to a broad functional group. Undiagnostic items are only quantified as fragments and not as objects. The finds from each site are treated separately.

Site assemblages

Site 1: Fiddington (Table 3.15)

The finds assemblage from Fiddington comprises 185 objects (189 frags) (4 copper alloy, 181 iron objects). Most of the finds are from contexts with spot dates within the Roman period. There are 11 finds from topsoil 1001 with post-medieval spot dating and 1 find from earlier ploughsoil 1002. The finds from topsoil 1001 comprise a small medieval copper alloy buckle and a copper alloy button of post-medieval date, a large horseshoe and a horseshoe nail, 3 links of an iron chain, 2 structural items, including a bolt with nut and washer, 2 nails and 2 miscellaneous fragments. There is a small iron fitting of uncertain purpose from ploughsoil 1002.

The finds from Roman contexts number 172 (176 frags). These finds include 162 hobnails (164 frags), all but one of which came from adjacent ditches in the central part of the site. Ditch 1023, probably of 2nd century date, contained 110 hobnails in fill 1046, and ditch 1020, dated to the 4th century, another 51, 50 (52 fragments) from the lower fill 1022 and 1 from 1021, the upper fill. Those in ditch 1023 clearly came from a boot discarded into the ditch. A single hobnail was also recovered from 1070, the fill of another 4th century ditch 1071. Other finds from Roman contexts comprise 8 nails (10 fragments), a small strip of iron (context 1051) and a small circular copper alloy object with a lip and 2 small pierced lugs (context 1043) (Cat. No.1). The function of this late object is uncertain; it came from the intersection of ditch 1020 with later furrow 1042, and it may be post-Roman.

Ref	Die axis	Condition	Comment
	12	W/W	in fragments
as LRBCI, 88	12	W/VW	damaged, ?irregular
	6	W/W	?irregular
	12	VW/VW	irregular, corroded

Table 3.15 Fiddington small finds: summary quantification by Context and Function, sorted by Spot Date

Spot Date	Context	Transport	Hobnails	Personal	Function Security	Structural	Nails	Misc	Query	Total
2C	1021		1				1			2
	1022		50							50
2C+	1166						+			+
Late 3rd	1160						+			+
4C	1046		110							110
4C	1051						5	1		6
4C	1070		1							1
4C	1100						1			1
RB?	1043						1		1	2
EAS?	1052						1			1
PMED	1001	2		2	1	2	2	2		11
PMED?	1002								1	1
Total		2	162	2	1	2	11	3	2	185

+ Nail stems only present. RB – Roman, EAS – Early Anglo-Saxon, PMED – post-medieval

Table 3.16 Bredon's Norton south (Area 3A) other metal finds: Summary quantification by Context and Function, sorted by Spot Date

Date	Context	Tool	Hobnails	Personal	Function Binding	Nails	Misc	Query	Undiagnostic	Totals
MIA	3301	1								1
RB	3276					4				4
1C	3163					3				3
1-2C	3271			1						1
2C?	3097					1				1
2C+	3068					2				2
	3298					2				2
3-4C	3188					2				2
	3332		4	1		2	1	2	*	10
240+	3019					13				13
	3040			1		2				3
270-400	3018					6				6
	3035						1			1
	3321				1					1
4C	3006			1		12	1			14
	3032					2		1		3
	3036					15				15
350+	3165					12	2	1		15
	3013					49			*	49
	3190					5	1			6
	3220					9				9
	3237					18	2		*	20
	3340						1			1
	3189					16				16
?	3049					+				+
Total		1	4	4	1	175	8	5	0	198

+ Nail stems only present; * undiagnostic small metal fragments present;
Query – object unidentified MIA – Middle Iron Age, RB – Romano-British, 1C – first century AD

Catalogue

Fig. 3.9.1 **Circular object with lip on one face**, 2 small pieced lugs on one edge. At least 2 rivets or pins on side or face with the lipped edge. Cu alloy. 19mm x 18mm. Ctx 1043. [Inv No. 111] Function and date uncertain.

Fiddington

0   50 mm

1:1

Site 2: Pamington

There are only 2 small finds from this area, a tapering iron spike or punch from ploughsoil 2001, and a possible fragment from a cast iron vessel from context 2040. The latter context also produced a single sherd of pottery. The cast iron is post-medieval or modern.

Site 3: Bredon's Norton

Southern area – site 3A

The finds assemblage from Site 3 comprises 198 objects (11 copper alloy and 187 iron objects) (Table 3.16). Most of the finds are from contexts with later Roman spot dates, or with no pottery dating, and comprise nails, presumably derived from the Roman building uncovered at the south end of the site.

Bredon's North Site 3A

Bredon's North Site 3B

Fig. 3.9 Metal, glass and worked bone objects

Nails

The bulk of the iron finds (175 in number) comprise nails, 113 of which are complete or very nearly complete and have been measured. Details can be found in the site archive. Most of the nails were recovered from contexts 3013 (n = 49), 3237 (n = 18), 3189 (n = 16), 3036 (n = 15), 3019 (n = 13), 3165 (n = 12) and 3006 (n = 12). Most of the nails from contexts 3013, 3189, 3036 and 3019 and many from context 3165 were complete, but only three each from contexts 3237 and 3006. All were simple wood nails with flat very nearly circular or oval heads (Manning Type 1; 1985, 134-35, fig. 32). They range in length from 26mm to 117mm, but most fall between 40mm and 86mm in length. The average length is 63.55mm. Contexts 3019 (av. = 65.9mm) and 3165 (av. = 64.57mm) have similar average lengths. The nails from context 3036 range in length from 40mm to 56mm and the average length is

48.33mm, while the average from context 3276 is 52.5mm. By contrast the average length of nails from contexts 3189 (av. = 71.6mm) and 3190 (av. = 74mm) is over 70mm. The average for all 113 measured nails from Bredon's Norton is 62.18mm.

The predominance of smaller nails between 40mm and 80-85mm is reflected in the nails found in a timber-lined pit in the *fabrica* at Inchtuthil, Perthshire. The pit contained 10 tons of nails, and the overall total of nails recovered is calculated to be at least 875, 428 (Manning 1986, 289). The nails ranged in length from 38mm (1½ ins) to 372mm (14 5/8 ins). The overwhelming majority of the nails (n = 848968 or 96.98%) measured 100mm (4 ins) or less,

Fig. 3.10 X-ray of iron saw fragment

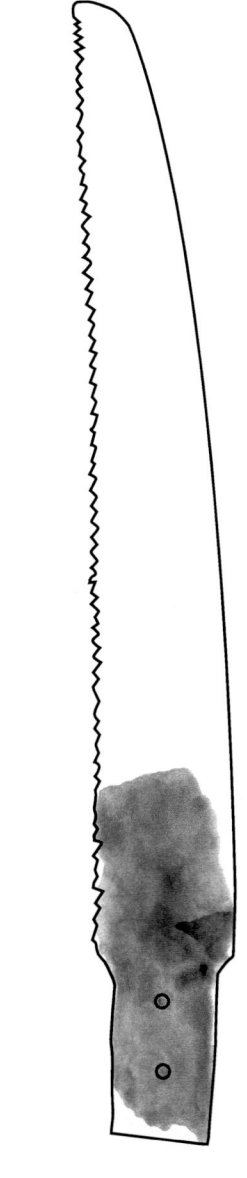

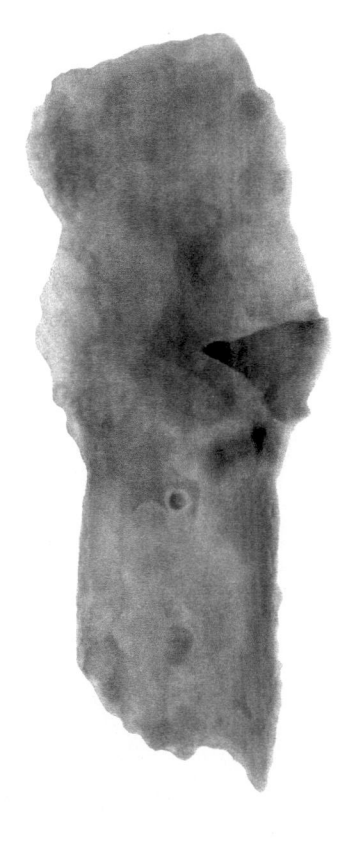

0   50 mm

1:1

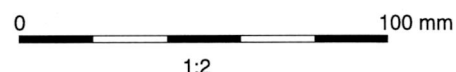

0   100 mm

1:2

and most were less than 70mm (2 ¾ ins) long (ibid., table xvii).

More locally, some 255 complete Type 1 nails were recovered, mainly from contexts of 3rd- and 4th-century date, from the excavation of a Roman building and associated settlement at Alfred's Castle. Most of the nails fell within the size range 30mm to 70mm (Scott in Gosden and Lock 2013, 113). At Frocester Court in Gloucestershire, 815 nails were found, a few being large Manning Type 1a nails, but the vast majority (768) of Manning Type 1b. Around half (359) were complete, and the most commonly used lengths ranged between 40-80mm (Price 2000, 77-81 and Fig. 3.7).

Other iron objects

The iron handle and part of the blade of a tool, probably a saw, was found with a middle Iron Age crouched burial (SF 3020, context 3301, Fig. 3.10.1). Bone from the skeleton gave a radiocarbon date range of 360-110 cal BC (SUERC-49694; 2167 ± 30 BP). Other iron finds include a small iron bow brooch with a hinged pin (sf 3019, context 3271; Fig. 3.9.2) of later 1st century AD date. The brooch was associated with 1st to 2nd century Roman pottery.

Copper alloy

Copper alloy finds include a piece of a pair of copper alloy tweezers of Roman type (SF 3034, context 3040, Fig. 3.9.3). There is also a small strip of copper alloy which might have been a fragment from another pair of tweezers (SF 3051, context 3165). Other copper alloy finds comprise a piece of copper alloy edge binding (context 3321), a post-medieval shanked button (context 3006) and 4 other miscellaneous fragments, and 5 objects of uncertain identification.

Context 3332, which was the fill of a shallow feature (context 3333) formed by the removal of flagstones from the floor of the sunken room 3184, produced fragments of a copper alloy pin or needle, a fragment of copper alloy ring or buckle frame and a fragment of part-melted copper alloy. The latter was provisionally identified as a fragment of a finger ring, but it is almost certainly nothing more

than a small curved fragment of melted copper alloy. Context 3332 also produced 4 hobnails; it also contained 3 sherds of late Roman thin-walled vessel glass and a small bead (see glass report).

Catalogue

Fig. 3.9 2 **T-shaped or Dolphin brooch probably with a hinged pin**. The bow is plain and the wings are also probably plain. Only part of the catchplate survives. Fe. L: 43mm; W: 19mm. Ctx 3271, SF 3019.
The form of T-shaped hinged pin brooch with plain wings probably dates to the 2nd half of the 1st century AD (Mackreth 2011, 88; see also ibid., pl. 58, nos 12074, 2238 and 2235).

Fig. 3.10. 1 **Possible saw blade fragment,** comprising incomplete plate tang with two rivets or pins, and incomplete blade. Blade is wider than tang and slightly angled. The preservation is not good and absence of visible teeth may be due to corrosion. With mineral preserved wood grain. Fe. L extant: 100mm; W: *c* 40mm. Ctx 3301, SF 3020. Skeleton radiocarbon-dated to 360-110 cal BC (SUERC-49694; 2167 ± 30 BP).
There is an example of a similar saw from Puddlehill, Beds, which was almost certainly from a middle Iron context (Darbyshire 1995, vol. 2, 169, fig. 60, L4; generally see ibid., vol 1, 407-53; vol.2, 167-200, figs 59-65). The best-preserved saw, complete with its wooden handle, comes from the Glastonbury Lake village, Somerset (Bullied and Gray 1917, 371, pl. lx, I53; see also pl lxi, I1 and I52). Another complete saw blade was recovered with a hoard of ironwork and other finds from a pit at Cadbury Castle, Somerset (Barrett et al. 2000, 62, 83,fig. 38,no. 3). There are similar saws from Danebury, Hants (Sellwood 1984, 351, fig. 7.11, no. 2.42; Cunliffe and Poole 1991, 342, fig. 7.12, 2.39-41). The latter come from contexts of Danebury ceramic period 7, currently dated to c 300 to 100 BC, and so of the same date range as the Bredon's Norton example. Other examples come from the hill forts of Hunsbury, Northants (Dryden 1885, 60, pl. vi, 16-7) and Hambledon Hill, Dorset (Manning 1985, 19-21, pl. 9, B21). The example found closest to the site is that from Bredon Hill, Glos. (Hencken 1938, 78, fig. 9, 1),

Table 3.17 Bredon's Norton north (Area 3B) metal finds: Summary quantification by Context and Function, sorted by Spot Date

Date	Context	Tool	Hobnails	Personal	Household	Binding	Nails	Misc	Waste	Total
					Function					
RB	5249						1			1
2C	5295		4				6			10
2C?	5180						1			1
mid 2C+	5176			1						1
240+	5247						1			1
?	5014					1				1
?	5256						2			2
Post-medieval	5001	1			1		1	3	2	8
	Total	1	4	1	1	1	12	3	2	25

where a saw was found at the tail of the outer rampart, but the construction of the outer rampart was dated (albeit on rather inexact grounds) to the very late Iron Age, rather than the middle Iron Age.

Fig. 3.9.3 **Tweezers fragment**, comprising one arm and the spring. Undecorated. Cu alloy. L: 40mm. Ctx 3040, SF 3034.

Northern area – Site 3B

In contrast to the southern area, there are only 24 metal small finds (3 copper alloy, 18 iron and 3 lead objects) from Site 3B. The copper alloy objects comprise an electrical connector (modern) and ring thimble of late medieval/early post-medieval date, both from ploughsoil 5001, and a fragment of edge binding from context 5014. The 3 lead finds comprise 2 pieces of melted lead waste and a thick piece of lead sheet with cut marks, all from the ploughsoil 5001. The ironwork comprises 12 nails, 4 hobnails and 2 pieces of iron strip, whose provenance, type and date are summarised in Table 3.17.

Six of the nails come from cremation 5295, and may indicate that this individual was buried in or with a box.

GLASS *by Ian Scott*

Introduction

A total of 16 sherds were recovered from the pipeline, comprising 13 sherds of vessel glass, one bead and 2 sherds that cannot be certainly identified to purpose. Perhaps surprisingly there is no window glass. The glass comes from all three sites, but only from the southern part of Bredon's Norton (area 3A). The glass from Fiddington and Pamington is all of post-medieval or modern date, and comes from plough furrows, ploughsoil or topsoil so is not reported upon in detail here.

Bredon's Norton South – Site 3A

The glass comprises 4 sherds of vessel glass and a bead. The vessel glass is all thin-walled and is colourless with a hint of yellow or green, but the sherds are too small to identify a form. It is probably of late Roman date. Three vessel sherds and the bead are from deposit 3332, which filled the space formed by the removal of flagstones from the floor of sunken room 3184. This context also produced a small assemblage of metal finds. The other vessel sherd is from context 3036, a demolition deposit within room 3184.

Catalogue

Fig. 3.9.4 **Glass bead**, bun-shaped with slightly off centre hole in translucent blue green glass. D: 7.2mm, L: 6mm. Ctx 3332, SF 3055

WORKED BONE *by Ian R Scott*

Only two worked bone objects were found in the excavations, both from Bredon's Norton. The bone objects are a fragment of a decorated bone handle and a dog tooth with hole drilled through the centre. Presumably the latter was suspended from a cord or formed part of necklace. It comes from context 5176 in the top of enclosure ditch 5292 and was associated with 2nd-century and later pottery. The decorated handle plate is from context 5044, a recut of the same enclosure, and associated with later 2nd-century pottery.

Catalogue

Fig. 3.9.5 **Dog tooth pendant or amulet**. Dog (or wolf) canine, pierced for suspension. Tooth. L: 46mm. Ctx 5176.
    Dog tooth pendants or amulets were found in the excavations on the Glastonbury lake village (Bulleid and Gray 1917, 480-85 and fig.158) and at Gravelly Guy, Oxfordshire an example was recovered from an early Iron Age pit (2118) with a disarticulated infant burial (Lambrick and Allen, 2004, 251, 341, 386, fig. 8.14, sf 630). They have also been recovered from Roman sites and contexts. There are examples of pierced dog canines from South Shields (Allason-Jones and Miket, 1984, 300-301, no. 6.3), from grave 278 in the Butts Road cemetery, Colchester (Crummy 1983, 51, fig. 54, no. 1803), and from grave 450 in the Lankhills cemetery, Winchester (Clarke, 1979, 296-97, and fig. 100, G450, nos 611-612). The Lankhills grave contained two pierced teeth and was dated to very late 4th century or very early 5th century (loc. cit.). The Butts Road grave 278, which dates no later than the early 4th century, contained a purse holding seven amuletic objects, including the canine tooth.

Fig. 3.9.6 **Bone handle plate**, decorated but incomplete. The handle plate is wider at one end. The narrower end is squared off end with rounded corners. It is decorated with 2 incised transverse panels of cross hatching and crosses. There is evidence of hatching along each edge of the plate. The decoration appears to be worn. The handle was fixed by at least two rivets. Bone. L: 71mm; W: 31mm. Ctx 5044, fill of N-S ditch 5045, 3rd phase of enclosure.
    The handle plate fragment comes from a knife with a plate tang. The decoration on the handle comprising transverse panels of lattice or cross hatch decoration and incised crosses is typical. See for example handle plates from Augst -Augusta Raurica, Switzerland (Deschler-Erb and Gostenčnik, 2008, fig. 10, nos 5-9), from Salzburg (Lang 2011, fig. 2) and from London (Manning 1985, 17-20, 22, and pls. 53-54, Q17Q20 and Q22) and Tokenhouse Yard, London (Wheeler 1930, 78, fig. 19, no. 1). One of the commoner knife forms associated with decorated bone handle plates has a downturned blade and often a handle terminating in a loop or ring (Deschler-Erb and Gostenčnik, 2008, fig. 10, no. 6; Manning 1985, loc. cit.). The blades are variants of Manning's Type 7 (Manning 1985, op. cit, 111-113, and fig. 28). Manning

suggested that the blade form is an early type and that smaller examples may be razors (op. cit., 112).

THE WORKED STONE *by Ruth Shaffrey*

Introduction

A small assemblage of stone totalling 71 items was recovered from the three excavations. These are reported upon site by site below. The material was studied to characterise the types of material present, whether structural stonework or stone objects, to provide information on the geographical distribution of materials utilised at the site, and to investigate whether this changed over time. The building materials from the Roman building at Bredon's Norton were also examined to help determine the materials from which it was constructed, roofed and decorated, and to provide information on the place of the building within the range of Roman villas from the region.

Pamington

A single probable saddle quern is the only object of worked stone from Pamington (2042). It is of a neat 'formed' variety with base that has been pecked into shape. The grinding surface was also pecked but is now concave and worn smooth. The stone is a medium to coarse grained feldspathic sandstone, probably Old Red Sandstone. As saddle querns from nearby sites such as Conderton Camp were mainly made from May Hill Sandstone or Old Red Sandstone (Thomas 2005 and Roe pers comm), this is in keeping with sources for the region in this period.

Catalogue

Saddle quern fragment, shaped (not illustrated). Medium to coarse grained sandstone with frequent feldspar, probably Old Red Sandstone. Concave pecked and smoothed grinding surface and pecked lower surface. Measures >190mm wide x >180mm long x 65mm thick. Ctx 2042.

Fiddington

Seven pieces of worked stone were retained during excavations at Fiddington. These comprise one rotary quern fragment, one hone and some structural stone. The rotary quern fragment (1045) is small and of indeterminate form, but is made from probable Old Red Sandstone, a typical quern material during the Roman period in this region. The hone is a smallish chunk of probable Old Red Sandstone that has been used for sharpening, resulting in two deep grooves (1022). It may have originated as roofing, although it is very thick.

The structural stone comprises three blocks of oolitic limestone, each with a worn face (1160). They are without obvious tool marks but were presumably employed as building stone. Another fragment of oolitic limestone is a fragment of roofing that may have been reused, possibly as a weight or lid as

it appears to have been deliberately modified into a generally circular shape (1001). Discs like this were also found at Bredon's Norton and are discussed further there. One further limestone slab has a worn surface suggesting use in a floor or other structure (1021).

The oolitic limestone used for the blocks and disc were probably obtained from the Lower Inferior Oolite that forms the upper reaches of Bredon Hill, although it is difficult to provenance the non-shelly oolitic limestones with accuracy due to the lack of variation in lithology over the region. The blocks from Fiddington, for example, match samples from both Bredon Hill and from the Roman quarries at The Querns in Cirencester, but a local source seems more likely in this instance. The Old Red Sandstone quern and hone probably came from the Forest of Dean and are typical of the stones we expect to see during the Roman period in this area.

Catalogue

Upper rotary quern fragment (not illustrated). Probable Old Red Sandstone. Small central fragment with eye measuring approx 50mm diameter. Grinding surface is slightly concave and worn very smooth. Upper surface is pecked and what remains slopes down gently towards eye. Ctx 1045. SF 375.

Hone (not illustrated). Probable Old Red Sandstone. Slab with smooth worn faces. Two grooves caused by use for sharpening. Measures 92 x 93 x 29mm. Ctx 1022, fill of ditch 1020. RB. SF 347.

Bredon's Norton

A total of 63 items of worked stone were retained during excavations at Bredon's Norton. These comprise mostly stone roofing (representing 34 stones) and tesserae (20).

Structural stone

Tesserae were recovered from contexts 3019 (1), 3165 (2), 3323 (1), 3332 (8), 3340 (7) and one unstratified. These are mainly of grey or white limestone (one is oolitic) with one of a red mudstone. Some showed signs of adhering mortar, so had clearly been used. The site also produced three roughly cuboid shaped lumps of tufa, all from destruction layer 3165. These were probably used structurally, perhaps in foundations. Tufa is a light, hard, porous material that forms when water leaches calcium carbonate out of limestone rocks and subsequently re-deposits it. This often occurs in relatively small quantities around springs and streams (North 1930, 302) and on the lower slopes of hills where the right conditions prevail. Although there are major exposures of tufa around Southstone Rock in the Shelsleys area to the northwest (Earp and Hains 1971, 100) and around Dursley in Gloucestershire to the south (North 1930, 302), the tufa blocks from Bredon's Norton were probably locally sourced from the lower levels of Bredon Hill.

Fig. 3.11 *Worked stone: roofing and objects*

The bulk of the stone assemblage is formed of roof slabs, 34 in total. Most are in a good state of preservation, with many complete or near complete, and five examples retaining the nails (or parts of the nails) with which they were fixed to the roof. The stones for which the original shape can be recorded (12) includes hexagonal (or octagonal/pentagonal), square/oblong and diamond shaped (Fig. 3.11.1-3). Two of the stones also have a curved upper edge suggesting their manufacture from potlids – concretionary lumps that were broken down into numerous roof-stones (Aston 1974, 20). There is no correlation between lithology and roof-stone shape.

Source of the stones

A variety of stone types were employed, falling into four broad groups. These comprise variations of oolitic limestone, two types of grey or cream calcareous sandstone (or sandy limestone) and a greyish red fine-grained sandstone. The oolitic limestones are variable but mostly match samples collected from the large outlier of Lower Inferior Oolite (Birdlip Limestone) that forms Bredon Hill. The similarity to these samples does not prove Bredon Hill is the source, as there are frequent exposures of Birdlip Limestone in other locales, but it seems a reasonable assumption.

The source of the sandy limestones/calcareous sandstones is problematic. Within the range of types present are one or two examples that, in hand specimen, match samples from Cleeve Hill (located about 10km south) from sandy beds within the Lower Inferior Oolite. A source within those beds is possible for a small number of this group. The vast majority, however are variations of brown and grey stones similar to Stonesfield Slate. There is some disagreement about the extent to which Stonesfield Slate was exploited by the Romans. Williams (1971 Table 2) cites several occurrences on buildings close to the Gloucester Pipeline, notably Whittington Court, Spoonley Wood and Wadfield. Aston however notes these are likely to be from more locally available beds of Cotswold stone and not specifically from Stonesfield (1974, 22). The roofing from Bredon's Norton, whilst being of a Stonesfield Slate 'type', is not identical in hand specimen, and is thus probably from another source such as that at Brimpsfield (the Througham Tilestone). If this is correct, these stones were transported in the region of 25km or more.

The greyish-red sandstone is from the Brownstones division of the Old Red Sandstone. This is likely to have had an equally distant source in the Forest of Dean, although it may have passed through an intermediary centre, as its main use was in buildings concentrated around Gloucester and Cirencester (Saunders 1998, Fig 5.1/5.2). It is the only lithology represented at sites such as Hucclecote and Brockworth (Roe 2003, 51; Rawes 1981, 73).

The presence of several different roof-stone lithologies is interesting, as it is more usual to find evidence for only a single type of stone at a site (Williams 1971,

Table 2: Hucclecote, Frocester, Painswick, Spoonley Wood, Wadfield, Whittington Court and Woodchester). There is often evidence for a combination of tile and stone, though it may be chronological, tile being earlier and stone later (Williams 1971). Barnsley Park and Witcombe are the only geographically close sites to have produced multiple stone types, and it is unclear what their associations with buildings were. At Bredon's Norton, many of the roof stones and the full range of stone types and stone shapes were deposited in contexts that were associated with structure 3184 including collapse or demolition (3013), subsequent levelling of the building (3019) and demolition of the room to the south of it (3165). This might appear to indicate significant variation on a single roof, however, it is also possible that some of the levelling material was introduced from the demolition of other buildings.

Although not uncommon, the use of stone roofing on Roman buildings would have been an indication of some prosperity. The evidence generally suggests the installation of stone roofs only from the mid-2nd century onwards (Williams 1971, 106), which would suggest that structure 3184 was not constructed before that time. The presence of a tesselated floor would have been a further display of wealth and the recovery of 20 tesserae, some with mortar still attached, is an indication that at least one building here had a mosaic floor.

The general picture of stone use at the three sites is one of a broad range of sources (Fig. 3.12). Local stones (such as the Oolite from Bredon's Hill) were used, but stones were also imported from the south (Cleeve Hill; Brimpsfield) and from the Forest of Dean/Wye Valley. Local stones must have made use of the road network, but it is likely that stones from the Forest of Dean travelled down the River Wye to the River Severn and then upstream to Gloucester and beyond. This pattern continues a tradition that began with the exporting of querns from the Forest of Dean and Wye valley in the Neolithic and continued into the Roman period with the exploiting and distributing of stone, coal and iron.

Objects

A single stone object recovered from a pre-Roman feature is a hone from mid to late Iron Age pit 3158 (3159, SF 3014). It has been made from a sandstone pebble, almost certainly gathered locally; the overall shape is natural, but it has been used along one edge so that it is now slightly bevelled.

All other stone objects were recovered from contexts of Roman date. Two naturally flat stones (SF 3052 and 3053) had been shaped into discs (Fig. 3.11.4 and 5). Both discs were found in deposit 3165, which sealed the whole of the Roman building south of structure 3184. A third fragment with a curved edge from the same context may also have been a disc. Neither disc has any evidence for burning or use wear and their function is not clear, although previous suggestions have included uses as lids for

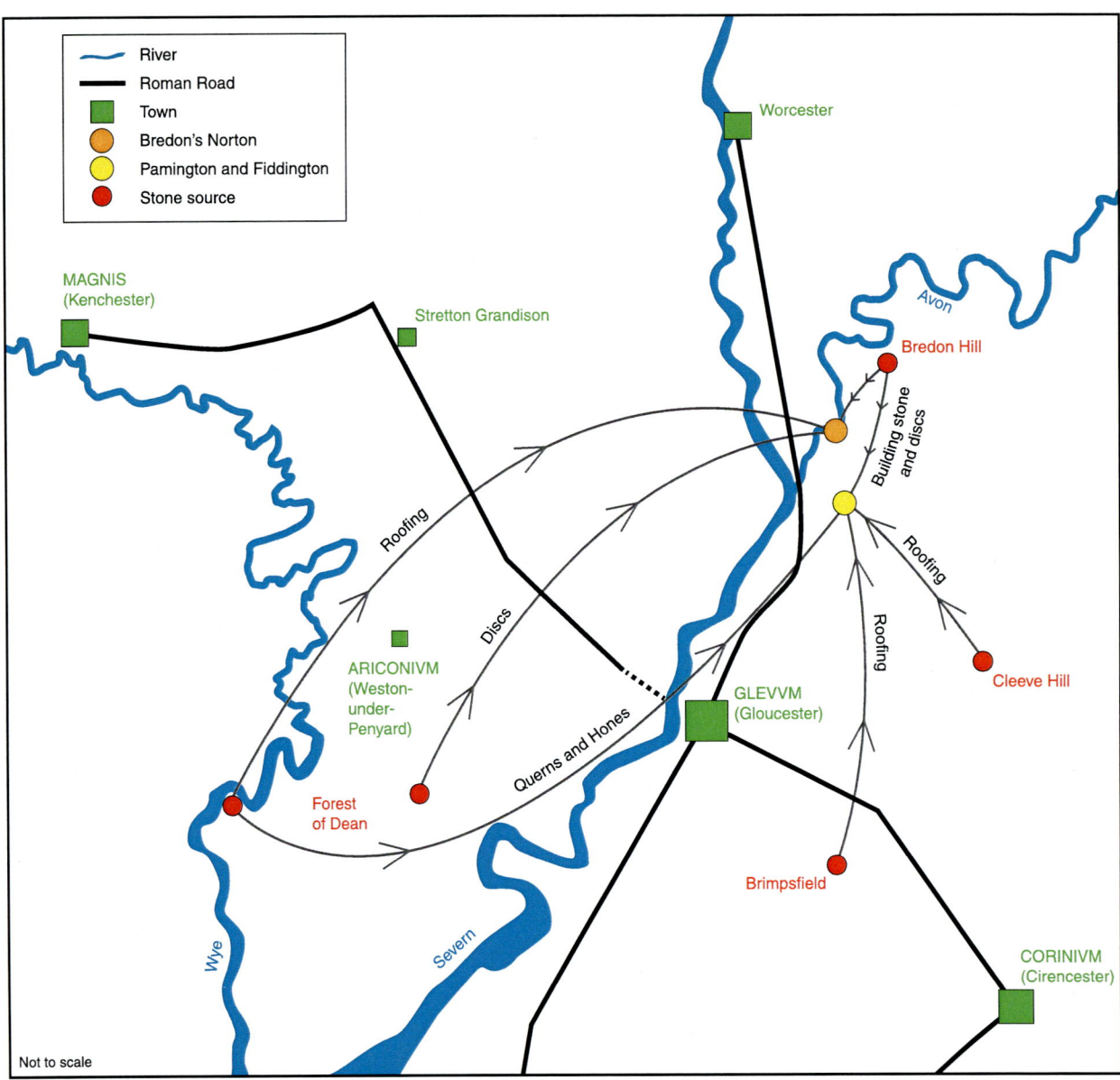

Fig. 3.12 Map showing the sources of the worked stone found at the three sites

pottery vessels or as bases to stand other items on. Both are made of micaceous sandstone, possibly Drybrook sandstone and quite different to any of the stone types used for roofing. Drybrook sandstone can be found on the northern edge of the Forest of Dean and therefore could have been transported alongside the Brownstones, used for roofing. A stone ring was recovered from levelling deposit 3019 representing final disuse of building 3184 (Fig. 3.11.6). Its purpose is unknown but it was presumably decorative (3019) and may have been worn as a pendant.

Given the structural evidence for significant buildings, one or more with stone roofs and areas of tesselated flooring, stone artefacts associated with occupation (such as querns, whetstones, spindle whorls etc) are conspicuous by their absence. This may suggest that domestic tasks evidenced by these tools did not occur in this part of the site and that

these buildings performed other functions, although it is also possible, given the extensive robbing of the building remains, that such objects were disposed of in areas outside the excavations.

WORKED FLINT *by Geraldine Crann*

A total of seven flints was recovered, two from Fiddington and five from Bredon's Norton, the latter including one burnt unworked pebble. All were residual finds in later contexts.

Both of the pieces from Fiddington were flakes, and one had subsequently been burnt. Both were recovered from ploughsoil (1001). The four worked pieces from Bredon's Norton included two small undiagnostic flakes (contexts 3004 and 3323) and two retouched pieces. One of these (context 3058, weighing 6g) was a tertiary flake on dark brown

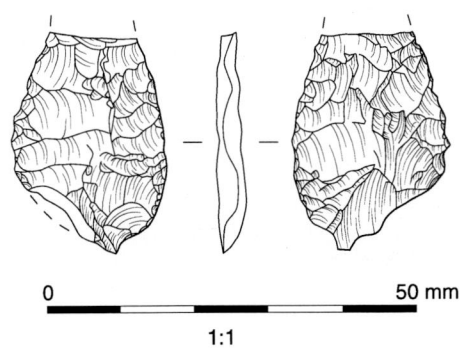

0   50 mm

1:1

Fig. 3.13 Flint arrowhead

flint, retouched along the left dorsal edge, and with usewear damage along dorsal/ventral right margin. The other (SF 3021 from context 5046, weighing 3g), was a fragment of leaf-shaped arrowhead on mid-brown flint, very lightly patinated. The piece is finely bifacially flaked, with the tip being fractured in antiquity and the base fractured more recently (Fig. 3.13). This is of early Neolithic date. The cleanly snapped tip suggests it was a functional arrowhead rather than a prestige piece. The retouched flake is also likely to be Neolithic in date.

Given the scale of investigation this is a remarkably sparse collection of flint, perhaps indicating a low level of prehistoric activity in the area.

Chapter 4

Environmental Reports

POST-EXCAVATION REGIONAL RESEARCH AIMS AND OBJECTIVES

Following the post-excavation assessment and during the analysis, the questions that could usefully be addressed became clearer. The sites dealt with in this volume span two regions, the West Midlands and the South West, but many of the research agenda aims are common to both, for example increasing use of scientific dating (Webster 2007, Research Aim 16, 281-2; Watt (ed.) 2011, Key Research Agenda Point 12, 121) and improving quality and quantity of environmental data (Webster 2007, RA17, 282-3; Watt (ed.) 2011, KRAP 8, 120).

For Gloucestershire, the potential of the narrow transects at Pamington and Fiddington were limited, but the analysis took account of regional Research Aims 29 (improving understanding of non-villa Roman settlement) and (for Fiddington) 26 (investigating changes in landscape at the end of the Roman period) (Webster (ed.) 2007, 285-6).

For Worcestershire, the data from Bredon's Norton clearly allowed a wider range of questions to be addressed. The key research agenda points for the Iron Age do not however include burials or detailed settlement morphologies, although the former are described, together with a distribution map (Hurst 2011, 109-110). The Romano-British resource assessment does not list specific questions, and the themes are too broadly drawn, or the evidence from this site too limited, to have much relevance to his broader themes (Esmonde-Cleary 2011, 127-147).

Some of the regional Research Aims for the South West were however particularly relevant, especially Research Aim 10 (Understanding transitional periods, Webster (ed.) 2007, 279-80) for the Iron Age-Roman transition and the very late Roman period, 14 (Widening understanding of Iron Age material culture, ibid., 281) for the burials and the saw, 20 and 21 (Improving understanding of cultivated plants; Improving understanding of the environmental aspects of farming, ibid., 284) for the late Roman grain deposit and 58 (Widening understanding of Roman burial traditions, ibid., 293) for the various groups of burials at Bredon's Norton.

THE HUMAN REMAINS *by Mark Gibson*

Introduction

The following report details the specialist analysis of human remains recovered during archaeological excavations at Bredon's Norton for the Gloucester SoS pipeline. In total, six adult inhumations, eight juvenile inhumations and two unurned cremation burials were recovered, along with disarticulated bone from three separate contexts (see Figs 2.16 and 2.19 for locations). All of the adult burials were in purpose-dug graves. Adult skeleton 3300 was dated to the middle Iron Age along with two of the deposits of disarticulated remains. Skeletons 5012 and 5198 were late Iron Age – early Roman, whilst adult skeletons 5202, 5223 and 153006 along with juvenile skeletons 5260, 5261, 5262, 5254, 5259, 5220, 5244 and 5284 were Roman. Cremation deposits 3064/3069 and 5295 were also dated to the Roman period, as were the remaining two deposits of disarticulated human remains.

Unburnt human remains

Methodology

Graves were planned on site, then human skeletons were exposed and photographed, including geo-rectified photography to enable subsequent planning. Grave fills were retained as soil samples and were processed for additional human bones, as well as for finds or other environmental materials. All remains were analysed by reference to the guidelines set out by Brickley and McKinley (2004) and Mays *et al* (2004). Analysis of the articulated skeletons involved examining the remains to make observations regarding their condition (Grade 0-5+, after McKinley 2004, 16), completeness (0-25%, 26-50%, 51-75%, 76-100%) and fragmentation ('low', <25% of the skeleton fragmented, 'medium', 25-75% of the skeleton fragmented, or 'high', >75% fragmented).

Relevant standards for estimation of age (Brooks and Suchey 1990; Brothwell 1981; Buckberry and Chamberlain 2002; Lovejoy *et al.* 1985; Miles 1962, 2001; Moorrees *et al.* 1963; Scheuer and Black 2003; AlQahyani 2009) and sex (Buikstra and Ubelaker

Table 4.1 Age categories employed to date unburnt human remains

Age category	Age range
Preterm	<37 weeks gestation
Neonate	Birth – 1 month
Infant	1 month – 1 year
Young child	1 – 5 years
Older child	6 – 12 years
Adolescent	13 – 17 years
Young adult	18 – 25 years
Prime adult	26 – 35 years
Middle adult	36 – 45 years
Mature adult	45 years +
Mature adult +	60 years +
Adult unspecified	>18 years

1994; Phenice 1969) were employed. All skeletons were assigned to one of the age categories given in Table 4.1.

A standard set of cranial and post-cranial measurements were taken wherever possible, as recommended by Brothwell and Zakrzewski (2004), primarily as a means of providing data for estimating biological sex of adults (Chamberlain 1994, 11; Bass 1987, 123) and for calculation of stature. Stature was estimated by employing the maximum length of available complete long bones and applying them to the regression equations devised by Trotter and Gleser (1952;1958) and revised by Trotter (1970). Bones with the lowest error margin were used and, in keeping with standard convention, calculations that used those from the left side were employed over those from the right side. Where possible, the platymeric and platycnemic indices were also calculated. These are indicators of proximal femur and tibia shaft shape respectively. In the femur, antero-posterior flattening of the shaft is assessed. The index of the femur has increased over time, that is, the femur has become more rounded. There are various hypotheses as to the reason for this, including mechanical stress, squatting and mineral/vitamin deficiencies (Brothwell 1981, 90-91; Waldron 2007, 46). In the tibia, transverse flattening is assessed. Again, there are various hypotheses as to the reason for tibial flattening, which include pathological change, muscular action and persistent squatting (*ibid.*, 1981, 91; 2007, 46).

Where possible, adult skeletons were examined for non-metric traits (minor variants in the skeleton) by following the guidelines set out by Berry and Berry (1967) and Finnegan (1978). Pathological lesions and bony abnormalities were described and differential diagnoses explored with reference to standard texts (for example Aufder-heide and Rodríguez-Martín 1998; Ortner 2003; Roberts and Connell 2004). Conditions were classified thus: infection, metabolic disorders, trauma, congenital and developmental conditions, joint disease, circulatory disorders, neoplastic disease,

miscellaneous conditions and unclassified pathology. Where appropriate, rates of disease are expressed in this report as crude prevalence rates (number of individuals with a condition out of the total number of individuals observed; CPR) and/or true prevalence rates (number of elements with a particular condition out of the number of elements observed; TPR). Whilst CPRs are not the most accurate way of assessing the rate of a particular disease in a population, because they do not account for missing or unobservable elements, they are useful for summarising patterns of disease within a population. They also allow for inter-site comparisons (e.g. using the data presented in Roberts and Cox 2003).

Results: Phase 1, Middle Iron Age

A single adult crouched burial (3300) was orientated north-south and had been cut into the upper fill of east-west aligned ditch 3305 close to the south end of the site (Fig. 2.17; Plate 2.10). The upper half of the skeleton had been removed by a later feature, although the head would have originally faced north. Radiocarbon dating gave a range of 360–110 cal BC (SUERC-49694; 2167 ± 30 years BP).

Disarticulated remains were also recovered from two features dating to the mid to late Iron Age. A single fragment was found in deposit 3121 in ditch 3120 only 5m south-east of grave 3300. Ditch 5073 was an east-west ditch in the northern part of the site, and contained five fragments of human bone within deposit 5071.

Skeleton 3300

Between 50% and 75% of skeleton 3300 survived, the skull and upper thorax, right arm and the majority of the left upper arm being missing. The surviving elements were moderately fragmented and the surfaces of the bones exhibited moderate, patchy surface erosion (Grade 2, McKinley 2004, 16).

All of the surviving epiphyses on skeleton 3300 had completely fused indicating that it was that of an adult. The morphology and erosion of the auricular surfaces, suggested that the individual had been a prime adult (26-35 years). The sexually dimorphic features of the pelvis were in keeping with an individual who was probably male (?M), especially the sciatic notch and features of the sacrum.

Due to the incomplete and fairly fragmentary nature of the bones, metrical and non-metrical data was limited. It was not possible to estimate stature or calculate the platymeric index. It was however possible to calculate the platycnemic index. In skeleton 3300 the platycnemic index was 63.2 (mesocnemic) indicating a moderately laterally flattened tibia (*ibid.* 1989, 89) Due to truncation its was only possible to record post-cranial non-metric traits: Allen's fossa on the right femur, double anterior facets on the left talus and both calcanei and a lateral squatting facet on the right tibia. These facets are thought to result from habitual adoption of the squatting position and the hyperdorsiflexed position of the ankle joint (Boulle 2001).

Spinal joint disease was observed in the form of Schmorl's nodes and vertebral body osteophytes in the thoracic and lumbar vertebrae of skeleton 3300. Schmorl's nodes are identified on dry bone as indentations on the vertebral end plates and are essentially 'pressure defects' arising from herniation of the intervertebral disc (Rogers and Waldron 1995, 27). Disc herniation is usually a gradual, age-related occurrence in adults, associated with weakening of the posterior longitudinal ligaments of the spine, but it may also occur in younger individuals as a result of activity or an injury, such as a jump or fall from height (Lovell 1997, 159; Jurmain 1999, 165).

A developmental anomaly, known as lumbarisation, was also observed, whereby the first sacral vertebrae takes on the morphological characteristics of the fifth lumbar vertebra. The degree of lumbarisation was significant enough for there to be six lumbar vertebrae. This sort of defect, known as vertebral border shifting, is not an uncommon finding in skeletal remains and the lumbo-sacral border is cited as the most frequently affected site (Barnes 1994, 79). In this case, the morphological abnormality was incomplete and unilateral, as an articulating facet with the sacral alae was maintained on the left side. It is suggested that unilateral sacralisation may lead to abnormal rotation/curvature of the lumbar spine, which in turn may cause low back pain and sciatica (ibid, 110), but no further abnormalities were observed in the lumbar spine of 3300.

Inflammation of the periostium (periostitis) was the only other pathology observed on this individual. It was present on the medial aspects of both tibial shafts. Periostitis may arise as a result of either a soft-tissue infection extending to the bone; a more generalised disease process; or by involvement from infection (osteitis or osteomyelitis) of the underlying bone (Aufderheide and Rodríguez-Martín 1998, 172). Thus it does not always relate to infection; trauma, neoplastic disease and haemorrhage may all produce periosteal new bone (ibid, 172). Periostitis is frequently observed on the tibia in archaeological material because it is more easily affected by mild recurrent trauma than other bones in the skeleton (Roberts and Manchester 1995, 130).

Disarticulated remains

The disarticulated bone from deposit 3121 was the distal half of a left humerus, whilst the five fragments of human bone from 5071 were all cranial vault fragments from the parietal bone (side could not be determined). In all cases the surface condition was Grade 2 (after McKinley 2004).

Sex could not be estimated on any of the disarticulated remains from this phase due to the paucity of elements, and the age could only be estimated as adult (given the size and robustness of the bones).

No metric nor non-metric data could be obtained from the disarticulated remains, and no pathological lesions were observed

Results: Phase 2, Late Iron Age to early Roman

Two adult skeletons are attributed to the late Iron Age or early Roman period, and were found in separate locations. The first (skeleton 5012) was located in an ovoid grave towards the north-west end of the site, and 36m north-west of ditch 5073. It lay on its left side in a crouched position with its head pointing to the north (Plate 2.16). Bone from this burial has been radiocarbon-dated to 50 cal BC-80 cal AD (SUERC-49695; 1983± 30 BP), confirming it as late Iron Age to early Roman. A second set of unburnt human remains (skeleton 5198) were recovered from ditch 5187, which ran east-west less than 10m north of ditch 5073 (Fig. 2.19). They were disarticulated, but were clearly from one skeleton that had been disturbed. Pottery finds from 5187 date the infilling of the ditch to the 2nd century AD.

Skeleton 5012

Over 76% of the bones of this skeleton were present, and all major elements, with only the middle portion of the left leg missing due to truncation during the stripping of the site. Despite this the remains were only moderately fragmented.

Both the auricular surfaces and the pubic symphyses survived on skeleton 5012. They gave a probable age range of between 35 and 45 years at death (middle adult). Attritional wear on the molars of 5012 was however much less than would be expected of an individual of that age, being more like that of a 17–25 year old. Attritional wear is however influenced by diet and was therefore discounted in this case.

Whilst the pelvic morphological traits were predominantly strongly male, the cranial traits were more mixed, exhibiting both female and indeterminate forms. Due to this skeleton 5012 was classified as a probable male (?M).

It was possible to estimate stature as well as both the platymeric and platycnemic indices of skeleton 5012. The only long bone complete enough to use for stature was the left radius which gave a stature of 1.63m (5 feet 4 inches). Roberts and Cox (2003, 142 and 396) calculated the ranges and means for male and female statures from a number of British Iron age and Roman sites. At 1.68m (c 5 feet 6 inches) during the Iron Age and 169cm during the Roman period, the stature of 5012 is considerably lower than would be expected for its date. The platymeric and platycnemic indices of skeleton 5012, were calculated to be 72.2 and 60 respectively. This means that its femur was platymeric (index below 84.9, Brothwell 1981, 89), indicating a flat or broad, proximal femur shaft. The tibia was platycnemic indicating transverse flattening, which is often seen in hunter gather groups and earlier man (ibid, 89).

Cranial and post-cranial non-metric traits were able to be observed on skeleton 5012. Whilst many of the locations for non-metric traits in the cranium could not be observed due to the fragmentation of the vault and the cranial base, it was noted that a maxillary torus was present adjacent to the right second molar. Post-cranially most locations were available for observation with a septal aperture being present on the right humerus. A septal aperture is a defect (a hole) in the septum that separates the olecranon of the ulna from the coronoid fossa of the humerus. It has been suggested this aperture arises as a result of impingement on the septum by the coronoid and olecranon processes, when the elbow joint is hyper-mobile (Mays 2008). Allen's fossae and third trochanters were present bilaterally on the femora. The latter is a distinct tuberosity located on the superior aspect of the gluteal ridge on the back of the femur. It seems to be related to bone size, being more common on gracile bones and females (Anderson, unpublished). Lateral squatting facets, which were present in both tibiae may be the result of the habitual adoption of the squatting position and the hyperdorsiflexed position of the ankle joint (Boulle 2001). Double anterior facets of the calcanei were also present on skeleton 5012.

Dental disease was observed in the form of calculus and dental enamel hypoplasia. Slight to moderate deposits of calculus were observed on all of the 31 observable teeth. Dental calculus, also known as plaque, is an extremely common disease. It has been linked to diets high in protein and/or carbohydrates (Hillson 1996, 254) and may, therefore, be an indication of diet, as well as of oral hygiene practices, or lack thereof. Dental enamel hypolasia (DEH) are lines, pits or grooves in the enamel which reflect disruption to the growth of the tooth during childhood. The disruption occurs as a result of physiological stress, such as a period of nutritional deficiency or disease, for example measles (Aufderheide and Rodríguez-Martín 1998, 405; Roberts and Manchester 1995, 58). In skeleton 5012 three of the second molars exhibited lines, as did both of the maxillary central incisors. The left maxillary third molar also exhibited pits. The position of all of these defects suggested that the periods of physiological stress occurred between two and four years of age.

Inflammatory reactions to either disease or soft tissue trauma was observed on the medial aspects of both tibial shafts and on the right femoral shaft. The new bone growth was dense and poorly defined with some striations and porosity over the surface indicating that the periostitis was well healed.

As well as periostitis, skeleton 5012 also exhibited developmental abnormalities and a metabolic disease. Vertebral border shifting was present in the form of partial lumbarisation of the first sacral vertebrae. Unlike the case in skeleton 3300 both of the alae of the first sacral vertebrae were fused to the rest of the sacrum, however the body had failed to completely fuse to that of the second sacral vertebrae and the arch had not completely coalesced with the rest of the sacrum. Further evidence of vertebral border shifting was seen as there were only 11 throacic vertebrae. The first lumbar vertebra did have very small and underdeveloped ribs, however its form was morphologically that of a first lumbar rather than a 12th thoracic vertebra.

Metabolic disease was present on skeleton 5012 in the form of cribra orbitalia in the left orbit. Cribra orbitalia is identified on dry bone as surface pitting on the orbital roof (the eye socket), accompanied by thinning of the compact bone (Ponec and Resnick 1984). These lesions have traditionally been attributed to iron deficiency anaemia in which marrow expansion causes diploic hyperplasia (thickening) and resorption of the outer table, which exposes the underlying trabeculae (porosity) (Mays 2012; Stuart-Macadam 1991). Aside from a diet deficient in iron, excessive blood loss through injury, chronic disease such as cancer, and malabsorption (for example, due to gastro-intestinal infection or parasites) may all have played a significant part in iron deficiency during this period (Roberts and Manchester 1995, 166; Roberts and Cox 2003, 140). However, more recently, Walker *et al.* (2009) have indicated that iron deficiency may not cause bone marrow hyperplasia and suggest that the lesion could relate to a deficiency in vitamin B12 and/or folic acid (megaloblastic anaemia) instead. In addition, unless expansion of the diploic space can be demonstrated, porosity of the orbital roofs may occur in a variety of other conditions, such as rickets or scurvy, which may also lead to thickening of the cranial bones, although not through marrow hyperplasia (Mays 2012, 293). Regardless of aetiology, cribra orbitalia is often considered as a skeletal indicator of non-specific health stress, and can be used to evaluate the overall burden of disease in archaeological populations (e.g. Steckel *et al.* 2009).

Skeleton 5198

As would be expected from a disturbed and disarticulated set of remains, skeleton 5198 was less than 25% complete, and the surviving elements were highly fragmented. Only both upper arms, part of the left forearm and lower leg, some right ribs and a couple of cervical vertebrae had survived. The surface condition of both of the individuals was however fairly good, having only moderate, patchy, surface erosion (Grade 2, McKinley 2004,16).

Due to a lack of surviving elements skeleton 5198 could only be aged as 'adult', although it was possible to tentatively suggest its sex. The length of the left scaplua glenoid cavity was 28mm, which is within the range for males. With no other metric or morphological sex indicators surviving, however, it was only possible to assign 5198 to the possible male category (??M).

Due to its high level of fragmentation and incomplete long bones it was not possible to gather any metric data from 5198 that could be used for either stature or any of the platymeric or platycnenmic indices, and the only locations which could be observed for non-metric traits were those of the scapula, humerus and calcaneus. Only the peroneal tubercle (an anterior outgrowth on bone on the lateral aspect of the calcaneus, (Finnegan 1978) on the left calcaneus was present.

Inflammatory reactions to either disease or soft tissue trauma was observed in both late Iron Age to early Roman individuals in the form of periostitis. In both cases the new bone growth was dense and poorly defined, with some striations and porosity over the surface indicating that the periostitis was well healed. On skeleton 5012 periostitis was found diffusely on the medial aspects of both tibial shafts and on the right femoral shaft, whilst on skeleton 5198 it was present on the left fibula shaft.

The only other pathology observed on the late Iron Age to early Roman assemblage was a well healed fracture to one of the right rib shafts of 5198. The two halves of the fracture had completely fused back together by the time of death, with only a slight misalignment inferio-medially

Results: Phase 3, Roman

One adult skeleton (5202) and eight juveniles dating to the middle Roman period were recovered, all in the northern part of the site. Bones from two further skeletons in a grave dated only as Roman by a single pottery sherd (5223 and 153006) were also found at the north-west end of the site. Seven of the juveniles, six neonates (5220, 5254, 5260, 5261, 5262, 5284) and an infant (5259), were recovered from the final silting of the ditches of an enclosure (group 5292) just north-west of ditch 5187. A further neonate (5244) was recovered from the upper fill (5046) of the adjacent recut ditch (group 5291). All these juveniles appear to have been deposited in the ditches while silting or infilling was occurring, rather than being in graves cut into the deposits after the ditches had fully silted. Radiocarbon dating gave a date range of 60-230 cal AD for skeleton 5244 and of 80-240 cal AD for skeleton 5262 (SUERC-49693; 1876 ± 30 years BP and SUERC-49696; 1853 ± 30 years BP). An attempt to date adult skeleton 5223 by radiocarbon dating failed due to lack of collagen (see also Radiocarbon Report, Nicholson Chapter 4).

The burial position and orientation of three of the juveniles (5254, 5260, 5262) could not be ascertained, partly due to their preservation, and partly due to disturbance. Neonate 5220 was lying on a south-east to north-west orientation, 5259 was lying with its head to the west and 5261 was lying with its head to the north. Both 5244 and 5284 occupied a crouched position, with 5244 lying on its left side, its head to the north and 5284 on its right, its head to the north-east (Plate 2.23; Plate 2.24).

Adult skeleton 5202 was located within the main enclosure (group 5292) on a north-south alignment in a crouched position (Plate 2.23). To the north of

5202 skeleton 5223 and disarticulated skeleton 153006, the latter found during evaluation, lay within a north-south aligned grave located just south of ditch 5209. Due to damage from evaluation trench 153 and disturbance from overlying ridge and furrow a burial position could not be determined for either.

Other adult and juvenile disarticulated human bones were also recovered from deposit 5049, the latest fill in enclosure ditch group 5292. One of the juvenile bones, a left humerus, was found in association with skeleton 5254. The minimum number of individuals was two, one adult and one juvenile.

Juvenile assemblage

Preservation

The completeness of the juvenile skeletons varied greatly and is summarised in Table 4.2. None of the skeletons were over 75% complete and only one was of a low fragmentation. The surface condition was good, however, with all skeletons being assigned to McKinley's Grade 1 or 2 (2004, 16).

Age

All but one of the juvenile assemblage were neonates, that is between 40 weeks in utero and 1.5 months old. Infant 5259 was estimated to have been between 1.5 and 3 months. In four skeletons (5244, 5254, 5262 and 5284) age was estimated using long bone length alone (Scheuer and Black 2003), because either no teeth were present or undamaged. The other four skeletons (ibid) were all aged using a combination of long bone/scapula measurements (Scheuer and Black 2003) and dental development (AlQahyani 2009).

Pathology

Skeletons 5220, 5244, 5261 and 5262 all had endocranial lesions affecting the parietal bones, and the occipital in skeleton 5261. Skeleton 5220 had fibre bone deposits, along with capillary and 'hair-on-end' lesions on its frontal bone, along with some additional 'hair-on-end' on its right parietal bone. Similar 'hair-on-end' lesions were also present on the frontal bones of skeletons 5244 and 5261,

Table 4.2 Preservation summary of the juvenile assemblage

Skeleton no.	Completeness (%)	Fragmentation	Surface condition (McKinley 2004)
5220	26–50	Medium	2
5244	51–75	Low	1
5254	26–50	Medium	1
5259	0–25	High	1
5260	51–75	High	1
5261	0–25	High	1
5262	51–75	High	2
5284	51–75	High	1

although the latter also had porous lesions on the crucifom eminance of its occipital. Deposits of fibre bone were present in skeleton 5262, on the endocranial surface of the left greater wing of sphenoid.

Endocranial lesions in juvenile skeletons are thought to result from inflammation or haemorrhage of the meninges, although the exact aetiology is a matter of debate. Trauma, infection and vitamin deficiencies, such as vitamin D deficiency, or rickets, are amongst the possibilities (Lewis 2004, 93; Brickley and Ives 2008, 103, Table 5.5).

As well as endocranial lesions skeleton 5261 also had cribra orbitalia bilaterally in the form of fine scattered foramina. It is possible that the cribra orbitalia and endocranial lesions resulted from the same condition, possibly a dietary deficiency.

The only other bony abnormality observed amongst the juvenile assemblage was an undiagnosed condition in infant skeleton 5259. There was a thickening of the frontal bone along both sides of the metopic suture with a thickening of the diploe and increased porosity to both the inner and outer tables. There was no new bone growth present on either of the two surfaces. It is possible that this may be part of the normal development of the frontal bone prior to the fusion of the metopic suture. Alternatively, it may refer to a systemic disorder, such as scurvy. However, no further evidence for this disease was observed on the individual.

Skeleton 5202

Adult 5202 was well represented, with over 75% of the bones being present and the surface only having undergone moderate, patchy erosion (Grade 2, McKinley 2004). It was however, highly fragmented with the skull, ribs and pelvis all consisting of only small fragments, the right hand and forearm were also mostly missing, with only the proximal half of the radius representing this region.

Despite its high level of fragmentation it was possible to estimate both the sex and age. Although relatively few morphological traits were observable in either the cranium or pelvis it was possible to estimate that this individual had probably been female (?F). The pubic symphysis and the auricular surface both indicated that this skeleton was that of a young adult (17-25 years) which was also confirmed by the medial clavicular epiphysis which was partly fused. When combined with the completed fusion of the iliac crest it was possible to narrow the age range to between 20 and 25 years.

It was only possible to gather metric data on the scapula and femur of adult 5202 due to fragmentation. Careful reconstruction of the femur allowed a stature estimation to be made. At 1.51m (*c* 4 feet 11 inches) this individual was 0.08m shorter than the female mean height of 1.59m (*c* 5 feet 3 inches) calculated for the Roman period (Roberts and Cox 2003, 142). It was also possible to calculate the platymeric index on the right femur. At 69.5 skeleton 5202 was platymeric, indicating a similar form to skeleton 5012.

The high level of fragmentation also prevented observations being made of the majority of cranial non-metric traits and some of the post-cranial traits. Cranially, a metopic suture was observed, along with a supraorbital foramen (the bridging over of a notch for vessels) on the right orbit. A metopic suture or metopism is the retention of the stature which divides the frontal bone vertically during early childhood. Variations in the sutures of the skull are considered to be under significant genetic control (Torgersen 1951a,b, 1954; Sjøvold 1984). Post-cranially, bilateral lateral tibial squatting facets and double anterior calcaneal facets were observed.

Both the maxillary and mandibular dentition of adult 5202 exhibited small flecks of calculus on all of the first and second molars, along with all of the mandibular premolars. In total 12/30 teeth were affected (TPR 40%).

Bilateral cribra orbitalia was also present in adult 5202 in the form of large and small foramina which had linked together into a trabecular like structure. Periosteal new bone growth was observed on the posterio-medial aspect of the right tibia. The new bone was light and woven in appearance with clear margins, indicating that the periostitis was active and unhealed at the time of death. The superior aspects of both acetabulae of skeleton 5202 also exhibited pathological lesions in the form of granular erosive lesions. There was no new bone growth present, nor any other indication of infection or trauma. The granular lesions differed from the porosity exhibited in degenerative joint disease and there was no corresponding lesion on the femoral heads; it may relate to inflammation in the joint, however its aetiology remains undiagnosed.

Skeleton 5223

Grave 5224, in which skeleton 5223 lay, had partly been excavated in CAT evaluation trench 153, fill 153006. Skeleton 5223 was poorly preserved and was less than 25% complete. It was highly fragmented with only fragments from the cranial vault, the right clavicle, both distal humerii, proximal ulnae and proximal femora present along with fragments from an unsideable tibia and fibula. The surface condition was however very good with only very slight erosion (Grade 1, McKinley 2004). The arrangement of the bones in the grave did not suggest that the skeleton was still articulated.

The high fragmentation and under-representation of elements of skeleton 5223 prevented any estimation of its sex and the gathering of metric and non-metric data. Age could only be estimated to be an adult due to the overall size and robusticity of the bone fragments.

Only one tooth survived on skeleton 5223, the right maxillary second premolar. It exhibited DEH in the form of a line indicating a period of physiological stress between the ages of 4.5 and 6.5 years of age. A portion of the right mandible of 5223 also survived with a single large periapiceal cavity at the apices of the sockets of both premolars. Periapiceal cavities develop as a result of pus-forming bacteria entering the pulp cavity, and tracking down the root of the tooth. Pulp cavities may be exposed to bacteria via caries, excessive attrition or trauma (Hillson 1986, 316). In addition, diets rich in carbohydrates are well known to promote this condition (Lukacs 1989, 261; Hillson 1986, 316; 1996, 255).

Despite its high level of fragmentation and low level of completeness pathological lesions were observed on skeleton 5223. The endocranial surface of a single fragment of cranial vault was entirely covered in new bone growth similar to the fibre bone described by Lewis (2004, 93), however, it was dense indicating that it had healed rather than still being active. Lewis (ibid) discusses the causes in non-adults and it is likely that these could be the same from skeleton 5223, although the lesion may be left over from childhood.

Skeleton 153006

Bones from this skeleton were retrieved during evaluation from a probable grave cut, whose position appears to correspond to that of grave 5224 containing skeleton 5223. The degree of completeness of skeleton 153006 was similar to that of skeleton 5223. It was also less than 25% complete and highly fragmented. The surviving elements consisted of fragments of cranial vault, along with facial bone and mandibular fragments. A partial left clavicle, left humerus and the midshaft of the left radius were also recovered as well as both femoral shafts and the majority of the anterior of the left tibia. The surface condition was moderate, with most of the surface showing some degree of erosion (Grade 3, Mckinley 2004).

Despite its high level of fragmentation it was possible to estimate both the sex and age. Although relatively few morphological traits were observable in the cranium and the pelvis was completely absent, the supraorbital ridge and the orbital margin tentatively suggest that this individual had possibly been male (??M). It was possible to estimate the age of this individual using dental attrition indicating that this individual was probably a middle adult (36-45 years).

Two teeth, the right mandibular second and third molars survived on skeleton 153006 along with six mandibular sockets. Both of the molars exhibited a slight build up of calculus.

No pathological lesions were observed on skeleton 153006.

Other disarticulated remains

The disarticulated remains consisted of a first metacarpal and the proximal half of a right ulna, both adult, along with the distal half of a right humerus, the distal half of a right femur and a complete left humerus, all juvenile. All of the juvenile bones could be aged between 40 weeks *in utero* and 1.5 months (neonate) based upon diaphyseal length measurements with reference to the bone lengths of individuals of known age given in

Scheuer and Black (2000, 289, 373, 394). The adult disarticulated remains could not be assigned to a more specific category. No metric or non-metric data could be gathered and no pathological lesions were observed upon them.

Cremated human remains

Methodology

In accordance with recommended practice (McKinley 2004, 9), contexts comprising or containing cremated bone were subject to whole-earth recovery. The deposits were wet sieved and sorted into fractions of >10 mm, 10-4 mm and 4-2 mm. As standard, the bone from the >10 mm and 10-4 mm fractions were separated from the extraneous material, which included flint and chalk fragments. Where 4-2 mm fractions comprised large total weights, bone weights within these fractions were estimated by separating the bone from 10g samples, and calculating the proportion present.

The bone was assessed for colour, weight and maximum fragment size. Each fraction was examined for identifiable bone elements and the presence of pyre and grave goods. The minimum number of individuals (MNI) present, and estimation of age and sex was attempted. Estimation of MNI was carried out by identification of repeated elements. Age estimations were based upon erosion of the auricular surface (Lovejoy *et al* 1985), although the latter is recognised as one of the less reliable ageing methods (Cox 2000, 66-68). Estimation of sex was possible in only one deposit. This was based on the observation of a sexually dimorphic trait of the skull (Buikstra and Ubelaker 1994).

Provenance

All of the cremation deposits were recovered from pits. Deposit 5295 was recovered from a pit cut into east-west orientated ditch 5301 in the northern part of the site. Hobnails recovered from the cremation deposit along with associated pottery place 5295 in the Roman period, probably the 2nd century AD. Contexts 3064 and 3069 were layers containing burnt remains related to a small pit (3063) in the southern part of the site. They represent a single cremation deposit and were treated as such. Pit 3063 was northernmost of three small pits, the central one of which is dated by pottery to the late Iron Age/early Roman period.

Results

A summary of the skeletal elements represented and the weight of bone present per fraction size is given in Table 4.3

Condition and fragmentation

In general, the cremated bone was very fragmented, with a large proportion of fragments under 10 mm.

Table 4.3 Summary of skeletal elements represented and weights of bone present

Deposit	Skeletal region	>10mm	10-4mm	4-2mm	Colour, MNI, age, sex, pathology
3064/ 3069	Skull	1.1g (Petrous portion)	7.8g (Vault, tooth root frags, maxilla)	-	95% white 3% blue 2% black
	Axial	-	-	-	MNI = 1
	Upper limb	-	-	-	Juvenile
	Lower limb	-	-	-	?
	Unid. long bone	-	2.5g	-	
	Unid. other	-	15.5g	7.2g	No pathology
	(Unid. total)	-	(18.0g)	(7.2g)	observed
	Total	1.1g	25.8g	7.2g	34.1g
5295	Skull	46.5g (Parietal, frontal, orbital rim, mandible, vault)	18.5g (Vault, mandible body, tooth root frags, molar root frags, mandibular premolar crown frag)	-	90% white 4% grey 4% blue 2% black
	Axial	5.9g (Vertebral arch frags, cervical arch frag, rib frags)	10.9g (Head of dens, vertebral body frags, vertebral arch frags, cervical spinus process, rib frags)	-	MNI = 1 Middle adult (35–39 years) ?F
	Upper limb	33.5g (Humeral head frags, humeral shaft frags, radial shaft frags, scapula frags, metacarpal head frag)	9.3g (scapula frags, humeral shaft frags, radial shaft frags, radial head frag, ulna shaft frags, metacarpal head frag, metacarpal shaft frag, proximal phalange, distal phalange)	-	
	Lower limb	43.0g (femoral shaft frags, tibial shaft frags, ilium frags, partial right auricular surface, first metatarsal head frags)	5.3g (Tibia shaft frags, fibula shaft frags, sesamoid, proximal phalange, distal phalange)	-	
	Unid. long bone	46.4g	36.9g		
	Unid. joint surface	1.5g	10.6g		
	Unid. other	24.7g	330.2g	144.6g	
	(Unid. total)	72.6g	377.7g	144.6g	
	Total	201.5g	421.7g	144.6g	767.8g

However, a significant proportion of the bone weight was yielded from the >10 mm fractions in deposit 5295 (26.2%). In both deposits the 10-4 mm fraction yielded the highest bone weights, comprising of 75.7 % of 3064/3069 and 54.9 % of deposit 5295.

The maximum fragment sizes from deposits 3064/3069 and 5295 were 15mm and 36mm respectively. In the case of 3064/3069 it was the single fragment of cremated bone over 10mm in size, a petrous portion of temporal bone, and for 5295 it was a femoral shaft fragment.

Fragmentation of cremated bone may result from a wide range of factors relating both to funerary practices and taphonomy. It is possible that the human remains were deliberately broken up by the mourners following cremation, as part of the funerary ritual, although there is a general lack of evidence for this in British cremation burials (McKinley 1994a, 342). Non-deliberate fragmentation of the bone may have occurred through any or several of the stages between collection from the funerary pyre to archaeological excavation and post-excavation processing. It is therefore important to regard the maximum fragment sizes given as post-excavation fragment sizes, not necessarily the size of fragments at the time of deposition (ibid, 342).

Weight of deposits

Investigations in modern crematoria have found that the bone weight of cremated adult individuals ranges between 1,000 g–2,400 g, with an average of 1,650 g (McKinley 2000a, 269). Predictably, individuals of smaller and more gracile build (such as many females and children) will usually have a lower bone weight, and poorer survival of the articular surfaces and spongy bone has been observed in modern older individuals with osteoporosis (McKinley 2000b, 404). In archaeological cremation burials, these factors play a role, as do funerary practices and taphonomic changes within the burial environment and excavation process. The thoroughness with which bone is collected from the pyre site following a cremation is a very significant determinant of the final weight of the cremation deposit (McKinley 1997, 139). How assiduous the mourners were in collecting bone from the pyre site was probably highly coloured by their beliefs in the afterlife and their perceptions of the relationship between the body and spirit after death, as well as the status of the deceased (McKinley 2000a, 270). Thus, all cremation burials are essentially 'token' as the entire skeleton is never truly represented.

Taphonomic changes, such as leaching of inorganic minerals from bone (most evident in trabecular bone) and mechanical disturbance and truncation also influence the final weight of the deposit. Archaeological machine stripping is a significant factor, as is the archaeological recovery of the deposit and subsequent processing.

The weight of both cremation deposits was below what would be expected for a modern cremation. Deposit 5295 was fairly moderate, at a total weight of 767.8g, whilst 3064/3069 was exceptionally low at a total weight of only 34.1g. A contemporary assemblage from Gill Mill, Oxfordshire contained cremation deposits with a weight range of 964.6–161.5g (Webb *et al.* forthcoming) and those from Westhampnett, West Sussex ranged between 190.9g and 687.1g (McKinley 2000a, 270). Given its low weight 3064/3069 may not represent a deliberate deposit.

All regions were represented in cremation deposit 5295, however, only skull fragments were specifically identified in deposit 3064/3069. McKinley (2004, 11) highlights that the distinctive appearance of parts of the skull, even as small fragments, invariably leads to a bias in the amount of skull identified. Skull fragments comprised the highest proportion of identified fragments in both cremation deposits at Bredon's Norton.

Demography

None of the cremation deposits appeared to comprise more than one individual, that is, no repeated elements were observed. The general size, surface texture of bone and thickness of cranial vault fragments in deposit 3064/3069 was consistent with those of a juvenile, though lack of epiphyses or identifiable tooth roots prevented a more accurate age estimation. A partial auricular surface in deposits 5295 allowed for a more specific age range to be estimated. The erosion of the surface was consistent with that which would be expected for a 35 – 39 year old (Lovejoy *et al* 1985), making this individual a middle adult.

Sex could be estimated for middle adult 5295. This was based upon a single fragment of the orbital margin on the frontal bone. The margin of the orbit was very sharp and gracile, making it more indicative of a female individual. However, it should be highlighted that an estimation of sex based on a single cranial feature only, should be treated with caution.

Pathology and non-metric traits

No pathology or non-metric traits were observed on either of the cremation deposits from Bredon's Norton.

Colour of the cremated bone

The degree of oxidation of the organic component of bone is related to the temperature acting upon the bone in an oxidising atmosphere (McKinley 2004, 11). The degree of oxidation is reflected macroscopically in the colour of the bone, hence the colour can be used as an indication of the efficiency of the cremation, in terms of such factors as the quantity of fuel used to build the pyre, the temperature attained in various parts of the pyre, and the length of time over which the cremation was undertaken (ibid, 11). Colours may range from brown/orange (unburnt), to black (charred: *c* 300°C), through hues of blue and grey (incompletely oxidised, up to *c* 600°C) to the fully oxidised white (>600°C) (ibid, 11).

In modern crematoria, where temperature, fuel availability and air circulation are optimised, full cremation of an adult corpse generally takes between 1–1.5 hours to complete when the temperature is maintained between 700-1,000°C (McKinley 2000b, 404). Here, the speed of full combustion depends upon the size and body mass of each individual as well as the proportion of fatty tissue present on the body (ibid, 404). In pyre cremations, maintenance of an optimal temperature and sufficient fuel and oxygen supply throughout the pyre is more problematic, often leading to less uniform combustion of the corpse (conspicuous in colour variation of different skeletal elements) (McKinley 2000a, 269). Both the length of time that the pyre will burn and the temperature attained are largely dependent on the quantity of fuel used in construction (ibid, 268).

Both of the cremation deposits included high proportions of buff-white fragments, indicative of complete oxidation of the majority of bones (*c* 90-95%). The non-white fragments from all four deposits were largely light grey or blue-grey in colour (incompletely oxidised), with fewer black (charred) fragments. In deposit 5295 the hand phalanges that were identified were most often black in colour, suggesting that they perhaps lay at the very edge of the pyre (McKinley 1989, 67; 2000a, 269).

Discussion

The human remains recovered from Bredon's Norton provide a valuable insight into the use of a small, rural site for burial from the middle Iron Age to the middle Roman period. To summarise, the middle Iron Age remains consisted of a single crouched inhumation of a prime adult, probably male, and two separate deposits of disarticulated adult bone, both from Iron Age ditches. Two further adults were dated to the late Iron Age/early Roman period, including one probable middle adult male, found in a crouched position, and a less well-preserved adult, who was tentatively sexed as male. Most of the burials were of Roman date and comprised seven neonates, one infant and disarticulated remains from at least one adult and one juvenile. These were all recovered from the latest deposits in enclosure ditch group 5292 and its recut 5291, dating to the middle of the Roman period. The enclosure ditches surrounded the crouched inhumation of a young adult, probably female. Two other highly disturbed adult inhumation was dated to this phase, as well as two cremation deposits, one juvenile and one middle adult, probably female.

Phase 1, middle Iron Age

The single articulated skeleton dating from this phase was osteologically unremarkable, Schmorl's nodes, periostitis and vertebral border shifting are all common pathologies observed amongst archaeological populations. The burial position, orientation and location of skeleton 3300 conforms with the recognised Iron Age funerary tradition of central Southern England in which single, crouched inhumations were placed within storage pits, shallow graves and ditches (Whimster 1981).

The disarticulated partial adult humerus and fragmented parietal bone recovered from ditches 3120 and 5073 respectively are also unremarkable in an Iron Age context. Isolated bones within settlement features such as pits, ditches and postholes, are common in the Iron Age, and perhaps represent opportune use of available space, rather than the utilisation of specially prepared graves (Hope 1999, 41). It has been suggested that the common discovery of isolated bones, in particular skull fragments, within Iron Age features may support the suggestion that the corpses during this period were exposed prior to burial (Carr and Knüsel 1997). Indeed, the evidence for Iron Age burial sites is very limited compared with those of other periods (Hope 1999, 42). However, the disarticulated remains had

no modifications (for example, scavenging marks or cut marks) to support this.

Phase 2, late Iron Age to early Roman

Due to its the high level of fragmentation and incompleteness little can be said about skeleton 5198, but skeleton 5012 was far better preserved. As with skeleton 3300 the position, orientation and location in terms of feature type conform with the Iron Age tradition of central Southern England (Whimster 1981). At only 1.63m skeleton 5012 was shorter than the average male height for this period (1.68 – 1.69m, as quoted in Roberts and Cox 2003, 142, 396). The skeletal health of this individual was generally fair; the dental disease, minor developmental anomaly of the lower spine, cribra orbitalia and periostitis are common, and in this individual none of them was severe.

Phase 3, Roman

The Roman burials include the most distinct group, seven middle Roman neonates and one infant in the final deposits of boundary ditch 5292 and its recut 5291. The position of these juveniles, within the final silting deposits of the ditches rather than within distinct graves cut into them, is certainly worthy of note. It is possible that these burials represent mere 'discarding' of newborns or infants (Soren and Soren 1999, 478). It has been suggested that infants were not regarded as true family members until they reached the age that they could walk, talk and interact, that is, they had no developed *persona* (ibid, 479; Esmonde Cleary 2000, 136). Plutarch (*Consolatio ad uxorum* 11, cited in Soren and Soren 1999, 483) even states that the laws forbade Romans to mourn for infants.

Five of the middle Roman juveniles exhibited endocranial lesions, which may be representative of severe, potentially fatal conditions, although this could not be confirmed. It is typical of Roman infant burial sites that it is impossible to establish the cause of death osteologically (Corney and Cox 2007, 12). It is possible that the assemblage may represent a normal infant mortality rate for the period of occupation, as suggested for the Barton Court Farm neonate burials (Miles 1984, microfiche plate 4:C12). Infanticide is also another possibility; Mays' (1993) research found strong evidence for the practice during the Roman period in Britain, based on the high proportions of full term perinates in Romano-British cemetery and non-cemetery populations. Documentary evidence for the practice of infanticide as a means of population control in the Roman Empire (Langer 1974, cited in Mays 1998, 66) further supports this. It was probably not uncommon for unwanted pregnancies to be continued to full term, with the unwanted newborns then left exposed, strangled or drowned (Soren and Soren 1999, 484; Taylor 2008, 94). Primitive methods of contraception may have been practised, although these would probably not have been used widely, and early-term abortifacients were considered risky or improper (ibid, 484). It may have been more common to kill off girls, rather than boys, particularly in poorer families where dowries might impoverish the family, although it has been noted that even rich families killed or exposed infants, perhaps to avoid having too many heirs of either sex (ibid, 484; Golden 1988, 157-159; Taylor 2008, 94-5). Infanticide has been suggested for the infant burials at Springhead, Kent (Penn 1967), Owslebury, Hampshire (Collis 1997) and Hambleden, Buckinghamshire (Cocks 1921).

Adult skeleton 5202, which lay within the enclosure and close to the juvenile group, was orientated north-south and lay in a crouched position, neither being typical of the burial rite in Roman Britain from the 2nd century AD, which was extended supine and orientated east-west. The position of skeleton 5202 is more in keeping with the previous Iron Age tradition (Whimster 1981). Osteologically skeleton 5202 also differs in stature from the average Roman female inhumation (1.59m or 5 feet 3 inches tall), being only 1.51m (*c* 4 feet 11 inches) tall. Skeleton 5202 was however taller than 1.47m (4 feet 10 inches), the modern clinical definition of dwarfism (Medline Plus 2013), nor did it exhibit other skeletal indicators of dwarfism, neither proportionate or disproportionate.

Given that skeletons 5223 and 153006 both appear to have originated from the same grave it seems likely that they would have been buried together, or within a short period of one another, and were perhaps related in some way. However, the high level of disturbance from evaluation trench 153 and the ridge and furrow has prevented this from being confirmed. It is also possible that they may have been from two intercutting graves, the grave containing 153006 being highly disturbed by the later activity.

The two Roman cremations contained only one individual each, one a juvenile and one a probable middle adult female. The cremation deposits follow the burial tradition most commonly seen in Roman Britain up to the 2nd century AD, after which cremation was largely replaced by inhumation (Millet 1995, 115). Neither of the cremation deposits were within the range observed in modern adult cremations, 5295 being just over three quarters of the expected minimum at 767.8g, and 3064/3069 being a mere fraction of it at 34.1g. However, it is rare, if ever, that the skeletal remains of an entire individual are present in a cremation burial (McKinley 1997, 137). Chemical destruction, and the possibility of some plough/machine truncation would have played some role in bone preservation and completeness, however it may have also been a deliberate choice by the mourners not to recover all of the remains from the pyre for burial. All skeletal regions were represented in deposit 5295; the only identifiable region in 3064/3069 was the skull. Combining this evidence with the significant proportion of fragments above

10mm in size in deposit 5295 and the very low proportion of such fragments in deposit 3064/3069, its seems likely that 5295 was a deliberate formal cremation burial, whilst 3064/3069 is more likely to be redeposited pyre debris. Both deposits did contain fairly large quantities of charcoal, but the proportion of charcoal to cremated bone was far higher in the case of 3064/3069.

No burnt animal bone was identified in either of the cremation deposits. Cremation 5295 contained a number of small iron nails, which were found in three out of the four samples in which this deposit was lifted. These indicated the presence of both hobnail sandals and nailed woodwork. Given their spread throughout the deposit it is most likely that the hobnails are from shoes that were either worn by the individual, or placed on the pyre during the cremation process, rather than being placed in with the cremated remains during deposition. The other nails may have belonged to a box or casket within the grave, or alternatively perhaps come from reused timbers burnt on the pyre.

Cremation was clearly fairly efficient, as neither cremation had much grey, black or blue bone. This level of efficiency is of note, because cremation burials of this period frequently exhibit uneven and incomplete burning (McKinley 2000c, 66). For example, this has been noted among those recovered from Gill Mill, Oxfordshire (Webb *et al.* forthcoming) and Westhampnett, West Sussex (McKinley 2000c, 66). That said, it was noted that some of the darkest (least burnt) fragments in deposit 5295 were the hand phalanges. Assuming that the body was laid on top of the pyre in a supine position, as is suggested to be the norm (McKinley 1997, 132), it could be inferred that one or both hands had slipped out of the pyre, or at least away from the centre of the heat. This seems especially likely considering the relatively thin flesh of the hands and the limited protection it would provide against fire.

ANIMAL BONES *by Lena Strid*

Introduction

All three sites excavated along the Gloucester Security of Supply pipeline had animal bone assemblages. The analysis of the assemblages focusses on bones that were recovered from features dated to the Iron Age and Roman periods, comprising a total of 2531 fragments. A full record of the assemblage can be found in the site archive.

Methodology

The bones were identified at Oxford Archaeology South using comparative skeletal reference collections, in addition to osteological identification manuals. All animal remains were counted and weighed, and where possible identified to species, element, side and zone (Serjeantson 1996; Strid 2012). Sheep and goat were identified to species

Table 4.4 Bone preservation grading methodology

Grade 0	Excellent preservation. Entire bone surface complete
Grade 1	Good preservation. Almost all bone surface complete
Grade 3	Fair preservation
Grade 4	Poor preservation. Most bone surface destroyed
Grade 5	Very poor preservation. No original bone surface remaining
Grade 6	Extremely poor preservation. Unlikely to be able to identify element

where possible, using Boessneck *et al.* (1964) and Prummel and Frisch (1986). They were otherwise classified as 'sheep/goat'. Ribs and vertebrae, with the exception of atlas and axis, were classified by size: 'large mammal' representing cattle, horse and deer; 'medium mammal' representing sheep/goat, pig and large dog; 'small mammal' representing small dog, cat and hare; and 'micromammal' representing animals such as rat and mouse.

The condition of the bone was graded on a 6-point system (0-5). Grade 0 equating to very well preserved bone, and grade 5 indicating that the bone had suffered such structural and attritional damage as to make it unrecognisable (Table 4.4).

For ageing, Habermehl's (1975) data on epiphyseal fusion was used. Three fusion stages were recorded: 'unfused', 'in fusion', and 'fused'. 'In fusion' indicates that the epiphyseal line is still visible. Tooth wear was recorded using Grant's tooth wear stages (Grant 1982), and correlated with tooth eruption (Habermehl 1975). In order to estimate an age for the animals, the methods of Halstead (1985), Payne (1973) and O'Connor (1988) were used for cattle, sheep/goat and pig respectively. Sex estimation was carried out based upon morphological traits on cattle pelves and pig canine teeth, using data from Schmid (1972) and Vretemark (1997). Measurements were taken according to von den Driesch (1976), using digital callipers with an accuracy of 0.01mm. Large bones were measured using an osteometric board, with an accuracy of 1mm.

Sieved samples were scanned and bones from bird and amphibians extracted, as well as mammal bones identifiable to species. The extracted bones comprised 18 fragments (1.6% of the total fragment count from the sieved samples).

Results: Bredon's Norton

The assemblage from Bredon's Norton was recovered from pits and ditches from a middle and late Iron Age and Roman settlement, the latter including a masonry building used in the late Roman period and the backfill from its demolition. A total of 1484 bones was recovered, of which 621 (41.8%) could be identified to taxon. The bones have been divided into four chronological groups for analysis: IA (middle and late Iron Age), LIA/ER (1st century AD either side of the Roman conquest), ER and MR (early and middle Roman) and LR (late Roman). This last group comes almost entirely from the masonry building.

Condition

The bones were generally well or fairly well preserved, regardless of time period. With the exception of one rodent-gnawed bone from late Roman demolition layer (3247), all other gnawed bones had been gnawed by carnivores, probably dogs or foxes. The late Iron Age/early Roman assemblage contained the highest frequency of gnawed bones, suggesting that waste disposal in this phase may have been treated in a different manner from that in other phases, and one in which scavenging animals had easier access to waste. The general scarcity of gnaw marks in the other phases suggest that butchery and kitchen waste had been disposed of rapidly and securely. A small number of burnt bones was found in the late Iron Age/early Roman and in the late Roman assemblages (Table 4.5).

Species present

The species present in the Iron Age to middle Roman assemblages included cattle (*Bos taurus*), sheep/ goat (*Ovis aries/Capra hircus*), pig (*Sus domesticus*), horse (*Equus caballus*), dog (*Canis familiaris*), domestic fowl (*Gallus gallus domesticus*) and frog (*Rana* sp.). A fragmented ulna from a small corvid, possibly jackdaw or magpie, was found in the fill of middle Iron Age grave 3299 (Table 4.6).

Although smaller in number, the late Roman assemblage contained the greatest species diversity (Table 4.6). All domestic animals in the late Iron Age

Table 4.5 Preservation level for bones from all phases in the Bredon's Norton assemblage, including number of burnt and gnawed bones

	N	0	1	2	3	4	5	Gnawed	Burnt
IA	37	5.4%	40.5%	48.6%	5.4%			8	
LIA/ER	884	4.0%	55.5%	38.8%	1.2%	0.5%		137	8
ER & MR	75	0.8%	77.3%	12.0%	2.7%			6	
LR (total)	488	9.8%	79.3%	9.8%	0.8%	0.2%		23	4
LRa	90	4.4%	87.8%	6.7%	0.1%			2	1
LRb	143	24.5%	66.4%	9.1%				13	2

Table 4.6 Number of fragments/taxon and phase in the Bredon's Norton assemblage

	IA	LIA/ER	ER & MR	LR (total)	LR a (M3-4C)	LR b (4C +)
Cattle	5	163	16	37	9	13
Sheep/goat	9	118	6	51	9	15
Sheep		3		2		
Pig	1	30	4	88	2	5
Horse	1	48	4	3	1	1
Dog		5	1			
Cat				4		3
Fox				3	3	
Field vole				1		1
Bank vole/field vole				1		1
Domestic fowl		1		1		
Duck				1		
?Woodcock				1	1	
Crow				1		
Crow/rook				1		
Small corvid	1					
Passerine				5	1	3
Indet. bird		1		1		1
Frog/toad		5		18		18
Frog		1				10
Micromammal				2		2
Medium mammal	5	93	5	99	14	17
Large mammal	7	148	9	90	32	32
Indet.	8	268	30	68	18	21
Total	37	884	75	488	90	143
Weight (g)	514	24563	2501	9971	1940	4042

to middle Roman assemblages were present, with the exception of dog and addition of cat (*Felis domesticus*). Wild taxa included fox (*Vulpes vulpes*), field vole (*Microtus agrestis*), duck (*Anatidae*), ?woodcock (*Scolopax rusticola*), crow (*Corvus corone*), crow/rook (*Corvus corone/Corvus frugilegus*) as well as frog/toad (*Rana* sp./*Bufo* sp.) and unidentifiable thrush-sized passerine (Table 4.6). The scarcity of wild fauna follows the general trend for rural Roman settlements (Grant 1989, 144). Parts of the late Roman assemblage could be divided into two phases: the earlier phase representing the construction of the building and the later phase representing its destruction. The bones from two phases are specified in Tables 4.5–6, but due to their small size they are not discussed further.

Additionally, a single eel (*Anguilla anguilla*) vertebra was identified by R. Nicholson from sample 5025, taken from layer 5049, the top fill of Roman ditch 5052 in group 5292.

Livestock

Studies have shown that an assemblage must contain at least 300 fragments of cattle, sheep/goat and pig, or a total MNI of 30 for these three taxa in order for an analysis of the inter-species frequency to be considered reliable (Hambleton 1999, 39-40). The late Iron Age/early Roman phase contains 302 fragments of these taxa, but the late Roman and other groups are too small for such analysis.

Iron Age faunal assemblages are sparsely represented in the upper Cotswold region. Nearby sites include the settlement at Aston Mill Farm and the hillfort at Conderton Camp, both from the middle Iron Age (Iles and Clark 2005; Lovett 1990). Their inter-species frequencies contrast greatly with Bredon's Norton as well as with each other (Fig. 4.1), suggesting that the three sites may represent settlements of different status or different animal husbandry focus. The Conderton Camp assemblage has a large variety of wild species, suggesting a higher-status site. The focus on cattle at Bredon's Norton could be related to the proximity of the river Avon, as wet floodplains are much more suitable for grazing cattle than for sheep. Aston Mill Farm is also situated near a flood plain, suggesting that the difference in frequency of sheep/goat between the two sites may be connected to accessibility of suitable sheep/goat pasture.

The few Roman faunal assemblages in the region mostly come from urban sites. Rural sites in Worcestershire and northern Gloucestershire have yielded too few bones to be considered for comparative material (University of York 2008). The urban assemblages from Worcester and Alcester show, as expected for urban sites from this period, high frequencies of cattle, followed by

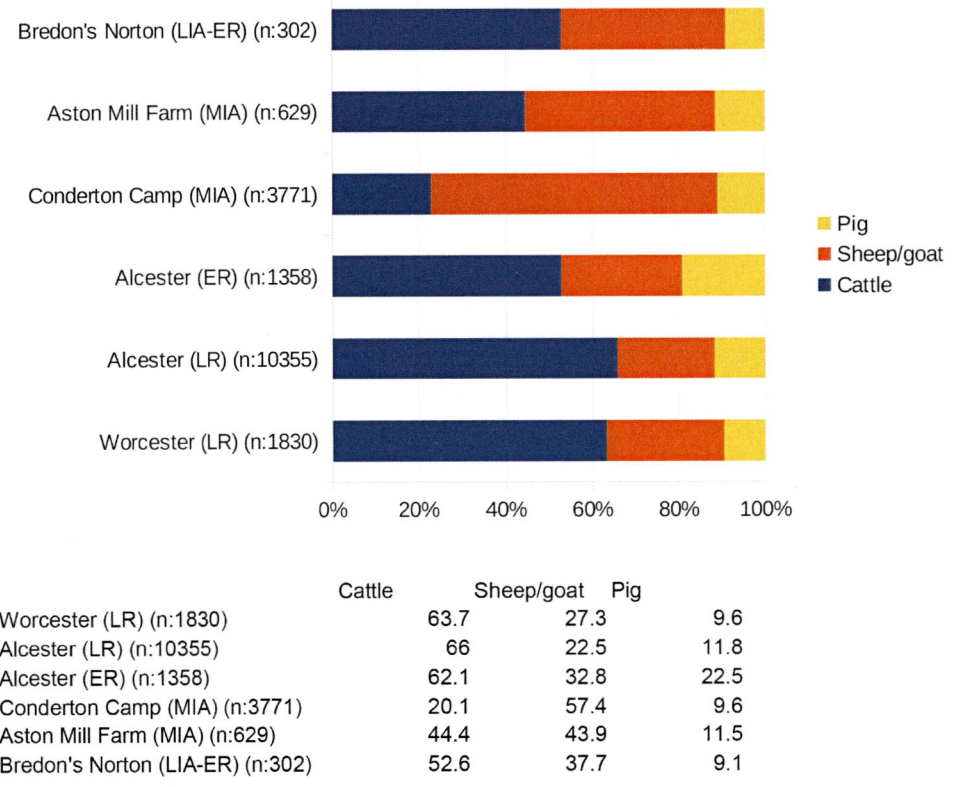

	Cattle	Sheep/goat	Pig
Worcester (LR) (n:1830)	63.7	27.3	9.6
Alcester (LR) (n:10355)	66	22.5	11.8
Alcester (ER) (n:1358)	62.1	32.8	22.5
Conderton Camp (MIA) (n:3771)	20.1	57.4	9.6
Aston Mill Farm (MIA) (n:629)	44.4	43.9	11.5
Bredon's Norton (LIA-ER) (n:302)	52.6	37.7	9.1

Fig. 4.1 Graph showing proportions of main domesticates and chronological trends at some Iron Age and Roman sites in the region

sheep/goat and pig (Fig. 4.1). Unfortunately, the late Roman assemblage from Bredon's Norton is below the recommended minimum of 300 fragments from cattle, sheep/goat and pig (Hambleton 1999, 39-40). The large proportion of pig bones is unusual for Roman sites in Britain as a whole, and has more in common with inter-species frequencies from Gaul (Hesse 2011) but it does mirror some assemblages from villas and other Romanised sites in Roman Britain (King 1999,40; Grimm in Barnett *et al.* 2011, 51-2). However, it is possible that the high frequency of

pig is dependent on skeletal element representation and does not accurately represent the living population at the end of the life of the settlement. Fragments from skull and feet are over-represented, whether due to ease of identification or excess of elements compared to sheep/goat and cattle. The majority of the pig fragments came from demolition layer 3165, suggesting that the remains may represent a single dumping event.

The ageing data is not very large (Table 4.7-4.10), but suggests that most cattle and sheep/goat were sub-adult or adult at the time of death, indicating

Table 4.7 Dental age data for cattle from all phases in the Bredon's Norton assemblage

	0-1 months	1-8 months	8-18 months	18-30 months	30-36 months	Young Adult	Adult	Old Adult	Senile
LIA/ER		4			1			4	1
ER&MR					1			1	1
LR (total)								1	1

Table 4.8 Dental age data for sheep/goat from all phases in the Bredon's Norton assemblage

	0-2 months	2-6 months	6-12 months	1-2 years	2-3 years	3-4 years	4-6 years	6-8 years	8-10 years
IA			1		1				
LIA/ER	1	1	2			2	3	2	
LR (total)			2			3			

Table 4.9 Dental age data for pig from all phases in the Bredon's Norton assemblage

	Juvenile	Immature	Sub-adult	Adult
IA			1	
LIA/ER			1	1
ER & MR		1		
LR (total)		1	4	2

that these animals were kept for multiple purposes, such as milk, wool, traction and meat. The younger animals probably represent surplus males raised for meat. Pig were raised solely for meat, and were often killed when reaching their full growth, or earlier. Bones from juvenile cattle, sheep/goat and pig, representing neonatal mortalities or deliberate culling were recovered in small numbers from the Iron Age to middle Roman and the late Roman assemblage.

Table 4.10 Epiphyseal closure of cattle, sheep/goat and pig from all phases in the Bredon's Norton assemblage

Cattle	IA		LIA/ER		ER&MR		LR (total)	
	N	% unfused	N	% unfused	N	% unfused	N	% unfused
Early fusion			21	0.0%	2	0.0%	6	0.0%
Mid fusion	1	100.0%	13	23.1%	1	0.0%	2	50.0%
Late fusion			8	25.0%	1	100.0%	3	33.3%
Sheep/goat	N	% unfused	N	% unfused	N	% unfused	N	% unfused
Early fusion			9	11.1%			6	0.0%
Mid fusion			4	25.0%	1	100.0%	6	33.3%
Late fusion			4	50.0%			11	27.3%
Pig	N	% unfused	N	% unfused	N	% unfused	N	% unfused
Early fusion			5	60.0%			5	20.0%
Mid fusion			3	66.7%			14	71.4%
Late fusion			2	50.0%	1	100.0%	2	100.0%

Table 4.11 Sexed animal remains in the Bredon's Norton assemblage

Species	Element	Phase	Male	Female
Cattle	Pelvis	LIA/ER		2
Pig	Mandibular canine	LIA/ER		1
		LR (total)	1	2

A small number of bones could be measured and/or sexed. The sample size is too small to yield any useful information regarding animal size, sex ratio and breed on the site. Measurements that were useful for comparison on a regional scale have been compiled in Tables 4.11 and 4.12.

Butchery marks were recorded on a total of 38 bones from cattle, sheep/goat, pig, large and medium-sized mammals. It was not possible to discern any pattern regarding inter-species variation of butchery methods nor changes in butchery practice over time. As expected in a rural late Iron Age/early Roman settlement, the main disarticulation of the carcass was carried out with knives (Maltby 2007, 60-61). There is some evidence for the use of cleavers for disarticulation in the late Roman assemblage, but knives seems to have been used as well. Indications of skinning include cut marks at the lower shaft on two cattle metatarsals. Chop marks and cut marks on the proximal metatarsal and the tarsal joint on four cattle suggest skinning or disarticulation. Sagittal splitting of the carcass was evidenced on one medium and one large mammal vertebra as well as on one cattle axis. Two pig skulls had been split sagitally, probably to extract the brain. Cut marks from disarticulation and filleting were noted on long bones from cattle, sheep/goat and pig. Cleavers had been used to disarticulate one late Iron Age/early Roman cattle radius and one late Roman cattle femur. The use of cleavers for filleting

Table 4.12 Measurements of cattle, sheep/goat, pig, horse and fox in the Bredon's Norton assemblage

Species	Element	Measurement		Phase		
Cattle	Tibia	Bd	LIA/ER	52.2		
			ER	54.5		
			LR (total)	55.3	55.7	
Sheep/goat	Metacarpal	GL	LR (total)	121.0		
		Bd	LIA/ER	22.8		
			LR (total)	22.1		
	Metatarsal	GL	LR (total)	131.0		
		Bd	LR (total)	20.7		
	Tibia	Bd	LR (total)	23.2	23.4	
Pig	Metacarpal IV	GL	LR (total)	74.4	74.8	
Horse	Metatarsal	Bd	ER	42.7		
			LR (total)	40.6	54.1	
	Tibia	Bd	LR (total)	56.8	60.7	
Fox	Humerus	GL	LR (total)	126.8		
		Bd	LR (total)	21.4		

were noted on one cattle radius and one cattle scapula, both from the late Roman assemblage. A late Iron Age/early Roman cattle horn core had been sawn off mid-horn core, suggesting that horn working took place at the settlement.

Pathological conditions were relatively scarce and were only found in the late Iron Age/early Roman and the late Roman assemblage. Exostoses at joints, probably from muscle strains, were noted on a horse metatarsal. A cattle metacarpal has small bone nodules on the posterior/lateral edge of the upper part of the shaft. A similar pathology was noted on a cattle metatarsal with bone nodules posteriorly on the lower part of the shaft. The aetiology is unknown, but a connection to muscle strain cannot be excluded. Degenerative joint disease was found on a cattle mandible, where the joint was slightly malformed and partly covered in small porosities. The proximal joint of a pig radius had exostoses laterally/anteriorly and an erosive lesion on the lateral/posterior side. The posterior part of the joint surface was mostly destroyed.

Eburnation occurred on the pubic part of the acetabulum on two cattle pelves. One of the pelves also had smooth extra bone growth around the rim of the acetabulum, suggesting increased wear and tear on the hip joint. The other pelvis had lipping and smooth extra bone growth around the rim as well as near-fusion of the pubic and ischial part of the acetabulum. The aetiology is uncertain, but the pathologies may be reactions to fracture of the femoral neck at a young age. Subluxation occurred on one cattle scapula, evidenced by extensive exostoses around the joint and eburnation on the medial half of the joint surface. Eburnation was also found on some of the exostoses (Fig. 4.2). A pig scapula had fractured across the neck and blade, but had healed well. Oral pathologies were relatively common. Pre-mortem tooth loss and pathological bone growth from infections occurred on mandibles from cattle, sheep/goat and pig, whereas irregular wear from malocclusion and/or tooth loss were noted on cattle and horse.

Other domestic mammals

The other domestic mammals, horse, dog and cat, were found in small numbers in most phases. The exception is the late Iron Age/early Roman assemblage, where horses were the third most numerous animal. As the fragmentation on many horse bones is similar to that of cattle, their flesh may have been used for food. One horse femur did indeed show cut

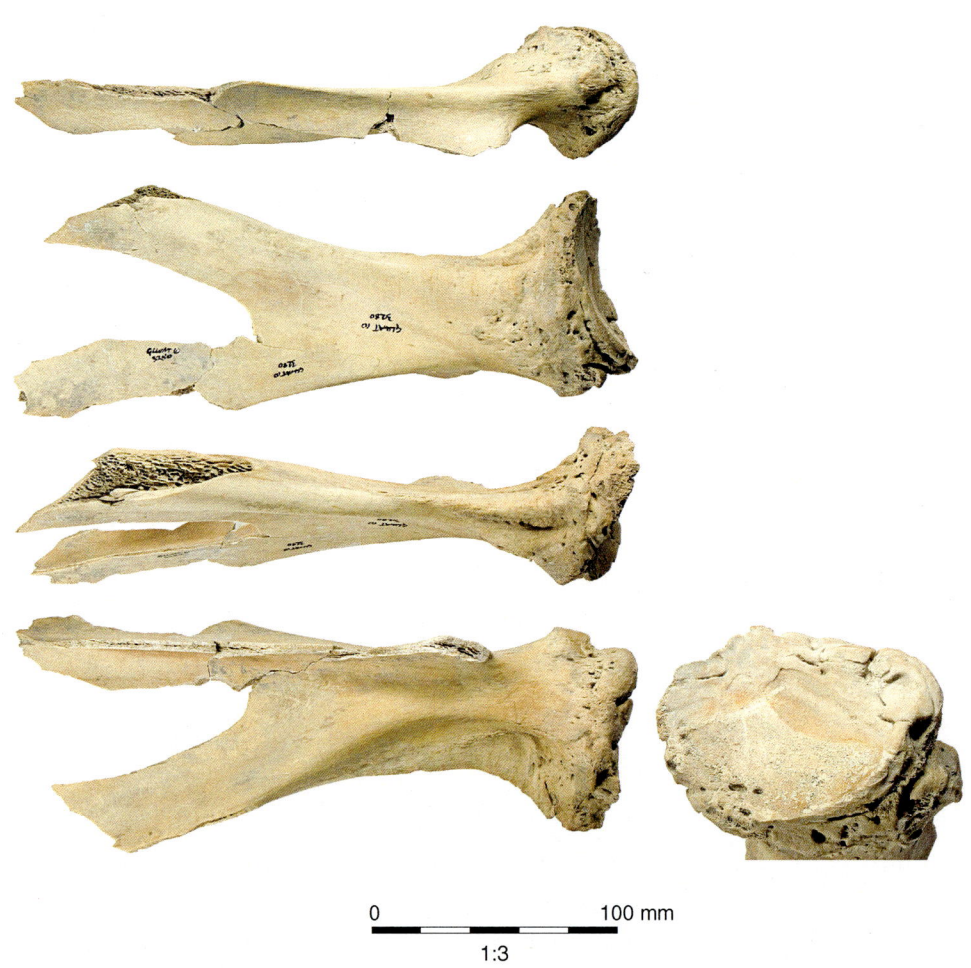

0   100 mm

1:3

Fig. 4.2 Cattle scapula with exostoses around the glenoid joint and eburnation on the joint surface

marks from filleting on the distal third of the shaft (Fig. 4.3). The shaft fragment was also burnt at both ends, possibly during cooking. However, there are also several entire meat bearing bones in the assemblages, suggesting that horse was not regularly on the menu. Other butchery marks on late Iron Age/early Roman horse remains include transverse chop marks ventrally on a pelvis, probably from disarticulation of the hind leg, and cut marks on a first phalanx, probably from skinning. All horse remains from Bredon's Norton came from adult animals. Pathologies only occurred in the late Iron Age/early Roman assemblage, comprising exostoses at the proximal joint of a metatarsal and irregular wear on two cheek teeth, the latter probably caused by malocclusion and/or tooth loss.

A single late Iron Age/early Roman dog pelvis represents a large canid. Wolf cannot be fully excluded, although due to the scarcity of wolf compared to dog in the zooarchaeological record and the emergence of large dogs in Roman Britain (Harcourt 1974, 164), this is less likely. The other dog bones in the assemblage probably represent dogs of medium size, used for guarding and/or herding.

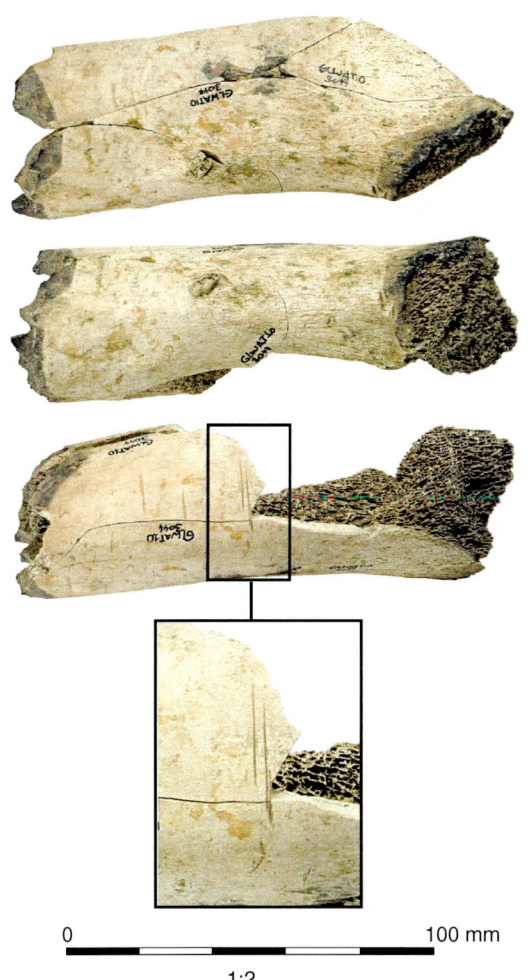

0   100 mm

1:2

Fig. 4.3 Fragment of horse femur illustrating burning at both ends and cut marks on the shaft

The fusion data and surface structure of the bones suggest that horses, dogs and cats were fully mature when they died. Horses were not normally bred for meat in the Iron Age or Roman periods, but were mainly utilised as riding animals or load carriers. However, one horse femur shaft in the late Iron Age/early Roman assemblage showed traces of charring at both ends. Two horizontal cleaver marks on the distal third of the shaft suggest disjointing and/or removal of meat. Cut marks or chop marks were not observed on any of the other horse, dog or cat bones.

Wild mammals

Wild mammals are only represented by fox and field vole, suggesting that hunting was a rare pastime and contributed very little, if anything, to the diet in the late Roman period. The fox may have been hunted for its fur and/or to prevent predation on domestic fowl.

Birds

The few avian remains suggest that neither poultry keeping nor wild fowling were of importance to the inhabitants of the settlements. However, bird bones are fragile and many may have been fragmented beyond recovery. Domestic fowl was introduced to Britain in the Iron Age but remained a very rare animal until the Roman period (Yalden and Albarella 2009, 101). The bones from duck, ?woodcock and passerine probably represent food waste, whereas the crow and crow/rook bones are more ambiguous. Young rooks have been eaten in post-medieval Europe, but there are no mention of any corvids in Roman cookbooks. Crows are predators on newborn lambs and large numbers of corvids were killed in the post-medieval period for this reason (Lovegrove 2007, 154-168). As the late Roman corvid bones were found in demolition layers they are less likely to represent ritual deposits – pits and ditches being more common features for such deposits (Morris 2011, 146; Serjeantson and Morris 2011). The middle Iron Age corvid wing bone however came from layer 3301, the fill of grave 3300, and may have been a ritual deposit.

Results: Fiddington and Pamington

The assemblages from Pamington (57 identifiable bones) and Fiddington (146 identifiable bones) came primarily from a series of enclosure and boundary ditches (Table 4.13). A small number of bones came from pits, postholes and layers. The bones from Pamington are all of the Iron Age, but those from Fiddington can be divided into early, middle and late Roman groups.

Due to the small size of the assemblages, especially once divided into phases, little can be said regarding animal husbandry practices. The bones from Fiddington also include parts of two

Table 4.13 Bones identified to species from the Pamington and Fiddington assemblages

| | Pamington | | Fiddington | |
	IA	ER	MR	LR
Cattle	25	21	13	15
Sheep/goat	22	7	12	23
Pig	2	1	3	4
Horse	8	29*	2	13**
Dog		2		
Fox				1
Total	57	60	30	56

* incl. 24 fragments from an articulated hind leg

** incl. 7 fragments from an articulated hind leg

articulated legs, reducing the number of bones for such analysis still further. However, the predominance of cattle and sheep/goat and scarcity of pigs is common on rural Iron Age and Roman sites.

Two articulated horse hind legs were found in the Fiddington assemblage, one in an early Roman ditch (1127) and the other in late Roman ditch (1101). Neither was measurable. Deposits of articulated animal limbs constitute one type of articulated animal bone group, possibly connected to ritual deposits, that are commonly found in Iron Age and Roman settlements (Hill 1995, 27-28; Morris 2011). The articulated limb in ditch 1127 was found in the upper fill of the ditches; the position within the ditch was not noted in ditch 1101, but the articulated limb was found together with other animal bones, pottery, charcoal and limestone fragments. It is therefore uncertain whether the articulated horse legs represent ritual deposits or disposal of dismembered carcasses.

SMALL MAMMAL REMAINS
by Rebecca Nicholson

A number of burnt small mammal bones were recovered from samples taken from the Roman sunken-floored room 3184, within deposits of charred grain and charcoal which relate to the secondary use of this building in the 4th century or beyond (Fig. 4.4; Table 4.14). The bone assemblage

Table 4.14 Small mammal bones by species and element found in samples from the late Roman burnt deposit in Building 3184

| Species | Samples | 3021 | 3032 | 3039 | 3040 | 3042 | 3043 | 3045 | 3047 | Total |
	Context	3013	3237	3237	3237	3237	3237	3237	3237	
common shrew	mandible	1		2						3
common/water shrew	humerus	1		1	1					3
	pelvis			1		1				2
	ulna			2			2			4
pigmy shrew	humerus		1			1				2
	mandible				1		1			2
	ulna						1			1
field vole	mandible			1			1			2
	maxilla	1								1
	pelvis			2						2
	tooth	2		3			2			7
bank vole	mandible				1					1
	maxilla						1			1
vole	humerus					1	2			3
	femur								1	1
	tibia	1								1
	tooth							2		2
cf. harvest mouse	maxilla			1						1
wood mouse	mandible						1			1
	maxilla			1						1
	pelvis			1						1
mouse	humerus						1			1
	tibia	1								1
vole/mouse	ulna						1			1
dog/fox (neonate/foetal)	femur			1						1
unidentified		80	10	80	10	85	51			316
Grand total		87	11	96	13	88	64	2	1	362

Fig. 4.4 Plan showing the grid used to sample the burnt deposit within Building 3184

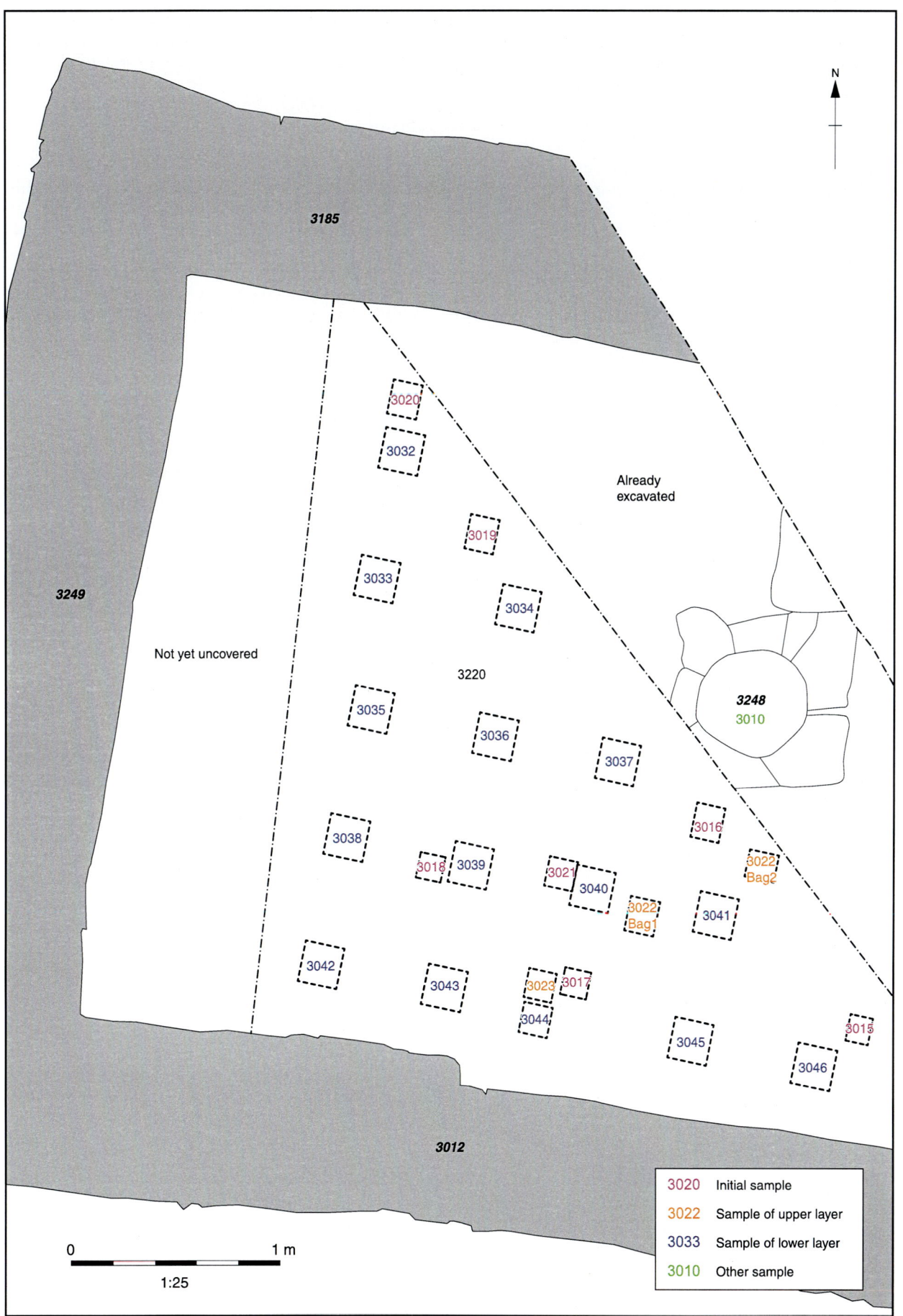

recovered from the fine residues and flots was scanned and diagnostic elements identified by comparison with skeletal material held at OAS and by the author as well as published guides (particularly Lawrence and Brown 1967). Only samples recovered from these burnt deposits are considered; while unburnt small mammal remains were relatively abundant across the sites, at least some of those recovered from other areas may be intrusive since these animals create underground burrrows.

Several samples from deposit 3237 and sample 3021 from deposit 3013 included fragments of charred or calcined small mammal bone, almost certainly from complete animals caught in the fire. Apart from a calcined femur from a foetal or neonatal puppy (smaller than a 3 day old collie) the remains came from rodents and insectivores. Field vole (*Microtus agrestis*), bank vole (*Myodes glareolus*), field mouse (*Apodemus sylvaticus*), a possible harvest mouse (*Micromys minutus*), common shrew (Sorex araneus) and pygmy shrew (*Sorex minutus*) have been identified, suggesting that the room was visited by a range of small animals. The bones ranged in colour from black (charred) through grey to white (fully calcined). A tibia from sample 3021 (3013) was only partially burnt, with both brown (unburnt) and white (calcined) bone present suggesting that the bone had not been exposed to the heart of the fire.

Although field and harvest mice may well have utilised the grain store as a source of both food and shelter, the relative abundance of voles and shrews is unusual for this kind of habitat; neither are commensals. Shrews are insectivores and while insects and arthropods may well have lived within the building a concentration of shrew remains is surprising (a minimum of one or two shrews was found in almost every sample which contained burnt bone). Both common and pygmy shrews are solitary animals, common shrews inhabiting grassland, woodland, scrub, hedgerows and banks while pygmy shrews are more usually found in open habitats (Lawrence and Brown 1967, 20-21). Cat bones are present though scarce at Roman sites (Yalden 1999, 125) but several have been recovered from Bredon's Norton South, late Roman contexts 3036 and 3018. While cats will readily catch shrews they rarely eat them, due to the foul-tasting and - smelling glands in the skin, and plausibly this could account for the collection of small mammal bones within the sunken-floored building.

PLANT MACROFOSSILS *by Kath Hunter*

Introduction, aims and summary

This report presents the analysis of plant remains recovered from three separate excavations along the route of the pipeline, at Pamington and Fiddington, Gloucestershire, and at Bredon's Norton South, Worcestershire. Pits, ditches, cremation and inhumation burials, and buildings – including a possible bath house re-used as a corndryer or grain store –

were excavated and sampled to provide information upon the crops and other plant materials grown and consumed at these sites over time, and to provide information on the local environment of these sites.

All of the deposits sampled for charred plant remains were processed, and charred plant remains were recovered from all of the sites. Silicified, mineralised and potentially dessicated cereal remains were noted in deposits associated with sunken Room 3184 (a possible plunge bath) at Bredon's Norton. Due to the extreme richness of the samples from this room, only 10L from each sample was processed.

The aim of the assessment was to characterise the quantity and quality of plant remains preserved in deposits along the pipeline in order to assess the value of the material to answer regional and site-based research questions. To do this, the following categories of information were considered:

- The quantity of the material preserved
- The quality and type of preservation
- The range of species represented
- Indicators of human activity such as domestic and agricultural practice
- Indicators of the local environment
- The potential for radiocarbon dating
- Other sites within the region that may have comparable assemblages

During the assessment stage all 77 samples for charred plant remains were assessed for the potential of the material for analysis. Overall the preservation of the plant remains was variable from very poor to excellent.

Only relatively small amounts of charred plants remains were recovered from Pamington (middle to late Iron Age samples) and from Fiddington (late Roman samples only), and on the basis of preservation and assemblage size two samples each were selected for further analysis from these sites.

At Bredon's Norton the pipeline uncovered a wider range of features, including part of a Roman stone building, possibly a bath house, in one room of which (3184) a very large quantity of charred cereal grains was discovered on the floor (Plate 2.49), and assessment suggested that this was predominantly Spelt wheat (*Triticum spelta*). The presence of burnt timbers above this deposit suggest that it is a stored crop that was burnt *in situ*, providing a very rare opportunity to study the remains of a stored Roman crop. Seventeen samples from this and associated deposits were selected for further analysis. Other deposits assessed for charred plant remains, but not further analysed, comprised context 5064 (from undated posthole 5060), context 5182 (from middle Roman ditch group 5290), context 5027 (fill of clay-lined pit 5025) and deposit 5258 on the floor of poorly-preserved corndryer (5255) (OA 2012, Appendix C.2 Table C.1.4).

Important period-based questions for further consideration at the analysis stage, with reference to the recommendations outlined by Campbell and Straker (unpublished, 2005) in their draft review of plant remains from the South of England, included:

- Evidence for crop processing
- Evidence for the nature of crop storage in late Roman Worcestershire (and the nature of the re-use of the bath house)
- Evidence for centralised food production and trade to Roman towns
- Potentially, evidence for malting/brewing
- Evidence for corn drying

Analysis confirmed that this was an almost pure deposit of spelt wheat (*Triticum spelta*) grains and chaff, which includes a relatively high number of single-grained spikelets. This could be either a genetic characteristic or the plants' response to their growing environment and could have reduced expected crop yields. The burnt grain lay upon the floor of the building directly below charred timbers and fallen wall plaster, and so grains were dated both to date the stored crop and the date of destruction of the building in which it was stored. Two radiocarbon dates obtained from spelt spikelets from the deposit have given a very late Roman date range, shedding light on Roman crop practices at the very end of the Roman period in northern Gloucestershire and southern Worcestershire.

Method

When the burnt deposit was first uncovered, a few initial samples were taken on an ad hoc basis across the interior of the building. Once the destruction deposits overlying the charcoal and ash layers had been removed, however, and the quantity of charred grain was appreciated, it was decided to sample the layer on a roughly 1m grid (see Table 4.17 for details). Two layers were distinguished on site, an upper black layer, with a more ashy greyish-white deposit below, and sampling was carried out on each of these. A plan showing the sampling grid and the numbers of the samples from both layers is illustrated (Fig. 4.4).

All of the samples were processed at OA South using a siraf style floatation machine and the flots were washed over a 250μm mesh sieve. The residues were retained in a 500μm flexible nylon mesh. The flots and heavy residues were dried in a heated drying room at *c* 25 °C. Both the flots and residues were analysed using low powered microscopes at a magnification of between x10 and x 20 (MTL10 and Leica EZ4D). The nomenclature for the plant remains follows Stace 2010. The identification of the plant remains was carried out using modern reference material and standard reference texts (Beijerinck 1947, Berggren 1981, Cappers *et al.* 2006, Jacomet 2006).

The samples from Pamington and Fiddington selected for full analysis from the initial assessment (Hunter in Sykes *et al.* 2011) were sorted by Julia Meen and Sharon Cook, who then carried out the preliminary identification under the supervision of the author, who checked and verified all identifications. The results are shown in Tables 4.15 and 4.16. Meen and Cook also sorted some of the samples from Bredon's Norton alongside the author. Because the grain deposit was so large, only a selection of the samples were analysed. Selection targeted three pairs of samples from the same locations, one from each of the two superimposed deposits, in order to assist in the interpretation of these apparently different assemblages. Preliminary identification was carried out to determine whether the deposit was all of one type, or whether it varied spatially. In order to gain as much information about the deposit as possible within a limited time scale, some of the samples selected were not sorted but were subjected to a comprehensive scan by the author, who recorded the frequency of different types of plant remains but did not extract them. This process also allowed species not represented elsewhere to be recorded. The results of the detailed analysis and the scan data are shown in Table 4.17.

During the scanning process, the frequency of the different types of charred plants remains was recorded using the following key:

| *1–5 items | ** 6–10 | *** 11–50 |
| **** 60–100 | ***** 101–500 | ! * ! 1000 + |

Results: Pamington

Following the assessment stage two ditch samples (2202 and 2203) were selected for full analysis, and both samples produced assemblages consisted with glume wheat processing waste, with chaff and some grain (Table 4.15). All of the cereal remains are of wheat apart from two cultivated oat floret bases (*Avena sativa*). This hints at a second crop which may have been grown separately from the wheat or may have been a relic within the wheat crop. Unfortunately, none of the wheat chaff was well enough preserved to securely identify it beyond emmer/spelt (*Triticum dicoccum/spelta*), both types of wheat which could have been grown in this period.

Weed seeds from the samples are mainly from plants associated with arable fields and grassland. The location of the material within ditch fills suggests secondary deposition and might be the result of a process or processes being carried out close by. The deposits might also be the result of several burning and dumping events. However, the nature of both assemblages suggests the processing of cereal or the subsequent burning of the waste happened close by. The weed seed assemblage also suggests the mixing of debris from several sources, such as burnt fodder or bedding as well as crop weeds that accumulated in the ditch fill.

Table 4.15 Charred plant remains from Fiddington

Fiddington late Roman samples Taxa	Common name	Componant	Habitat	Pit fill 1067 Sample 1006	Ditch fill 1070 Sample 1005
Triticum sp.	wheat nfi	grain	Cult		10
Triticum sp.	wheat	grain	Cult	121	
cf. *Triticum* sp.	possible wheat	grain	Cult		8
Hordeum sp.	barley	grain	Cult	8	
cf. *Hordeum* sp	possible barley	grain	Cult	2	
Avena sp.	oat	grain	Cult	36	5
cf. *Avena* sp.	possible oat	grain	Cult/Grassland	61	46
Cereal NFI	unidentified cereal	grain fragments (charred)	Cult	220	150
Triticum cf. *dicoccum*	possible emmer	spikelet fork	Cult	16	
Triticum cf. *dicoccum*	possible emmer	glume base		12	
Triticum spelta	spelt	glume base	Cult	157	31
Triticum cf. *spelta*	spelt	glume base		4	
Triticum spelta	spelt	spikelet fork	Cult	24	
Triticum spelta/dicoccum	spelt/emmer	spikelet fork	Cult	97	35
Triticum spelta/dicoccum	spelt/emmer	glume base	Cult	57	100+
Triticum sp.	free threshing	rachis fragment		1	
Triticum sp.	wheat	lemna/palea fragments (silicified)	*		
Triticum sp.	wheat	awn fragments	Cult	*	
Hordeum sp.	barley	rachis fragment (2-row lax-eared hulled)	Cult	2	
Hordeum sp.	barley	rachis fragment (hulled)	Cult		
Hordeum sp.	barley	rachis fragment	Cult	15	
Avena cf. *sativa* L.	oat	floret base		1	
Avena sp.	oat	floret base		15	
Avena sp.	oat	awn fragments	C, arable, rough and waste ground	**	
Avena fatua L.	wild oat	floret base	arable, rough and waste ground	10	
Cereal NFI	unidentified cereal	detached embryo	C	39	6
Cereal NFI	unidentified cereal	detached coleoptile	C	40	10
Cereal NFI	unidentified cereal	straw culm node		1	
Vicia/Lathyrus sp. (4mm)	vetch/pea	seed (fragments)	Da, Cult		2(4)
Vicia/Lathyrus sp. (2mm)	vetch/pea	seed	Da, Cult	5	1
Vicia/Lathyrus sp. (1mm)	vetch/pea	seed		2	
Trifolium/melilotus sp. L	clover/medick	seed			1
Raphanum raphanistrum L.	wild radish	mericarp	cultivated and rough ground, waste places and tips	1	
Persicaria sp.	knotweeds	Achene			
cf. *Persicaria* sp.	knotweeds	Achene		1	
cf. *Fallopia convolvulus* (L.) Love	possible black bindweed	Achene		1	
Rumex cf. *acetosella* L.	possible sheep's sorrel	Achene/(tepal)			8
Rumex sp.	dock type	Achene	DaGMSW	15	
cf. *Rumex* sp.	dock type	Achene		3	
Chenopodium album L.	fat hen	seed	Da,n	58	
Atriplex sp.	orache	seed	n	7	
Chenopodium sp.	goosefoots	seed	n	5	9
Chenopodium/Atriplex sp.		seed	n	7	
Caryophyllaceae		seecapsule fragment		1	
Stellaria sp.	stichworts	seed		1	
Agrostemma githago L.	corn cockle	seed capsule fragment	Da		1
		Achene			1
Cirsium sp.	thistle	Achene		1	
Anthemis cotula	stinking chamomile	Achene	A heavy soils	71	9

162

Table 4.15 (continued)

Fiddington late Roman samples Taxa	Common name	Componant	Habitat	Pit fill 1067 Sample 1006	Ditch fill 1070 Sample 1005
cf .*Anthemis cotula*	stinking chamomile	Achene		17	
Tripleurospermum inodorum (L.) Scultz-Bip	scentless mayweed	Achene	Da		1
	grass	Caryopsis		6	1
cf. Poaceae	possible grass	Caryopsis		12	
Lolium sp.	rye grass	Caryopsis		3	
cf. *Lolium* sp	possible rye grass type	caryopsis			2
cf. *Danthonia decumbens* (L.) DC	heath-grass	cayopsis			1
Unident		seed			6

Table 4.16 Charred plant remains from Pamington

Pamington mid-late Iron Age ditches Taxa	Common name	Componant	Habitat	Ditch fill 2012 Sample 2002	Ditch fill 2039 Sample 2003
Triticum sp.	wheat nfi	grain	Cult	2	1
cf. *Triticum* sp.	possible wheat	grain	Cult		2
Avena/Bromus sp.	oat/brome	grain	Cult/grassland		3
Cereal NFI	Unidentified cereal	grain fragments (charred)	Cult	25	38
Triticum spelta/dicoccum	spelt/emmer	spikelet fork	Cult	1	5
Triticum spelta/dicoccum	spelt/emmer	glume base	Cult	67	116
Avena sativa L.	oat	floret base	Cult		2
cf. *Papaver* sp.	poppy	seed		1	
Vicia/Lathyrus sp. (4mm)	vetch/pea	seed	Da, Cult		2
Vicia/Lathyrus sp. (2mm)	vetch/pea	seed	Da, Cult	2	
Trifolium/Lotus sp. L	clover/birdsfoot trefoil	seed		1	1
cf. *Potentilla* sp.	cinquefoil type	achene		1	1
Corylus avellana L.	hazelnut	shell frags	SW		5
Polygonaceae					2
Atriplex sp.	orache	seed	n	1	
Chenopodium sp.	goosefoots	Seed	n	1	
Caryophyllaceae				2	
cf. *Stellaria* sp.	stichworts	seed		1	
Galium aperine L.	cleavers	nutlet		1	
Plantago lanceolata L.	Ribwort Plantain	seed	G short or grazed, Da	1	
Euphrasia/Odontites L.	Eyebright/ Bartsia	seed	Da G	1	
Asteraceae				2	1
Poaceae	Grass	Caryopsis			9
Unident		seed		2	5
		nut fragment			1
Unident		bread like fragments		2	

Results: Fiddington

The two samples analysed were sample 1006 from fill 1067 in Enclosure C and sample 1005 from fill 1070 of late Roman ditch 1071. The assemblages identified from these features fit into a pattern often seen in this period. There is a mixture of cereal grain and chaff with weed seeds within both samples (Table 4.16).

Sample 1006 from enclosure fill 1067 produced wheat, oat and hulled barley grains. The chaff suggests that two types of wheat, spelt and possibly emmer, are present, together with a six row type of barley. This is consistent with evidence of crops from this period. A single possibly cultivated oat floret base may suggest a third crop. However, all the other identifiable oat floret bases are clearly of a wild type with the distinct sucker at the end. This suggests a weed with a similar habitat to the cultivated crop that was inadvertently harvested and the seed retained during the subsequent processing of the grain. A single rachis fragment of free threshing wheat may suggest another potential crop. The free threshing nature of this plant means that it is less

Table 4.17 Charred plant remains from Bredon's Norton Building 3184 (late 4th century)

Taxa	Common name	Componant	sample / context / layer no. / FA/ Scan / feature type and no. — vol. Flot / % sorted/ scanned / Habitat
Triticum spelta	spelt	single spikelet fork with grain	Cult
Triticum spelta	spelt	double spikelet fork with grain	Cult
Triticum spelta	spelt	articulated ear fragment	
Triticum spelta	spelt	immature spelt spikelet (articulated)	
Triticum spelta	spelt	primary (sterile) spikelet	
Triticum cf.spelta	possible spelt	grains from a double spikelet (sprouted)	9
Triticum cf.spelta	possible spelt	grain (sprouted) [insect damage]	Cult
Triticum sp.	glume wheat type	grain (sprouted)	Cult
Triticum sp.	glume wheat type	tail grain	
Triticum sp.	wheat nfi	Grain	Cult
Triticum cf. *spelta/ dicoccum*	spelt/emmer glume wheat type	tail grain	
Triticum sp.	wheat	grain	Cult
cf. *Triticum* sp.	possible wheat	grain	Cult
cf. *Hordeum* sp	possible barley	grain	Cult
Avena fatua L.	wild oat	grain in floret	weed of arable,waste and rough ground
Avena sp.	oat	grain (mineralised)	Cult
cf. *Avena* sp.	possible oat	grain	Cult/Grassland
Cereal NFI	unidentified cereal	grain fragments	cult
Triticum dicoccum Schubl	emmer	glume base	Cult
Triticum cf. *dicoccum*	possible emmer	spikelet fork	Cult
Triticum spelta	spelt	glume base	Cult
Triticum spelta	spelt	glume fragments no base	5
Triticum spelta	spelt	single spikelet fork	Cult
Triticum spelta	spelt	double spikelet fork	Cult
Triticum spelta	spelt	spikelet fork	Cult
cf. *Triticum spelta*	possible spelt	palea/lemma fragments charred	1000+
cf. *Triticum spelta*	possible spelt	palea/lemma fragments silicified	!*!
cf. *Triticum spelta*	possible spelt	palea/lemma fragments mineralised	
cf. *Triticum spelta*	possible spelt	articulated rachis	1
cf. *Triticum spelta*	possible spelt	primary rachis nodes	
cf. *Triticum spelta*	possible spelt	rachis	
cf. *Triticum spelta*	possible spelt	sterile spikelets	1
cf. *Triticum spelta*	possible spelt	glume base	
cf. *Triticum spelta*	possible spelt	spikelet fork	
Triticum spelta/dicoccum	spelt/emmer	spikelet fork	Cult
Triticum spelta/dicoccum	spelt/emmer	glume base	Cult
Triticum cf. *aestivum*	bread wheat	rachis fragment	Cult
Triticum sp.	wheat	awn fragments charred	Cult
Triticum sp.	wheat	awn fragments silicified	1000+
Triticum sp. 10	wheat	partially charred rachis and glumes	
Triticum sp.	wheat	partially charred glumes	1
Triticum sp.	wheat	partially charred spikelet (sterile)	
Triticum sp.	wheat	silicified chaff fragments	

3009 3220 FA burnt layer	3010 3247 FA tank	3016 3013 2 Scan lower ash layer	3020 3189 2 Scan lower ash layer	3021 3013 2 FA ash (below 3040)	3025 3331 FA structure	3026 3331 Scan structure	3031 3237 1 Scan grain layer	3032 3237 1 FA grain layer	3036 3237 1 Scan grain layer	3039 3237 1 FA grain layer	3040 3237 1 FA grain layer	3042 3237 1 FA grain layer	3044 3237 1 Scan grain layer	3046 3237 1 FA grain layer	3049 3340 FA* drain	3050 3332 Scan floor
										25% sorted						
2		*			*		**	*	*	21	34	14	***		7	
4							*	*	**	20	46	24	***		8	
					*			1	21							
				*												
							11									
								1(1)				-1				
							1(1)						18			
114	17									778[1](1)	727(2)	(3)[4]	995	237		
				23												
2																
49	5				****		***	*!*		1000+					58	
13	4	*				*		53			20			16		
		***	***			***		233	*****				*****	307		**
65						****		127				105		220	21	***
				3												
					1	1			*	1						
9							*	1	*	29	9	24	***(*)	6		
2														1		
1000+			****	23			****		*!*	1000+	1000+	1000+	*!*		23	***
1				1												
35	1	*	*	1			***	17		93	96	63	***	31	11	
2												3		6		
16												81		15		
36	2		*		**	*	***	29	***	107	173	118	***	82	6	
						**				!*!	500+		1000+			
!	******	!*!		*		****	****		**	****		1000+				
				**						*	500+					
								*		4		***	12			
									6	3	***					
				*												
							1	*		2	7		****			
1														3		
														6		
	2		*	2			**	3		1000+	16	44	*	31	9	
		**			*	**	**	7		1000+	44	35	*	6	10	*
											6					
					***	***		*				**				
!*!	***	*!*	!*!	*		**	***	****		****		****	****			
										4						
								2(1)								
			*										!*!			

Table 4.17 *(continued)*

			sample *context* *layer no.* *FA/ Scan* *feature type and no.*
Taxa	*Common name*	*Componant*	*vol. Flot* *% sorted/ scanned* *Habitat*
Triticum sp.	wheat	mineralised chaff fragment	
cf. *Hordeum* sp.	barley	rachis fragment	
Avena sp.	oat	awn fragments	Cult ,arable, rough and waste ground
Avena sp.	oat	oat stem	
Avena fatua L.	Wild oat	floret base	arable, rough and waste ground
Wild oat	pedicel		
Avena sp.	oat	floret base	
cf. *Secale cereale*	possible rye	rachis fragment	
Cereal NFI	Unidentified cereal	detached embryo (sprouted)	C
Cereal NFI	Unidentified cereal	detached coleoptile	C
Cereal NFI	Unidentified cereal	straw internode	
Cereal NFI	Unidentified cereal	straw culm node	
Papaver sp.	poppy	seed capsule lid	
Vicia/Lathyrus sp. (4mm)	vetch/pea	seed	Da,Cult
Vicia/Lathyrus sp. (2mm)	vetch/pea	seed	Da,Cult
Trifolium/melilotus sp.	clover/ medick	seed	
Viola sp.	violet type	seed	
Fallopia convolvulus (L.) Love.	black bindweed.	achene	Da
Rumex sp.	dock type	achene (tepal)	DaGMSW
Chenopodium sp.	goosefoots	seed	n
cf. *Stachys*sp.	possible woundwort	nutlet	
Cirsium cf. *Palustra* (L.) Scop.	possible marsh thistle	achene	marshes,damp grassland and open wood
cf. *Serratula tinctoria*	possible saw-wort	achene	grassland, scrub, open woodland, cliff tops and rocky stream sides on well-drained soils.
cf. *Anthemis cotula*	possible stinking chamomile	flower head	
cf. *Tripleurospermum inodorum*	Scentless mayweed	flower head	
cf .*Senecio vulgaris*	possible groundsel	flower head	open and rough ground
cf. *Apium* sp.	possible marshwort	fruit	
	Grass	Caryopsis	
	fern	frond fragments	1
Unident		?flower head	
Unident		charcoal	
Unident		ashy concretions with silicified chaff	*
		mineralised ashy concretions with chaff	*****
		fuel ash slag	

3009	3010	3016	3020	3021	3025	3026	3031	3032	3036	3039	3040	3042	3044	3046	3049	3050
3220	3247	3013 2	3189 2	3013 2	3331	3331	3237 1	3237 1	3237 1	3237 1	3237 1	3237 1	3237 1	3237 1	3340	3332
FA burnt layer	FA tank	Scan lower ash layer	Scan lower ash layer	FA ash (below 3040)	FA structure	Scan structure	Scan grain layer	FA grain layer	Scan grain layer	FA grain layer	FA grain layer	FA grain layer	Scan grain layer	FA grain layer	FA* drain	Scan floor

25% sorted

3009	3010	3016	3020	3021	3025	3026	3031	3032	3036	3039	3040	3042	3044	3046	3049	3050
												***				
									1		1					
20+													*			*
									*	4		4	**	7		
1	2								*	2		6	***	1 *Avena fatua* L.		
									3	3	12		5			
											2					
												*				
(3)101			*						*	213(2)	1(1)	239	***(*)	136	1	
1											2					
							1	*	3	2			3			
							1									
											1					
								1								
										1						
														1		
										1						
														1		
												7(20)				
				2								2			1	*
										1						
	1															
													1			
										1						
											*					
										1						
									*					1		
			7			*****	15	*	2	7	3	*	9			
										1						
		(**)****		(***)****		(*****)****		(***)****		(**)**		(*)****			(**)**	
(*)****			(*)		*!*		(***)*****									
		*				*			*							
***					**	***										
	*	*		*	*		**		*							

likely to come into contact with fire than the glume type wheats. It also produces more palatable chaff that could potentially be used as fodder. This might result in an under-representation of this crop in assemblages of this date or earlier. The relatively large number of stinking chamomile seeds (*Anthemis cotula*), in the assemblage might suggest the burnt debris of the fine sieving of the cereal crop. A small quantity of fragile silicifed wheat awns and palea/lemma fragments, also possibly of wheat origin, are present in sample 1006. This might also suggest that the assemblage is from a crop processed relatively close by, and that the deposit has not been subjected to much disturbance after deposition.

The smaller assemblage from sample 1005, ditch 1071, contains only evidence of wheat including spelt and oat. Unfortunately there is no diagnostic oat chaff. Again the mixture of grain chaff and wheat seeds suggests the deposit of glume wheat processing waste. As with the deposit from Pamington, this is probably the result of secondary deposition. Whilst the assemblage suggest cereal processing waste it is possible that this could have been used with other plant material as fuel and then subsequently dumped into the ditch. The stinking chamomile in both assemblages is a plant that prefers a heavy base soil which may indicate where in the area it was grown. A single scentless mayweed seed found in sample 1005 however prefers a lighter soil.

Results: Bredon's Norton

Preservation

It was evident during excavation that the charred grain deposit in the building at Bredon's Norton was exceptionally well preserved (Table 4.17; Plate 2.50). During the assessment and analysis stages four types of preservation of the plant remains were identified within the deposit from building (3184). The majority of material was charred, but there was also silicified, mineralised and possibly waterlogged preservation represented. The silicified material was indicative of silica-rich cereal chaff that has been burnt in high-temperature reducing conditions, such as at the centre of a hearth, oven or bonfire. This can lead to all but the silica bodies within the plant tissue being burnt away, and these then fusing to create a fragile subfossil. The most commonly preserved parts of the cereal plants preserved are the Lemna, palea and awns and glume beak (Boardman and Jones 1990; Robinson and Straker 1991). The palea and lemna tend to be destroyed by the lower temperature burning in oxygenated conditions that tends to char grains, spikelets and glume bases.

Two distinct layers were identified during excavation. The upper layer consisted of charred cereal grains and some charcoal. The layer below contained abundant grey/white ashy material. During the analysis stage it has been confirmed that the majority of the charred plant remains, where identifiable, are of spelt wheat with some wild oat (*Avena fatua*).

The ashy layer contained mainly small fragments of silicified chaff, including wheat awn, lemma and palea. Some of this material also appears to have been encrusted with a carbonate-rich deposit (it reacted strongly with cold dilute hydrochloric acid). This material appears to be similar to mineralised plants remains. Also amongst the charred material some of the remains, and in particular immature spelt rachis fragments, appeared to have been only partially charred. The material was brown and fibrous and some of the original cell structure of the plant remains had survived. It is possible that the material was partially charred whilst surrounded by material that ended up fully charred, and that this inhibited the action of aerobic bacteria that might have resulted in the decay of this material.

The author has seen similar preservation in a deposit of partially charred and waterlogged cereal grains found in lake silts associated with a Dark Age crannog at Llangorse, Powys (Dowse 1993; Casledine forthcoming).

The fact that the floor of the building was liable to flooding from the central cistern on occasion may explain the presence of partially charred and waterlogged remains here, and also the calcium carbonate encrustation, due to the reaction between groundwater and the limestone of the flagged floor.

Morphology of the spelt

Where the preservation of cereal remains was sufficiently good, it was possible to identify most of it as spelt. There was no evidence of any insect damage to any of the grains and only a few examples of sprouting were observed. This included single- and double-grained spikelets and empty but almost intact spikelets, which suggests that at least some of the spelt was being stored in a partially processed state. Boardman and Jones (1990) suggest that the effect on charring on wheat still held in the glume may result in the grain swelling, forcing the glumes apart and causing them to fracture, so that the grain is released. This may well have happened in the grain deposit on this site and resulted in a higher incidence of loose grains than was originally present.

Both single- and double-grain spikelets were identified (Plate 4.1). The ratio of the different types are shown in Table 4.18 below. Double-grained spikelets are considered to be the norm with Spelt, but single-grained spikelets may occur either as a genetic trait which might be amplified by the use of seed corn from a restricted gene pool, or as a response by the plant to unfavourable growing conditions (Mark Robinson and Rachel Ballantyne pers. comm.). Dr Ballantyne has noted the presence of single-grained spikelets from Fen-edge sites in Cambridgeshire. A combination of the single- and

Table 4.18 Ratio of single to double spelt spikelet forks

	Sample 3031	Sample 3032	Sample 3036	Sample 3039	Sample 3040	Sample 3042	Sample 3044	Sample 3046
Single spikelet	2	1	1	1	1	1	1	1
Double spikelet	1	1	2	1	1	2	1	1

2000 μm

Plate 4.1 Enlarged photograph of single- and double-grained spelt spikelets from Bredon's Norton

double-grained spikelets was also found in late Roman deposits from South Gloucestershire (Gray 2006) and at London Gateway, Essex (Hunter 2012). Also present were immature or sterile spikelet fragments which suggest that whole ears of spelt were present at Bredon's Norton.

A single emmer glume base fragment was recovered from the ashy layer at the base of the grain deposit (sample 3021). This represents the only identifiable wheat remain other than spelt from Bredon's Norton. Rye (*Secale cereale*) may be represented by a single rachis fragments from sample 3040.

Other plant remains

The high level of preservation has allowed several examples of plants remains not usually preserved by charring to have survived (see Table 4.17). Three seed heads tentatively identified as Stinking chamomile (*Anthemis cotula*) in sample 3040, scentless mayweed (*Tripleurospermum inodorum*) in sample 3044 and grounsel (*Senecio vulgaris*) in sample 3046, along with the lid of a poppy seed capsule (*Papaver* sp.) in sample 3042, all suggest that the grain deposit was burnt *in situ*. Several samples taken from the grain deposit also contained fern type fronds probably bracken (*Pteridium aquilinum*), and these were particularly numerous and well-preserved in sample 3031. These may represent plants gathered for bedding, fodder or packaging. The wild oats (*Avena fatua*), some still within their florets, are of a similar size to the cereal grains, and were probably a weed of the growing crop that was

not removed by crop processing. The presence of their pedicels and oat type inflorescence stems suggest that whole oat ears were present.

Taphonomy

During excavation the grain deposit and the lower ash deposit were identified as different contexts, but it is probable that the two deposits were originally mixed, and have been separated by the action of gravity and/or percolation of rain water down through the deposit, resulting in the accumulation of the finer ashy material at the base. It is also possible that calcium-rich ground water has also contributed to this sorting and resulted in the mineralisation of some of the remains.

The exceptionally good preservation particularly of the charred remains suggest that the deposit was either burnt *in situ* or was moved very soon after burning, and had remained undisturbed ever since. The excavation identified the remains of probable charred timbers overlying the grain deposit, protected by large fragments of wall plaster which had in turn covered them. The charred timbers were found at right angles to one another, either along the main axis of the building or lying across it, and so have plausibly been interpreted as part of the roof or of an upper floor of the building, rather than timbers dumped from elsewhere (see Fig. 2.35 and Boardman this volume). Whilst charcoal was found in many of the grain samples, there was no trace of a wooden floor beneath the grain deposit, and the absence of reddening from burning, despite the cracking of many of the flagstones of the stone floor below the deposit, suggests that the fire was not lit on the floor. This might suggest that the grain had been stored in a loft within the building, and that the fire occurred in the loft, the charred material falling through the burning floor onto the flagged stone floor below.

That some burning continued at ground level is shown by the burning upon the areas of wall plaster that had fallen from the walls on top of the deposit. As not all of the building or the charred grain deposit have been excavated, it is also possible that the seat of the fire was elsewhere and the assemblage analysed in this report is from the periphery of the burning event.

Having both charred and silicified remains within a single deposit suggests that at least two burning environments were present. Boardman and Jones (1990) suggest that well-preserved charred cereal remains occur in conditions of relatively low temperature burning whilst silicified remains tend to be formed in high temperature oxygen poor conditions. Robinson and Straker (1991) also discuss the kind of conditions that produce silicified remains; they identify the centre of bonfires, kilns and ovens as being the most likely place to recover them. Given that the two types of preservation represented here need such different conditions to occur, a mixing of material seems to have taken place. It is possible that hot up- draughts from the seat of the fire have carried the ashy material away to the edges and this has become incorporated with the charred material.

There is also no evidence of the grain having been stored in sacks, baskets or by partition. The excellent preservation of the plant remains in this deposit indicates that other organic material was not present, rather than that it had been destroyed. The fact that the spelt appears to have mostly been preserved within the glume suggests that it was either being stored prior to being processed or it was stored as seed corn.

Morris (1979) suggested that the storage of seed corn might occur in upper storeys of villa buildings, rather than in separate agricultural buildings. A charred grain deposit at Dinnington Villa, Somerset, with a single radiocarbon date of 410-570 cal AD (King with Grande forthcoming), was found overlying a mosaic floor, and like the Bredon's Norton deposit appears to have been accidentally destroyed by fire. A villa site at Truckle Hill, Wiltshire (Andrews 2009) has two deposits of spelt processing waste associated with a corndryer that has been set into an earlier bath house building. It is possible that the deposit at Bredon's Norton was being stored while awaiting parching in a similar drying oven. The one oven found so far at Bredon's Norton (at the very north-west end of the site) has a radiocarbon date that suggests it was probably not still in use as late as the date of the charred deposit found on the bath house floor (see Radiocarbon Dating below). A fire in a granary from the last quarter of the third century in South Shields produced an assemblage of apparently cleaned wheat grains with some spelt chaff associated with it; this assemblage also had evidence of sacks and partitions within the granary (van der Veen 1992).

The radiocarbon dates from spelt spikelets have produced two consistent dates, which when combined give a tight date range of 379-427 cal AD at 89% confidence (1646± 17 BP; see also Radiocarbon Dating, Nicholson Chapter 4), suggesting that the grain deposit was charred at the very end of the Roman period (or possibly very early in the post-Roman period). This indicates the continuing production of a pure spelt crop until that date. The proportion of single to double grained spelt spikelets seen at this site may suggest that there was limited access to genetically variable seed corn and a genetic trait which might reduce the crop yield was now being exhibited.

WOOD CHARCOAL *by Sheila Boardman*

Introduction

Seventy seven samples from the 2010 excavations at Bredon's Norton, Pamington and Fiddington were assessed for wood charcoal and other plant remains, of which nine samples from Bredon's Norton were recommended for full wood charcoal analysis (Hunter 2011). Three of the nine samples came from two Late Iron Age to early Roman (*c* 50 BC–AD 120) cremations and six were from late Roman destruction layers within Building 3184.

The destruction layers included two main horizons: a dense charred layer with wood charcoal and much charred grain and chaff (3331), and an ash rich layer, again with charred grains/chaff, plus much silicified chaff and awns, and smaller charcoal fragments (3237). A plan showing the sample grid for charred plant remains and charcoal is shown in Figure 4.4. The heavily charred layer (3331) also included the remains of several charred planks and other structural timbers (Fig. 2.35; Plates 2.50 and 2.51). Unfortunately, due to their fragility, it was not possible to retrieve these remains intact. The original form(s) and possible functions of these materials must be reconstructed from the plans and the flotation samples. Other samples come from destruction, collapse or demolition layers within Building 3184 (e.g. 3013, 3251), or destruction material which fell into the tank or cistern (3247). Due to the nature of the remains recovered in Building 3184 and the relative rapidity with which the material could be analysed, a larger number of samples were investigated (via full analysis and rapid assessment) than originally planned. Greater attention was also given to assessing the maturity and possible uses of several (largely oak) structural components.

Aims

The wood charcoal investigation was undertaken with view to addressing a number of questions. Firstly, what fuels/pyre materials were used in the Roman cremations, and do these indicate that specific taxa were selected for this purpose?

Secondly, does the wood charcoal evidence shed light on the structure, function and destruction of Building 3184, and what was its chronology?

Thirdly, on the basis of the wood charcoal results from Bredon's Norton, and from other sites in the Vale of Gloucester and South Worcestershire, what inferences can be drawn about the nature of the surrounding landscape during the late Iron Age and Roman periods?

Methodology

The samples were processed at Oxford Archaeology using a modified Siraf-type water separation machine. The flots were collected on a 250 micron mesh and the heavy residues on a 500 micron mesh. When dry the fractions were sieved at 4 and 2 mm and wood charcoal fragments greater 2 mm in size were extracted for identification. These were fractured by hand and sorted into groups based on features observed in transverse section. This was generally sufficient for the identification of oak charcoal, and for assessing its maturity, i.e. whether heartwood, sapwood and/or roundwood were present. Non-oak fragments were sectioned again longitudinally, along their radial and tangential planes, and examined at magnifications of up to x300. Identifications were made using keys in Schweingruber (1990), Hather (2000) and Gale and Cutler (2000). Nomenclature follows Stace (2010).

The proportions of the total charcoal analysed varied from sample to sample. For the fully analysed samples, at least 100 fragments were identified, or all charcoal greater than 2 mm in the case of two poorer samples. Selections of larger (greater than 10mm, 4–10 mm) and smaller (2-4 mm) charcoal fragments were made from the flots and residues. For the rapidly assessed samples, 25 to 35 fragments of flot charcoal were examined. Nearly one third of these were from the 2-4 mm size

fraction, so it is possible that rarer taxa or smaller roundwood fragments have been missed.

Results

The wood charcoal results from the fully analysed samples are listed by fragment count in Tables 4.19 and 4.20. The results of the rapidly scanned samples are presented as presence/absence data in Tables 4.21 and 4.22, where the large bold **X** denotes the most common taxon/component and the smaller **x**'s, the other material present. Table 4.22 provides more detail for the maturity of the oak fragments and range of material in each sample. Many factors affect charcoal preservation, so it not reliable to provide quantified data on maturity for individual samples. Preservation condition of the wood charcoal was generally poorer for the cremation samples. There were significant numbers of partly vitrified or iron pan encrusted fragments, making it impossible to assess wood maturity in all but a few cases. Charcoal from the destruction layers in Building 3184 was generally very well preserved, although all samples contained occasional sooty or crumbly fragments.

Table 4.19 Charcoal from cremations at Bredon's Norton

	Sample No	3005	3006	5015
	Context No	3064	3069	5295
	Period and phase	ER?	ER?	Roman
	Sample vol. (litres)	9	20	60
Rosaceae	**Common name**			
Prunus spinosa type	blackthorn type	3r		
Prunus sp.	cherry/blackthorn	3r		
cf. *Prunus* sp.	cf. cherry/blackthorn	1		
Pomoideae* (see key below)	hawthorn type	1		12
cf. Pomoideae	cf. hawthorn type	1		
Fagaceae				
Quercus	oak	89(hs)	12	90(h)
cf. *Quercus*	cf. oak		2	4
Betulaceae				
Corylus avellana	hazel	9	3	
Alnus/Corylus	alder/hazel	3		
Sapindaceae				
Acer campestre	field maple		2	
Oleaceae				
Fraxinus excelsior	ash			1
cf. *Fraxinus excelsior*	cf. ash			1
Indet. charcoal fragments		10	5r	11
Total charcoal fragments		120	24	119

Key: ER = Early Roman Symbols used in fragment counts: h = heartwood, s = sapwood, r = roundwood *Pomoideae (syn. Maloideae) include: Pyrus (pear), Malus (apple), Crataegus (hawthorn) and Sorbus (rowan, service, whitebeam)

Table 4.20 Charcoal from timbers within late 4th century burnt layer on floor of Room 3184

	Sample No	3036	3038	3039	3041	3042	3043	3030	3021
	Context No	3237	3237	3237	3237	3237	3237	3331	3013
	Feature type	Ash rich burnt layer	Ash rich burnt layer	Ash rich burnt layer	Ash rich burnt layer	Ash rich burnt layer	Ash rich burnt layer	Burnt layer/ deposit	Collapse/ demolition
Sample vol. (litres)		2	1	4	1	1	1	0.25	4
Fagaceae	**Common name**								
Quercus	oak	104(h)	108shr	108hsbr	100h(sb)	106hs	19h	102hs	104h
cf. *Quercus*	cf. oak			2					
Indet. charcoal fragments				5	1				
Total charcoal fragments		104	108	115	101	106	19	102	104

Symbols used in fragment counts: h = heartwood, s = sapwood, r = roundwood, b = bark

At least eight taxa are represented in Tables 4.19-4.22. By far the most numerous in all the fully analysed and rapidly assessed samples were fragments of oak (*Quercus*). The other taxa were blackthorn/cherry (*Prunus* sp.), hazel (*Corylus avellana*), alder/hazel (*Alnus/Corylus*), ash (*Fraxinus*), field maple (*Acer campestre*) and hawthorn type (Pomoideae). The last includes pear (*Pyrus*), crab-apple (*Malus*), hawthorn (*Crataegus*) and rowan/whitebeam/service (*Sorbus* spp.).

Cremation samples (Table 4.19)

Three samples were examined from two crema-tions. Neither was radiocarbon dated, but hobnails were recovered from cremation deposit 5295, and the other cremation (3063/3069), although undated, is thought to belong to the late Iron Age–early Roman (*c* 50 BC–AD 120 AD) phase.

Bredon's Norton: Sample 3005 (context 3064) from pit 3063

This was the most varied of the three cremation samples in terms of the taxa present but more than four fifths of identifiable fragments were oak. As noted above, much of this was poorly preserved. Of less than 20 fragments where maturity could be considered, two thirds were probable heartwood and a third possible sapwood. The main cremation fuel therefore appears to be oak. The other taxa were blackthorn, blackthorn/cherry, hazel, alder/hazel, and hawthorn type. These may represent a mixture of additional fuels, kindling materials and incidental inclusions. This sample and sample 3006 below belong to the same cremation, that of a single juvenile (see Gibson above).

Table 4.21 Charcoal from other late 4th century destruction-related deposits within Room 3184

Sample No	3011	3016	3021	3024	3025	3026	3027	3028	3029	3030	3050
Context No	3251	3013	3013	3331	3331	3331	3331	3331	3331	3331	3331
Feature type	Burnt deposit	Collapse/ demolition	Collapse/ demolition	Burnt layer	Burnt layer	Burnt layer	Burnt layer	Burnt layer	Burnt layer	Burnt layer	Burnt layer
Sample vol. (litres)	40	10	4	2	3	2	2	4	0.25	0.25	20
Rosaceae											
Pomoideae (hawthorn type*)	x										
Fagaceae											
Quercus (oak) heartwood	X	X	X	X	x	x	X		x	X	
Quercus sapwood	x	x			X	X		X	X	x	X
Quercus roundwood	x		x								
Quercus with bark											
Quercus indet.	x	x	x	x	x	x			x	x	x
Oleaceae											
Fraxinus excelsior (ash)									x		

Key: Pomoideae - hawthorn type (inc. *Pyrus* [pear], *Malus* [apple], *Crataegus* [hawthorn] & *Sorbus* [rowan, whitebeam, service, etc.); *Quercus* - oak; *Fraxinus* - ash (see Tables 4.19 & 4.20)

Bredon's Norton: Sample 3006 (context 3069)

Layer 3069 was the natural clay into which cremation pit 3063 was cut, and was sampled to recover material derived from 3064 that had percolated through root action into the natural. There was very little charcoal in this sample, all poorly preserved. Half of the fragments were oak but with so few remains it was not possible to assess maturity. The other taxa were hazel and field maple.

Bredon's Norton North: Sample 5015 (context 5295)

The identifiable material here was generally very small (in the 3-4 mm range) and this was again dominated by oak. A few fragments of oak heartwood were noted but this may not be the only material present. Hawthorn type charcoal may indicate a secondary cremation fuel, and there were single pieces of ash and possible ash. The cremated bone came from a mature female, 35–39 years in age (see Gibson this report).

Bredon's Norton, Building 3184: Destruction layers, demolition and collapse – Contexts 3331, 3237, 3251, 3013, 3247 (Tables 4.20-4.22).

Context 3331

During excavations, several large charred planks or rafters, some with associated nails/nail holes, were seen in destruction level 3331. These were photographed and planned (Fig. 2.35; Plates 2.50 and 2.51). The wider planks or rafters, which were aligned east-west along the long axis of the room, measured between 140 and 220mm wide, with narrower charred timbers 60-80mm wide parallel to these. The longest continuous length recorded was 0.72m, but fragments of similar width in line indicate timbers originally at least 1.2m long. At right angles to these, in other words aligned north-south across the room, were fragments of two widths, one 140mm wide, the others 50-60mm wide. None of these survived more than 0.48m long (Fig. 2.35). These may be the remains of purlins or another type of roof brace, wall laths/timbers, part of a collapsed loft, or possibly a mixture of these. The charred timbers were too fragile and fragmentary to lift intact, so they were bulk sampled, the samples including varying amounts of other destruction material (charred cereal grains and chaff), and processed using the methods described above. The possible planks/rafters were included in samples 3024, 3025, 3026, 3027, 3030 and possibly 3050, and the other timbers (purlins/braces/laths, etc.) were included in samples 3028 and 3029. A date of 130-310 cal. AD at 95% confidence (SUERC 49691[GU32270]; 1810 +/-26 BP) was obtained from a fragment of oak sapwood from sample 3030.

It is extremely difficult to record and study worked wood preserved as charcoal, even when this was recovered intact. Such material is very fragile, difficult to handle, and often very distorted. Any evidence for wood working, including tool marks, tends to be very indistinct or to have disappeared altogether. Following flotation, the timbers from context 3331 became very fragmented and split, largely along radial planes. Original flat surfaces were only occasionally visible but no nail holes were seen following flotation. We are thus reliant on original plans for the wood *in situ*, a few remaining timber fragments with flattened sides, breakdowns of maturity of the oak fragments and an assessment of ring curvature, to reconstruct the

3032	3033	3034	3036	3038	3039	3041	3042	3043	3010
3237	3237	3237	3237	3237	3237	3237	3237	3237	3247
Ash rich burnt layer	Ash rich burnt layer	Ash rich burnt layer	Ash rich burnt layer	Ash rich burnt layer	Ash rich burnt layer	Ash rich burnt layer	Ash rich burnt layer	Ash rich burnt layer	Cistern/tank
10	10	1	2	1	4	1	1	1	1
x	x	x	xx	x	x	x	X	x	
x	x	x	x	x	x	x		x	
				x					
	x			x	x		x		
X	X	X	XX	X	X	X	X	x	X

173

Table 4.22 Charcoal from burnt deposits within late 4th century Room 3184

Sample no	Context no	Feature type	Sample vol. (l)	Rosaceae Pomoideae	Fagaceae Quercus heartwood	Quercus sapwood	Quercus roundwood	Quercus inc. bark	Quercus indet.	Oleaceae Fraxinus excelsior
3011	3251	Burnt deposit	40	x	X	x	x		x	
3016	3013	Collapse/demolition	10		X	x			x	
3021	3013	Collapse/demolition	4		X		x		x	
3024	3331	Burnt layer/deposit	2		X				x	
3025	3331	Burnt layer/deposit	3		x	X			x	
3026	3331	Burnt layer/deposit	2		x	X			x	
3027	3331	Burnt layer/deposit	2		X					
3028	3331	Burnt layer/deposit	4			X				
3029	3331	Burnt layer/deposit	0.25		x	X			x	
3030	3331	Burnt layer/deposit	0.25		X	x			x	
3050	3331	Burnt layer/deposit	20			X			x	x
3032	3237	Ash rich burnt layer	10		x	x			X	
3033	3237	Ash rich burnt layer	10		x	x			X	
3034	3237	Ash rich burnt layer	1		x	x		x	X	
3036	3237	Ash rich burnt layer	2		x				X	
3038	3237	Ash rich burnt layer	1		x	x			X	
3039	3237	Ash rich burnt layer	4		x	x	x	x	X	
3041	3237	Ash rich burnt layer	1		x	x		x	X	
3042	3237	Ash rich burnt layer	1		x	x			X	
3043	3237	Ash rich burnt layer	1		X			x	x	
3010	3247	Cistern/tank	1		x	x			X	

timber components. As Figure 2.35 shows, five plank remnants are represented in samples 3024, 3025, 3026, 3027 and 3030. These had varying proportions of oak heartwood and sapwood. From the transverse sections of plank fragments which had one or two flat sides, it appears that some of these came from radially split, hewn or sawn timbers. They had been worked along the lines of least resistance preserving the original strength of the timber. Some half/quarter sawn timbers may also be present. The material in samples 3028 and 3029, meanwhile, were either all or largely from oak sapwood, and from the reasonably wide growth rings and ring curvature observed, it is likely that they came from immature trees or branches.

Other destruction-related deposits (contexts 3237, 3251, 3013, 3247)

The samples from these contexts included some large fragments, which also may be the remains of planks, rafters or other structural timbers. However, these samples were more mixed generally, and the charcoal more poorly preserved, so they may include a wider range of destruction debris. Only limited assessments could be made of wood maturity. The presence of bark in four samples from (3237) may point to the inclusion of more small, unworked or roughly worked timbers (see Tables 4.21 and 4.22). The other destruction deposits produced a similar picture. Sample 3010, from a fill of the tank/cistern (3247), did not produce evidence

for a wooden cover burnt *in situ*, and only 32 (>2 mm) charcoal fragments were recovered in total. However, there were a couple of uncharred oak fragments, indicating that the tank had held water at the time or before the destruction of the building. The remains in this sample were very similar to those in the surrounding ashy layer 3237.

Roman wood working and construction techniques

Planks/rafters from the Bredon's Norton building overlaid the main destruction levels, so most likely came from a wooden roof or loft. There is little evidence for timber roofs in Roman Britain, so this has to be extrapolated from elsewhere. Simple, double or close-coupled roofs are most likely (Perring 2001; Adams 1999). In simple roofs, rafters rest directly on horizontal timbers or purlins which run from one gable wall to another (Adam 1999). In double roofs, purlins are used to support (brace) the rafters, and in close-coupled roofs, paired rafters (or trusses) are braced by collar beams to form A frames (Perring 2001). If constructed of timber, a double roof is most likely at Bredon's Norton, as the smaller timbers (braces?) lay at right angles to the larger timbers/rafters. However, this is highly conjectural.

Other sites

In Bronze Age cremations, a single woody taxa often seems to have been selected for cremating

Comments

Bulk sample – mixed structural/other debris?
Inc. structural timbers?
Inc. structural timbers?
Mostly from single burnt oak plank/rafter
Mostly from single burnt oak plank/rafter
Mostly from single burnt oak plank/rafter
Mostly from single burnt oak plank/rafter
Structural timber – brace/lath, etc.
Structural timber – brace/lath, etc.
Mostly from single burnt oak plank/rafter
Bulk sample   mixed structural/other debris?
Mixed structural/other burnt debris
Ditto
"
"
"
"
"
"
"

Mixed debris, no evidence for wooden cover

bodies (Thompson 1999), a practice that may have continued into the Iron Age and Roman periods in some areas (Challinor 2011). The main taxon selected in the prehistoric cremations was oak, but hawthorn type (Pomoideae/Maloideae) charcoal dominated samples were also common (Challinor 2011a). In later periods, the picture becomes more mixed. At the Roman Cemetery at Pepper Hill, Southfleet, Kent, cremation samples produced almost exclusively oak (Challinor 2006), whereas at Latton Lands, north Wiltshire, they each had an average of five taxa, including elm (*Ulmus*), unusually, plus hawthorn type, blackthorn/cherry, oak, ash, holly (*Ilex*) and alder (Challinor 2008). At Bredon's Norton, both of the Roman cremations were dominated by oak. It was suggested above that the other charcoal taxa could represent kindling or incidental inclusion, but this may also include deliberate offerings. The range of taxa in the Bredon's Norton cremations seem to include some of the main taxa present in the Iron Age and Roman landscape of the region.

At Saxon's Lode Farm, at nearby Ripple, in the Severn Valley, 36 samples were analysed for wood charcoal from deposits dating from the Iron Age to early third century AD (Gale 2008). Preservation conditions were generally poor and very few fragments (often only three) were identified per sample, so it is surprising that such a wide range of taxa was identified. This included oak, blackthorn, hawthorn type, alder, hazel, field maple, ash and holly. Gale suggested that the area probably

supported oak, ash, maple woodland, while high proportions of blackthorn and hawthorn type charcoal suggests open woodland/scrub, or presence of stock-proof hedgerows (Gale 2008: 69). At Bradley Stoke, south Gloucs., while largely from prehistoric and Saxon deposits (including possible Saxon charcoal clamps), the charcoal evidence revealed a similar range of woody taxa to that from Bredon's Norton and Ripple, but it lacked alder and hazel, and there was some beech (*Fagus sylvatica*) in earlier samples (Challinor 2011). Southeast of Bredon's Norton, the picture is similar, for example around Horcott Quarry, near Fairford (Challinor 2012). A Roman cremation from Horcott also produced concentrations of roundwood of blackthorn/wild plum (*Prunus spinosa/domestica*), cherry, hawthorn group and dogwood/cornel (*Cornus* sp.).

At the Cotswold Community sites in south Gloucestershire and north Wiltshire, purging buckthorn (*Rhamnus cartharica*) was present as roundwood in most middle Iron Age to early Roman samples, and there were large amounts of hawthorn type, blackthorn and blackthorn/cherry roundwood charcoal, which probably reflects fuels collected from hedgerows and/or scrub (Challinor 2010). Early evidence for hedgerows in the wider region comes from an analysis of seeds and pollen from a middle Iron Age ditch at Alcester, near Stratford upon Avon, which revealed a flora rich in hawthorn, blackthorn, field maple and purging buckthorn, suggesting a hedged boundary (Greig 1994).

RADIOCARBON DATING *by Rebecca Nicholson*

A total of nine samples from Bredon's Norton were submitted to the Scottish Universities Environmental Research Centre (SUERC) AMS Facility, Glasgow for AMS radiocarbon dating. The samples were sent in two batches, the original eight samples comprising five samples from human skeletons, one of which failed due to insufficient carbon, one upon seeds from the layer of charred grain overlying the floor of structure 3184, one upon charcoal from one of the charred timbers overlying the grain, and the last upon grain found in the flue of a corn-drying oven. An additional sample of charred grain from the layer on the floor of structure 3184 was submitted later as a priority sample to obtain better resolution of the radiocarbon date range obtained from the previous sample.

The samples upon human bone were taken to date three inhumation burials without other dating, and two of a group of cremation burials found in close proximity in the top of an enclosure ditch. The sample from the corndryer was intended to date the last use of the structure, and the sample of charcoal from a charred timber was taken to date the cutting of the timber, and indirectly to assist in dating the construction, or possibly the repair, of structure 3184. The dating of the charring of the layer of grain

Table 4.23 Conventional and calibrated radiocarbon dates

Lab. ID	Context	Sample	Feature	Material
SUERC-49691	3331	3030	3184	Charcoal (oak sapwood, 2 rings)
SUERC-49692	3237	3040	3184	Charred grain (spelt, double- grained in spikelet)
SUERC-49693	SK 5244			Human bone (neonate left tibia)
GU-32273	SK5223			Human bone (right femur and tibia shaft fragments)
SUERC-49694	SK3300			Human bone (right femur shaft)
SUERC-49695	SK5012			Human bone (right femur shaft)
SUERC-49696	SK5262			Human bone (left distal femur, neonate)
SUERC-49697	5249	5023		Charred grain (indeterminate cereal)
SUERC-51413	3237	3042	3184	Charred grain (spelt wheat, spikelet)

found upon the floor of structure 3184 was important both to date the stored crop, and, as this directly underlay charred timbers, fallen wall plaster and other destruction materials, the date of destruction of the building.

The samples selected for dating comprised short-lived material including charred grain, some still within the spikelet, charred sapwood and human bone. The results of the eight dated samples and one failed sample are presented in Figure 4.5 and Table 4.23. The results are conventional radiocarbon years BP (Stuiver and Polach 1977), quoted according to the international standard known as the Trondheim convention (Stuiver and Kra 1986). The error, which is expressed at the one sigma level of confidence, includes components from the counting statistics on the sample, modern reference standards, background standards and the random machine error. In all cases the measured $\delta13C$ results are within the expected ranges for the materials dated, suggesting that preservation was good enough to justify confidence in the radiocarbon determinations. The

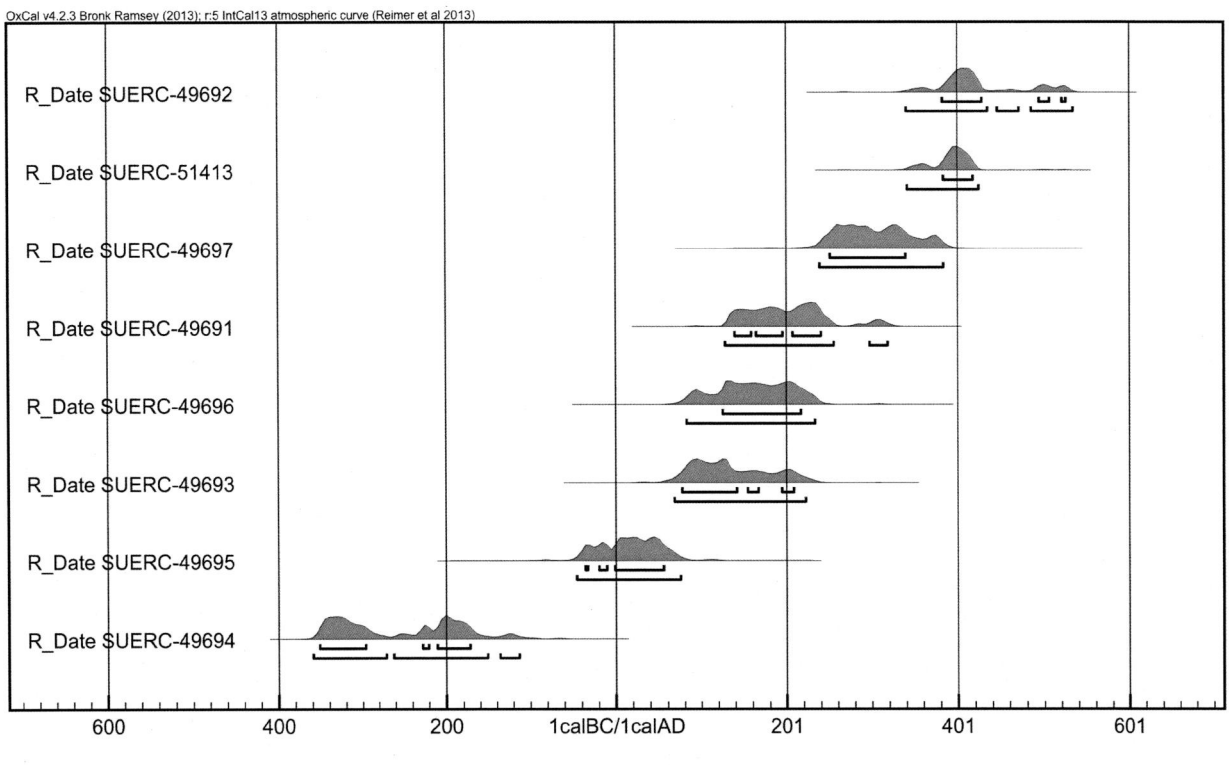

Fig. 4.5 Calibrated distributions of radiocarbon determinations

δ13C (0/00)	Radiocarbon age (BP)	Calibrated date (95.4 % confidence)	Calibrated date (68.2% confidence)
-23.7	1810 ± 26	cal AD 120–260 (90.4%)	cal AD 140–250 (68.2%)
		cal. AD 290–320 (5%)	
-22.6	1635 ± 28	cal AD 340–540 (95.4%)	cal AD 380–430 (59.8%)
			cal. AD 490–510 (6.3%)
			cal. AD 520–530 (2.2%)
-20	1876 ± 30	cal AD 60–230 (95.4%)	cal AD 70–170 (60.7%)
			cal. AD 190–210 (7.5%)
		Failed (insufficient carbon)	Failed (insufficient carbon)
-20.7	2167 ± 30	360–150 cal. BC (92.4%)	360–290 cal BC (37.4%)
		140–110 cal BC (3%)	220–170 cal BC (30.8%)
-21.1	1983 ± 30	50 cal BC–cal AD 80 (95.4%)	40–30 cal. BC (2.3%)
			20 cal. BC–cal AD 60 (65.9%)
-20.1	1853 ± 30	cal AD 80–240 (95.4%)	cal AD 120–220 (68.2%)
-22.7	1736± 29	cal AD 230–390 (95.4%)	cal AD 250–340 (68.2%)
-24.7	1652 ± 20	cal AD 340–425 (95.4%)	cal AD 380–420 (68.2%)

calibrated calendar age ranges were determined using the University of Oxford Radiocarbon Accelerator Unit calibration program OxCal 4.2.3 (Bronk Ramsey 1995; 2001; 2009; Bronk Ramsey and Lee 2013) and the IntCal13 atmospheric curve (Reimer *et al.* 2013) and are quoted at both 68.2% confidence (1 sigma) and 95.4% confidence (2 sigma), with the end points rounded out to the nearest 10 years, or 5 years for error terms of less than 25 radiocarbon years.

Two spatially separate samples of charred grain (spelt wheat) from the apparently homogeneous deposit on the floor of the sunken floored room (SUERC-49692 and SUERC-51413) were compared statistically using the R-Combine function of OxCal. One of these (sample 3042) had been submitted for high precision radiocarbon dating. The resulting $\chi 2$ result of T=0.2 at 1 df confirms that the two samples could have been charred during a single event. The combined date for these samples is 1646 ±17 BP, which at 95.4% probability equates to cal. AD 345–430 or cal. AD 390–420 at 68.2%, indicating that the building burnt down at the end of the Roman era in Britain or very shortly thereafter.

Chapter 5

Discussion

by Tim Allen

INTRODUCTION

The results of the pipeline excavations have provided important new information on a number of topics, and useful additions to the corpus of information on others in both the later Iron Age and the Roman periods. The scale of investigation, and thus the finds and environmental assemblages, was not however sufficiently large to warrant discussion of all aspects of later Iron Age and Roman activity on these sites. As a result, the discussion will confine itself to those aspects that offer a significant addition to the current knowledge of the region. The discussion follows a broadly chronological format, drawing in evidence from whichever of the sites provides relevant new data.

MIDDLE IRON AGE

Enclosure ditches

Clearly middle Iron Age activity is limited to the south end of the site at Bredon's Norton, where a ditch was cut by grave 3300 containing a crouched skeleton, probably a male, on his left side with head to the north, accompanied by part or all of an Iron Age saw. Bone from the skeleton was radiocarbon dated to 360-110 cal BC. The ditch was picked up on the geophysical survey west of the site, and may have joined onto a curvilinear enclosure some 25-30m across, one of several indicated by the geophysical surveys (Figs 2.14 and 2.16).

The crouched burial accompanied by a saw

Middle Iron Age burials are still very rare in Worcestershire; a single middle-late Iron Age example from Church Lench was radiocarbon-dated to 190 Cal BC-20 Cal AD (Griffin *et al.* 2002). A number of Iron Age inhumation burials are reported from Beckford (Britnell 1973; Wills 1976; Wills 1978), but none has yet been published in detail, and their date within the Iron Age is still unclear. The four adults and a child reported from the 1972-3 excavation are described as crouched within small and shallow bowl-shaped pits (Britnell 1973, 10), and these may well have been purpose-dug graves.

In Gloucestershire such burials are more numerous, but are usually pit burials, for example at Bourton-on-the-Water Primary School and Greystones Farm, Bourton-on-the-Water (Nichols 2006; Nichols 2013; Cotswold Archaeology 2015), Bourton-on-the-Hill (Gloucester Echo 2013), Salmondsbury (Dunning 1976) or Home Farm, Fairford (Headland Archaeology 2014). Both of the Home Farm crouched burials were in a pit alignment, and were radiocarbon-dated to the middle Iron Age (ibid, 9). Both were in the tops of the surviving pits, and one of these was in an oval cut (ibid., 10), so was perhaps a purpose-dug grave. The Iron Age burials at West Kemble were described as pit burials, but Burial 22 occupied most of a circular cut only 1m square, and Burial 21 was found in a secondary grave cut only 1m long and 0.6m wide within a half-filled pit that already contained human bones in the base (King *et al.* 1996, 19-23 and fig. 4). Both of these are therefore probably in purpose-dug graves. Three other inhumations are now known here, and Cunliffe (2005 552) describes this as a small cemetery.

Single examples of crouched burial in purpose-dug graves have been found at the Lynches Trackway north-east of Cirencester, at Uley Bury and (probably) at Badgeworth on the north side of Crickley Hill (Allen *et al.* 1999, 76-7; Moore 2006, 85; RCHM 1976, 5). One of the pits containing a human skeleton at Bourton-on-the-Water in 2000, pit 76, was also believed to have been a purpose-dug grave (Nichols 2013, 25). Otherwise the clearest examples in purpose-dug graves are on the Gloucestershire Thames river gravels. Two crouched inhumations in graves, one of which was dug into the fill of a boundary ditch, were found adjacent to one another at Horcott Pit (Lamdin-Whymark *et al.* 2009, fig. 21). These were both radiocarbon-dated, a possible female to 380-160 cal BC (SUERC 3427/GU-12108; 2195 + 180 BP) and a juvenile of 15-17 years to 370-110 cal BC (SUERC 3552/GU12110; 2175 + 130 BP). Burial 1215 from Roughground Farm, Lechlade was radiocarbon-dated to 350-40 cal. BC (Allen *et al.* 1993, 45).

The burial at Bredon's Norton is particularly unusual, both in being in a purpose-dug grave, and in containing grave goods. Grave goods are gener-

179

ally rare with middle Iron Age burials in this part of England; none of the Iron Age burials from Beckford, for example, had accompanying grave goods (Britnell 1973; Wills 1978). Two perforated sheep bones were found with Burial 22 at West Kemble (King *et al.* 1996, 21-2), while in Oxfordshire a child at Spring Road, Abingdon was accompanied by a bone ring, and at Gravelly Guy, Stanton Harcourt one adult by a bone toggle and another by a shale spindlewhorl (Allen and Kamash 2008, 16-17; Lambrick and Allen 2004, 224 fig. 6.1 and Table 6.3). The deposition of iron objects in any type of context in the Iron Age is rare, and suggests that such objects were valuable, and their deposition represents acts of especial significance. The grave at Badgeworth was apparently accompanied by an iron pot-hook, a bracelet and two short pointed rods, but is only described as 'probably Iron Age' (RCHM 1976, 5). Metal grave goods other than brooches in middle Iron Age burials are otherwise almost unknown, and to the author's knowledge the accompaniment of a saw is unique in Britain. There are simply too few accompanied burials to determine whether the choice of object was relevant to the role of the individual in life, although it is tempting to imagine that this person was a carpenter. Another Iron Age saw was found at Bredon Hill Camp close by, but was apparently deposited in the very late Iron Age (Hencken 1938, 19), although the finds were not closely datable. An overlap with the radiocarbon range for the Bredon's Norton burial is therefore possible.

The presence of a corvid bone in this grave is also of interest, given the predominance of these species amongst the birds associated with special deposits in the Iron Age at Danebury (Grant 1984, 540), and the recent recognition of their wider association with deliberate deposition in the Iron Age (Serjeantson and Morris 2011, 85-94). An association between these birds and death, probably because they are carrion-feeders, has occurred in various past societies, including the Celtic world (Green 1997, 166 and 174), and an association with human remains was noted by Serjeantson and Morris at Danebury (Serjeantson and Morris 2011, 90-91). These authors stressed the role of corvids in excarnation, now widely believed to have been practised in Iron Age Britain, as a reason for this association (ibid., 101-2). Unsurprisingly, it has been whole skeletons or articulated wings that have been recognised as significant, but once recognised as creatures with particular associations, there is no reason why single bones may not have been used as symbols. No instances of Iron Age graves including corvid skeletons or bones were listed by Serjeantson and Morris, but they noted that their researches were not comprehensive for all parts of Britain (ibid., 92).

The tradition of crouched burial in purpose-dug graves continued into the late Iron Age or very early Roman period at Bredon's Norton. Skeleton 5012, which lay at the north-west end of the site, was buried in a very similar position and orientation to middle Iron Age burial 3300, and was also a male individual. There were however no accompanying grave goods. The largest group of late Iron Age burials in Worcestershire is the fifty or more young adult male skeletons found at Kemerton Camp hillfort on Bredon Hill, which were not formally buried, and are interpreted as the victims of a massacre, now known to have occurred at the time of the Roman conquest of the region (Hencken 1938; Thomas 2005, 257). Otherwise, late Iron Age burials are also rare in Worcestershire, the only published parallel being that already mentioned at Church Lench, further details of which were reported in 2006 (Griffin *et al.* 2006, 1-9). As already mentioned, a number of flexed burials were found at Beckford, but are only known from interim reports.

In the wider region, crouched burials are known from Latton Lands in Gloucestershire, where they were cut into an enclosure ditch, and at Gravelly Guy, Stanton Harcourt, Oxon, (Lambrick and Allen 2004, 169 and 223-236). Burial 309 at the latter site was accompanied by a brooch. Another possibly late Iron Age burial was recently found at the Horse and Groom, Bourton-on-the-Hill (Hurst 2013). Three cist-burials from Birdlip represent the largest group from the region (Bellows 1881), but are of a much more elaborate grave type than the example from Bredon's Norton, one including a mirror. Crouched burials continuing into the 2nd century AD are now known from Hucclecote, Gloucestershire (Thomas *et al.* 2003, 20).

LATE IRON AGE AND ROMAN

Sub-rectangular and sub-circular enclosures

The two sub-rectangular enclosures at Pamington were both probably dug in the late Iron Age, although enclosure 2077 clearly remained in use until the later 1st century AD, when a dump of pottery and stones was placed in the upper fill of the ditch. Similar enclosures are known from the later Iron Age of the region at several sites. At High Street, Evesham, a sub-rectangular enclosure 16-17m by 11-14m was revealed with a single narrow entrance on the narrow west side (Edwards and Hurst 2000, fig. 2.3). At Rudgeway Lane, Walton Cardiff near Tewkesbury, late Iron Age Enclosure 3 was of similar shape (Hart and McSloy 2008, fig. 6). This consisted of two concentric ditch circuits, the smaller of which was 14m by 11m across, the larger and later 17-18m long and perhaps 16m wide. No details of the depth, profile or fills of the enclosure were given, but the transitional late Iron Age to early Roman date of enclosure 2077 was mirrored here, as an early Roman carinated bowl was recovered from the outer ditch fill and from an inhumation cut into its base. No certain entrances were found in either circuit, but the southern side of both phases was cut away by later ditches.

Other early Roman examples include Enclosure A at Fiddington, which is of very similar size and shape. The dated 1st-2nd century Malvernian pottery was from secondary fills, so it is possible that this enclosure too could have been dug very early in the Roman period, or conceivably in the late Iron Age. The ditches at Enclosure A are also of similar depth, and, like those at Pamington, the entrance appears to have been on the west or north-west side. Several similar sub-enclosures, ranging from 12 by 15m to 16 by 18m, but of 2nd century AD date, were found at Leylandii House Farm, Norton and Lenchwick (Jackson *et al.* 1996). One of these had a narrow entrance on the west. Another enclosure of similar shape, and also of 2nd century date, was found at Blenheim Farm, Moreton-in-Marsh (Hart and Alexander 2007, 10-11 and fig. 8). This was slightly larger (26 by 20m across), and had an entrance only 0.7m wide on the east side.

At Leylandii House Farm there was an oven within one enclosure, but otherwise none of these examples seems to have been accompanied by many internal features. Only at Pamington Enclosure 2077, where gully or slot 2019 appears to have been dug in alignment with, and equidistant from, the surrounding ditch, is it almost certain that any of these internal features was contemporary. Those that were present at Pamington and Fiddington would have allowed the possibility of a bank along the inner edge of the ditch of their respective enclosures, and the same is true of the enclosures at High Street, Evesham and Rudgeway Lane, Walton Cardiff.

Although not exactly similar in size and shape, sub-rectangular or oval enclosures of early Roman date are also common in the Upper Thames Valley (Lambrick and Allen 2004, 174-6). Here evidence of structures is rarely found, and it has been suggested that buildings were either slightly-founded, or had mass walls at this period (ibid., 175; Allen *et al.* 1984, 100), making it difficult to use the presence or absence of structural remains within such enclosures as an indicator of domestic function. Although precise details are difficult to derive from the report, it appears that a fair quantity of pottery and animal bone was recovered from Enclosure 3 at Rudgeway Lane, in contrast to the small assemblages from the other sites. This may be a better indicator of the presence or absence of a domestic function than evidence of buildings. On these grounds neither the examples at Pamington nor the early-middle Roman examples at Fiddington would appear to have had a domestic function, although it must be remembered that in both the Pamington and Fiddington examples, the ditch termini, where concentrations of material are often found, lay outside the area investigated.

Although more nearly circular, Enclosure C at Fiddington is another related example, being 14.5 by 12.5m across. This is of later 4th century AD date, and shows that the tradition of small curvilinear enclosures continues right to the end of the Roman period in this area. A number of pits and a ditch were found within this enclosure, though it is not certain that they did not predate it. It seems probable, however, that in this case, the enclosure was defining and marking off an area of pits. Quantities of pottery, animal bone and charred plant remains were associated with this enclosure, indicating proximity both to cereal processing and to domestic activity, unlike many of the earlier enclosures. The fill of this enclosure did however also include an articulated horse limb, which is perhaps less likely to have been the result of simple rubbish disposal. It is alternatively possible that deliberate deposition was being carried out in this enclosure, as is also possible at Rudgeway Lane earlier, where the enclosure ditch contained a largely complete carinated jar and an inhumation burial.

The penannular enclosure at Bredon's Norton

Penannular enclosure 3150 at Bredon's Norton, of which only part was revealed within the excavation, has mixed dating evidence. Much of the pottery recovered was of late Iron Age date, which appears to be consistent with the date of the large irregular pit 3158 that was approximately in the centre of its interior. The Malvernian decorated pot (Fig. 3.3) that was found at the base of the pit was clearly deposited either whole, or was broken only during the act of deposition, and thus provides a good date for the infilling of the pit. Despite the late Iron Age material, the southern terminal contained 2nd century Roman pottery, and tile from one of the other cuts also indicates a clearly Roman date.

Penannular and circular gullies of Roman date are relatively common in Gloucestershire. There are both early Roman and middle Roman examples near Tewkesbury, at Areas C and D (Walker *et al.* 2004, 42-44) and at Rudgeway Lane, Walton Cardiff (Hart and McSloy 2008, 10-15 and figs 6 and 7). Examples such as Fiddington, Birdlip Quarry and Barnsley Park continue into the late Roman period (see above; Mudd *et al.* 1999, 157-202 and 257-9). The Bredon's Norton example was at the lower end of the size range (only 9-10m across), similar to the smallest examples at Sites C and D; those from Rudgeway Lane were 11 and 12m across, and the later examples from Fiddington and Birdlip larger still. There was no indication of internal features at Rudgeway Lane, and only pits at Area D-Site 1, but the Birdlip examples generally included lines of stakeholes or postholes inside that strongly suggested that they surrounded circular buildings. The evidence at Bredon's Norton is equivocal, as the internal arcs of gully are not concentric to the outer enclosure, and the internal postholes do not form an obvious wall line.

The quantities of material recovered from the penannular gully are not large, with the exception of the central pit (see below). The varied character of the material from the adjacent gullies, which included clear evidence of hearths (including a decorated example) and ovens, pottery and a brooch, suggests that there was a domestic focus close by, if not within the penannular enclosure itself.

A deliberately deposited vessel?

The burial of the pot in a pit in the interior of the penannular enclosure does not appear to have been related to the vessel's function, as is sometimes the case with vessels used for water storage, storage of dry goods, or even as flowerpots on later prehistoric and early Roman sites. Such vessels normally sit in a pit dug almost exactly to the size of the pot, which despite the evidence of later disturbance, does not appear to have been the case here. They are also normally plain, rather than decorated like the example at Bredon's Norton, while vessels intended as flowerpots have their bases removed for drainage, which was not the case here.

Complete, or almost complete, vessels are also relatively common in larger pits and in ditches on later prehistoric sites, and are increasingly regarded as evidence of deliberate ritual deposition. Vessels deposited in this manner can be placed whole as in pits 4969 and 3676 at the A2 in Kent or Alfred's Castle in Oxfordshire (Allen *et al.* 2013, 311 figs 3.57 and 3.60; Gosden and Lock 2013, fig. 4.5) or can be smashed in place; at Suddern Farm in Hampshire, for example, sherds of a complete but broken middle Iron Age saucepan pot were found across the base of a pit, their arrangement suggesting that it had been dropped onto the pit base (Cunliffe and Poole 2000, 104, fig 3.46). A local example was present at Conderton Camp on Bredon Hill, where Pit A contained almost all of a very large handmade storage jar close to the base, but smashed into over 100 pieces (Morris in Thomas 2005, 130-131 fig. 44 and Plate 54, and 144-5). This vessel was of a very similar form to that at Bredon's Norton, and like it, was decorated with a row of impressions around the neck, though these were not the classic Malvernian duck-stamped type. A copper alloy penannular brooch was also found close to the base of the pit, and was classified as Fowler's Type A3iii, ie Romano-British (Thomas 2005, 150 and fig. 49). The pot may therefore represent a very late Iron Age or very early Romano-British vessel.

The purpose of such deposits is open to interpretation, prominent among which is that they were offerings to cthonic deities (Cunliffe and Poole 1991, 162; Cunliffe 2005, 570) related to agriculture, particularly as closure deposits at the end of use. Deposits related to enclosures could equally have been foundation offerings, but given our ignorance of late Iron Age religion, it would be unprofitable to speculate further.

Context of the small enclosures

At Pamington, the two sub-rectangular enclosures are right next to one another, but were some distance from any other archaeological features

along the pipeline, and the geophysical survey also suggested that no other small enclosures lay in the immediate vicinity (Figure 2.1). There were, however, sizeable ditches running east-west both to the north and the south, the southern ditch having an inturned entrance possibly with two large gate-postholes, raising the possibility that the excavated small enclosures lay within a much larger one, approximately 75m across from north to south, and at least the same east-west (Fig. 5.1). The northern ditch contained a single sherd of Iron Age pottery, which while not strong dating evidence, does not rule out the possibility that this was a contemporary boundary ditch. The character of the southern inturned entrance also supports an early date for this boundary.

None of the comparative late Iron Age or early Roman local examples described above definitely lay within a contemporary larger enclosure, but were often incorporated within a later Roman large enclosure or enclosure group, as for example at Rudgeway Lane (Hart and McSloy 2008, see also below).

Fiddington, however, shows no good evidence of larger enclosures, instead indicating a succession of small circular or curvilinear enclosures throughout the RB period, including some definitely later 4th century activity. The revealed evidence at Fiddington suggests a settlement consisting of small domestic or stock enclosures linked to short lengths of ditch, perhaps defining paddocks or ancillary agricultural enclosures. There is no evidence of major enclosures, and this model of settlement appears to continue right through the Roman period. Although the quantities of material from the middle Roman enclosures are not large, the variety of material perhaps tends towards interpretation as domestic in function, and this is very likely for the late Roman enclosure here.

The settlement at Rudgeway Lane, which lies less than 2km due west, begins in the middle Iron Age with a slightly larger enclosure, but in the late Iron Age/early Roman period has a cropmark complex of similar small enclosures to those already described above south of the excavated area, most of them curvilinear but some rectilinear, many of which are linked by short lengths of ditch. This cellular arrangement of enclosures is also seen in the Gloucestershire Thames Valley, for instance at Thornhill Farm (Jennings *et al.* 2004). Locally, then, this type of settlement is not uncommon. The cropmark complex is also not unlike the cellular enclosures found by geophysical survey at Bredon's Norton east of the Roman rectilinear enclosures (Figs 2.14 and 2.16). Where dated, the other examples quoted above are, as at Fiddington, of the late Iron Age or early Roman periods; middle Iron Age examples, as appear to be present at Bredon's Norton, are fewer.

At the other end of their timescale, the Rudgeway Lane site sees a progression from these small curvilinear enclosures to a larger rectilinear arrangement

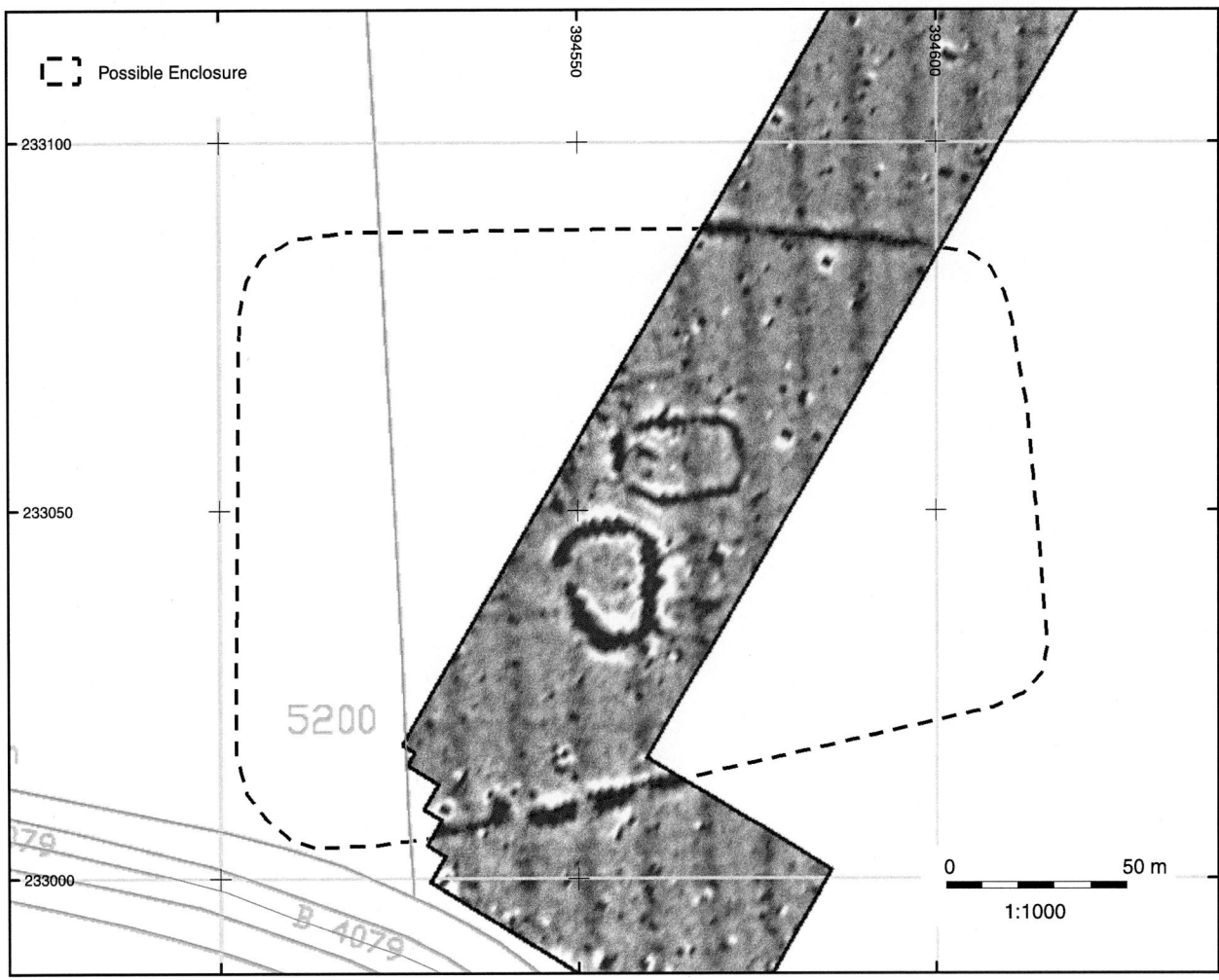

Fig. 5.1 Plan showing possible larger enclosure at Pamington

in the 2nd/3rd century AD (Hart and McSloy 2008, figs 5 and 6). At Bredon's Norton the rectilinear enclosure system appears to have been established by the late 1st or early 2nd century AD. This slightly earlier date may support the evidence from building materials for a higher status site with at least one villa building being constructed at this time, but it would be unwise to place too much emphasis on the morphology of ditched enclosures, and the point within the 2nd century at which the rectilinear enclosures appeared at Rudgeway Lane is not specified.

Romano-British burials

All of the burials of Roman date came from Bredon's Norton, and all but two were inhumations. The predominance of inhumations is however skewed by the group of neonates, for whom cremation was not customary in the Roman period; Pliny the Elder states that children who have not cut their teeth are not cremated, and Juvenal echoes this (Pearce 2001, 126). Excluding the neonatal burials, there were three inhumations (or five including the two late Iron Age or very early Roman examples), and two

cremations. One of the two cremations came from the north-west end of the site, the other from the southern part; both were Roman, but neither was closely dated. The inhumations all came from the north-western part of the site, and two of the three adults were found within 5 metres of one another in the south-west corner of a large enclosure surrounded by ditch groups 5288 and 5290-2. One of the adults (skeleton 5202) was of 2nd century date, the other consisted only of disarticulated bones within a 2nd century or later ditch, suggesting that the burial was somewhat earlier. The surrounding enclosure had at least three phases, all of them Roman, but it is likely that it was already in existence when the burials, of at least skeleton 5202, were made.

The placing of burials at the edges of Romano-British enclosures within settlements, as at Rudgeway Lane, Walton Cardiff, near Tewkesbury (Hart and McSloy 2008, figs 6 and 7), at Gilder's Paddock, Bishop's Cleeve (Parry 1999) and at Tockington Park Farm (Masser and McGill 2004, fig. 4), or within fields or enclosures close by, as at Cotswold Community, South Gloucestershire (Powell *et al.* 2010, vol. 1, 136-8 and fig. 3.30), is not uncommon in the region, or in Roman Britain as a whole (Pearce 2013, 102-3). At the first of these sites, the corners of several enclosures were occupied by single burials, though that at the south-west corner of the site had a second burial just outside, while at Tockington Park Farm there were at least 5 individuals, and at least 7 at Gilder's Paddock. Pearce also noted that burials were sometimes deliberately placed at the approaches to settlements, on or beside trackways (Pearce 2013, 104-5), and the geophysical survey evidence at Bredon's Norton indicates that the burials lay immediately adjacent to a trackway into the settlement between two enclosures from the south-west (see Fig. 2.14).

Adjacent to the two adult inhumations in close proximity at Bredon's North, was the group of 8 neonates, all of late 2nd century or later date, found in close proximity to one another in the top of enclosure ditch 5192/5191. No evidence of grave cuts was found during the excavation, perhaps suggesting that the bodies were disposed of casually in the ditch top, and were covered gradually by successive deposits of refuse from the adjoining settlement. There was however no evidence of animal gnawing on the bones, as might have been expected had the bodies been left exposed for any length of time. The burial of single infants, each with a deliberate covering of soil and domestic refuse is more plausible, although no evidence of the separate dumps was visible during excavation.

Another possibility is that although the bodies were dumped on the exposed ditch top, this area was enclosed in some way that protected them from interference by animals. If the nine infants were deposited individually, as seems most likely, then this protection must have continued for a considerable period of time. The only postholes that were observed within the excavation, however, were clearly cutting the ditch top, so how this might have been achieved is unclear.

Alternatively, it is possible that the burials were made as a group together with the surrounding soil as a single event. Pottery from the middle fill of the ditch indicates a date in the later 2nd century or later. The radiocarbon dates from the two skeletons that have been dated have a wide range that includes the late 2nd and early 3rd centuries, so would allow this, even if this falls towards the end of their ranges at 95% probability. Although all of the skeletons were incomplete, they did not however consist simply of a scatter of redeposited disarticulated bones, so this was not an accumulation of redeposited material that happened to incorporate newborn babies.

The deposition of the juveniles as a group would certainly have reduced the possibility of disturbance of the burials, but it then begs the question as to why so many newborns were being buried at one time, or at least within a short period of time.

Roman neonatal burials in Britain have been found in a variety of contexts, few of them clearly formal, and their status is uncertain. Groups or scatters of neonatal burials, usually unaccompanied by grave goods, are often found in peripheral locations, such as towards the corners of enclosures surrounding villas, as at Barton Court Farm, Oxfordshire (Miles 1984) or in the ditches around farmsteads, as at the Eton Rowing Course near Dorney, Buckinghamshire (Allen *et al.* 2000). Those at Barton Court occurred as a group of 8, and were of 3rd century date, while those at the Eton Rowing Course were more scattered both in location and date, from the mid-1st century to the late 2nd century AD. At the latter site, as at Bredon's Norton, they were mixed in with deposits containing domestic rubbish, and also occurred in hollows within the settlement, which does not suggest particular care in their burial.

The most famous group of neonatal burials in Roman Britain is that of 97 individuals of late Roman date at the Yewden villa, Hambleden, Buckinghamshire (Cocks 1921). Most of these were found in a yard adjacent to the villa buildings. Recent investigation of 33 of these suggests that they were the product of deliberate infanticide, and the presence of both boys and girls made the researchers conclude that there was no preferential treatment of either sex (Mays and Eyers 2011). Possibly these were the children of female slaves working at the site.

The apparently casual disposal of neonatal infants has led to considerable debate about the significance attached to newborn fatalities in the Roman world. Certainly the classical world has plenty of stories about the exposure of unwanted newborn infants, although this was usually in forested or mountainous areas remote from settlement. The Roman author Pliny the Elder believed that a child 'did not obtain a soul until.....the age of teething.... ' (Philpott 1991, 101), and this has suggested to some that no special significance was attached to the burial of newborns in Roman Britain. Pearce (2001) however argues that the evidence from Romano-British cemeteries gives a more complex picture, and a more varied attitude to the burial of young infants. McKinley has noted the high numbers or neonates in association with shrines and other ritual sites at Springhead, and suggests that this association may not have been accidental (McKinley in Barnett *et al* 2011, 8-9).

The clustering of the group at Bredon's Norton does suggest that a specific area was chosen for the disposal of these infants, even though, as at Barton Court Farm, it was peripheral to the main settlement focus. In discussing Roman infant burials in the Thames Valley, Booth stated that burials of infants were normally segregated from those of adults, as at Barton Court Farm, the distinction only breaking down in the later 4th century AD (Booth *et al.* 2007, 229-231). At Bredon's Norton, however, the earlier burial of adults adjacent to the infant cluster, indicates that this was already an area known for burials, and that the disposal of infants was not kept separate from that of some at least of the adult community, though only one or two adult burials lay adjacent within the stripped area. A distinction between the burial of adults and neonatal infants may not therefore, on this site, have been important.

The scatter of adult burials in the north-west part of the site perhaps indicates a zone of the settlement that was considered appropriate for burial, rather than a particular enclosure, as was the case on some other sites such as Northfield Farm, Long Wittenham, Oxfordshire (Gray 1977), and perhaps at Tockington Park Farm, where the enclosure containing the burials lay *c* 100m from the main villa buildings (Masser and McGill 2004, fig. 3). The villa at Roughground Farm, Lechlade combined both of these, burials being scattered throughout two groups of subsidiary occupation enclosures, but with a concentration in one particular enclosure, and a third larger cemetery group as well (Allen *et al*. 1993, fig. 69).

Date of construction of the Roman building at Bredon's Norton

Only one ditch, 3037=3310, was certainly cut by the construction of the sunken-floored room. This contained sherds of early Roman date. This ditch was also overlain by 3303, the western room of the building, consisting of robber trench 3297 and 3047, and of the western end of platform cut 3025. Room 3303 also cut ditch 3305 and grave 3300, both of which were Iron Age.

The southern platform, on which a hypocaust was constructed, cut ditches 3279 and 3120. Ditch 3279 contained only Iron Age and late Iron Age/early Roman pottery, but ditch 3120 included a probable backfill that contained early Roman pottery, and the top fill included further early Roman pottery, large box flue and flat tile fragments. This last deposit might represent a spread of construction debris from the adjacent building. It was cut by ditch 3118.

If the interpretation of the deliberate infilling of 3120, and the subsequent spread of building material is as part of the construction of the platform, then construction may have been later 1st century (or early 2nd century) AD. The absence of any features later than the 1st century cut by the building would support this. The excavation of a cut for the building will, however, have removed much of the evidence for earlier Roman activity under the building, and as the floors of the building were not removed, we do not know what features later than the early Roman period might lie beneath it.

A phase of Roman building construction in the late 1st century or early 2nd century AD is also suggested by the presence of box flue tile in ditch 3081=3126 to the south. The debris within ditch 3120 was cut by gully 3118, which ran west-east parallel to the main axis of the building just south of the end of drain 3167, and may have taken water from it. The fill of this gully contained only a single

sherd of 1st/2nd century AD pottery. Though not strong, this evidence would also fit with an early date for the building.

Ditch 3055, which was traced from the SE corner of the building, ran SE down to ditch 3081=3126, and cut into it, but was not traced beyond it. It may have drained into the top of this ditch, or into the 2nd century parallel ditches to the south. It is even possible that gully 3118 had originally continued eastwards to join 3055, but was later infilled and the cobbling extended over it, at the same time that a stone 'bridge' was laid over the infilled ditch 3055.

It is alternatively possible that the tiles from layer 3124/3125 were misattributed, and in fact came from late ditch 3031, belonging to the destruction of the building instead. The presence of similar tile in the ditches to the south, however, which are clearly of early date, makes their presence in 3124/5 less contentious. The presence of the tiles in these other early ditches certainly suggests that a Roman building was being constructed somewhere on the site in the late 1st/early 2nd century AD; the possibility that at this early date this material had been brought in as rubble or as leftovers from elsewhere, perhaps for use in other structures such as corndryers, is relatively unlikely. Other local candidates for early Roman urban or villa construction are rare.

Given that a Roman building was being constructed on the site at this early date, and that the fabrics being used were the same as those in the destruction levels of the excavated building, the simplest interpretation would be that the tiles in the early contexts, including those immediately adjacent to the excavated building, come from that building.

This need not however confirm an early date for the excavated building. It is possible that the excavated building may have made use of materials from a much earlier building nearby, hence the similarity of the tile fabrics. It is also possible that local clays were used for many types of tile throughout the Roman period, so that the similarity of fabrics is irrelevant, although the pink grogged ware tiles were clearly imported.

The date of the pink grogged ware large tiles used in the hypocaust is believed by Paul Booth to be 4th century, although no comprehensive study of ceramic building material in this fabric has been carried out. In the absence of *in situ* tiles of this fabric, however, those that were found could represent later repairs to the structure, rather than dating its original construction.

Pottery from the silt on the floor of the hypocaust, however, which is described as sealed in places by mortar on which the hypocaust was constructed, also includes mid-4th century material. There is unfortunately no conclusive proof that the late pottery came from below one of the mortar patches, but unless this was intrusive from the destruction soils where these directly overlay the silt, this would date the hypocaust to the later 4th century. The ditch running S from the end of the drain (4030) contains later 4th century material, showing that it was infilled at this date. It cut 3118, a possible predecessor of 1st/2nd century or later date, again leaving the possibility of an earlier construction date open.

One final piece of evidence needs to be taken into consideration. One of the charred timbers from the layer overlying the floor of room 3184, which appear to represent structural timbers from the ceiling of the room, was radiocarbon-dated to 120-320 cal AD at 95% confidence. As oak is much easier to work when green, ie freshly cut, it is unlikely that the ceiling would have been constructed later than the early 4th century, and could have been as early as the first half of the 2nd century AD. There is a 90% probability that the oak was felled before AD 260.

The date of the charred timber strongly argues for the construction of the Room 3184 between the early 2nd and the mid-3rd century AD. The absence of render on the south side of wall 3012, the southern wall of room 3184, also suggests that both this room and the hypocaust to the south were constructed together. The 4th century large bricks of pink-grogged ware found associated with the destruction of the hypocaust must then represent repairs or reflooring in the 4th century, repairs which also provided the context for the dropping of the later 4th century dish onto the sub-floor beneath.

Construction and function of the building

Due to the very heavy robbing of all but the sunken-floored room 3184, no floors, internal features or associated finds from the period of use of the building, or of its initial abandonment, survive. It is in any case likely that materials used and broken during the life of the building would have been disposed of outside the building, rather than left on the floors. Only a limited part of the area surrounding the building lay within the easement of the pipeline, and this mainly contained features of early Roman date, and certainly no concentrations of high quality Roman finds such as are often associated with masonry villa buildings.

The destruction deposits did contain a small number of finds, and these included one certain pair of tweezers and a possible fragment from a second. These are usually considered to be related to personal hygiene, but with only one certain example do not provide strong evidence of function. Other than these, the few finds are not specific as to function. For these reasons, interpretation of the function of this building is almost entirely reliant on the limited structural evidence.

The sunken-floored room 3184

Many of the characteristics of this room are shared by cold plunge baths at other sites. The floor of this room is flagged, and would have been at least 0.8m below that of the adjacent hypocausted rooms. A quarter-round moulding was found sealing the junction of the floor and walls, again a common feature in such baths, and a drain was provided through one wall at ground level. The plunge bath at Spoonley Wood, Gloucestershire, less than 20km from Bredon's Norton, also had a flagged floor and a quarter-round moulding (RCHM 1976, 114). At Bancroft, Milton Keynes, and at Lullingstone, the floor was of inverted tegulae, but otherwise all of these features were present (Williams and Zeepvat 1994, 139-140; Meates 1979, 92-5). At Bredon's Norton waterproofing below the flagstones was provided by a thick layer of clay, whereas opus signinum concrete was used at Bancroft, at Lullingstone and at many other sites. The evidence for opus signinum on the walls of Room 3184 at Bredon's Norton is uncertain; a red layer of mortar was certainly found behind the surface skim of fine white mortar that was painted, and this red mortar was harder than the underlying mortar layer, but did not contain the visible tile fragments usually so characteristic of opus signinum proper. The use of three layers of mortar on the walls, one of which was red, does however suggest that the intention was to provide a waterproofing layer, even if the execution was not up to the usual standard of opus signinum.

If this interpretation is correct, then it is possible that the original function of room 3184 was as the cold plunge bath of a bath house complex, of which fragments of several other rooms were also recovered in the excavation. At 3.5m by at least 6m long, room 3184 was among the larger plunge-baths known at villa sites in Britain, but is broadly comparable to that at Spoonley Wood, which was 5.5m long and 3.5m wide. Larger pools are known, for example the pool 5m by 6m at Ebrington, Gloucestershire (RCHM 1996, 52-3), and/or those at Bucknowle and Halstock, Dorset, the first of which was 3.3m by 7m long in the 4th century AD (Light and Ellis 2009, 39-40 and fig. 19) the second having a pool 8m long by over 4m wide (Lucas 1993, fig. 54).

The central cistern

The central cistern or well is however a most unusual feature to find within a cold plunge bath. At the Honeyditches villa in Devon, Henrietta Miles suggested that there had been a small cold plunge bath in the south-east corner, adjacent to a well (Miles 1977, fig. 8 and 117-121). The well was however some 2.4m in diameter, so was intended to provide considerably more water than the small cistern at Bredon's Norton. Stuart Foreman has suggested that the water for the plunge bath at Bredon's Norton may have welled up from the cistern, as the room lies at a local change in the underlying geology, which may have meant that a spring line existed at this point, and was made use of when constructing the cold plunge bath. A similar arrangement was found at the bath-building at Baston Manor, Hayes in Kent (Philp 1973, 82-3). It is however unlikely that at Bredon's Norton this would have been sufficient to fill the pool, as otherwise construction of the bath itself would have been all but impossible.

At a later stage the bath was clearly drained, as the groove cut into the flagstones of the floor from the central cistern or well to the drain makes no sense had the bath still held water. The groove implies that, even at the wettest season of the year, the cistern would only have overflown to a very limited degree.

Unless a dramatic change in the local water table within the late Roman period is invoked, it seems very unlikely that the cistern could have filled the bath. Without this sudden change, the cistern is best seen as a secondary addition to the room, added when its function as a plunge bath ended.

A similarly shallow well or cistern was found in Building C at Shakenoak, Oxfordshire (Brodribb *et al.* 2005, 279-294 and fig. IV.14). Building C was built (as at Bredon's Norton) on low-lying ground, and was interpreted as a bath house. The well here was rectangular rather than circular, but was only 0.75m by 0.4-0.5m across and just less than 1.2m deep, bottoming on the natural limestone. It was believed that this would have generally held 0.3m of water, and may have been used to fill a tank in one of the adjacent rooms of this bath-house. The cistern at Bredon's Norton could well have been intended for a similar purpose.

A shallow cistern, projecting 6" above the floor, was also found in Room 1 adjacent to the bath house at Great Witcombe (RCHM 1976, 60-61), in a room floored with Old Red Sandstone. It was 0.57m by 0.52m across, with a large stone slab on the base, and another forming each side of the cistern. This cistern, which was constructed in the early 2nd century AD, was however fed with water via a channel, rather than from groundwater, and had an outlet drain 0.25m above the base, so that it would only have held a limited volume of water (Clifford 1954, 16-18). The cistern is believed to have had a ritual function due to the existence of niches along one wall and a pottery model of a fir cone found in the same room (ibid., fig. 2). Another sunken room of 2nd century date in the region with a probably ritual function is the cellar with painted plaster and niches in the villa at Wortley in Wotton-under-Edge in South Gloucestershire, (Wilson *et al.* 2014, 12-17), where it is suggested there was a central water tank or font above a cruciform arrangement of drains. This was however a fully underground room, rather than a partly sunken structure, and appears to have been designed with a ritual function from the start. The distinction between ritual and other bathing is unlikely to have been clear-cut in the Roman world, however, so the Bredon's Norton example may also have fulfilled such 'ritual' purposes.

The rooms to the south

South of Room 3184 the building was constructed on a limestone platform. This was probably partly due to the ditches that had previously been dug across this area, some possibly only infilled for the building's construction, and also perhaps in part due to a change in underlying geology, which may have meant that a spring line existed in this area, making the ground liable to flooding. A similar platform was used in a low-lying area at Shakenoak Farm, Oxfordshire, to provide a firm footing for the 2nd century bath-house Building C (Brodribb *et al.* 2005, 278-9).

Due to the extensive robbing, the function, and indeed even the layout, of the rooms in this area is uncertain, but it seems likely that there was one main hypocausted room adjacent to the cold plunge bath, which was 6.4m long (east to west) and 5.5m wide. If correctly interpreted, the heavily-robbed western room at Bredon's Norton may well have been a stokehole, and the room adjacent to the plunge bath the hot room or *caldarium*. This arrangement is a common one within the bath complex, as at Spoonley Wood (RCHM 1976, 114), Bancroft (Williams and Zeepvat 1994, figs 89 and 95) and at Northfleet, Kent, in its later stages (Andrews *et al.* 2011, fig. 4.6 and 220-221). The curving edge of the platform on the south-west may indicate that the original intention was to have a small semicircular plunge bath on this side of the caldarium, possibly a hot bath, but if so, nothing has survived.

East of the main room the platform extended to define a small room 2.5m by 2m, with an area of uncertain dimensions to the north where the natural had not been truncated for a platform. There was no surviving evidence of a north wall to this room, but the very straight edge of the platform, and the higher level of the natural to the north, strongly suggests that there must have been a wall of some sort here. The level of the platform suggests that the small room on the south-east must either also have been hypocausted, or have had a sunken floor in relation to the main adjacent room. No trace of any finished floor survived, and on balance, the former seems more probable. The area to the north may have been external to the building, or may have been another room without underfloor heating, whose floor has been completely truncated.

Interpretation of the building layout

A Roman bath house requires at least two heated rooms, the *caldarium* (hot room) and *tepidarium* (warm room), plus an unheated *frigidarium* (cold room), and normally a cold plunge pool and *praefurnium* (furnace-room) (Rook 2002). There are usually also *apodyteria* (dressing rooms), and the complex can be much larger than this. The exposed remains do not fall easily into this arrangement (see Figure 5.2). The main room, interpreted as the *caldarium* as it is immediately adjacent to the

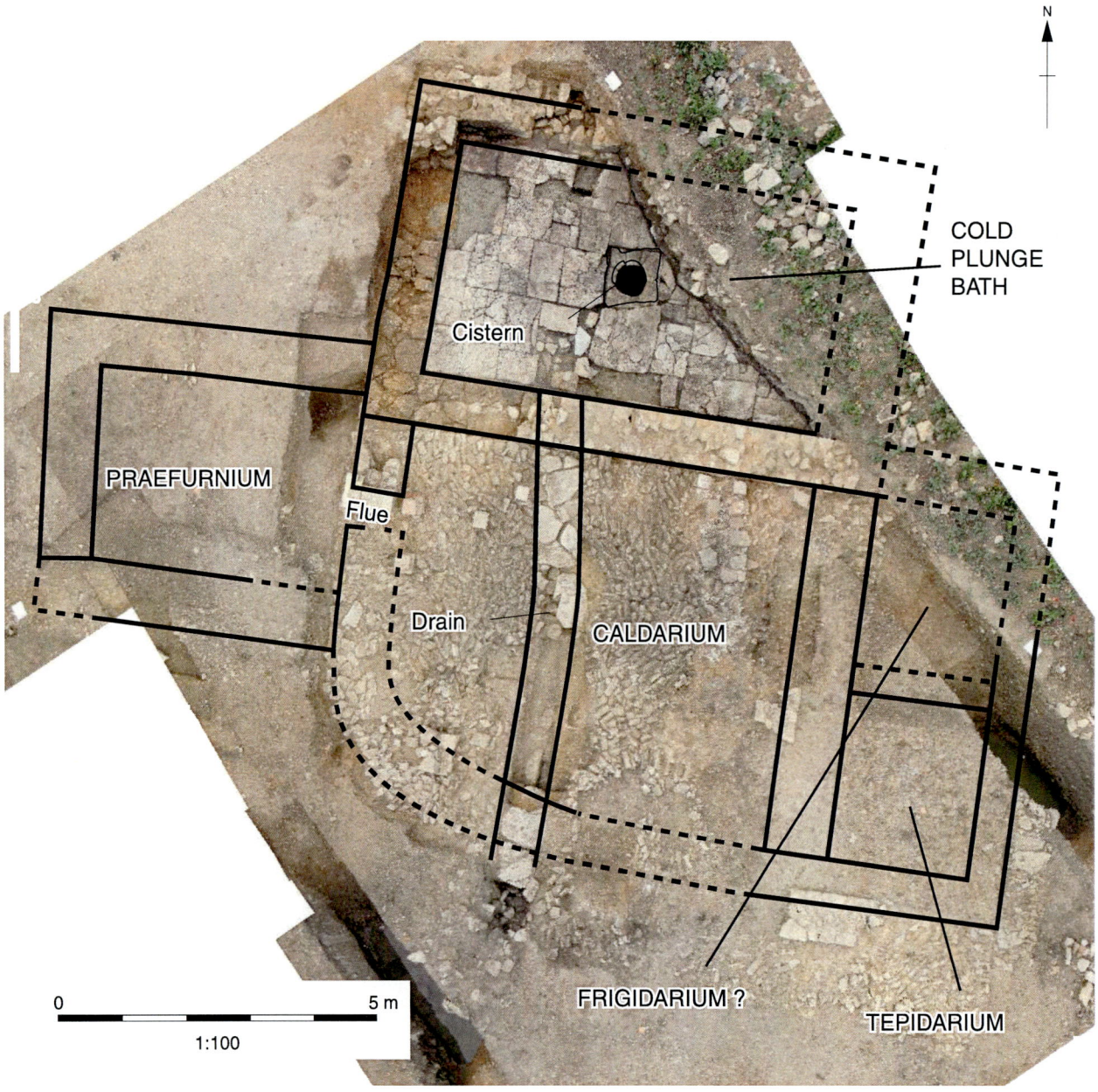

Fig. 5.2 Tentative interpretation of the Roman building at Bredon's Norton

furnace in the room on the west, has no evidence of a subdivision in its original form. Later on, wall 3337 may indicate that this room was divided into two, allowing for a *caldarium* on the west, and a *tepidarium*, which was always further from the *praefurnium*, on the east. In the original arrangement, however, the function of the *tepidarium* would have had to have been met by the small south-east room, which is disproportionately small in relation to the adjacent *caldarium*. If internal, the unheated area to the north of this could then have been the *frigidarium*, but this is also very small when compared to the usual arrangements, and makes the cold plunge bath enormous in comparison. While the sizes of the different rooms varied considerably in Romano-British bath houses (Rook 2002, 22-3), this would represent an extreme departure

from the norm. There is no surviving evidence that the complex continued further east than wall foundation 3021, but that this was really the case seems very unlikely, and it is more probable that the bath-house extended further east, but that the part within the excavation has now been completely destroyed.

The burnt grain deposit

This was found directly overlying the flagged floor in Room 3184, suggesting that the floor had remained in use until the fire that burnt the grain occurred. This event is dated by radiocarbon assay to 345-430 cal AD at 95% confidence, and most likely between AD390 and AD420, ie at the very end of the Roman occupation of Britain (Figure 4.5).

As argued above, the grain is unlikely to have been stored on the floor of the building, both because of the likelihood of flooding on occasions, as shown by the central cistern and the groove for drainage cut across the floor slabs, and because it underlay the remains of charred timbers, showing that it had not been stored on a wooden floor raised above the stone flags. The central cistern appears to have remained open until this fire took place, and the fact that the charred material largely overlay the rubble collapse within it is attributed to standing water inside it, such that the charred material floated on the top, while the rubble sank to the bottom of the open cistern. Temporary storage immediately after harvest is theoretically possible, but the choice of a sunken room liable to be damp seems a poor one. Temporary use of this environment might perhaps have favoured the sprouting of grain for malting, but there was no evidence in the charred material for sprouted grain.

The timbers may instead have belonged to a wooden ceiling, grain spilling through gaps in the planks as they burnt, and falling onto the floor before the main structure of the ceiling collapsed. This might also explain the absence of very high temperature burning on the plaster still adhering to the south wall. It is however noticeable that all of the timbers that were planned lie at right angles to one another, and parallel either to the east-west or north-south walls surrounding room 3184. While this is consistent with an arrangement of principal joists and planks forming the ceiling structure, and a floor at first floor level on which the grain might have been stored, it is odd that all of the collapsing timbers should have preserved their original orientation if they had collapsed from above. The same objection however also rules out the possibility that both the grain and the timbers were dumped from a fire elsewhere, which might otherwise explain the absence of intense burning on the plaster.

Perhaps the explanation is that most of the ceiling came down in one piece, and subsequently continued to burn until only fragments of the structure remained. This would suggest that the ceiling was already weakened at the edges, so that it burnt through more quickly here. This may have been the result of partial rotting of the timbers where they were supported upon, or within, the walls, or perhaps indicates that the fire was set deliberately, rather than being accidental. In support of the first suggestion, the charred timber from the roof that was radiocarbon-dated gave a date range of 120-260 cal AD at 93% confidence. Oak is much easier to work when green ie fresh, so it is unlikely that the date at which the ceiling was constructed was later than 260AD, and quite possibly considerably earlier. Use as a plunge pool would have meant that the atmosphere was damp, so that by the late 4th century it is plausible that the joists were already beginning to decay. The effects of decay are often found to be worst where the surrounding environment changes, in this case where the timbers entered the wall.

If this was not the case, the collapse of most of the ceiling in one piece would suggest that the structure had been deliberately weakened around the edges, either by chopping partway through the joists, or by setting the fire around the edges, so that the joists here burnt through first. The latter is not however consistent with the presence of grain below the surviving timbers across most of the floor. Unfortunately not enough of the timbers from the excavated part of this room survived to determine whether the joists had been deliberately weakened, and it leaves open the question of accidental or deliberate destruction of the building.

The reuse of Roman buildings for agricultural or industrial purposes in the late Roman period is relatively common, for example by the insertion of corndryers, but evidence for the storage of grain in such buildings is not. A layer of charred grain was found directly upon a mosaic floor at Dinnington villa in Somerset (King with Grande forthcoming), though in this case the grain has been provisionally dated to 410–570 cal AD, so the reuse of this room would be post-Roman. The evidence at Bredon's Norton clearly relates to the Romano-British period, albeit at the very end. This could plausibly be seen as another instance of the late Roman change of use that has been observed within a number of Roman villas, when formerly domestic buildings (including bath houses) are turned over to agricultural or industrial use. Examples include Truckle Hill, North Wraxall, Wilts, where a corndryer was built up against the side of a bath house, the charred remains from which were dumped in the *frigidarium* (Andrews 2009).

There is however documentary evidence for the use of lofts to store grain. According to Black (1981), Columella in his *Rei Rusticae* describes grain as stored *tabulatis*, ie at a raised level, while liquids are stored *in planis*, at ground level (I, VI, 9-16), and recommends access to the loft by ladder. Black suggests that such granaries will be built into the structural framework of buildings built for other purposes, leaving no archaeological trace. While Columella was writing in the 1st century AD, and is unlikely to have been thinking primarily of bath houses when he wrote, the principle of storage in lofts, and over rooms containing liquids, was clearly well-established at the start of the Roman occupation of Britain, and may have been common. As Black has pointed out, however, the archaeological evidence for such practices in Britain is likely to be *nil*. We are thus fortunate to have encountered an exceptional fire such as this.

Late Roman use of the sunken-floored room

A corollary of the interpretation suggested here is that the excavated part of the sunken-floored room was empty, or held only highly combustible materials, when the fire occurred, as no traces of storage jars, charred barrels or other containers was found within the burnt debris. Whether this part of the building was abandoned, or whether the insertion of the central cistern, together with the presence of its painted walls, made it suitable for other, perhaps ritual purposes, is uncertain. The date of insertion of the cistern is unknown, though likely to have been considerably later than those at Great Witcombe and Shakenoak cited above. What is clear is that its narrowness, and the possibility of a central spanning timber, make use as a late Roman baptistry extremely unlikely.

Consideration of the wider settlement at Bredon's Norton (Fig. 2.14)

The 2006 geophysical survey demonstrated that there was an extensive settlement here. As already mentioned, the possible misalignment of readings from adjacent grid squares gives a somewhat blurred appearance to the survey plot, making it difficult to be certain about the details of the settlement layout in places. The results of the later geophysical survey transect along the line of the pipeline however largely agrees with the results of the 2006 survey, giving added confidence to the survey outside this area. There was clearly a series of circular or oval enclosures running SSW-NNE along the east side of the surveyed area, possibly flanked on the west by a series of curving longer ditches in the northern part of the area. West of these were two main rectilinear enclosures with a gap between that possibly represents a trackway entering the heart of the settlement from the west. These rectilinear enclosures consist of several parallel ditches on all sides.

Where the pipeline transect crossed the area of the geophysical survey, excavation has confirmed the main layout indicated by the geophysical survey, and has demonstrated that this was a long-lived settlement with evidence for occupation from the middle Iron Age until the very end of the Roman period. The transect ran diagonally across the settlement area, so that it only crossed the westernmost part of the settlement on the north, but ran over the central part further south. A middle Iron Age ditch and burial were found towards the south end of the transect, apparently related to a curvilinear enclosure visible from the geophysical survey.

In the late Iron Age or early Roman period activity was more widespread, including lengths of the ditches of several curvilinear enclosures visible on the geophysical survey plot in the southern part of the site, together with associated small pits and postholes. Similar circular or oval enclosures are visible all along the east side of the geophysical survey plot in the northern field, but do not extend to the western edge of the settlement, and it is therefore probably not surprising that no certain middle-late Iron Age features were found in the excavated transect across the northern part of the settlement, although a few ditches and a burial of possibly very late Iron Age date were found at the south-east end of the northern part of the transect. The use of the curvilinear enclosures clearly continued through the 1st century AD and into the early 2nd century at Bredon's Norton.

The excavation indicates that the reorganisation into at least two large rectangular enclosures divided by a trackway occurred during the late 1st century or 2nd century AD. Although less of the ditches of the southern enclosure was excavated, the dating is reasonably consistent between the two enclosures, supporting the idea that the long narrow area between them was intended as a trackway or droveway into the settlement, and that the construction of both enclosures may have taken place at much the same time. The curvilinear enclosures in the south-eastern part of the site were still active in the late 1st and early 2nd centuries AD, so it is possible that the larger rectilinear enclosures were originally laid out alongside the curvilinear ones.

The date of construction of the substantial masonry building further to the south-east is still poorly defined, but such evidence as there is indicates that it might also have been part of this reorganisation, or have followed shortly afterwards. More excavation would however be needed to confirm the relative dates of these elements.

An area of 2 ha. was surveyed by earth resistance in an attempt to identify further evidence of Romanised masonry buildings on the site (Smalley 2011). The survey highlighted several areas that the authors of the survey believed indicated the likely presence of structural remains, and their interpretation of the survey is also shown in Figure 5.3. The outline of possible buildings is not however very clear, and the fact that the gradiometer survey was not obscured to a greater degree in the areas indicated on the interpretation casts some doubt on this interpretation. It remains possible that some of the east-west and north-south lines east and north-east of the excavated building do belong to further rooms, but due to the excavated evidence for heavy robbing, it would be unwise to over-interpret the survey results. An area of possible stonework was also recorded just over 100m to the north-west, towards the north-west corner of the more northerly rectilinear enclosure, and although little of this was interpreted as representing surviving stonework, this may perhaps mark the former position of a separate building within the settlement.

One might speculate that each of the two rectilinear enclosures had its own masonry building, and there were a few fragments of Roman ceramic building material in early contexts at, or just beyond the very south end of the northern enclosure, but these were closer to the known building to the south-east, so do not really support this hypothesis. Only further excavation will clarify the nature and organisation of the surveyed part of the Bredon's Norton Roman settlement.

The 2006 geophysical survey shows the limits of the settlement on the west side clearly, and there is very little at all west of this that might be archaeological. Fieldwalking in the western part of the field

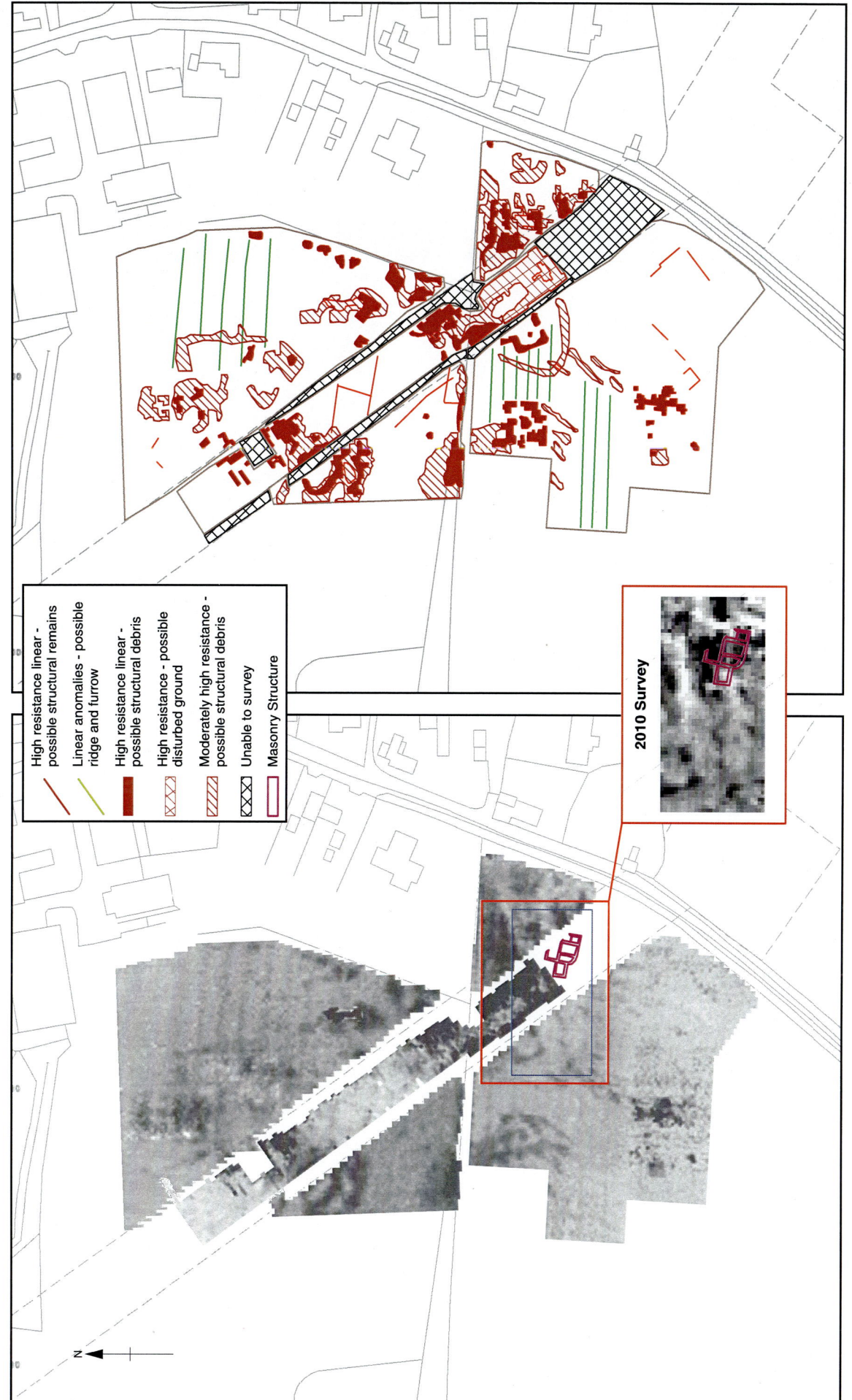

2010 Survey

High resistance linear - possible structural remains

Linear anomalies - possible ridge and furrow

High resistance linear - possible structural debris

High resistance - possible disturbed ground

Moderately high resistance - possible structural debris

Unable to survey

Masonry Structure

N

Fig. 5.3 Earth resistance survey of Bredon's Norton by Stratascan and provisional interpretation

191

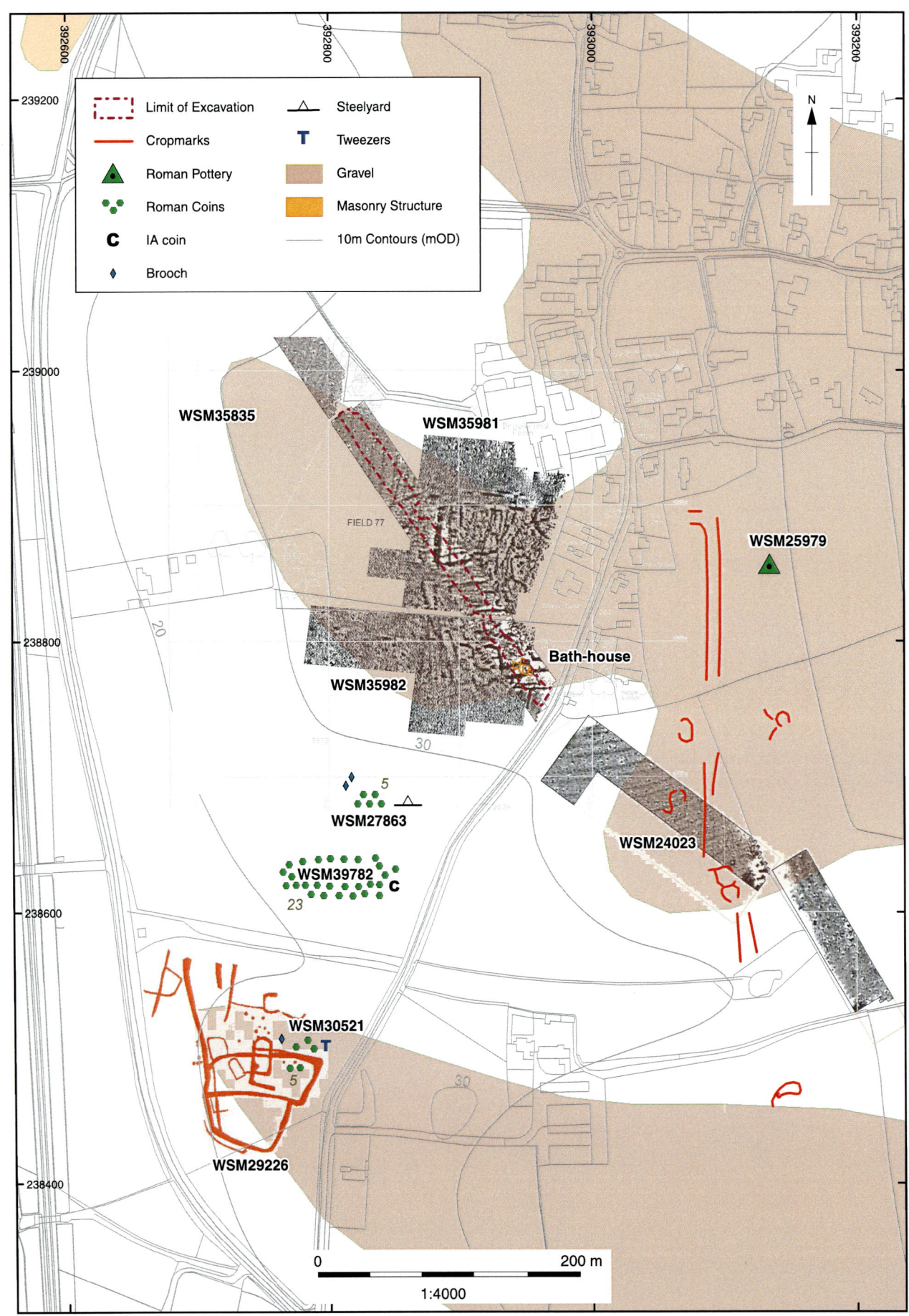

recovered very little material (WSM35835). Evidence for the extent of the settlement beyond the surveyed areas may be provided by cropmarks. In the field east of the modern road that bounds the excavation on the south-east, two oblique aerial photographs (WSM24023: AS850 and 851) show a pair of parallel ditches probably representing a trackway running north-south some 140m east of the excavated building over a distance of at least 300m before fading out to the south. There is no direct evidence that this trackway is Roman, but Roman pottery has been recovered from the more northerly of the fields crossed by the trackway (HER WSM25979).

South-east of the pipeline several possible curvilinear enclosures are visible on the west side of the trackway. The photographs are obscured by natural areas of deeper soil, so the definition of the curvilinear enclosures is poor, but an outline interpretation is given in Figure 5.4.

Some 300m to the south-west of the excavated building, a double enclosure attached to the east side of a linear boundary is plotted (WSM 29226; Fig. 5.4), and this also has other rectilinear ditches, small enclosures and groups of pits. Although not excavated, five 4th century Roman coins were found by metal detecting in the area of this enclosure, and a 2nd century Roman brooch in the north-east corner. The enclosure is similar in character to one at Butler's Field, Lechlade, Gloucestershire, although only a peripheral trackway was excavated (Boyle *et al.* 1998, 3-4 and Fig. 1.3).

Another five Roman coins, a brooch and a steelyard, and a further twenty four Roman coins and one late Iron Age coin were also found in the field north of this, between the excavation and cropmark enclosure (WSM 27863; WSM 39782). The character of these metal-detected finds indicate further Roman settlement between the two known settlement areas, although it is also possible that they represent the results of manuring fields with materials from the main settlement to the north. Only further geophysical survey or excavation is likely to resolve this.

Given the limited scope of the excavations, further speculation on the building, and indeed on its place in relation to the remainder of the site, is unprofitable. Hopefully these investigations have highlighted the potential of this settlement for further, more detailed investigation in the future.

Wider context of the excavated sites

Bredon's Norton lies only 3km south-west of the hillfort of Bredon Hill Camp, otherwise known as Kemerton Camp, and is 4.3km west of Conderton Camp (Figure 5.5). Both Conderton Camp and Kemerton Camp are known to have been occupied during the middle Iron Age, and Kemerton Camp

continued until occupation was brought to an abrupt end by the Roman army in the mid-1st century AD (Thomas 2005, 257). Both hillforts have evidence of numerous storage pits during these periods; Conderton Camp has clear evidence of domestic occupation, while Kemerton Camp, whose interior has not been extensively investigated, is larger and multivallate. Thomas suggested that Kemerton Camp was a central place for the Iron Age communities of the surrounding area, performing the functions of centralised storage, a focal point for redistribution and for the manufacture of superfluous goods for exchange (Thomas 2005, 247-8). The site at Bredon's Norton is within an hour's walk from these hillforts, and a relationship between them is very likely.

South of Bredon Hill a number of sites of Iron Age and Romano-British date are known from Bredon eastwards to Beckford and Ashton-under-Hill, with a particular concentration strung out along the north side of the Carrant Brook (ibid., 1-3; Bishop 2009). This was clearly a densely populated area from the middle Iron Age onwards, becoming even more so in the Roman period.

Pamington is 5km south-west of Conderton Camp, the nearest of the hillforts on Bredon Hill, and so may also have fallen within its sphere of influence, but is south of the Carrant and Tirle brooks, and is only 3km from The Knolls Camp, Oxenton to the south-east. Fiddington, which lies just over 3km from Pamington, is also a similar distance from The Knolls Camp. This site occupies high ground projecting from the edge of the Gloucestershire Cotswolds into the Carrant valley. Only limited excavation has taken place on this site, and may have examined redeposited material, but the pottery recovered indicates activity in the middle Iron Age (Dunning 1933; Moore 2006). The RCHM Gloucestershire Cotswolds volume however discounted this as a hillfort (RCHM 1976, xxix-xxxi), as the earthworks were at the foot of a hill. South-east of The Knolls Camp is the much larger hillfort at Nottingham Camp, which is only 5.5-6km from both Pamington and Fiddington, and if The Knolls Camp was not a hillfort, this may instead have been a focus for the inhabitants of both sites. Iron Age activity is becoming increasingly common in excavations at and around Bishop's Cleeve (Barber and Walker 1998; Parry 1999; Lovell *et al.* 2007), and it seems probable that this also represented a focus of settlement in the later Iron Age. If Nottingham Hill was the focus for Iron Age settlement south of the Carrant Brook, the cluster of settlements around Bishop's Cleeve are likely to have comprised those most closely linked to it during the Iron Age.

The Roman villa at Bredon's Norton is one of only two known for certain in south Worcester-

Fig. 5.4 (opposite) Bredon's Norton: pipeline excavation and geophysical survey in relation to cropmarks and field-walking evidence

shire, the other being at Childwickham, some 11km to the east (Patrick and Hurst 2004). The Bredon Hill Hoard, a hoard of several thousand later 3rd century Roman silver coins, was found in 2011 about 0.5km north of Bredon Hill Camp within a pot in a hole dug into the rubble overlying a succession of buildings with stone foundations, possibly indicating another villa (Fig. 5.5). Details of the stratigraphic sequence, which is not fully published, vary, but it appears that the hoard was

accompanied by a coin minted in AD 355-361, suggesting that the villa had gone out of use by the mid-4th century (British Archaeology 2012; Worcestershire Hub online). A courtyard villa is also suspected east of the river Isbourne north of Wormington (*ibid*, fig. 17), but is only known from cropmark evidence. Geographically Bredon's Norton lies at the periphery of the much larger group of villas known from Gloucestershire, the closest being those in Sudeley parish at Wadfield

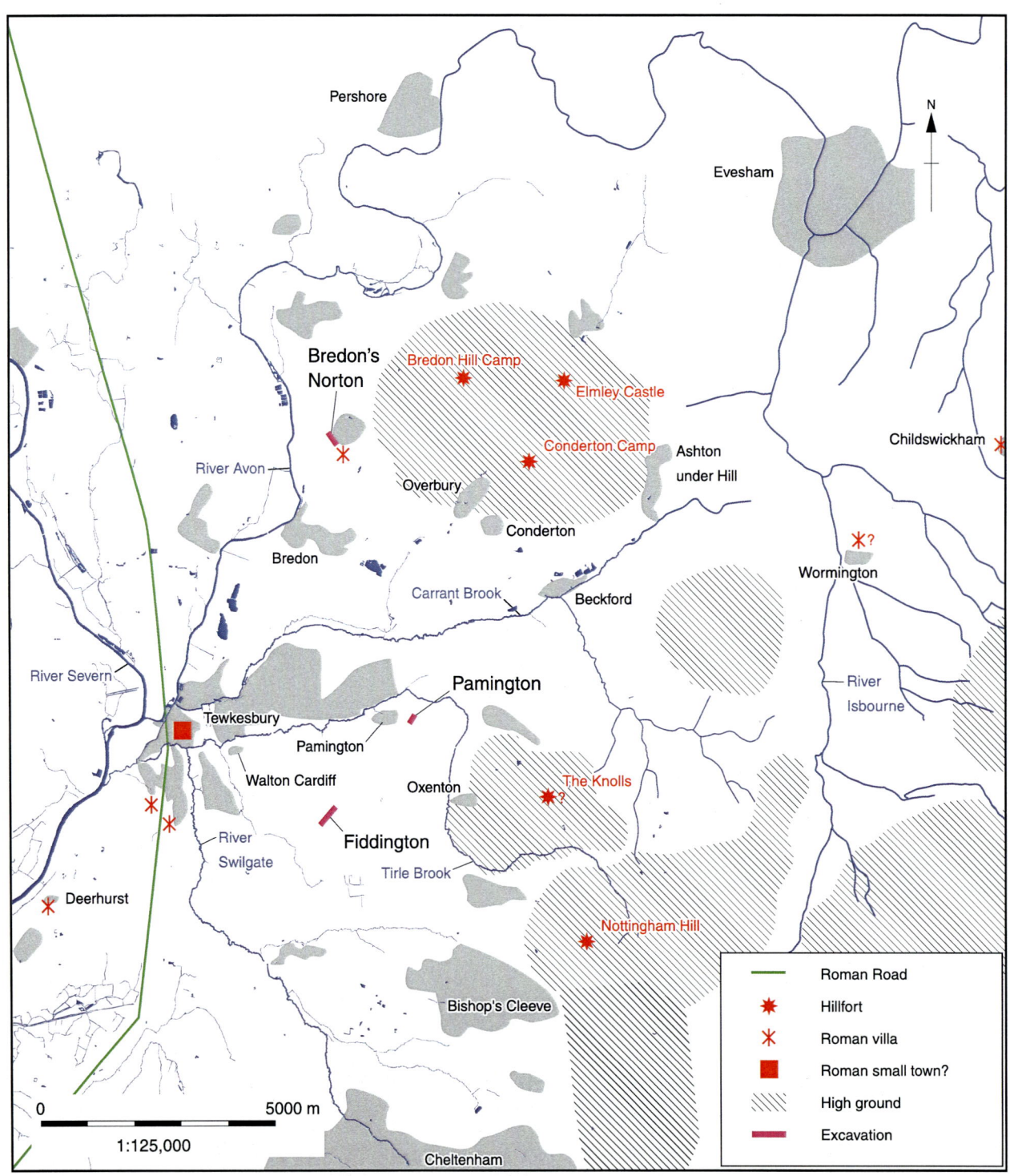

Fig. 5.5 *Excavated sites in relation to sites in the surrounding area*

and Spoonley Wood, 16km and 18.5km to the south-east.

Closer evidence of Roman buildings has been found at Tewkesbury, some 6.5km to the south-west, where a small town is suspected from discoveries in the Oldbury district close to the confluence of the rivers Avon and Severn (Walker *et al.* 2004; Copeland 2011, 99). Tewkesbury also lay on the line of a Roman road linking Worcester to Gloucester (ibid., 107, fig. 57). If there was a Roman small town under the Oldbury part of Tewkesbury, then this will have provided the local market for the villa, and for the native settlement at Fiddington, which lay only 4km to the east.

In addition, evidence of high-status Roman buildings has been recovered at both Tewkesbury Park and Southwick Park, on the southern side of Tewkesbury, which Copeland suggests may represent a pair of villas (ibid., 99). Similar evidence also comes from Deerhurst only another 4km downstream, leading Copeland to speculate that river transport down the Severn to Gloucester was important to this group of sites. It is plausible that proximity to the river Avon, which is only 100m west of Bredon's Norton, was also a factor in the positioning of this villa.

Extensive rural settlement of late Iron Age and Romano-British date has been revealed at Bishop's Cleeve in the Gloucestershire Severn Vale (Barber and Walker 1998; Parry 1999; Cullen and Hancocks 2007; Lovell *et al.* 2007; Parry pers. comm.). A villa is suspected here from building materials found at Home Farm (Barber and Walker 1998, 125-35). This complex of settlements lies only 4 km south-east of Fiddington and 5.5km from Pamington, and though not so well served in terms of the transport network, may have provided an additional focus for contact and exchange for these settlements.

Bibliography

Adam, J-P, 1999 *Roman Building: Materials and Techniques*, London

Allason-Jones, L, and Miket, R, 1984 *The catalogue of small finds from South Shields fort*, The Society of Antiquaries of Newcastle upon Tyne, Monograph series No. **2**, Newcastle

Allen, J R L, and Fulford, M G, 1996 The distribution of south-east Dorset Black Burnished category 1 pottery in south-west Britain, *Britannia* **27**, 223-282

Allen, T G, 1990 *An Iron Age and Romano-British enclosed settlement at Watkins Farm, Northmoor, Oxon*, Thames Valley Landscapes: the Windrush Valley Volume **1**, Oxford Univ. Committee for Archaeology, Oxford

Allen, T, with Hacking, P, and Boyle, A, 2000 Eton Rowing Course at Dorney Lake. The Burial Traditions, *Tarmac Papers* **4**, 65-106

Allen, T G, Darvill, T C, Green, L S, and Jones, M U, 1993 *Excavations at Roughground Farm, Lechlade, Gloucestershire: a prehistoric and Roman landscape*, Oxford Archaeological Unit Thames Valley Landscapes: the Cotswold Water Park, Volume **1**, Oxford

Allen, T G, and Kamash, Z 2008 *Saved from the grave: Neolithic to Saxon discoveries at Spring Road Municipal Cemetery, Abingdon, Oxfordshire, 1990–2000*, Oxford Archaeology Thames Valley Landscapes Monograph **28**

Allen, T, Miles, D, and Palmer, S, 1984 Iron Age buildings in the Upper Thames Region, in *Aspects of the Iron Age in Central Southern Britain* (eds B Cunliffe and D Miles), University of Oxford Committee for Archaeology Monograph **2**, 89-101

Allen, T, Lupton, A, and Mudd, A, with Muir, J, and Mortimer, S, 1999 Chapter 3: The Later Prehistoric Period, in *Excavations along Roman Ermine Street, Gloucestershire and Wiltshire. The archaeology of the A419/A417 Swindon to Gloucester Road Scheme, Volume 1: Prehistoric and Roman activity* (A Mudd, R J Williams and A Lupton) Oxford Archaeological Unit, 35-97

Allen, T, Donnelly, M, Hardy, A, Hayden, C, and Powell, K, 2013 *A Road through the Past: Archaeological discoveries on the A2 Pepperhill to Cobham road-scheme in Kent*, Oxford Archaeology Monograph **16**

AlQahtani, S J, 2009 *Atlas of Tooth Development and Eruption*, online at www.smd.qmul.ac.uk/dental

Andrews, P, 2009 The discovery, excavation and preservation of a detached Roman bath-house at Truckle Hill, North Wraxall, *Wilts Archaeol Nat Hist Mag* **102**, 129-49

Andrews, P, Biddulph, E, Hardy, A, and Brown, R, 2011 *Settling the Ebbsfleet Valley. High Speed 1 excavations at Springhead and Northfleet, Kent: the Late Iron Age, Roman, Saxon and Medieval Landscape. Volume 1: the Sites*, Oxford Wessex Archaeology

Aston, M, 1974 *Stonesfield Slate*, Oxfordshire County Council Department of Museum Services Publication 5, Oxford

Aufderheide, A C, and Rodríguez-Martín, C, 1998 *The Cambridge Encyclopedia of Human Paleopathology*, Cambridge University Press, Cambridge

Ballantyne, R M, (in press) The plant remains, in *Prehistoric and Roman Fen-edge Communities at Colne Fen, Earith. The Archaeology of the Lower Ouse Valley Volume 1* (eds C Evans, G Appleby, S Lucy and R Regan), McDonald Institute Monograph Series, Cambridge

Barber, A J, and Walker, G T, 1998 Home Farm, Bishop's Cleeve. Excavation of a Romano-British occupation site, 1993-4, *Trans Bristol Gloucestershire Archaeol Soc* **116**, 117-139

Barber, A R, and Watts, M, 2008 Excavations at Saxon's Lode Farm, Ripple (2001-2): Iron Age, Romano-British and Anglo-Saxon rural settlement in the Severn Valley, *Trans Worcestershire Archaeol Soc* **21**, 1-90

Barclay, A, and Wait, G A, 2004, Fired clay, in *Gravelly Guy, Stanton Harcourt, Oxfordshire: the development of a prehistoric and Romano-British community*, (G Lambrick and T Allen) Oxford Archaeology Thames Valley Landscapes Monograph **21**, 376-86, Oxford

Barfield, L, 2006 Bays Meadow villa, Droitwich: excavations 1967-77, in *Roman Droitwich: Dodderhill fort, Bays Meadow villa, and roadside settlement*, (ed. D Hurst), Counc Brit Archaeol Res Rep **146**, 78-242, York

Barnes, E, 1994 *Developmental Defects of the Axial Skeleton in Palaeopathology* University Press of Colorado, Colorado

Barnett, C, McKinley, J I, Stafford, E, Grimm, J M, and Stevens, C J, 2011 *Settling the Ebbsfleet Valley. High Speed 1 Excavations at Springhead and Northfleet, Kent, The Late Iron Age, Roman, Saxon and Medieval landscape. Volume3: Late Iron Age to Roman Human Remains and Environmental Reports*, Oxford Wessex Archaeology

Barrett, J C, Freeman, P W M, and Woodward, A, 2000 *Cadbury Castle, Somerset. The late prehistoric and early historic archaeology*, English Heritage Archaeological Report 20, London

Bass, W M, 1987 *Human Osteology. A Laboratory and Field Manual* (3rd edition), Special Publication No. 2 of the Missouri Archaeological Society, Missouri

Beijerinck, W, 1947 *Zaden Atlas der Nederlandsche Flora*. Wageningen, Biol. Stat Wijster 30

Bellows, J, 1881 On some Bronze and other articles found near Birdlip, *Trans Bristol and Gloucestershire Archaeol Soc* **5**, 137

Berggren, G, 1981 *Atlas of seeds and small fruits of Northwest-European plant species with morphological descriptions. Part 3, Salicaceae-Cruciferae*, Berlings

Bertrand, I, (ed) 2008 *Le travail de l'os, du bois de cerf et de la corne à 'époque romaine: un artisanat en marge? Actes de la table ronde instrument, Chauvigny (Vienne, F), 8-9 Décembre 2005*, Montagnac

Berry, A C, and Berry, A J, 1967 Epigenetic variation in the human cranium, *Journal of Anatomy* **101**, 361-379

Biddulph, E, 2011 Wall plaster from Northfleet Roman villa, in *Settling the Ebbsfleet Valley. High Speed 1 excavations at Springhead and Northfleet, Kent: the late Iron Age, Roman, Saxon and medieval landscape. Volume 2: Late Iron Age to Roman finds reports*, (E Biddulph, R Seager Smith and J Schuster), Oxford Wessex monograph, Oxford and Salisbury, 352-4

Bidwell, P T, 1979 *The legionary bath-house and basilica and forum at Exeter*, Exeter Archaeological Reports 1, Exeter

Bishop, S, 2009 *The Carrant Valley Landscape NMP, National Mapping Programme Report*, Research Department Report Series **30**, English Heritage

Black, E W, 1981 An Additional Classification of Granaries in Roman Britain, *Britannia* **12**, 163-5

Boardman, S, and Jones, G, 1990 Experiments on the Effects of Charring on Cereal Plant Components, *Journal of Archaeological Science* **17**, 1-11

Boessneck, J, Müller, H-H, and Teichert, M, 1964 Osteologische Unterscheidungsmerkmale zwischen Schaf (Ovis aries Linné) und Ziege (Capra hircus Linné), *Kühn-Archiv* **78**

Booth, P, 1991 Inter site comparisons between pottery assemblages in Roman Warwickshire: ceramic indicators of social status, *J Roman Pottery Stud* **4**, 1-10

Booth, P, 2004 Quantifying status: some pottery data from the Upper Thames Valley, *J Roman Pottery Stud* **11**, 39-52

Booth, P, 2007 Cotswold Water Park Roman ceramic assemblages in their regional context, in *Iron Age and Roman settlement in the Upper Thames Valley: Excavations at Claydon Pike and other sites within the Cotswold Water Park* (D Miles, S Palmer, A Smith and G P Jones) Oxford Archaeology Thames Valley Landscapes Monograph **26**, Oxford, 319-335

Booth, P, 2011 Oxford Archaeology Roman pottery recording guidelines, Oxford Archaeol unpublished document (revised October 2011)

Booth, P, 2013 Roman pottery, in A Simmonds, Excavations at Stallards Place, Dymock, 2007, *Transactions Bristol and Gloucestershire Archaeol Soc* **131**, 97-98

Booth, P, forthcoming The pottery, in *Later prehistoric landscape and a Roman nucleated settlement in the lower Windrush valley at Gill Mill, near Witney, Oxfordshire* (P Booth and A Simmonds) Oxford Archaeology Monograph, Oxford

Booth, P M, and Green, S, 1989 The Nature and Distribution of Certain Pink, Grog Tempered Vessels, *J Rom Pottery Stud* **2**, 77-84

Booth, P, Boyle, A, and Keevill, G D, 1993 A Romano-British kiln site at Lower Farm, Nuneham Courtenay, and other sites on the Didcot to Oxford and Wootton to Abingdon water mains, Oxfordshire, *Oxoniensia* **58**, 87-217

Boulle, E, 2001 Osteological features associated with ankle hyperdorsiflexion, *International Journal of Osteoarchaeology* **11 (5)**, 345-349

Boyle, A, Jennings, D, Miles, D, and Palmer, S, 1998 *The Anglo-Saxon Cemetery at Butler's Field, Lechlade, Gloucestershire. Volume 1: Prehistoric and Roman Activity and Anglo-Saxon Grave Catalogue*, Oxford Archaeology Thames Valley Landscapes Monograph **10**, Oxford

Brickley, M, and Ives, R 2008 *The Bioarchaeology of Metabolic Bone Disease*, Oxford and London

Brickley, M, and McKinley, J, 2004 *Guidelines to the Standards For Recording Human Remains*, IFA Paper No. 7 British Association for Biological Anthropology and Osteoarchaeology and the Institute of Field Archaeologists

Britnell, W, 1973 Beckford, South Worcs, *West Midlands Archaeological News Sheet* **16**, CBA Group 8, 10-11

Brodribb, A C C, Hands, A R, and Walker, D R, 2005 *The Roman Villa at Shakenoak Farm, Oxfordshire. Excavations 1960-1976*, BAR Brit Ser **395**, Oxford

Brodribb, G, 1987 *Roman brick and tile*, Gloucester

Bronk Ramsey, C, 1995 Radiocarbon calibration and analysis of stratigraphy: the OxCal program, *Radiocarbon* **37(2)**, 425–30

Bronk Ramsey, C, 2001 Development of the radiocarbon calibration program, *Radiocarbon* **43(2A)**, 355–63.

Bronk Ramsey, C, 2009 Dealing with outliers and offsets in radiocarbon dating. *Radiocarbon*, **51(3)**, 1023-1045

Bronk Ramsey, C, and Lee, S, 2013 Recent and planned developments of the program OxCal, *Radiocarbon* **55**, 3-4

Brooks, S, T, and Suchey, J, M, 1990 Skeletal age determination based on the os pubis: a comparison of the Acsádi-Nemeskéri and Suchey-Brooks Methods, *Human Evolution* **5**, 227-238

Brothwell, D R, 1981 *Digging up bones*, Oxford University Press, Oxford

Brothwell, D, and Zakrezewski, S, 2004 Metric and non-metric studies of archaeological human bone, in *Guidelines to the Standards for Recording Human Remains* (M Brickley and J McKinley), IFA Paper 7, British Association for Biological Anthropology and Osteoarchaeology and the Institute of Field Archaeologists, 27-28

Brown, A, 1994 A Romano-British shell-gritted pottery and tile manufacturing site at Harrold, Beds, *Bedfordshire Archaeol* 21, 19-107

Brown, K, and Timby, J, 2007 Pottery, in Simmonds 2007, 226-228

Bryant, V, and Evans, J, 2004a Iron Age and Roman pottery, in Dalwood and Edwards 2004, 240-280

Bryant, V, and Evans, J, 2004b Slab built vessels, in Dalwood and Edwards, 366

Buckberry, J, and Chamberlain, A, 2002 Age estimation from the auricular surface of the ilium: a revised method, *American Journal of Physical Anthropology* 119, 231-239

Buikstra, J E, and Ubelaker, D H, (eds.) 1994 *Standards for data collection from human skeletal remains* Arkansas Archaeological Survey Research Series 44, Arkansus

Bulleid, A, and Gray, H St G, 1917 *The Glastonbury Lake Village, a full description of the excavations and the relics discovered, 1892-1907, Vol. 2*, Glastonbury

Campbell, G, and Straker, V, 2005 *A review of Macroscopic Plant Remains In Southern England*, unpublished

Cappers, R T J, Bekker, R M and Jans, J E A, 2006 *Digitale Zandenatlas Van Nederland*, Groningen University

Carr, G, and Knüsel, C, 1997 The ritual framework of excarnation as the mortuary practice of the early and middle Iron Ages of central southern Britain, in *Reconstructing Iron Age Societies: New Approaches to the British Iron Age* (A Gwilt and C Haslegrove), Oxbow Monograph 71, 167-173, Oxford

Carter, G A, 1998 *Excavations at the Orsett 'Cock' Enclosure, Essex, 1976*, EAA report 86, Essex County Council

Caseldine, A E, and Griffiths, C J, 2010 *The Charred Plant remains from Llangorse Crannog*. Report for the National Museum of Wales, University of Wales, Lampeter

Catchpole, T, 2007 Excavations at the Sewage Treatment Works, Dymock, Gloucestershire, *Trans Bristol and Gloucestershire Archaeol Soc* 125, 137-219

Catchpole, T, Simmonds, A, and Copeland, T, 2007 Dymock: its origins and function, *Trans Bristol and Gloucestershire Archaeol Soc* 125, 235-237

Challinor, D, 2006 Charcoal from Pepper Hill Roman cemetery, in *Palaeoenvironmental evidence from Section 1 of the Channel Tunnel Rail Link, Kent, CTRL Scheme-wide Specialist Report Series, in ADS* (eds J Giorgi and E Stafford) http:// archaeologydataservice.ac.uk/archiveDS/ archiveDownload?t=arch-335-1/dissemination/ pdf/PT1_Int_Site_Reps/02_Pepper_Hill/PHL_ ISR_Text/PHL_ISR_Text.pdf

Challinor, D, 2009 The wood charcoal, in A late Neolithic/Early Bronze Age enclosure and Iron Age and Romano-British settlement at Latton Lands, Wiltshire (K Powell, G Laws and L Brown) *Wiltshire Archaeological & Natural History Magazine* 102, 97-8

Challinor, D, 2010 Chapter 14. Charcoal, in *Evolution of a Farming Community in the Upper Thames Valley. Excavation of a Prehistoric, Roman and Post-Roman Landscape at Cotswold Community, Gloucestershire and Wiltshire. Volume 2: The Finds and Environmental Reports* (eds A Smith, K Powell and P Booth), Oxford Archaeology, 195-202, Oxford

Challinor, D, 2011 The Charcoal, in Prehistoric, Roman and Anglo-Saxon Activity at the Willow Brook Centre, Bradley Stoke, South Gloucestershire, (A Simmonds) *Trans Bristol and Gloucestershire Archaeol Soc* 129, 27-29

Challinor, D, 2012 Wood charcoal [from Horcott Quarry, Fairford, Gloucestershire], in Hayden *et al.* forthcoming

Chamberlain, A, 1994 *Human Remains*, British Museum Press, London

Clarke, G, 1979 *The Roman cemetery at Lankhills*, Winchester Studies 3: Pre-Roman and Roman Winchester Part III, Oxford

Clifford, E M, 1954 The Roman Villa, Witcombe, Gloucestershire, *Trans Bristol and Gloucestershire Archaeol Soc* 73, 5-69

Cocks, A, H, 1921 A Romano-British homestead in the Hambleden Valley, Bucks, *Archaeologia* 71, 141-198

Coleman, L, and Watts, M, 2008 Romano-British agriculture at the former St James's Railway Station, Cheltenham: excavations in 2000-2001, in N Holbrook (ed.) 2008, 85-105

Coleman, L, Hancock, A, and Watts, M, 2006 *Excavations on the Wormington to Tirley pipeline, 2000*, Cotswold Archaeology Monograph 3, Cirencester

Collis, J, 1977 Owslebury (Hants) and the problems of burials on rural settlements, in *Burial in the Roman World* (ed. R Reece), CBA Research Report 22, 26-34, London,

Cooper, N J, 1998 The supply of pottery to Roman Cirencester, in *Cirencester: the Roman town defences, public buildings and shops* (ed. N Holbrook) Cirencester Excavations V, Cirencester, 324-350

Copeland, T, 2011 *Roman Gloucestershire*, The History Press

Corney, M, and Cox, P W, 2007 *Colliton Park Roman Town House – A Preliminary Description of the Building, Archaeology, Setting and Reconstruction*, AC Archaeology Report No. 7406/1/3, Salisbury

Cotswold Archaeology, 2009 Gloucester Security of Supply Pipeline, Worcester and

Gloucestershire. Archaeological evaluation, unpublished report prepared on behalf of ARCUS for Severn Trent Water

Cotswold Archaeology 2015 Greystones Farm (Parlour Building), Bourton-on-the-Water, Gloucestershire: Archaeological Excavation, unpublished client report 15752

Council for British Archaeology, 2012 News, Coin find raises questions about Roman hoards, *British Archaeology* Issue **122**

Cox, M, 2003 Aging adults from the skeleton, in *Human Osteology in Archaeology and Forensic Science (*M Cox and S May), 61-81, London

Crummy, N, 1983 *The Roman small finds from excavations in Colchester 1971-9*, Colchester Archaeological Report **2**, Colchester

Crummy, N, Crummy, P, and Crossan, C, 1993 *Excavations of Roman and later cemeteries, churches and monastic site in Colchester, 1971-88*, Colchester Archaeological Report **9**, Colchester 1993

Cullen, K, and Hancocks, A, 2007 Prehistoric and medieval remains at 21 Church Road, Bishop's Cleeve: excavations in 2004, in *Prehistoric and medieval occupation at Moreton-in-Marsh and Bishop's Cleeve, Gloucestershire* (ed. M Watts) Bristol and Gloucestershire Archaeol Rep No. **5**, 73-94

Cunliffe, B, 2005 *Iron Age Communities in Britain*, 4th edn, Routledge, London and New York

Cunliffe, B, and Poole, C, 1991, *Danebury: an Iron Age hillfort in Hampshire Vol. 4 The excavations, 1979–1988: the site*, CBA Res Rep **73**

Cunliffe, B, and Poole, C, 2000 *Suddern Farm, Middle Wallop, Hants, 1991 and 1996. The Danebury environs programme: the prehistory of a Wessex landscape*, English Heritage and OUCA monograph 49, Oxford

Dalwood, H, and Edwards, R, 2004 *Excavations at Deansway, Worcester, 1988–89 Romano-British small town to late medieval city*, CBA Res Rep **139**, York

Darbyshire, G, 1995 *Pre-Roman iron tools for working metal and wood in Southern Britain*, unpublished PhD thesis, University of Wales, Cardiff

Deschler-Erb, S and Gostenčnik, K, 2008 Différences et identities de la vie quotidienne dans le provinces romaine: 'example de la tabletterie, in Bertrand, I (ed) 2008, 283-309

Dinn, J, and Evans, J, 1990 Aston Mill Farm, Kemerton - excavations of ring-ditch, middle Iron-Age enclosure and Grubenhaus, *Trans Worcestershire Archaeol Soc* **12**, 5-66

Dowse, K, L, 1991 *Llangorse Crannog: A study of the carbonised plant remains and environmental evidence from a Dark Age crannog in Wales*, unpublished BA Honours dissertation, St Davids University College, Lampeter

von den Driesch, A, 1976 *A guide to the measurement of animal bones from archaeological sites*, Harvard University

Dryden, Sir Henry, 1885, Hunsbury or Danes Camp

and discoveries there, *Reports and Papers of the Architectural and Archaeological Societies*, **18**, 53-61

Dunning, G C, 1933, Oxenton Hill Camp, with drawings of pottery, *Transactions of the Bristol and Gloucestershire Archaeological Society* **55**, 383-4

Dunning, G C, 1976 Salmondsbury, Bourton-on-the-Water, Glos, in *Hillforts: Later Prehistoric Earthworks in Britain and Ireland* (ed D W Harding), 75-118

Earp, J R, and Hains, B A, 1971 *British Regional geology. The Welsh Borderland*, HMSO, London

Edlin, H L, 1949 *Woodland crafts in Britain: an account of the traditional uses of trees and timber in the British Countryside*, London

Edwards, R, and Hurst, D, 2000 Iron Age Settlement and a Medieval and later Farmstead: Excavation at 93-97 High Street, Evesham, *Trans Worcestershire Arch Soc* **17**, 73-110

Elrington, C R, (ed.) 1968 *Victoria County History of Gloucestershire*, Vol. VIII

Esmonde Cleary, S, 2000 Putting the dead in their place: burial location in *Roman Britain, in Burial, Society and Context in the Roman World* (J Pearce, M Millett and M Struck), 127-142, Oxbow Books, Oxford

Esmonde Cleary, S, 2011, The Romano-British period: an assessment, in Watt (ed.), 127-147

Evans, C J, Jones, L, and Ellis, P, 2000 *Severn Valley ware production at Newland Hopfields*, BUFAU Mono Ser **2**, Brit Archaeol Rep Brit Ser **313**, Oxford

Evans, C J, Garland, N, Millward, J, and Reynolds, S, 2011 Roman pottery [from 14-24 The Butts], in *Life and industry in the suburbs of Roman Worcester*, (eds S Butler and R Cuttler), BAR Brit Ser **533**, Oxford, 83-108

Evans, J, 1994 Discussion of the pottery in the context of Roman Alcester, in *Roman Alcester: Southern extramural area 1964-1966 excavations, Part 2* (eds S Cracknell and C Mahany), CBA Res Rep **97**, 144-49

Evison, V I, and Hill, P, 1996 *Two Anglo-Saxon Cemeteries at Beckford, Hereford and Worcester*, CBA Research Report **103**, York

Feugère, M, and Prévot, P, 2008 Les matières dures animals (os, bois de cerf et ivoire) dans la vallée de l'Hérault: production et consummation, in Bertrand, I (ed) 2008, 231-268

Finnegan, M, 1978 Non-metric variation of the infracranial skeleton, *Journal of Anatomy* 125, 23-37

French, A, 2006 Oxfordshire parchment and colour-coated wares, in Barfield 2006, 154

Gale, R, 2008 Charcoal, in Excavations of Saxon's Lode Farm, Ripple (2001-2): Iron Age, Romano-British and Anglo-Saxon rural settlement in the Severn Valley (A Barber and M Webb), *Trans Worcestershire Archaeol Soc* **21**, 68-9

Gale, R, and Cutler, D, 2000 *Plants in Archaeology:*

Identification manual of vegetative plant materials used in Europe and the southern Mediterranean to c 1500, Westbury and Kew

Gelling, P S, and Peacock, D P S, 1970 The pottery from Caynham Camp, near Ludlow, *Trans Shropshire Archaeol Soc* **58** (for 1965-1968), 96-100

Gentil, P, and Slowikowski, A M, 2000 Kiln Furniture and Ceramic Building Material, in *Iron Age and Roman Settlement on the Stagsden Bypass*, (M Dawson) Beds Arch Monograph **3**, 86-92

Gillam, J P, 1976 Coarse fumed ware in North Britain and beyond, *Glasgow Archaeol J* **4**, 57-80

Giorgi, J, forthcoming Charred and Waterlogged Plant Remains [from Arkell's Land (Coln Gravel)], Kempsford, in Hayden *et al.* forthcoming

Gloucestershire Echo, 2013 (posted November 30th) Human remains from Iron Age discovered at Cotswold Pub by LP Archaeology, http://www.gloucestershireecho.co.uk/Human-remains-discovered-Cotswold-pub/story-20098708-detail/story.html

Golden, M, 1988 Did the ancients care when their children died?, *Greece and Rome* **35**, 152-163

Gosden, C, and Lock, G, 2013 *Histories in the making: Excavations at Alfred's Castle 1998–2000*, OUCA monograph **79**

Grant, A, 1982 The use of toothwear as a guide to the age of domestic ungulates, in *Ageing and sexing animal bones from archaeological sites* (eds B Wilson, C Grigson and S Payne), BAR Brit. Ser. **109**, 91-108, Oxford

Grant, A, 1984, The animal husbandry, in *Danebury: an Iron Age hillfort in Hampshire, 2: The excavations, 1969-78: the finds*, (B W Cunliffe), CBA Res Rep **52**, 494-548, London

Grant, A, 1989 Animals in Roman Britain, in *Research on Roman Britain: 1960-89* (ed M Todd), Britannia Monograph Series **11**, 135-146, London

Gray, L, 2006 The Plant Macrofossils in Wessex Water Oldbury-on-Severn to Aust discharge pipeline, South Gloucestershire: archaeological surveys and excavations 2003-4, *Annual report of the Severn Estuary Levels research Committee* **17**, 77-142

Green, M J, 1997 *Dictionary of Celtic Myth and Legend*, Oxford

Greig, J, 1994 A possible hedgerow flora from an Iron Age ditch at Alcester, Warwickshire, *Circaea, The Journal for the Association for Environmental Archaeology* **11** (1), 7-16

Griffin, S, Mann, A, and Western, G, 2002 *Excavation at Old Yew Hill Wood, Church Lench, Worcestershire*, Worcestershire County Archaeological Report, **904**

Griffin, S, Western, G, Mann, A, and Dalwood, H, 2006 A Late Iron Age burial at Old Yew Hill Farm, Church Lench, *Trans Worcestershire Archaeol Soc* **20**, 1-9

Habermehl, K-H, 1975 *Die Altersbestimmung bei Haus- und Labortieren* (2nd edn), Berlin, Hamburg

Halstead, P, 1985 A Study of Mandibular Teeth from Romano-British Contexts at Maxey, in *Archaeology and environment in the lower Welland Valley*, (ed F Pryor), East Anglian Archaeology Rep **27**, 219-224

Hambleton, E, 1999 *Animal husbandry regimes in Iron Age Britain. A comparative study of faunal assemblages from British Iron Age sites*, BAR Brit Ser **282**, Oxford

Hancocks, A, 1999 The pottery, in Iron-Age, Romano-British and medieval occupation at Bishop's Cleeve, Gloucestershire: excavations at Gilder's Paddock, 1989 and 1990-1 (C Parry), *Trans Bristol and Gloucestershire Archaeol Soc* **117**, 104-109 and 112-115

Hannan, A, 1993 Excavations at Tewkesbury, 1972–74, *Trans Bristol and Gloucestershire Archaeol Soc* **111**, 21-75

Hannan, A, 1997 Tewkesbury and the Earls of Gloucester: Excavations at Holm Hill, 1974–5, *Trans Bristol and Gloucestershire Archaeol Soc* **115**, 79–231

Harcourt, R A, 1974 The dog in prehistoric and early historic Britain, *Journal of Archaeological Science* **1**, 151-175

Hart, J, and Alexander, M, 2007 Prehistoric, Romano-British and medieval remains at Blenheim Farm, Moreton-in-Marsh, Gloucestershire: Excavations in 2003, in *Prehistoric and Medieval occupation at Moreton-in-Marsh and Bishop's Cleeve* (ed M Watts), Bristol and Gloucestershire Arch Report **5**, 1-72

Hart, J, and McSloy, E R, 2008 Prehistoric and early historic activity, settlement and burial at Walton Cardiff, near Tewkesbury: excavations at Rudgeway Lane in 2004-2005, in Holbrook 2008, 1-84

Hather, J G, 2000 *The Identification of Northern European Woods: A Guide for Archaeologists and Conservators*, London

Hayden, C, Early, R, Biddulph, E, Booth, P, Dodd, A, Smith, A, Laws, G, and Welsh, K, forthcoming *Horcott Quarry, Fairford and Arkell's Land, Kempsford: Prehistoric, Roman and Anglo-Saxon settlement and burial in the Upper Thames Valley in Gloucestershire*, Oxford Archaeology Thames Valley Landscapes Monograph

Headland Archaeology 2014 Land at Home Farm, Fairford, Gloucestershire. Archaeological excavation, unpublished client report prepared for The Environmental Dimension Partnership on behalf of Bloor Homes

Hencken, T C, 1938 The excavation of the Iron Age camp on Bredon Hill, Gloucestershire, 1935-1937, *Arch J* **95**, 1-111

Henig, M, Soffe, G, and Adcock, K (eds), forthcoming *Villas, sanctuaries and settlement in the Romano-British countryside: new perspectives and controversies*

Hesse, R, 2011 Reconsidering animal husbandry

and diet in the northwest provinces, *Journal of Roman Archaeology* **24**, 215-248

Hey, G, Booth, P, and Timby, J, 2011 *Yarnton: Iron Age and Romano-British Settlement and Landscape. Results of Excavations 1990-98*, Oxford Archaeology Thames Valley Landscapes Monograph **35**

Hill, J D, 1995 *Ritual and rubbish in the Iron Age of Wessex. A study of the formation of a specific archaeological record*, BAR Brit Ser **242**

Hillman, G, 1984 Reconstruction of crop husbandry practices from charred remains of crops, in *Farming Practice in British Prehistory* (ed R Mercer), Edinburgh: University Press, 123-161

Hillson, S, 1986 *Teeth*, Cambridge

Hillson, S, 1996 *Dental Anthropology* (3rd ed.), Cambridge

Holbrook, N, 2006 The Roman period, in Holbrook and Juřica, 97-131

Holbrook, N, (ed.), 2008a *Iron Age and Romano-British agriculture in the North Gloucestershire Severn Vale*, Bristol and Gloucestershire Archaeol Rep No. **6**

Holbrook, N, 2008b Iron Age and Romano-British [discussion], in Hart and McSloy 2008, 69-75

Holbrook, N, 2013 Interpreting the archaeology of late Roman and early post-Roman Cirencester, in *Living and working in the Roman world Essays in honour of Michael Fulford on his 65th birthday*, (eds H Eckardt and S Rippon), JRA Supplementary Series No. **95**, Portsmouth, Rhode Island, 31-46

Holbrook, N, and Juřica, J, (eds), 2006 *Twenty-five years of archaeology in Gloucestershire A review of new discoveries and new thinking in Gloucestershire South Gloucestershire and Bristol 1979-2004*, Cotswold Archaeology, Bristol and Gloucestershire Archaeological Report No. **3**

Hooke, D, 1990 *Worcestershire Anglo-Saxon Charter Bounds*, Woodbridge

Hope, V, M, 1999 The Iron and Roman Ages *c* 600 BC to AD 400, in Death in England (eds P C Jupp and C Gittings), 40-64, Manchester

Hunter, K, 2012 Plant macrofossils, in *London Gateway Iron Age and Roman salt making in the Thames Estuary excavation at Stanford Wharf Nature Reserve, Essex*, (E Biddulph, S Foreman, E Stafford, D Stansbie, and R Nicholson) Oxford Archaeology Monograph **18**, Digital Volume Specialist report 19, http://library.thehuman journey.net/909

Hurst, D, 2011 Middle Bronze Age to Iron Age: a research assessment overview and agenda, in Watt 2011, 101-126

Hurst, D, 2013 Middle Bronze Age to late Iron Age Worcestershire, West Midlands Regional Research Framework for Archaeology Research Seminar **2**

Hurst, D, and Jackson, R, 2006 Assessment and Updated Project Design for the Bredon hillfort (Worcestershire) archive - Unlocking the past: Collections and HER Enhancement (Stage 3b); 1935–7 excavations by Thalassa Cruso Hencken,

Worcestershire Historic Environment, Archaeology Service, Archaeology Data Service

Iles, M, and Clark, K, 2005 The animal bone, in Thomas 2005, 183-223

Jackson, R A, Hurst, J D, and Pearson, E A, 1996 A Romano-British settlement at Leylandii House Farm, Norton and Lenchwick, *Trans Worcestershire Arch Soc* **15**, 63-72

Jacomet, S, 2006 *Identification of cereal remains from archaeological sites* (2nd edn), Archaeobotany Lab IPAS, Basel University English translation

Jennings, D, Muir, J, Palmer, S, and Smith, A, 2004 *Thornhill Farm, Fairford, Gloucestershire; an Iron Age and Roman pastoral site in the Upper Thames Valley*, Oxford Archaeology Thames Valley Landscapes monograph **23**

Jurmain, R, D, 1999 *Stories from the Skeleton – Behavioural Reconstruction in Human Osteology*, Gordon and Breach, Netherlands

King, A, with Grande, C, forthcoming Dinnington and Yarford: two villas in south and west Somerset, in *Villas, Sanctuaries and Settlements in the Romano-British Countryside: New Perspectives and Controversies* (M Henig, G, Soffe, and K Adcock), Oxford

King, R, Barber, A, and Timby, J, 1996, Excavations at West Lane, Kemble: an Iron-Age, Roman and Saxon burial site and a medieval building, *Trans Bristol and Gloucestershire Archaeol Soc* **114**, 15-54

Lambrick, G, and Allen, T G, 2004 *Gravelly Guy, Stanton Harcourt, Oxfordshire. Development of a Prehistoric and Romano-British Community*, Thames Valley Landscapes Monograph **21**, Oxford

Lamdin-Whymark, H, Brady, K, and Smith, A, 2009 Excavation of a Neolithic to Roman Landscape at Horcott Pit near Fairford, Gloucstershire, in 2002 and 2003, *Trans Bristol & Gloucestershire Archaeol Soc* **127**, 45-129

Lang, F, 2011 Activity not Profession. Considerations about bone working in Roman times, in *Written in bones. Studies in the technological and social contexts of past faunal skeletal remains*, (eds J Baron and B Kufel-Diakowska), Wrocław

Lawrence, M J, and Brown, R W, 1967 *Mammals of Britain. Their Tracks, Trails and Signs*, London

Lewis, M E, 2004 Endocranial lesions in non-adult skeletons: understanding their aetiology, *International Journal of Osteoarchaeology* **14**, 82-97

Light, T, and Ellis, P, 2009 *Bucknowle, a Romano-British villa and its antecedents: excavations 1976-1991*, Dorset Natural History and Archaeological Society Monograph **18**

Liversidge, J, 1969 Furniture and interior decoration, in *The Roman villa in Britain* (ed A L F Rivet), London, 127-72

Lovegrove, R, 2007 *Silent fields. The long decline of a nation's wildlife*, Oxford

Lovejoy, C, O, Meindl, R, S, Pryzbeck, T, R, and

Mensforth, R, P, 1985 Chronological metamorphosis of the auricular surface of the ilium: a new method for the determination of adult skeletal age at death, *American Journal of Physical Anthropology* **68**, 15-28

Lovell, J, Wakeham, G, Timby, J, and Allen, M J, 2007 Iron-Age to Saxon farming settlement at Bishop's Cleeve, Gloucestershire: excavations south of Church Road, 1998 and 2004, *Trans Bristol and Gloucestershire Archaeol Soc* **125**, 95-129

Lovell, N, 1997 Trauma analysis in palaeo-pathology, *Yearbook Physical Anthropology*, 40, 139-70

Lovett, J, 1990 Animal bone, in Dinn and Evans 1990, 48-54

Lowther, A W G, 1935 Notes: An Early Iron Age Oven at St Martha's Hill, near Guildford, *Surrey Archaeological Collections* **XLIII**, 113-5

Lucas, R N, 1993 *The Romano-British villa at Halstock, Dorset. Excavations 1967-1985*, Dorset Natural History and Archaeological Society Monograph **13**

Lukacs, J R, 1989 Dental palaeopathology: methods of reconstructing dietary patterns, in: *Reconstruction of Life from the Skeleton*, (eds M Y Iscan and K A Kennedy), 261-286, New York

Masser, P, and McGill, B, 2004 Excavations of Romano-British Sites at Tockington Park Farm and Westerleigh, South Gloucestershire, in 1997, *Trans Bristol and Gloucestershire Archaeol Soc* **122**, 95-116

McKinley, J I, 1994a Bone fragment size in British cremation burials and its implications for pyre technology and ritual, *Journal of Archaeological Science* **21**, 339-342

McKinley, J I, 1997 Bronze Age 'barrows' and funerary rites and rituals of cremation, *Proceedings of the Prehistoric Society* **63**, 129-145

McKinley, J I, 2000a Cremation burials, in *The Eastern Cemetery of Roman London. Excavations 1983-1990* (B Barber and D Bowsher), MoLAS Monograph **4**, 264-277

McKinley, J I, 2000b The analysis of cremated bone, in *Human osteology in archaeology and forensic science* (eds M Cox and S Mays), 403-421, London

McKinley, J I, 2000c Funerary practice, in *The Eastern Cemetery of Roman London. Excavations 1983-1990* (B Barber and D Bowsher), MoLAS Monograph **4**, 60-81

McKinley, J I, 2004 Compiling a skeletal inventory: cremated human bone, in *Guidelines to the Standards for Recording Human Remains* (eds M Brickley and J I McKinley), IFA Paper No. 7, BABAO and IFA, Southampton and Reading, 9-13

McSloy, E R, 2006 The pottery, in Coleman *et al.* 2006, 37-57

McSloy, E R, 2007 The pottery, in Cullen and Hancocks, 80-85

McSloy, E R, 2008a The late Iron Age and Roman pottery, in Hart and McSloy, 29-40

McSloy, E R, 2008b Pottery, in Coleman and Watts, 94-98

McSloy, E R, 2008c Prehistoric and Roman pottery, in Barber and Watts 2008, 35-53

Maltby, M, 2007 Chop and change: Specialist cattle carcass processing in Roman Britain, in *TRAC 2006. Proceedings of the sixteenth annual Theoretical Roman Archaeology Conference* (eds B Croxford, N Ray, R Roth and N White), Oxford, 59-76

Manning, W H, 1985 *Catalogue of the Romano-British iron tools, fittings and weapons in the British Museum*, London

Manning, W H, 1986 The iron objects, in *Inchtuthil. The Roman legionary fortress. Excavations 1952-65* (L Pitts and J K St Joseph) Britannia Monograph series No. **6**, London, 289-99

Marshall, A, 1976 Southwick Park Settlement, *Glevensis* **10**, 30

Mays, S, 1993 Infanticide in Roman Britain, *Antiquity* **67**, 883-888

Mays, S, 1998 *The Archaeology of Human Bones*, London

Mays, S, 2008 Septal aperture of the humerus in a mediaeval human skeletal population, *American Journal of Physical Anthropology* **136** (4), 432-40

Mays, S, 2012 The relationship between palaeopathology and the clinical sciences, in *A Companion to Paleopathology*, (ed A L Grauer), First edition, Chichester, Wiley-Blackwell, 285-309

Mays, S, Brickley, M, and Dodwell, N, 2004 *Human Bones from Archaeological Sites. Guidelines for Producing Assessment documents and Analytical Reports*, English Heritage, London

Mays, S, and Eyers, J, 2011 'Perinatal Infant Death at the Roman Villa site at Hambleden, Buckinghamshire, England, *Journal of Archaeological Science* **38**, 1931–8

Meates, G W, 1979 *The Roman Villa at Lullingstone, Kent. Volume* **1** *– The Site*, Kent Archaeological Society

Medline Plus 2013, *Dwarfism*, online at: http://www.nlm.nih.gov/medlineplus/dwarfism.html, [accessed: 22/11/13], Maryland, USA, Medline Plus, service of the National Library of Medicine, National Institute of Health

Miles, A, 1962 Assessment of age of a population of Anglo-Saxons from their dentition, *Proc Royal Society of Medicine* **55**, 881-6

Miles, D, (ed.) 1984 *Archaeology at Barton Court Farm, Abingdon, Oxon.*, Oxford Archaeological Unit Report 3, CBA Research Report **50**

Miles, H, 1977 The Honeyditches Villa, Seaton, Devon, *Britannia* **8**, 107-148

Millet, M, 1995 *Roman Britain*, Batsford, London

Moore, T, 2006 The Iron Age, in Holbrook and Juřica 2006, 61-96

Moorees, C F A, Fanning, E A, and Hunt, E E, 1963

Age variation of formation stages for ten permanent teeth, *Journal of Dental Research* **42**, 1490-1502

Mora, P, Mora, L, and Phillpot, P, 1994 *Conservation of wall paintings*, London

Morris, E, 2005 Pottery and briquetage, in Thomas, N, 2005, 117-47

Morris, J, 1979 *Agricultural buildings in Roman Britain*, BAR Brit Ser **70**

Morris, J, 2011 *Investigating animal burials. Ritual, mundane and beyond*, BAR Brit Ser **535**

Mudd, A, Williams, R J, and Lupton, A, 1999 *Excavations along Roman Ermine Street, Gloucestershire and Wiltshire. The archaeology of the A419/A417 Swindon to Gloucester Road Scheme, Volume 1: Prehistoric and Roman activity*, Oxford Archaeological Unit, 35-97

Musty, J W G, 1974 Medieval pottery kilns, in *Medieval Pottery from Excavations* (V I Evison, H Hodges and J G Hurst), London, 41-65

Needham, S, and Spence, T, 1996 *Refuse and disposal at Area 16 east Runnymede. Runnymede Bridge research excavations, Volume 2*, London

Nichols, P W, 2006 An archaeological excavation at Bourton-on-the-Water Primary School, Gloucestershire, 2003, unpublished report by Gloucester County Council Archaeology Service for Wildin Partnership

Nichols, P, 2013 An archaeological excavation at Bourton-on-the-Water Primary School, School Hill, Bourton-on-the-Water, Gloucestershire, 2000, unpublished report by Gloucestershire County Council Archaeology Service for Gloucestershire County Council

North, F J, 1930 *Limestones. Their origins, Distribution and uses*, London

O'Connor, T, 1988 *Bones from the General Accident site, Tanner Row*, Archaeology of York Vol. **15/2**, York Archaeological Trust/Council for British Archaeology

Ortner, D J, 2003 *Identification of Pathological Conditions in Human Skeletal Remains*, Academic Press, London and San Diego

Oxford Archaeology 2012 Gloucester Security of Supply Water Pipeline, Worcestershire and Gloucestershire: Post-Excavation Assessment and Updated Project Design V.3, unpublished report prepared on behalf of Severn Trent Water

Page, W, (ed) 1913 *Victoria County History of Worcestershire*, Vol. III

Parry, C, 1999 Iron Age, Romano-British and Medieval Occupation at Bishop's Cleeve, Gloucestershire: excavations at Gilder's Paddock 1989 and 1990-1, *Trans Bristol and Gloucestershire Archaeol Soc* **117**, 89-118

Patrick, C, and Hurst, D, 2004 Archaeological Survey and Excavation along the Cotswold Spring Supply Trunk Main, unpublished archive report prepared by the Historic Environment and Archaeology Service,

Worcestershire County Council for Severn Trent Water Ltd

Payne, S, 1973 Kill-off patterns in sheep and goats: the mandibles from Aşwan Kale, *Anatolian studies* **23**, 281-303

Peacock, D P S, 1967 Romano-British pottery production in the Malvern district of Worcestershire, *Trans Worcestershire Archaeol Soc* **1**, 15-28

Peacock, D P S, 1968 A petrological study of certain Iron Age pottery from western England, *Proc Prehist Soc* **13**, 414-427

Pearce, J, 2001 Infants, Cemeteries and Communities in the Roman provinces, in *TRAC 2000, Proceedings of the Tenth Annual Theoretical Roman Archaeology Conference, London 2000* (G Davies, A Gardner and K Lockyear eds), 125-142

Penn, W, S, 1967 Possible evidence from Springhead for the Great Plague of A.D. 166, *Archaeologia Cantiana* **82**, 263-271

Perring, D, 2001 *The Roman House in Britain*, London

Phase Site Investigations Limited, 2009a Gloucester Security of Supply Scheme, Tewkesbury and the Vale of Avon, Archaeological Geophysical Survey, Coombe Hill to Fiddington, Project No. ARC/218/147, on behalf of ARCUS/Severn Trent Water

Phase Site Investigations Limited, 2009b Gloucester Security of Supply Scheme, Tewkesbury and the Vale of Avon, Archaeological Geophysical Survey, Revised Pipeline Route, Project No. ARC/288/166, on behalf of ARCUS/Severn Trent Water

Phenice, T W, 1969 A newly developed visual method of sexing the os pubis *American Journal of Physical Anthropology* **30**, 297-301

Philp, B, 1973 SITE 13. A Roman Bath-Building near Baston Manor, Hayes, Kent, in *Excavations in West Kent 1960-1970* (B Philp), Second Research Report in the Kent Series, Dover, 80-93

Philpott, R, 1991 *Burial practices in Roman Britain*, BAR Brit Ser **219**, Oxford

Ponec, D J, and Resnick, D, 1984 On the etiology and pathogenesis of porotic hyperostosis of the skull, *Investigative Radiology* **19**, 313-317

Poole, C, 1995 Study 14: Loomweights versus oven bricks, in *Danebury: an Iron Age hillfort in Hampshire Volume 6 A hillfort community in perspective* (B Cunliffe), CBA Res Rep **102**

Poole, C, 2010a Structural fired clay and clay objects in *Evolution of a Farming Community in the Upper Thames Valley Volume 2: The Finds and Environmental Reports* (K Powell, A Smith and G Laws), OA Monograph **31**

Poole, C, 2010b, Prehistoric Fired Clay, in *Castle Hill and its Landscape; Archaeological Investigations at the Wittenhams, Oxfordshire* (T G Allen, K Cramp, H Lamdin-Whymark, and L Webley), Oxford Archaeology Monograph **9**, Oxford, 164-168

Poole, C, 2010c The fired clay, in Roman settlement, pottery production, and a cemetery in the Beam valley, Dagenham (E Biddulph, K Brady, B M Ford, and P Murray), *Transactions of the Essex Society for Archaeology and History* **1**, 109-65

Poole, C, 2015 Chapter 12, The structural fired clay and briquetage, in *Digging at the Gateway. Archaeological landscapes of south Thanet: the Archaeology of East Kent Access Phase II. Volume 2: The Finds and Environmental Reports* (P Andrews, P Booth, A Fitzpatrick, and K Welsh) Oxford-Wessex Archaeology monograph **8**, 289-323

Powell, K, Smith, A, and Laws, G, 2010 *Evolution of a farming community in the Upper Thames Valley. Excavation of a Prehistoric, Roman and Post-Roman landscape at Cotswold Community, Gloucestershire and Wiltshire*, Thames Valley Landscapes Monograph **31**

Price, E, 2000 *Frocester. A Romano-British Settlement, its Antecedents and Successors, Volume 2 The Finds*, Gloucester and District Archaeological Research Group, Stonehouse

Prummel, W, and Frisch, H-J, 1986 A guide for the distinction of species, sex and body side in bones of sheep and goat, *Journal of Archaeological Science* **13**, 567-577

Rackham, O, 1983 *Trees and Woodland in the British Landscape*, London

Rawes, B, 1981 The Romano-British site at Brockworth, Gloucestershire, *Britannia* 12, 45-79

Reimer, P J, Bard, E, Bayliss, A, Beck, J W, Blackwell, P G, Bronk Ramsey, C, Brown, D M, Buck, C E, Edwards, R L, Friedrich, M, Grootes, P M, Guilderson, T P, Haflidason, H, Hajdas, I, Hatte, C, Heaton, T J, Hogg, A G, Hughen, K A, Kaiser, K F, Kromer, B, Manning, S W, Reimer, R W, Richards, D A, Scott, E M, Southon, J R, Turner, C S M, van der Plicht, J, 2013 Selection and Treatment of data for radiocarbon calibration: An update to the International Calibration (INTCAL) Criteria, *Radiocarbon* **55 (4)**,1-23

RIB, 1965 *The Roman inscriptions of Britain. Volume I: Inscriptions on stone* (eds R G Collingwood and R P Wright), Clarendon Press, Oxford

Roberts, C, and Connell, B, 2004 Guidance on recording palaeopathology, in *Guidelines to the Standards for Recording Human Remains*, (M Brickley and J McKinley), IFA Paper No. 7, British Association for Biological Anthropology and Osteoarchaeology and the Institute of Field Archaeologists, 34-39

Roberts, C, and Cox, M, 2003 *Health and Disease in Britain from Prehistory to the Present Day*, Sutton Publishing, Stroud

Roberts, C, and Manchester, K, 1995 *The Archaeology of Disease* (second edition), Sutton Publishing, Stroud

Robinson, M, and Straker, V R, 1991, Silica skeletons and macroscopic plant remains from Ash, in *New Light on early Farming* (ed J Renfrew), Edinburgh University Press, 3-13

Roe, F, 2003 Worked Stone in *Later prehistoric and Romano-British burial and settlement at Hucclecote,*

Gloucestershire: excavations in advance of the Gloucester Business Park Link Road, 1998 (A Thomas, N Holbrook, and C Bateman), Cotswold Archaeology Bristol and Gloucestershire Archaeological Report 2, Cirencester, Cotswold Archaeological Trust, 50-51

Rogers, J, and Waldron, T, 1995 *A field guide to joint disease in archaeology*, Chichester, New York

Rook, T, 2002 *Roman Baths in Britain*, Shire Archaeology, Aylesbury

Royal Commission on Historical Monuments England 1976 *Ancient and Historical Monuments in the County of Gloucester. Volume 1: Iron Age and Romano-British Monuments in the Gloucestershire Cotswolds*, HMSO, London

Saunders, R L, 1998 *The Use of Old Red Sandstone in Roman Britain. A Petrological and Archaeological study*, Unpublished PhD thesis, University of Reading

Scheuer, L, and Black, S, 2000 *Developmental juvenile osteology*, Elsevier Academic Press, Oxford

Schmid, E, 1972 *Atlas of animal bones. For prehistorians, archaeologists and quaternary geologists*, Amsterdam, London, New York

Schweingruber, F H, 1990 *Microscopic wood anatomy* (3rd Edition), Birmensdorf: Swiss Federal Institute for Forest, Snow and Landscape Research

Scott, I, 2013 Metal finds, other than copper alloy, in Gosden and Lock 2013, 113

Sellwood, L, 1984, Objects of iron, in *Danebury: an Iron Age hillfort in Hampshire, Vol. 2. The excavations 1969-1978: the finds* (B Cunliffe), CBA Research Report **52**, London, 346-71

Serjeantson, D, 1996 The animal bones, in Needham and Spence 1996, 194-253

Serjeantson, D, and Morris, J, 2011 Ravens and crows in Iron Age and Roman Britain, *Oxford Journal of Archaeology* **30**, 85-107

Simmonds, A, 2007 Excavations at land adjacent to the Rectory, Dymock, Gloucestershire, 2002, *Trans Bristol and Gloucestershire Archaeol Soc* **125**, 220-235

Simmonds, A, 2011 Prehistoric, Roman and Anglo-Saxon Activity at the Willow Brook Centre, Bradley Stoke, South Gloucestershire, *Trans Bristol and Gloucestershire Archaeol Soc* **129**, 11-35

Simmonds, A, Thacker, G, and Shepherd, N, 2010 An investigation of the evolution of the wetland environment of Longdon Marsh, Worcestershire and the excavation of a late Iron Age/Romano-British farmstead, *Trans Worcestershire Archaeol Soc* **22**, 1-58

Smalley, R, 2011 Geophysical Survey Report, Bredon's Norton, Worcestershire, unpublished report by Stratascan Limited for Severn Trent Water on behalf of Oxford Archaeology, February 2011

Soren, D, and Soren, N (eds), 1999 *A Roman Villa and a Late Roman Cemetery. Excavation at Poggio*

Gramignano (Lugnano in Teverina), Rome: Le'Erma di Bretschneider

Sjøvold, T, 1984 A report on the heritability of some cranial measurements and non-metric traits, in *Multivariate Statistical Methods in Physical Anthropology* (ed G N van Vark), Groningen: Reidel, 223-246

Stace, C, 2010 *New Flora of the British Isles*, 3rd Edition, Cambridge

Steckel, R, H, Kjellström, A, Rose, J, Larsen, C, S, Walker, P, L, Blondiaux, J, Grupe, G, and Maat, G, 2009 Summary measurement of health and wellbeing: the health index, *American Journal of Physical Anthropology Supplement* **48**, 247

Stuart-Macadam, P, 1991 Anaemia in Roman Britain: Poundbury Camp, in *Health in Past Societies, Biocultural Interpretations of Human Skeletal Remains in Archaeological Contexts* (H Bush and M Zvelebil), BAR International Series **567**, Tempvs Reparatvm Archaeological and Historical Associates Limited, 101-113

Stuiver, M, and Kra, R S, 1986 Editorial comment, *Radiocarbon*, **28** (2B), ii

Stuiver, M, and Polach, H A, 1977 Reporting of C14 data, *Radiocarbon*, **19**, 355–63

Sykes, D, Booth, P, and Foreman, S, 2011 Gloucester Security of Supply Pipeline. Post-excavation assessment and updated project design, unpublished report by Oxford Archaeology

Taylor, A, 2008 Aspects of deviant burial in Roman Britain, in *Deviant Burial in the Archaeological Record* (ed E M Murphy), Oxbow Books, Oxford, 91-114

Taylor, J, 2004 The distribution and exchange of pink, grog-tempered pottery in the East Midlands: an update, *J Roman Pottery Stud* **11**, 60-66

Thomas, A, Holbrook, N, and Bateman, C, 2003 *Late prehistoric and Romano-British burial and settlement at Hucclecote, Gloucestershire*, Trans Bristol and Gloucestershire Archaeol Rep **2**, Cotswold Archaeology

Thomas, N, 2005 *Conderton Camp, Worcestershire: a small middle Iron Age hillfort on Bredon Hill*, CBA Research Report **143**

Thompson, I, 1982 *Grog-tempered 'Belgic' pottery of South-eastern England*, Brit Archaeol Rep Brit Ser **108**, Oxford

Thomson, G B, 1999 The analysis of wood charcoals from selected pits and funerary contexts, in *Excavations at Barrow Hills, Radley, Oxfordshire, vol. 1: The Neolithic and Bronze Age Monument Complex* (A Barclay and C Halpin), Oxford Archaeology Thames Valley Landscapes monograph **11**, 247-253

Timby, J, 1990 Severn Valley wares: a reassessment, *Britannia* **21**, 243-251

Timby, J, 1998 Pottery (and fired clay), in Barber and Walker 1998, 126-9

Timby, J R, 2000 Pottery, in Price 2000, 125-162

Timby, J, 2002 The pottery, in Excavations at West Drive, Cheltenham, Gloucestershire, 1997-9 (T

Catchpole), *Trans Bristol Gloucestershire Archaeol Soc* **120**, 92-6

Timby, J, 2004 Romano-British pottery, in Walker *et al.* 2004, 66-75

Timby, J, 2007a Pottery fabrics, in Lovell *et al.*, 118-122

Timby, J, 2007b Pottery, in Catchpole 2007, 155-171

Timby, J, 2010, The pottery, in Simmonds *et al.*, 23-32

Tomber, R, and Dore, J, 1998 *The national Roman fabric reference collection: a handbook*, Museum of London Archaeol Services Mono No **2**

Torgersen, J H, 1951a The developmental genetics and evolutionary meaning of the metopic suture *American Journal of Physical Anthropology* **9**, 193-205

Torgersen, J H, 1951b Hereditary factors in the sutural patterns of the skull, *Acta Radiologica* **36**, 374-382

Trotter, M, 1970 Estimation of stature from intact long bones, in *Personal Identification in Mass Disasters* (ed T D Stewart), Smithsonian Institution Press, Washington, D.C., 71-83

Trotter, M, and Gleser, G, 1952 Estimation of stature from long-bones of American Whites and Negroes *American Journal of Physical Anthropology* **9**, 427-440

Trotter, M, and Gleser, G, 1958 A re-evaluation of estimation of stature based on measurements of stature taken during life and of long bones after death, *American Journal of Physical Anthropology* **16**, 79-123

University of York, 2008 Environmental Archaeology Bibliography, Archaeology Data Service collection 385, Collection doi 10.5284/1000225 http://archaeologydata service.ac.uk/archives/view/eab_eh_2004/

Upex, S, Mudd, A, and Hart, J, 2010 A middle Iron Age settlement at Grange Farm, Bredon, Worcestershire: excavations in 2003, *Trans Worcestershire Archaeol Soc* **22**, 65-76

van der Veen, M, 1992 *Crop Husbandry Regimes. An Archaeobotanical Study of Farming in Northern England: 1000 BC - AD 500*, Sheffield

Vretemark, M, 1997 Från ben till boskap. Kosthåll och djurhållning med utgångspunkt i medeltida benmaterial från Skara, Skrifter från Länsmuseet Skara **25**

Waldron, T, 2007 *St Peter's, Barton-upon-Humber, Lincolnshire. A Parish Church and its Community. Volume 2: the Human Remains*, Oxford

Walker, G, Thomas, A, and Bateman, C, 2004 Bronze Age and Romano-British sites south-east of Tewkesbury: evaluations and excavations 1991-7, *Trans Bristol and Gloucestershire Archaeol Soc* **122**, 29-94

Walker, P, L, Bathurst, R, R, Richman, R, Gjerdrum, T, and Andrushko, V, A, 2009 The causes of porotic hyperostosis and cribra orbitalia: A reappraisal of the iron-deficiency-anemia hypothesis, *American Journal of Physical Anthropology* **139** (2), 109-125

Watt, S, (ed.), 2011 *The archaeology of the West Midlands A framework for research,* University of Birmingham, Oxford

Webb, H, Loe, L, Clough, S, and Gibson, M forthcoming Human remains, in *Later Prehistoric landscape and a Roman nucleated settlement in the lower Windrush Valley at Gill Mill, near Witney, Oxfordshire* (P Booth and A Simmonds), Oxford Archaeology Thames Valley Landscapes monograph

Webster, G, 1976 (ed.) *Romano-British coarse pottery: a student's guide,* Counc Brit Archaeol Res Rep **6,** London

Webster, P V, 1976 Severn Valley ware: a preliminary study, *Trans Bristol and Gloucestershire Archaeol Soc* **94,** 18-46

Webster, P, 1996 *Roman samian pottery in Britain,* Counc Brit Archaeol Practical Handbooks **13,** York

Webster, C J (ed.), 2007 *The Archaeology of South West England. South West Archaeological Research Framework: Resource assessment and Research Agenda,* Somerset County Council, http://www1. somerset.gov.uk/archives/hes/downloads/ swarfweb.pdf

Wessex Archaeology, 2010 Gloucester Security of Supply - Strensham Water Treatment Works to Coombe Hill Pipeline. Written Scheme of Investigation for Archaeological Mitigation Works, unpublished document prepared by Wessex Archaeology for Severn Trent Water, April 2010

Wheeler, R E M, 1930 *London in Roman Times,* London Museum Catalogues **3,** London

Whimster, R, 1981 *Burial practices in Iron Age Britain: A discussion and gazetteer of the evidence,* c *700 B.C.–A.D. 43,* B A R Brit Ser, Oxford

Wild, F, 1993 The samian stamps and decorated ware, in Hannan 1993, 48-55

Williams, J H, 1971 Roman Building Materials in the South West, *Transactions of the Bristol and Gloucestershire Archaeological Society* 90, 95-120

Williams, R J, and Zeepvat, R J, 1994 *Bancroft. The Late Bronze Age and Iron Age settlement, Roman Villa and Temple-Mausoleum, Vol. 1: Excavations and Building Materials,* Buckinghamshire Archaeol Soc Monograph Series No. **7**

Willis, S, 2012 The Iron Age and Roman pottery, in *Ariconium, Herefordshire. An Iron Age settlement and Romano-British 'small town'* (R Jackson), Oxford, 40-110

Wills, J, 1976 Beckford, Hereford and Worcester, *West Midlands Archaeological News Sheet* **19,** Council for British Archaeology Group 8, 35

Wills, J, 1978 Beckford 1978, *West Midlands Archaeological News Sheet* **21,** 43-5

Wilson, D, Bagnall, A, and Taylor, B, 2014 *Report on the Excavation of a Romano-British Site at Wortley, South Gloucestershire,* BAR Brit Ser **591**

Yalden, D, 1999 *The History of British Mammals,* Poyser Natural History, London

Yalden, D W, and Albarella, U, 2009 *The history of British birds,* Oxford

Young, C J, 1977 *The Roman pottery industry of the Oxford region,* BAR (Brit Ser) **43,** Oxford

Index